QUALITATIVE RESEARCH

Theory, Method and Practice

edited by David Silverman

SAGE Publications
London • Thousand Oaks • New Delhi

First published 1997
Reprinted 1997, 1998

SAGE Publications Ltd
6 Bonhill Street
London EC2A 4PU

SAGE Publications Inc
2455 Teller Road
Thousand Oaks, California 91320

SAGE Publications India Pvt Ltd
32, M-Block Market
Greater Kailash – I
New Delhi 110 048

British Library Cataloguing in Publication Data

A catalogue record for this book is available
from the British Library

ISBN 0 8039 7665 8
ISBN 0 8039 7666 6 (pbk)

Library of Congress catalog record available

Typeset by Mayhew Typesetting, Rhayader, Powys
Printed in Great Britain by Biddles Ltd, Guildford

QUALITATIVE RESEARCH

Contents

Notes on Contributors

Paul Atkinson is Professor of Sociology in the School of Social and Administrative Studies, University of Wales, Cardiff. His research interests include: the microsociology of knowledge, the analysis of sociological texts, and qualitative research methods. His recent publications include *Medical Talk and Medical Work* (1995, Sage).

Carolyn Baker is a Reader in the Graduate School of Education, the University of Queensland, Brisbane, Australia. Her interests include studies of talk and interaction in classrooms, meetings and other educational settings. In her research on literacy she has applied ethnomethodology and conversation analysis to instances of 'talk around text'. One recent publication, with Jayne Keogh, is 'Accounting for achievement in parent–teacher interviews', *Human Studies*, 18 (2/3), 1995.

Isabelle Baszanger is a sociologist at the CNRS (Centre National de la Recherche Scientifique), Paris. Her main research interests are sociology of medicine, sociology of pain, interactionism. Her recent publications include *Médecine et douleur: La fin d'un oubli* (1995, Seuil).

Michael Bloor is Reader and Director of the Social Research Unit, University of Wales, Cardiff. His research interests are HIV-related risk behaviour, occupational health and safety, and substance misuse. He is author of *The Sociology of HIV Transmission* (1995, Sage).

Amanda Coffey is a lecturer in sociology in the School of Social and Administrative Studies, University of Wales, Cardiff. Her research interests include: the sociology of professional work, gender and education, and qualitative research methods. She is currently directing ESRC-funded research on young people and citizenship. Her recent publications include *Making Sense of Qualitative Data* (1996, Sage).

Nicolas Dodier is a sociologist at the INSERM, Paris. His research interests are sociology of technology, sociology of medicine and science and theory of action. His recent publications include *L'expertise médicale: Essai de sociologie sur l'exercice du jugement* (1993, Métailié) and *Les hommes et les machines: La conscience collective dans les sociétés, technicisées* (1995, Métailié).

Barry Glassner is Professor and Chair, Department of Sociology, University of Southern California. His areas of interest are qualitative methodology, culture and deviance. His current research is on the promotion of fears in American society. His publications include *Career Crash* (1994, Simon & Schuster).

Jaber F. Gubrium is Professor of Sociology at the University of Florida. His research focuses on the descriptive organization of personal identity, family, the life course, illness and aging. With James A. Holstein, he is author of *The New Language of Qualitative Method* (1997, Oxford University Press), which explores the theoretical and methodological implications of researchers' choices of analytic and conceptual vocabularies.

Christian Heath is Professor of Sociology at the University of Nottingham. He is currently undertaking various projects concerned with work, interaction and technology, including studies of the media, health care and telecommunications; see, for example, 'Convergent activities: (collaborative work and multimedia technology in London Underground Line Control Rooms', in David Middleton and Yrjö Engestrom (eds), *Cognition and Communication at Work: Distributed Cognition in the Workplace* (1997, Cambridge University Press).

John Heritage is Professor of Sociology at the University of California, Los Angeles. He works in the fields of conversation analysis, mass media and medicine. His current research includes work on the news interview in Britain and the United States, and on various aspects of primary health care. He is co-editor with Paul Drew of *Talk at Work: Interaction in Institutional Settings* (1992, Cambridge University Press).

James A. Holstein is Professor of Sociology at Marquette University. He has conducted qualitative research in a variety of people processing and social control settings, including courts, juries, schools and mental health agencies. He is co-author, with Jaber F. Gubrium, of *The Active Interview* (1995, Sage) which brings a social constructionist perspective to the research interviewing process.

Gale Miller is Professor of Sociology in the Department of Social and Cultural Sciences, Marquette University. His research interests involve theoretically informed qualitative studies of everyday life in contemporary organizations and institutions. His recent research focuses on how personal and social problems are rhetorically constructed and remedied in organizational and institutional settings. He is author with James A. Holstein of *Dispute Domains and Welfare Claims: Conflict and Law in Public Bureaucracies* (1996, JAI Press).

Jody Miller is Assistant Professor in the Department of Criminology and Criminal Justice, University of Missouri at St Louis. Her main areas of interest are gender, adolescence and delinquency and she is currently studying female gang involvement. A recent paper is 'Gender and power on the streets: Street prostitution in the era of crack cocaine', *Journal of Contemporary Ethnography*, 23 (4), 1995.

Anssi Peräkylä is Associate Professor in Sociology at the University of Helsinki. His areas of interest include medical interaction and current research focuses on doctor–patient interaction in Finnish primary care. He is author of *AIDS Counselling: Institutional Interaction and Clinical Practice* (1995, Cambridge University Press).

Jonathan Potter is Professor of Discourse Analysis in the Department of Social Sciences at Loughborough University. He has had a long-standing interest in discourse analysis, fact construction, interaction in natural settings and social psychological theory. His most recent book is *Representing Reality: Discourse, Rhetoric and Social Construction* (1996, Sage).

Lindsay Prior is Senior Lecturer in Social Research Methods at the University of Wales, Cardiff. His research interests centre on various aspects of the sociology of health and illness, and issues of social research. He is currently researching into images of risk in twentieth-century social and medical sciences. His is author of *The Social Organization of Mental Illness* (1993, Sage).

David Silverman is Professor of Sociology at Goldsmiths College, University of London. His research interests are focused on professional–client interaction, medicine and counselling, and qualitative research methods. He is author of *Interpreting Qualitative Data: Methods for Analysing Talk, Text and Interaction* (1993, Sage) and of *Discourses of Counselling: HIV Counselling as Social Interaction* (1996, Sage).

Rod Watson is currently Reader in Sociology, Victoria University of Manchester. In 1996 he was awarded the Francqui Medal and Francqui Inter-University Professorship in Belgium. He has published in ethnomethodology, conversation(al) analysis and interactional ethnography. His substantive research projects have included analyses of murder interrogations, telephoned calls to 'crisis intervention' centres, interaction and locomotion in public space, risk management in mountain and forest driving, classroom interaction, the textual analysis of sociological writings and ethnographic texts on Afro-American speech practices.

In memory of Phil Strong
A fine sociologist and a true friend

PART I INTRODUCTION

1 Introducing *Qualitative Research*

David Silverman

This text aims to build on the success of the editor's *Interpreting Qualitative Data* (*IQD* – Silverman, 1993). Like that book, it was generated by a number of assumptions which I feel I ought to put before the reader. Namely:

1 The centrality of the relationship between analytic perspectives and methodological issues and the consequent requirement to go beyond a purely 'cookbook' version of research methods.
2 The need to broaden our conception of qualitative research beyond issues of subjective 'meaning' and towards issues of language, representation and social organization.
3 The desire to search for ways of building links between social science traditions rather than dwelling in 'armed camps' fighting internal battles.
4 The belief that a social *science*, which takes seriously the attempt to sort fact from fancy, remains a valid enterprise.
5 The assumption that we no longer need to regard qualitative research as provisional or never based on initial hypotheses. This is because qualitative studies have already assembled a usable, cumulative body of knowledge.
6 The commitment to a dialogue between social science and the community based on a recognition of their different starting points rather than upon a facile acceptance of topics defined by what are taken to be 'social problems'.

Each of these assumptions is, implicitly or explicitly, highly contested within contemporary qualitative research. This is largely, I believe, because such research has become a terrain on which the diverse schools of late twentieth-century social theory have fought their mock battles. Ultimately, the assumptions set out here try to extricate us a little from such battles by appealing to a kind of aesthetics of research whose details I attempt to sketch out in the final chapter of this book.

Of course, avoiding such battles, in the context of a commitment to a cumulative social science, is far more likely to make our trade appear relevant to the wider community. As we look outwards rather than inwards, with confidence rather than despair, the way is open for a fruitful dialogue between social scientists, practitioners and community groups.

Moreover, it is worth noting that we present ourselves not only to the wider community but also to the students we teach. Both *IQD* and the idea for this present book derive from twenty-five years of teaching methodology courses and supervising research projects at both undergraduate and graduate levels. That experience has reinforced the wisdom of the old maxim that true learning is based upon *doing*. In practice, this means that I approach taught courses as workshops in which students are given skills to analyse data and so to learn the craft of our trade. This means that assessments of students' progress are properly done through data exercises rather than the conventional essay in which students are invited to offer wooden accounts of what other people have written.

It follows that I have little time for the conventional trajectory of the PhD in which students spend their first year 'reviewing the literature', gather data in year two and then panic in year three about how they can analyse their data. Instead, my students begin their data analysis in year one – sometimes in week one. In that way, they may well have 'cracked' the basic problem in their research in that first year and so can spend their remaining years pursuing the worthy but relatively non-problematic tasks of ploughing through their data following an already established method.

Like *IQD*, my hope is that this book will be used by students who are not yet familiar with the approaches involved, their theoretical underpinnings and their research practice. In *IQD*, student exercises were designed to allow readers to test their understanding of each chapter. In this book, worked through examples of research studies make the arguments much more accessible. Moreover, the chapters are not written in standard edited collection style as chapters addressed to the contributors' peers but inaccessible to a student audience. This means that the presentation is didactic but not 'cookbook' in style.

The particular contribution of this reader lies in its assembly of a very well-known international team of researchers who share my commitment to rigorous, analytically derived but non-polarized qualitative research. Six US researchers join seven from the UK, two from France and one each from Finland and Australia.

While the majority of the contributors are sociologists, the disciplines of social psychology (Potter) and educational studies (Baker) are also represented. In any event, I believe that all have succeeded in making their presentations accessible to a multidisciplinary audience. Rather than denying their own analytic position in favour of some woolly centre ground, these authors have clearly set out the assumptions from which they proceed while remaining open to the diverse interests of their readers.

Each has written a chapter which reflects on the analysis of each of the kinds of data discussed in *IQD*: observations, texts, talk and interviews.

Following *IQD*, each author uses particular examples of data analysis to advance analytic arguments.

The two chapters on observational methods seek to rescue observational work from the pitfalls of mere 'description' and lazy coding and towards exciting methodological and analytic directions for observational research. In Chapter 2, Isabelle Baszanger and Nicolas Dodier begin with the need to ground research in field observations. The question they then raise is how the ethnographer actually goes about relating partial observations to broader generalizations about the 'whole'. Baszanger and Dodier show how ethnography has been dominated by traditions which seek to integrate observations either by an appeal to the concept of 'subculture' or by the understanding or writing of the individual author. Rejecting such appeals to 'culture' or 'the self', they depict a 'combinative ethnography' which seeks to generalize by applying the comparative method to groups of situations or activities collected in the ethnographic 'casebook'.

In Chapter 3, Gale Miller shows how cumulative observation can be combined with analytic vitality. In this chapter, 'Building Bridges', Miller raises the possibility of dialogue between ethnography, conversation analysis and Foucault. Beginning with the focus on naturally occurring data used by discursively oriented ethnographers, Miller points to what each of these three traditions have in common and to how they can provoke a set of fascinating research questions for the ethnographer. He then shows how these questions can be addressed in the single case study as well as in comparative or longitudinal studies.

Part III on 'texts' follows Miller's call for building bridges by showing how ethnographic reading of texts can fruitfully work with a diverse set of analytic traditions. Paul Atkinson and Amanda Coffey apply theories from literary theory of narrative and genre to the documents through which organizations represent themselves and the records and documentary data they accumulate. Taking the example of 'audit', they show how we can fruitfully analyse financial statements produced by accountants and accounts of their work by university departments. They also remind us of the 'audit trail' as documents refer to other documents. Following Atkinson and Coffey, we are given the tools to explicate systematically how texts are organized through the concepts of 'authorship', 'readership', 'intertextuality' and 'rhetoric'.

In Lindsay Prior's chapter on texts, we move from literary theory to Foucault's theory of discourse. However, unlike the stultifying theoretical level of some introductions to Foucault, Prior has written a delightful, accessible chapter which shows, in practice, what it is like to use such a method. Avoiding references to a knowing 'subject', Prior shows us how we can instead focus on how a text instructs us to see the world. Using examples as diverse as a star atlas, a statistical summary of 'causes of death' and a psychiatric interview, he reveals how Foucault's work can properly be used as a thought-provoking toolbox.

Like Prior and Atkinson and Coffey, Rod Watson's chapter on texts takes us through many empirical examples – from newspaper headlines, to police reports, to the social organization of public space. Watson argues that texts are so pervasive that, ironically, we may not properly attend to them. Drawing on the ethnomethodological work of Garfinkel and Sacks, he reminds us of how texts depend upon the common-sense properties of everyday language. Moreover, like the previous two chapters, Watson shows how texts and readers are active in encouraging or producing particular interpretations.

This idea of the 'active' reader is carried over into Part IV on interviews. All three chapters in this section remind us that both interviewees and social scientists actively construct meaning in each other's talk. Jody Miller and Barry Glassner address the issue of finding 'reality' in interview accounts. As I argued in *IQD*, the desire of many researchers to treat interview data as more or less straightforward 'pictures' of an external reality can fail to understand how that 'reality' is being represented in words. Miller and Glassner set out a position which seeks to move beyond this argument about the 'inside' and the 'outside' of interview accounts. Using their own research on adolescents' social worlds, they argue that interview accounts may fruitfully be treated as situated elements in social worlds, drawing upon and revising and reframing the cultural stories available in those worlds. For Miller and Glassner, the focus of interview research should be fixed upon what stories are told and how and where they are produced.

In their chapter, James Holstein and Jaber Gubrium show us how a focus on story and narrative structure demands that we recognize that both interview data and interview analysis are *active* occasions in which meanings are produced. This means that we ought to view research 'subjects' not as stable entities but as actively constructed through their answers. Indeed, in Holstein and Gubrium's telling phrase, both interviewee and interviewer are 'practitioners of everyday life'. Using examples from their research on nursing home residents and on carers of elderly family members, they invite us to locate the interpretive practices which generate the 'hows' and the 'whats' of experience as aspects of reality that are constructed in collaboration with the interviewer to produce a 'narrative drama'.

The final chapter on interview data is by Carolyn Baker. In common with Holstein and Gubrium, Baker treats interview talk as social action in which all parties draw upon their cultural knowledge in doing their accounting work. Baker's particular contribution is to show how interview data may be analysed in terms of the categories that participants use and how those categories are routinely attached to particular kinds of activity. Using this form of Sacks's 'membership categorization analysis', Baker shows how we can describe the interpretive work present in data taken from parent–teacher interviews and research interviews with teenagers and the Chair of a school welfare committee. Like the previous two chapters,

Baker appeals to the 'cultural logics' drawn upon by members in accounting for themselves and assembling a social world which is 'recognizably familiar, orderly and moral'.

Part V is concerned with audio and video data. Jonathan Potter discusses discourse analysis (DA) as a way of analysing naturally occurring talk. Potter shows the manner in which DA allows us to address how versions of reality are produced to seem objective and separate from the speaker. Using examples drawn from television interviews with Princess Diana and Salman Rushdie and a newspaper report of a psychiatrist's comment, he demonstrates how we can analyse the ways in which speakers disavow a 'stake' in their actions.

In its focus on how reality is locally constructed, DA shares many concerns with conversation analysis (CA). John Heritage's chapter presents an accessible introduction to how conversation analytic methods can be used in the analysis of institutional talk. After a brief review of the main features of such talk, Heritage devotes the rest of his chapter to an illuminating analysis of a short telephone conversation between a school employee and the mother of a child who may be a truant. He shows how, using CA, we can identify the overall structural organization of the phone call, its sequence organization, turn design, the lexical choices of speakers and interactional asymmetries. Finally, Heritage demonstrates how each of these elements fits inside each other – 'rather like a Russian doll', as he puts it.

The elegance of Heritage's account of institutional talk is matched by Christian Heath's discussion of the analysis of face to face interaction through video. Beginning with a clear account of CA's focus on sequential organization, Heath shows how CA can be used to study visual conduct and how the physical properties of human environments are made relevant within the course of social interaction. Like Heritage, Heath uses an extended example. In a medical consultation, a patient's movements serve to focus the doctor's attention on a particular aspect of her account of her symptoms. The example also shows that, while the visual aspect of conduct is not organized on a turn by turn basis, as Heath puts it: 'the sequential relations between visual and vocal actions remain a critical property of their organization'. Heath concludes by showing the relevance of these insights to studies of the workplace, including human–computer interaction.

The final three chapters of this book, by Peräkylä, Bloor and myself, each deal with a self-contained theme. Anssi Peräkylä discusses how qualitative research can seek to offer reliable and valid descriptions. Following Heritage's chapter, Peräkylä illustrates his argument with CA research on institutional interaction. He shows how good transcripts of audio-recorded interactions can maintain the reliability of the data. However, Peräkylä also shows how we can accommodate the fact that tapes do not necessarily include all aspects of social interaction and addresses such 'nitty gritty' questions as the selection of what to record, the technical quality of recordings and the adequacy of transcripts. Finally, validity questions are discussed in terms of conventional 'deviant case analysis' as well as specifically CA methods, such as validation through 'next turn'. Overall, Peräkylä is right to claim that his chapter is the first systematic attempt to discuss such matters in relation to CA. At the same time, his discussion has a much broader relevance to all serious qualitative research.

Michael Bloor's chapter also deals with a topic that concerns most qualitative researchers: the ability of our research to contribute to addressing social problems. Bloor argues that our focus on everyday activities makes it particularly relevant in helping practitioners to think about their working practices. He demonstrates his argument by detailed discussions of case studies which he conducted of male prostitutes in Glasgow and of eight therapeutic communities. Both sets of studies illustrate Bloor's point about the ways in which rigorous qualitative research can have relevance for service provision, even if, at least in Britain, it is unlikely to have much impact upon policy debates at the governmental level. Finally, Bloor reviews (and rejects) the argument that social scientists should not be practitioners' helpers.

Not all of the contributors to this volume are in agreement about every issue. We particularly see this within Parts II and V, where contrasting views of each kind of data analysis are advanced. None the less, I believe that the contributors to this volume share enough in common to make this a coherent volume.

Many of my contributors, I suspect, would agree with most of the six points at the start of this chapter. With more certainty, I would claim that we share a fairly common sense of what constitutes 'good' qualitative research. For instance, even though we come from different intellectual traditions, I would be surprised if we were to have any fundamental disagreement about, say, the assessment of an article submitted to us for refereeing.

This common sense of what we are 'looking for' derives, I believe, from an aesthetic of social research. Therefore, this volume concludes with a Postscript in which I sketch out some of my thoughts on what this aesthetic might be. Most of my other authors have not seen this Postscript (although I thank Paul Acourt, Anne Murcott, Jonathan Potter and Ros Gill for their helpful comments on an earlier draft) and I must beg their pardon if they find it fails to match their own sense of their purposes. But I hope (and think) that, by and large, it does.

I want to conclude this Introduction by referring to an absent friend. To my delight, Phil Strong had accepted my invitation to contribute a chapter to this book. His topic was to be: 'Frames and Ceremonial Orders: Observational Work after Goffman'. Tragically and unexpectedly, Phil died before he could write this chapter. I did think about finding another author to cover Phil's topic. Very quickly, however, I decided that Phil's contribution was irreplaceable. This book is, therefore, dedicated to him.

Finally, I would like to thank my Editor at Sage, Stephen Barr, who had the original idea for this book, and Greer Rafferty at Goldsmiths, who, as usual, has helped a great deal in getting the typescript together. As always, my thanks are due to Gilly and Arthur for putting up with me and to my friends at the Nursery End for giving me summers I can look forward to.

Reference

Silverman, D. (1993) *Interpreting Qualitative Data: Methods for Analysing Talk, Text and Interaction*. London: Sage.

PART II OBSERVATION

2 Ethnography

Relating the Part to the Whole

*Isabelle Baszanger and Nicolas Dodier**

By the beginning of the twentieth century, the anthropological tradition, primarily through the influential work of Bronislaw Malinowski, Edward Evans-Pritchard and Margaret Mead, had conferred an abiding legitimacy on field observations integrated into a 'cultural whole'. The subsequent crisis in this model corresponds to two lines of questioning. First, ethnomethodological studies undermined the conventional view by revealing the interpretations and negotiations needed to decontextualize observation situations at all junctures of fieldwork. Whether that work is ethnographic or statistical, it involves invisible operations that do not generally appear in social studies texts. Secondly, analysis of field notes starting in the 1980s forced a revision of the traditional views of the anthropologist in the field and served as a basis for a very critical reassessment, even within the field of ethnology itself, of the authority of the ethnographer. Since that time, new conceptions of ethnography have emerged. They reassert the value of fieldwork, but focus more on demonstrating the relationship between forms of heterogeneous action rather than trying to identify a culture as a whole. This chapter will sum up new developments in ethnography, particularly in terms of the concept of fieldwork, the status it confers on ethnographic data and the way it envisages the aggregation of cases.

An initial characterization of ethnographic research

Ethnographic studies are carried out to satisfy three simultaneous requirements associated with the study of human activities:

1 the need for an empirical approach;
2 the need to remain open to elements that cannot be codified at the time of the study;
3 a concern for grounding the phenomena observed in the field.

Each requirement is briefly discussed below.

---

* Translated by Philippa Cruchley-Wallis.

The need for an empirical approach

This first need is dictated by the fact that the phenomena studied cannot be deduced but require empirical observation. This is undoubtedly what Durkheim really meant by his well-known injunction to 'treat social facts as things', meaning not so much that sociology should be conducted along the same lines as the natural sciences, but as a way of distinguishing it from philosophy and the introspection that takes place upstream of an empirical approach.[1] In the current debate over the resources people mobilize to understand the world and to make reference to it, this is the major difference between the social sciences, on the one hand, and the philosophy of language, phenomenology and hermeneutics, on the other.

The need to remain open

Beyond any methodical planning of observations, the fieldworker must remain open in order to discover the elements making up the markers and the tools that people mobilize in their interactions with others and, more generally, with the world. By markers, we mean representations of the world, or normative expectations, but also the linguistic and para-linguistic resources that are displayed in contact with the environment (Bessy and Chateauraynaud, 1995; Thévenot, 1994). The objective here is to distinguish between openness to new data (*in situ studies*) and its opposite, as when individual activities are studied according to strict schedules and on the basis of previously defined items and rules (*a priori codified studies*). This second approach is intrinsically incapable of revealing the unexpected elements that come to light as a study progresses. In methodological terms, a study can be described as *in situ* if it allows each subject to behave in an endogenous manner, that is, one that is not influenced by the study arrangements. There are many reasons for not 'aligning' the subjects of a study in compliance with the study arrangements, just as there are many theories calling for recourse to ethnographic studies: discovery of other cultures that cannot be understood in the light of pre-existing knowledge (anthropological tradition), the contingency of continually negotiated human activities (interactionist tradition) and observation of how people handle the contingencies of a given situation (ethnomethodology), and so on.

This principle of openness to what cannot *a priori* be pre-codified results in the basic tension underlying *in situ* studies. The flexibility required by this openness conflicts with the need to maintain at least a minimum of method in the conduct of the study, that is, a certain guide for the behaviour both of the fieldworker and the people observed, depending on the plan of the study. This duality is an implicit part of the general situation of the *in situ* fieldworker. The tension is primarily epistemological. The principle of non-alignment of the people observed does not sit easily with the principle of planning that has governed the experimental sciences since the idea of scientific 'reproduction' or 'reproducibility' was elevated to the rank of a major, normative requirement of scientific research (Licoppe, 1996). Social scientists who wish, none the less, to continue openly to observe the endogenous development of human activities approach this problem in a number of different ways. Some seek to conform as closely as possible to the requirements of experimental reproducibility. Even if they allow open activity sequences to take place, they try as much as possible to standardize the time intervals of these sequences and record this activity by automatic means (tape recorder or VCR used in conversation analysis). Others oppose this requirement of alignment and even the whole idea of observation corresponding to the current canons of science. They insist on an approach that is opposed to any type of planning, leaving the study completely open to the uncertainties of the field. Still others recognize the need for some sort of compromise between method and openness to situations, and see ethnographic tensions as a more extreme but, ultimately, a quite banal example of the sort of negotiation that is omnipresent in science (e.g. scientists' negotiation between the need to follow standard rules, which in any case always demand local interpretations and adjustments, and the concrete course of any scientific endeavour).[2] It is worth noting that this duality underlying the ethnographer's work also has moral implications beyond the epistemological dimension. To satisfy this principle of openness, which is deliberately taken quite far, the ethnographer must graft his/her study onto pre-existing systems of activity. As opposed to the researcher, who channels subject matter into the laboratory, the ethnographer leaves the laboratory and tries to make his/her data gathering compatible with the study population's other commitments. By definition, ethnographic study design is a hybrid approach in which the fieldworker is present in two agencies, as data gatherer and as a person involved in activities directed towards other objectives.[3]

Grounding observed phenomena in the field

A study becomes ethnographic when the fieldworker is careful to connect the facts that s/he observes with the specific features of the *backdrop* against which these facts occur, which are linked to historical and cultural contingencies. Not all *in situ* studies are field studies. Distinctions can be made between different sorts of empirical study carried out in the social sciences. Some attempt to universalize, that is, are formal in nature, while others, resolutely grounded in a specific context, can be considered as ethnographic – or field – studies. Formal studies dissociate collected data from any context in order to access a universal, human level from the outset. This is the approach characteristic of the philosophy of language, of Austin's pragmatics, of phenomenological analyses or ordinary language analysis based on analysis of conversations. It is also characteristic of the 'nomothetical' approach that uses empirical observation to demonstrate consistencies between facts and to formulate general laws. Nevertheless, the ethnographic study is not only empirical or only 'open'. It is, like history, embedded in a field that is limited in time and space (Ricoeur, 1983). Returning to a concept that Darbo-Peschanski (1987) applies to the studies of Herodotus, it is a 'science of the particular' and describes itself as such. This does not exclude a second step, in which a series of ethnographic studies can serve as sources for defining universal, human phenomena, in the true sense. This is, for example, the position of Lévi-Strauss: ethnographic studies provide elements for ethnological texts that study societies one after the other – on this basis and starting from a systematic comparison between societies, anthropological work attempts to arrive at a theory of the structure of the human spirit. In *in situ* studies, this reference to field experience nevertheless distinguishes ethnographic studies from other observation methods that are not grounded in a specific field (conversation analysis, situated cognition and ethnomethodology). This raises a question about fieldwork: what is the status of this 'specific' context in which the study takes place? How is it described? How is this framework delineated, since it is not a here-and-now situation, nor a situation in which humankind as a whole is characterized through the fundamental properties of every one of its activities? This question is the focal point of any analysis of the process of generalization in ethnography, particularly through the question of how a cultural whole is depicted. This is sometimes called the process of 'totalization', an operation whereby the ethnographer integrates the different observation sequences into a global referential framework.

Integrative ethnography

The ethnographic tradition has long considered that it is possible to integrate sequences of ethnographic observations by relating them to a cultural whole: a global reference which encompasses these observations and within which the different data throw light on each other. This vision of an integrative ethnography has been developed in social and cultural anthropology, particularly in the study of non-Western societies, but also in similar studies carried out in Western countries. It also involves the most culturally oriented part of the interactionist tradition: that is, the study of microcultures or subcultures, and, more generally, all references in the interactionist tradition to the existence of communities of people sharing the same rules and the same understanding of the world (e.g. deviant communities). Integrative ethnography proposes a monographic totalization that is distinct from statistical totalization or summation. In general, the latter does not meet the requirement of openness, and is therefore excluded from our classification of '*in situ*' study methods.[4]

A number of methods have been proposed to achieve this monographic totalization. First, it can result from the fieldworker's reflections, whereby s/he achieves an integrated vision of his/her subjective experience. This is the meaning behind calls for empathy with the people encountered: the fieldworker tries to immerse him/herself in the field conditions and gain access to the point of view of the others, seen as 'natives', that is, people who share a similar cultural perspective, one that differs from the perspective of the newly arrived fieldworker. As Clifford noted, a professional anthropologist is supposed to successfully 'infiltrate the expressional universe of the other' (1983: 100). By understanding the other through an empathetic relationship, the fieldworker would be able to reconstruct this other's point of view, and therefore culture (or the contents of this other's collective consciousness). The assumption of empathy as the process through which the point of view of the other becomes transparent to the fieldworker is vulnerable to criticisms arising from hermeneutic interpretation of texts and actions (Gadamer, 1976; Ricoeur, 1986). The act of gaining access to the point of view of the other always implies an initial period of questioning, which is itself embedded in a certain tradition, that of the interpreter – s/he is always caught in the 'hermeneutic circle' of the initial questioning of the text (or action), and of its transformation, in return, as a result of this encounter. Although certain relationships or certain moments can be better qualified as empathetic, in the sense of a type of harmony between persons, we cannot therefore conclude that the point of view of the other will be conveyed in total transparency or that it can be expressed in words. Any interpretive act is influenced, consciously or not, by the tradition to which the interpreter belongs. Lévi-Strauss (1974) proposes a variation on this process by considering the moment the experience is integrated into a whole not as a moment of access to the point of view of the other, but as a moment when the entire set of results experienced and memorized by the fieldworker crystallize into a single, unified experience. That event takes place at the conclusion of the fieldworker's ethnographic apprenticeship in the society studied. The ethnographer's field experience 'represents a crucial moment in his/her education, prior to which he may have accumulated dissociated knowledge that might never integrate into a holistic experience; only after this moment will this knowledge "take definitive form" and suddenly acquire a meaning that it previously lacked' (Lévi-Strauss, 1974: 409). In other words, what we are dealing with here is a genuine 'internal revolution' (Lévi-Strauss, 1974: 409).

By treating participant observation as a method rather than 'a clinical talent' resulting from an empathetic stance,[5] a number of authors have helped to provide a new explanation for the position of the ethnographer, which becomes one of his/her own methodological tools. Just like the ethnographer in remote societies, the observer has to accept a separation from his/her familiar universe, not only in order to be physically present in the new environment, but also in order to achieve personal proximity.[6]

The observer has to enter into the group and find the right distance between him/herself and the group. There is a close relationship here between the observer's presentation of him/herself (to enter the field and throughout the study), and the place accorded to the observer by the other. While it is paramount for a fieldworker to be attentive to the expectations and role projections of the people being observed,[7] this is less in order to achieve an empathetic attitude than because the interrelations themselves and, finally, the fieldworker and the work done on his/her experience are the preferential instruments of observation. There is nothing romantic or intuitive here. This is conscious work on the part of the observer, who has to control his/her emotional reaction to what is observed and also develop a finely tuned introspection to fully understand the process of transformation which s/he undergoes by being constantly present in the field. Hence, understanding a cultural whole is achieved through this reciprocating motion of the observer and the phenomena that s/he is observing, or, as Fox puts it, the process 'by which a participant observer gradually makes organized sense out of what he sees, hears and becomes a part of it' (1974: 230). The observer establishes a sort of parallel between what s/he feels and what the people observed feel, or the phases they pass through. S/he uses a form of introspection to reveal how s/he develops new attitudes or borrows new roles and what that 'does for him/her'. In this way, s/he has fleeting insights into the possible functions and meanings for the people observed, which s/he then tries to verify in the field, at which point s/he either recognizes their validity or rejects them.[8] The duration of the observation enables the fieldworker in a sense to immerse him/herself in the subject being observed, but this is closer to a process of socialization than a direct access to the point of view of the other. In order to achieve a comprehensive understanding of a group, the fieldworker has to work his/her way through the dense fabric of the culture observed, in order to arrive later at an objective understanding and, hence, a monographic totalization.[9] This brings us back to a slightly modified form of Lévi-Strauss's position.

Geertz (1973) also distances himself from the empathetic schema and reintegrates the concept of culture in a hermeneutic process: activities can be read like texts, as far as both the actors themselves and the fieldworker are concerned; the concept of 'culture' is also a tool for the actors, who use it to interpret their reciprocal behaviour. It is the discovery of the hermeneutic role of the concept of culture for all individuals in their daily relationships – based not on a representation of lived experience or on their point of view, but on a description of their oral or written production – that allows us to relate a sequence of specific scenes to a culture. In any case (empathy, the integrative experience of the ethnographer, the participant observation of the sociologist, the hermeneutic approach), access to the major outlines of the culture being studied, as can be seen in all ethnography manuals, implies using methods to go beyond a disparate set of ethnographic observations and discover an integrated culture which is different from other cultures.[10]

Because of its capacity to satisfy the need for concrete facts in the study and at the same time produce a discourse taking in collective wholes, this approach has for a long time exerted a great deal of fascination over the social sciences. However, it does not stand up very well to two criticisms. First, it is only valid if we are dealing with so-called 'mechanical' solidarity between individuals (Durkheim), that is, a society or group in which people are assumed to share the same elements of the collective consciousness. Difficulties arise if the coordination between human activities conforms to other types of logic. In contemporary worlds, one now has to take into account the fact that several possible references can coexist despite their contradictions, sometimes within the same person, and that they can slot into the normative guidelines for action depending on the constraints of the actual situation (Boltanski and Thévenot, 1991). The very notion of society becomes problematical when solidarity between people is established along socio-technical networks in which individuals coordinate their activities step by step according to functional objectives and without reference to a single common framework (Dodier, 1995a). Moreover, at the methodological level, the moment at which data are integrated into a whole occurs at an unknown, almost mysterious point of the process. Some ethnographers cultivate this sense of mystery by affirming their lack of interest in any account of methods. But others take a more ambiguous stand: monographic totalization may conceal implicit statistical totalization performed, as it were, behind the scenes. We see this particularly in the rhetoric of cultural ethnographic studies, which very easily use frequency markers when describing behaviour (often, sometimes, from time to time, always, etc.) without making more than a token attempt to justify them. These problems have been taken very seriously by some historians of ethnography and by certain ethnographers, to the point of casting doubt on the tradition of totalization presented more or less as a foregone conclusion in ethnology and field sociology.

Narrative integration

An attentive reading of ethnographers' field notes, particularly the famous example of Malinowski's notebook (1985), has led some authors to hark back to the question of the status that should be accorded to the process of monographic totalization. Hence was revealed the very personal nature of the act of totalization, perceived in an almost ritual form by anthropologists as an experience associated with solitude. For a long time, this experience in the field was perceived as a necessary moment of immersion in a culture for which the anthropologist could then become the legitimate representative. An analysis of field notes shows that the switch from this experience in the field to the ethnographic text is more complicated than had been thought until then. The role of the actual individual history of the ethnographer in his/her manner of identifying the culture became more apparent, as did the influence of the actual work of writing on the identification of cultural types, based on much vaguer and more varied encounters than might be imagined from the simple accounts given in the published texts (Clifford, 1985). Once this observation was acknowledged, several channels were explored.

The first consists of claiming that the writing work itself is an essential part of ethnography. The ethnographic text is deliberately considered to be a work of fiction, stylizing people and events as a way of emphasizing their cultural traits. The ethnographer is seen as an author and due emphasis is given to the profoundly personal nature of his/her account (Clifford, 1983, 1985). Another channel consists of seeing the fieldwork itself not as the hidden face of ethnography, perhaps reported in a personal diary, but as the actual material of the ethnographic text. This text is no longer the 'picture' of a culture or a society revealed to the ethnographer at the end of a learning process by which, finally, s/he is able to see it as a whole, but the 'account' of events confronting the ethnographer as the inquiry progresses. The narrative is now seen as integrating these events (Ricoeur, 1983); it preserves their temporal dimension and does not banish the ethnographer from his/her text – quite the opposite, in fact. This narrative ethnography can take the form of an approach that we might call hyper-reflexive, more preoccupied in fact with questioning and reporting on the operations performed by the ethnographer in his/her attempt, through concepts such as 'culture' or 'society', to confer some meaning on activities, than really acknowledging the existence of the other (Moerman, 1975). The encounter between ethnologist and study population is viewed as a dialogue initiated between individuals who themselves belong to different collective wholes. The concept of 'culture' is not abandoned, but the ethnologist does not try so much to acknowledge an 'other culture' as to reveal the dialogue that is established between different cultures during the fieldwork (Dwyer, 1979).

Finally, the narrative approach in ethnography is influenced by psychoanalysis (Favret-Saada, 1977; Favret-Saada and Contreras, 1981[11]). The study is described as a process profoundly linked to the individual history of the ethnographer. The text may be a history of the events occurring in the course of the fieldwork, that is, the field notes (Favret-Saada and Contreras, 1981). Alternatively, in an approach that is closer to the anthropological tradition, the narrative dimensions of the ethnological study are fitted into or alternate with analyses giving a representation of the logic of the relationships (in this case, the framework surrounding enunciations about sorcery) encountered by the ethnographer (Favret-Saada, 1977). This form of narrative is interesting because it does not unfairly remove the ethnographer from his/her text, particularly if s/he is closely involved in the activities described therein. It also avoids limiting the inquiry to the trajectory of a specific person, without at least suggesting why this experience is exemplary and in what way it provides information about the type of relationship the people studied have with the world. Hence, this form of text transcends the alternative between a purely singular 'I', characteristic of narrative ethnography, and the absence of the 'I', which is typical of classic ethnography. The work of reflexivity is not limited to narratives in the first person. Through the study itself, and in a retrospective vision, the author becomes capable of describing, in the series of events which s/he is reporting, in what capacity s/he was present or what place s/he occupied in these events (and, notably, in the case of Jeanne Favret-Saada, the place of her work in the framework surrounding enunciations). Here, we are dealing, in the field of the social sciences, with texts that have the same force as 'evidence'. Often, these texts also suggest what part of this evidence is representative of a more general condition, by using all the possibilities of first-person narration and by identifying the role played by the author.[12]

The ethnographic casebook

There is another way of looking at the aggregation of specific events collected in an ethnographic study. The context of the events observed is considered neither as a 'whole' to be discovered (integrative ethnography) nor as a grounding point for an individual history (narrative ethnography), but as a disparate collection of resources between which individuals have to navigate. Unlike the cultural approach, we do not presume here that the resources mobilized by people in their behaviour can be linked up to a coherent whole. Unlike narrative ethnography, we leave behind the first-person account, the aim being to generalize from the study. This approach could be described as *combinative ethnography*. It takes several different forms in ethnographic work. In point of fact, it is present from the very beginning of the interactionist tradition. Compared with the anthropological tradition, the originality of the first works in the Chicago tradition was that they did not necessarily integrate the data collected around a collective whole in terms of a common culture, but in terms of territory, of geographic space.[13] The problem with which these sociologists were concerned was based on human ecology: interactions of human groups with the natural environment and interactions of human groups in a given geographical milieu. Their key concept, the unit of reference, so to speak, was the biotic community, with its notion of territory.[14] The main point here was to make an inventory of a space by studying the different communities and activities of which it is composed, that is, which encounter and confront each other in that space. Hence, the ethnographic material aimed to identify certain cases (and notably life histories) as examples of more general phenomena,[15] but with quite a high degree of freedom to circulate between different levels of generalization.[16] It should be noted that the ethnographer's participation in daily activities is seen as much, if not more, as a way of collecting facts as of gaining access to the meaning of situations for the subjects being studied. In this respect, we are still some distance away from the movement that was to become participant observation in the 1950s (cf. Platt, 1983) and the position of integrative ethnography.[17]

In the theory of action proposed by Glaser and Strauss (1967) as well as in its methodological implications, the method known as 'constant comparison' does not necessarily concern collective entities, but rather situations or types of activity, classified by the sociologist and studied in their relationships to each other, with a view to revealing their compatibility or the contrasts between them. Individuals can switch from one line of activity to another and the aim of the sociological study is to demonstrate the combinations – whether harmonious or conflictual – between these multiple commitments.

This methodological orientation has also emerged within the framework of new developments of the sociological theory of action. Here, in the context of 'sociological pragmatics', it is considered that individuals can be involved in different 'regimes of action', that the arrangements that provide a framework for these situations direct people towards certain forms of commitment, but that tensions or combinations can emerge between these regimes of action (Boltanski and Thévenot, 1991; Dodier, 1993, 1995b). For example, the actual work of a doctor could be studied as the articulation between different 'framings' of his or her patient (Baszanger, 1992; Dodier, 1994; Silverman, 1987). From this viewpoint, recourse to the ethnographic study is no longer concerned with the search for references shared by the actors, as in the integrative approach. It aims to take stock of the dynamic relationship between the real activities of individuals within the framework of complex, normative references, which are related to the situation and are not unified. Although the arrangements framing the action are assumed to have a historical origin and a particular distribution in space, they are not automatically assigned to a culture. This type of schema, which breaks with the concept of a collective consciousness shared from the outset, assumes that individuals, and their actions, are located at the intersection of a non-harmonized plurality of references, which are examined in their existential commitment.

A common characteristic of these three types of ethnographic study (the Chicago tradition, the form of interactionism inspired by Anselm Strauss, sociological pragmatics) is to *distinguish between generalization and totalization*. The study method consists of accumulating a series of individual cases, of analysing them as a combination between different logics of action that coexist not only in the field under consideration, but even within these individuals or during their encounters. Accumulation and processing of these cases can be likened to an *ethnographic casebook*, which is gradually enriched by new examples displaying new forms of activity and patterns of articulation. The survey aims at producing a combinative inventory of possible situations. The researcher has not chosen an integrated field constituting a central point from which s/he will reconstitute a collective whole. Instead, s/he circulates between several sites, depending on which dimensions appear relevant in the analysis of each case. Although s/he sometimes seeks a field that will allow him/her to study a regime of action or a form of activity in greater depth, s/he is not surprised if this field proves to be more disparate than anticipated, a factor that forces him/her to take into consideration the way in which it is related to other forms of action. The material collected often appears as a rather vast corpus of textual data coming from very disparate sources, in terms of situations and the media used[18].

Combinative ethnography and totalization

Several responses have been proposed, in ethnography, to the question of the aggregation of observations. Integrative ethnography suggests that it is possible, thanks to monographic totalizations, to gain access to the collective wholes that govern behaviour. Narrative ethnography has quite radically challenged any pretension to totalization on the part of the social sciences – it integrates itself in a vaster movement of critiques of totalization in the social sciences,[19] and focuses on the production of highly individualized accounts gathered in the course of the study. Finally, various ethnographic practices have sought to implement forms of generalization, which, starting from work on series of cases, aim not so much at the totalization of data as the revelation of a combinative mechanism between disparate or even contradictory forms of action within a given society. Methodologically speaking, these last-mentioned works refer back to a non-cultural concept of the field already present in the Chicago tradition, but with a greater concern for theoretical clarification concerning the concept of action and the methods for gathering and processing data. They avoid both the mysteries of monographic totalization and the excesses of focusing on the person of the fieldworker evident in some narrative ethnographic works, or the escape back towards hyper-reflexivity.

Nevertheless, it is difficult to avoid these approaches being confronted if not with the question of totalization, at least with that of the distribution in space and time of the forms of action encountered. A purely 'combinative' approach to activities does not really respond to the question of the empirical grounding of these activities. It gives indications as to the diversity of possible situations within a reference field and allows analysis of the dynamic relationship between actions as a function of the figures formed by the encounter of different regimes of action, but it does not respond to the question: who is concerned by this or that logical framework? Where and when? At this point, we can see two possible ways of taking the grounding requirement into account. On the one hand, we can imagine statistical enumerations which, on the basis of ethnographic studies, can give indications as to the distribution of the micro-phenomena studied. Contrary to a 'closed' use of statistics, which does not correspond to the requirement of openness incumbent on fieldwork, we are dealing here with statistics based on categories initially generated by ethnographic work with human actors.[20] On the other hand, we can imagine forms of historical narration which can be used both as a genesis of resources available to contemporary observers and as a way of acknowledging combinations between disparate arrangements, without necessarily falling back into the totalization of historical periodization, history's equivalent of the cultural totalizations of ethnography (Baszanger, 1995; Desrosières, 1993). This suggests the possibility of reintegrating ethnographic observations of the present in history, and hence in the consciousness of historical time.

Appendix: characterization of the ethnographic study

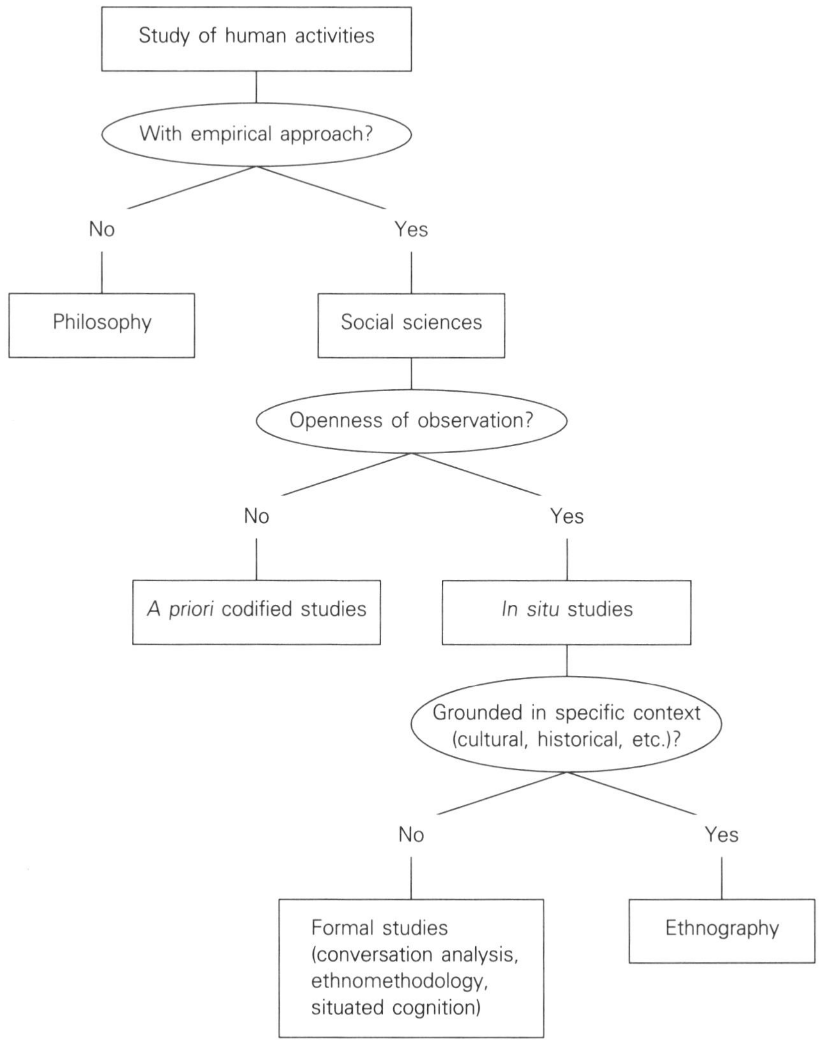

Notes

1. 'To treat facts of a certain order as things is not then to place them in a certain category of reality but to assume a certain mental attitude toward them on the principle that when approaching their study we are absolutely ignorant of their nature, and that their characteristic

properties, like the unknown causes on which they depend, cannot be discovered by even the most careful introspection' (Durkheim, 1967: xiii).

2. This last argument is reinforced, on the epistemological level, by the fact that the negotiated character of the design and implementation of an experiment has, in any case, generally come to light thanks to work in sociology of science. Even in the most detailed experimental plans, negotiations are often eliminated from reports, in spite of the fact that they actually exist (Collins, 1985; Knorr-Cetina, 1981; Latour and Woolgar, 1979).

3. This is why themes of duplicity, treachery and manipulation are at the heart of such narratives (Leiris, 1981). An implicit part of the ethnographer's condition is that s/he has to resolve these tensions as they appear.

4. On the opposition between monograph and statistics, see Desrosières (1993).

5. 'There is a general tendency to think of a study based on participant observation as largely the product of an esoteric, personal kind of clinical talent on the part of the field worker, who is considered to be endowed with qualities usually referred to as "sensitivity", "intuition" and "empathy"' (Fox, 1974: 231).

6. This separation is achieved via an initial work on oneself. 'On several afternoons and evenings at Harvard, I found myself considering a trip to Cornerville and then rationalizing my way out of it. . . . then too, I had to admit that I felt more comfortable among these familiar surroundings than I did wandering around Cornerville and spending time with people in whose presence I felt distinctly uncomfortable at first. When I found myself rationalizing in this way, I realized that I would have to make a break. Only if I lived in Cornerville would I ever be able to understand it and be accepted by it' (Whyte, 1981: 293–4).

7. It is clearly shown in the example in the appendix of Bosk (1979).

8. The way in which Renée Fox describes her understanding (discovery) of the meaning and function of black humour for sick people nicely illustrates this phenomenon: 'At a non-hospital gathering one evening, I *caught myself* in the act of making a macabre joke, and I can remember speculating on the source of my unlikely new talent. The next morning, as I moved to [the ward], for the first time I *noticed* how much of the ward's conversation was phrased in the language of the grim joke and how often I responded in kind. Without realizing it, I had learned to speak to the men of [the ward] in the same way that they talked to each other. Long before this insight occurred, my field notes contained many samples of ward humor. But it was only by virtue of *self-observation* that I became sufficiently *aware* of its prevalence to regard it as a phenomenon central to my study' (1974: 231; emphasis added).

9. This point appears clearly in the relationship between the initial field notes, which, in many ways, already contain 'everything', and the final analysis which came months later: 'From the very start . . . my notes contained almost all the components of the ward picture I was ultimately to assemble. However, at the time that I recorded this observation, I was not yet aware of the patterned interconnections between them. At what point did I begin to see the ward in a coherently structured way? In the sense of month and day, I cannot really answer that question. But I do know that the so-called "understanding" of [the ward] which I eventually attained was not simply the result of coming to know more about the ward in a cognitive sense. It also involved a process of attitude learning (very much akin to what social scientists mean when they refer to the process of "socialization")' (Fox, 1974: 217–18).

10. We can, for example, refer to the classical manuals of Griaule (1957), Maget (1962) or Mauss (1947).

11. See also Certeau (1987) concerning the relationship between history and narrative.

12. Evidence about working-class lifestyles are remarkable in this respect in their capacity to combine accounts of individual histories anchored in very specific contexts and preservation of a general framework of discussion (Linhart, 1978; Navel, 1945; Weil, 1951).

13. The sociological objective of this tradition was an attempt to understand the new urban space emerging as a result of industrialization and the double phenomenon of immigration that accompanied it (from the south and rural zones towards the north and the dawning metropolises, on the one hand, and from the European continent with its multiple ethnic components, on the other). Chicago, with its mosaic of ethnic groups and its different socio-ethnic neighbourhoods, was emblematic of this phenomenon. The aim was to analyse the ways

in which this space in which different groups confronted each other and mixed together was structured and to study their reactions to these totally new living conditions.

14. For example, Thrasher (1927) started from the question of the geographical localization of juvenile delinquency: some sectors are more affected than others, how can this be explained?

15. The preferred approach is the study of natural history followed by a study of the community (understood here in the sense of a biotic community with its notion of territory): a town, a neighbourhood, an ethnic community located in a given geographical space (the ghettos). The central method used is the case study, which is based essentially on a life history and, to a lesser extent, on non-structured interviews using the actual words of the subject and all sorts of personal documents (personal letters, evidence collected in community notebooks, etc.).

16. The important point was to gather intensive data – for example, for *The Hobo* (1923), Anderson collected sixty life histories, made a preliminary study of 400 tramps, one use of which was to establish a list of the apparent physical defects of hobos and to identify both individual and more general traits. Alongside these life histories, the facts were collected via a study of administrative statistics, archives, local newspapers and the case files of social workers.

17. The fieldworker's position is different from the empathetic position of the participant-observer and is closer to that of the stranger, if we refer to Sombart and especially to Simmel. In a text written during his 1927 survey and published in 1983, Cressey shows how he attempted to build up a position as stranger in his ethnographic relationships to study the environment, the world of taxi dance halls. Referring to Sombart's analysis of 'the cultural stranger', he distinguishes between two 'stranger positions' which he used in his research. The 'sociological stranger' is a stranger with a particular status as commonly used by lawyers, doctors, social workers, public school counsellors, etc. The second, which he used much more often, is that of the 'anonymous stranger'. This is an ordinary relationship in big cities where isolated people meet up in transient relationships and with free time on their hands. For the researcher: 'it provides an opportunity for exploring aspects of human nature not ordinarily revealed' and has the effect of a 'catharsis'. This ethnographic relationship allows the fieldworker to access revelations that Cressey calls 'impersonal confessions'.

18. The work of processing these data can benefit from the development of automated techniques designed to facilitate constant two-way communication between the encoding of the material and ethnographic concentration on its special features (Chateauraynaud and Charriau, 1995).

19. On the critique of statistical totalization and its limitations, see Dodier (1996).

20. See for example, the enumerations made in Becker et al. (1961), and, in a more general sense, for the relationships between qualitative and quantitative data in theoretical elaboration, see Glaser and Strauss (1967: Chap. 8).

References

Anderson, N. (1923) *The Hobo*. Chicago: University of Chicago Press.

Baszanger, I. (1992) 'Deciphering chronic pain', *Sociology of Health and Illness*, 14: 181–215.

Baszanger, I. (1995) *Médecine et douleur: La fin d'un oubli*. Paris: Seuil.

Becker, H., Geer, B., Hughes, E. and Strauss, A. (1961) *Boys in White: Students' Culture in Medical School*. Chicago: University of Chicago Press.

Bessy, C. and Chateauraynaud, F. (1995) *Experts et faussaires: Pour une sociologie de la perception*. Paris: Métailié.

Boltanski, L. and Thévenot, L. (1991) *De la justification: Les économies de la grandeur*. Paris: Gallimard.

Bosk, C. (1979) *Forgive and Remember: Managing Medical Failure*. Chicago and London: University of Chicago Press.

Certeau, M. de (1987) *Histoire et psychanalyse entre science et fiction*. Paris: Gallimard.

Chateauraynaud, F. and Charriau, J.P. (1995) *PROSPERO (Programme de Sociologie*

Pragmatique Expérimentale et Réflexive sur Ordinateur). Version 1.0 pour Windows. Paris: Association Doxa-Centre d'Études de l'Emploi.
Clifford, J. (1983) 'De l'autorité en ethnographie', *L'Ethnographie*, 2: 87–118.
Clifford, J. (1985) 'De l'ethnographie comme fiction: Conrad et Malinowski', *Études Rurales*, 97–8: 47–67.
Collins, H. (1985) *Changing Order: Replication and Induction in Scientific Practice*. London: Sage.
Cressey, P. (1983) 'A comparison of the "sociological stranger" and the "anonymous stranger" in field research', *Urban Life*, 12 (1): 102–20.
Darbo-Peschanski, C. (1987) *Le discours du particulier: Essai sur l'enquête hérodotéenne*. Paris: Seuil.
Desrosières, A. (1993) *La politique des grands nombres: Histoire de la raison statistique*. Paris: La Découverte.
Dodier, N. (1993) 'Acting as a combination of common worlds', *Sociological Review*, 41 (3): 556–71.
Dodier, N. (1994) 'Expert medical decisions in occupational medicine: A sociological analysis of medical judgement', *Sociology of Health and Illness*, 16 (4): 489–514.
Dodier, N. (1995a) *Les hommes et les machines: La conscience collective dans les sociétés technicisées*. Paris: Métailié.
Dodier, N. (1995b) 'The conventional foundations of action. Elements of a sociological pragmatics', *Reseaux, The French Journal of Communications*, 3 (2): 147–66.
Dodier, N. (1996) 'Les sciences sociales face à la raison statistique', *Annales: Histoire, Sciences Sociales*, 2: 409–28.
Durkheim, É. (1967) *The Rules of Sociological Method*, trans S. Solway and J. Mueller. New York: The Free Press.
Dwyer, K. (1979) 'The dialogic of ethnography', *Dialectical Anthropology*, 4 (3): 205–24.
Favret-Saada, J. (1977) *Les mots, la mort, les sorts*. Paris: Gallimard.
Favret-Saada, J. and Contreras, J. (1981) *Corps pour corps: Enquête sur la sorcellerie dans le bocage*. Paris: Gallimard.
Fox, R.C. (1974) *Experiment Perilous*. Philadelphia: University of Pennsylvania Press.
Gadamer, H.G. (1976) *Vérité et Méthode: Les grandes lignes d'une herméneutique philosophique*. Paris: Seuil.
Geertz, C. (1973) *The Interpretation of Cultures*. New York: Basic Books.
Glaser, B. and Strauss, A. (1967) *The Discovery of Grounded Theory*. Chicago: Aldine.
Griaule, M. (1957) *Méthode de l'ethnographie*. Paris: PUF.
Knorr-Cetina, K. (1981) *The Manufacture of Knowledge*. Oxford: Pergamon.
Latour, B. and Woolgar, S. (1979) *Laboratory Life: The Production of Scientific Facts*. London: Sage.
Leiris, M. (1981) *L'Afrique fantôme*. Paris: Gallimard.
Lévi-Strauss, C. (1974) *Anthropologie structurale*. Paris: Plon.
Licoppe, C. (1996) *La formation de la pratique scientifique*. Paris: La Découverte.
Linhart, R. (1978) *L'établi*. Paris: Minuit.
Maget, M. (1962) *Guide d'étude directe des comportements culturels (ethnographie métropolitaine)*. Paris: Éditions du CNRS.
Malinowski, B. (1985) *Journal d'ethnographe*. Paris: Seuil.
Mauss, M. (1947) *Manuel d'ethnographie*. Paris: Payot.
Moerman, M. (1975) 'Accomplishing ethnicity', in R. Turner (ed.), *Ethnomethodology*. Harmondsworth: Penguin.
Navel, G. (1945) *Travaux*. Paris: Stock.
Platt, J. (1983) 'The development of the "participant observation" method in sociology: Origin myth and history', *Journal of the History of the Behavioral Sciences*, 19 (October): 379–93.
Ricoeur, P. (1983) *Temps et récit*. Vol. 1. Paris: Seuil.
Ricoeur, P. (1986) *Du texte à l'action: Essais d'herméneutique II*. Paris: Seuil.

Silverman, D. (1987) *Communication and Medical Practice: Social Relations in the Clinic*. London: Sage.
Thévenot, L. (1994) 'Le régime de familiarité: Des choses en personne', *Genèses*, 17: 72–101.
Thrasher, F.M. (1927) *The Gang*. Chicago: University of Chicago Press.
Weil, S. (1951) *La condition ouvrière*. Paris: Gallimard.
Whyte, W.F. (1981) *Street Corner Society* (3rd edn). Chicago: University of Chicago Press.

3 Building Bridges

The Possibility of Analytic Dialogue Between Ethnography, Conversation Analysis and Foucault

Gale Miller

While it is sometimes dismissed as 'only descriptive and impressionistic', I consider qualitative research to be an analytic enterprise. Qualitative research offers sociologists and others distinctive opportunities to develop analytic perspectives that speak directly to the practical circumstances and processes of everyday life. It may also be used to apply and evaluate general theory, including macroscopic perspectives concerned with the broad sweep of history, culture and social structure. Indeed, qualitative research is a unique arena for assessing these perspectives because it requires that they speak to issues of everyday life and practice. Serious questions should be raised about sociological perspectives that purport to speak with authority about social life, but which cannot minimally inform research on how that life is lived (Giddens, 1976).

This chapter extends and elaborates the analytic potential of qualitative research by considering how it may be used to construct bridges between different theories of social life, particularly perspectives that focus on macro- and microscopic issues. The analysis deals with the ways in which the microsociological insights of ethnomethodology (Garfinkel, 1967; Heritage, 1984; Mehan and Wood, 1975; Zimmerman, 1969) and conversation analysis (Atkinson and Heritage, 1984; Boden and Zimmerman, 1991; Button and Lee, 1987; Sacks, 1992; Sacks et al., 1974) may be linked with the macro-historical emphasis of Foucauldian discourse studies (Dreyfus and Rabinow, 1982; Foucault, 1972, 1980; Lindstrom, 1990; Shumway, 1989).

I use the bridging metaphor self-consciously. Bridges link distinctive land formations, making it possible for people to traverse between them. While opening new opportunities for residents on each side, bridges do not blend the formations or otherwise make them indistinguishable. Where possible, bridges are also built to span the shortest distance between the land formations. The same conditions hold for this analysis. My purpose is to show how two or more analytic formations may be linked and made mutually informative, while also respecting the distinctive contributions and integrity of each perspective. The analysis is also intended to identify the areas of greatest complementarity between these distinctive perspectives and methodological strategies.

This goal may be contrasted with triangulation, a research strategy that involves using several methods to reveal multiple aspects of a single empirical reality (Denzin, 1978). A major assumption of the triangulation strategy is that sociological research is a discovery process designed to get at an objective truth that may be systematized as a formal theory of social structure and process. Triangulation assumes that looking at an object from more than one standpoint provides researchers and theorists with more comprehensive knowledge about the object. This approach also assumes that 'there is an overwhelming need for a single set of standards by which the methodological act can be evaluated' (Denzin, 1978: 339).

The bridging approach discussed here differs from triangulation in its focus on using several methodological strategies to link aspects of different sociological perspectives, not to discover indisputable facts about a single social reality. I do not assume that the objects of ethnomethodological, conversation analytic and Foucauldian analyses are the same, that they can be integrated into a larger and more comprehensive perspective, or that there should be a single standard for evaluating the methodological emphases of these approaches to qualitative research. The central issue involves providing a venue for dialogue between different interpretive frameworks. Its promise is interpretive insight, particularly into the ways in which meaning is implicated in our mundane everyday lives and activities.

Discourse and ethnography

Ethnomethodology, conversation analysis and Foucauldian discourse studies are, in my judgement, three of the most important developments in the sociology of the latter half of the twentieth century. Their significance is related to their concerns for how language and knowledge are related and are constitutive aspects of social life. While different in many ways, each of these perspectives stresses how social life may be organized within multiple social realities, how the realities are socially constructed through our use of language, and the reflexivity of our accounts of social settings, realities and issues. The concept of reflexivity refers to the ways in which our portrayals of social realities simultaneously describe and constitute the realities (Garfinkel, 1967). Our descriptions of social realities, then, cannot be separated from the objects, persons or circumstances that they describe or the languages that we use to describe them.

While informed by aspects of philosophy (particularly hermeneutics and ordinary language philosophy), ethnomethodology and conversation analysis are oriented towards (and recast) classic sociological issues (Hilbert, 1992). They also emphasize how social realities are built from the 'bottom up' (from ordinary interactions to general social processes). Foucauldian discourse studies, on the other hand, are part of the philosophical movement sometimes called poststructuralism (Eagleton, 1983) and at other times postmodernism (Best and Kellner, 1991). This approach also treats social realities as embedded in generalized discourses into which interactants enter in conducting their everyday activities and interactions. Indeed, Foucauldian discourse studies might be characterized as moving from the 'top down' (from culturally standardized discourses to the reality-constructing activities of everyday life).

These perspectives are also similar in their treatment of empirical research and analysis as interrelated. Ethnomethodology, conversation analysis and Foucauldian discourse studies are offered not as integrated, all-encompassing or grand theories of society (defined as an abstract structure or entity), but as distinctive standpoints from which concrete, empirical aspects of social life may be seen and analysed. Their empirical focus is also reflected in the differing methodological strategies associated with each perspective. The strategies are designed to produce data that might be used to apply, extend and elaborate on issues that are central to the perspectives. While some proponents of these perspectives and strategies describe their research as inductive (e.g. Merry, 1990) because it involves careful analysis of data, it is important to recognize that qualitative data – like other depictions of social reality – are social constructs. Thus, they are influenced by researchers' assumptions about social reality and methodological practices.

Taken together, these perspectives provide qualitative sociologists with interpretive resources for writing ethnographies of institutional discourse (Miller, 1994). These ethnographies focus on the ways in which everyday life is organized within, and through, language. They involve attending to both the discursive categories and practices associated with social settings, and how setting members use them (sometimes in distinctive ways) to achieve their practical ends. Thus, social settings might be said to 'provide' their members with discursive resources and opportunities for constructing a variety of social realities. Situationally 'provided' discourses shape and guide (but do not determine) what might be said in social settings (Silverman, 1987). Social realities are always locally constructed and contingent. They are 'built up' through setting members' organization and use of the discursive resources and opportunities that are made available to them in concrete social settings.

This analytic focus has, at least, three major implications for qualitative sociologists' orientations to their research. First, ethnographic studies of institutional discourse need to be differentiated from qualitative studies that focus on the distinctive values and perspectives of cultural and subcultural groups. These studies provide readers with 'insider' knowledge about how cultural and subcultural groups orient to social reality, and explain the social significance of their distinctive practices. Schwartz and Jacobs (1979) aptly characterize this ethnographic approach as reality reconstruction, because it is concerned with accurately representing the meanings expressed by group members. The ethnography of institutional discourse, on the other hand, better fits within Schwartz and Jacobs's (1979) formal sociology category, which focuses on setting members' interpretive and interactional competencies, including those that are so taken-for-granted that members are unlikely to mention them to one another or to qualitative researchers.

Ethnographies of institutional discourse might also be compared and contrasted with qualitative research strategies which treat every study as a unique case, and those that are designed to produce context-free generalizations. The first strategy treats every case study as sociologically interesting in itself, whereas the second assumes that a single case study only becomes sociologically informative when it is compared and contrasted with other case studies. Ethnographic research informed by ethnomethodology, conversation analysis and Foucauldian discourse studies gets beyond this opposition by treating every instance of reality construction as a distinctive event that warrants its own analysis. But it also considers how every instance of reality construction involves knowledge about transsituational skills and issues which are, to some degree, context-free.

Finally, ethnographies of institutional discourse extend the long-standing emphasis on observational methods in qualitative sociology. These methods are central to diverse qualitative research strategies, including reality reconstruction, formal sociology, case studies concerned with the uniquenesses of particular social worlds, and those designed to produce generalizations. The observational methods used in these studies also vary. They include, for example, participant observation, various types of non-participant observation and the use of less obtrusive observational techniques (such as observation from behind one-way mirrors or other 'hidden' sites). Frequently (perhaps usually), qualitative researchers combine these observational strategies with other qualitative methods, such as interviews and life histories.

Ethnographers of institutional discourse also rely on observational methods (usually non-participant observation) in conducting their research. But the focus of discursively oriented ethnographers' observations is different than those of other qualitative researchers. One way of understanding this difference is by considering what it means to study social settings versus social worlds. The latter research topic assumes that everyday life is organized within relatively stable and integrated ways of life (Unruh, 1983). Qualitative researchers of social worlds use observational and related methods to identify and reconstruct the perspectives and patterns of action and interaction that organize diverse social worlds.

Discursively focused research on social settings, on the other hand, emphasizes how social realities are always under construction. It considers how setting members continuously assemble and use the interactional and interpretive resources 'provided' by social settings to construct, defend, repair and change social realities. These reality-constructing activities may involve practices that are so taken-for-granted by setting members that they go unnoticed and unreported. Hence the emphasis by discursively oriented ethnographers on observing (directly, by means of audio and video recordings, and through the careful reading of texts) the actual ways in which setting members construct social realities by making sense of practical issues.

I elaborate on these issues in the next three sections by discussing some of the major emphases of ethnomethodology, conversation analysis and Foucauldian discourse studies. The discussion is selective, emphasizing those aspects of the perspectives that might be used to construct dialogue between them. Later, I use this discussion to identify areas of complementarity between the perspectives, and then consider how they might be bridged through comparative research. I conclude by discussing some of the general implications of the analytic strategy outlined here for other qualitative researchers.

Ethnomethodological concerns and strategies

The ethnomethodological project focuses on the common-sense methods that we use to make sense of our experiences and constitute social realities (Garfinkel, 1967). The methods of special interest to ethnomethodologists are the various interpretive procedures that we routinely use to classify aspects of our experience and to establish connections between them. Smith (1978), for example, takes an ethnomethodological stance in analysing how persons are assigned to mental illness categories by way of contrast structures. Contrast structures are oppositional distinctions that cast some circumstances, behaviours or persons as normal, natural or preferred and cast others as abnormal, unnatural or undesired. An example is the following statement made by Angela about K:

(i) We would go to the beach or pool on a hot day,
(ii) I would sort of dip in and just lie in the sun
(iii) while K insisted that she had to swim 30 laps. (Smith, 1978: 43)

This example can be read to reveal four additional aspects of ethnomethodological analysis. First, notice that Angela's claims are expressed as straightforward, declarative statements that might be treated as descriptive of her own and K's behaviour. They might, in other words, be treated as dealing with matters of fact and not evaluation. For ethnomethodologists, however, such descriptive practices are reality-creating activities through which behaviours, circumstances and persons are cast as instances of cultural categories and may be assigned moral and political significance. Secondly, while Angela does not specify them, her description and contrast involve several assumptions (or background expectancies) about mental illness. Two of the most significant are that mental illness is a departure from what might be called a normal state of mind, and that signs of mental health and illness may be discerned from persons' behaviour.

The third ethnomethodologically interesting feature of Angela's account involves its reflexivity and localness. I have already noted how the description creates the social reality of mental illness by treating K's behaviour as an instance of this cultural category. But the reflexivity of the account involves more than this. It also constructs a social world in which Angela and K are assigned distinct, contrastive and hierarchical positions and identities. In this world, Angela is positively positioned as normal and K as mentally ill. The account is local because its meaning is inextricably linked to the practical circumstances in which it was voiced and interpreted by others. These circumstances might be analysed as the contingencies to which Angela oriented in offering the account, and to which others orient in interpreting it.

Finally, ethnomethodologists emphasize that all constructions of social reality are potentially open to contest and change. Thus, Angela's description might not always be treated as evidence of K's mental illness. Notice, for example, how the meaning of Angela's description changes if we assume that K is an Olympic swimmer in training or that swimming is part of K's rehabilitation from an accident. In these cases, the contrast between Angela's and K's orientations to swimming might be taken as evidence of K's great (and admirable) commitment to athletic excellence or to recovering from her accident. Two major questions asked by ethnomethodologists, then, involve the circumstances, and the ways in which socially constructed realities change. Both questions point to the potential instability of meaning in everyday life, and the practical, moral and/or political implications that different social realities might have for individuals and groups.

Ethnomethodologically informed studies of institutional and other social settings also focus on the social and political contexts within which members use available interpretive methods to construct social realities. These studies analyse how social settings are organized as interpretive hierarchies (Dingwall et al., 1983), local cultures (Gubrium, 1989) or rhetorical domains (Miller and Holstein, 1995, 1996) within which some orientations to practical issues are usually privileged over others. The result is that some definitions of social reality are more likely to emerge in institutional settings than others, a probability that may have significant, practical implications for clients and other institutional actors (Gubrium, 1992; Miller, 1991).

Emerson and Messinger (1977), for example, analyse how troubles are defined and responded to in human service and social control organizations as a micro-political process. Central to the process is organizational officials' usual orientation to potential trouble definitions and remedies as hierarchically arrayed along continua, ranging from the most preferred to the least preferred. In these settings, then, all possible definitions of reality (and interpretive methods) are not equally available to organizational officials because they must offer justifications for recourse to less preferred definitions and remedies that are not likely to be required of those advocating for typical and preferred definitions and remedies. As Emerson (1969) shows in his study of decision-making by juvenile court officials, dispreferred definitions and remedies may be so devalued in these settings that they are rejected in favour of more typical responses if only one setting member speaks against them.

While they analyse their data from a different standpoint, ethnomethodologists usually observe social settings and interactions in much the same ways as do traditional ethnographers. That is, they observe and take notes about the everyday activities and relationships of their research subjects. The difference, as Coulon (1995) notes, lies not in their field techniques, but in the kinds of questions that conventional and ethnomethodological ethnographers ask about social settings and processes, and the types of data that their questions generate. As the above discussion suggests, ethnomethodologists are more likely than other ethnographers to focus on the interpretive practices of setting members, a focus that requires that they attend to (and record in their field notes) the details of setting members' interactions. A similar concern is central to the methodological strategies of conversation analysis.

Conversation analytic concerns and strategies

Developed simultaneously with ethnomethodology, conversation analysis focuses on the ways in which social realities and relationships are constituted through persons' talk-in-interaction (Sacks et al., 1974). The focus of this perspective is on the social organization of talk-in-interaction, the interactional and interpretive competencies of the interactants, and how they collaborate to construct social realities. While conversation analysts share ethnomethodologists' interest in interpretive methods, they treat these methods as emergent from the distinctive structure and processes of talk-in-interaction. In its most basic form, talk-in-interaction is organized as sequentially organized turns at talk through which speakers reflexively construct a context for their interactions as they go about the practical activities that make up the interaction. These activities include displaying situationally 'appropriate' orientations to others' talk, taking and finishing one's turn at talk at situationally 'appropriate' points, and using one's turn in situationally 'appropriate' ways.

Consider, for example, the following interaction occurring in a plea bargaining meeting, and involving a public defender (PD2) and district attorney (DA3). In such meetings, prosecuting and defence attorneys negotiate and agree upon the charges to be made against defendants (in this case Delaney), and punishments that will be given to defendants after they plead guilty to the charges. For instance:

1 *PD2:* Okay uh is there an offer in Delaney
2 *DA3:* Yeah plea to Mal Mish and Uh uhm modest fine and uh restitution
3 *PD2:* Okay
4 (0.8)
5 *PD2:* Fifty dollars?
6 *DA3:* Yes.
(Maynard, 1984: 80)

While this exchange might be seen as unremarkable, it displays several of the collaborative skills that we routinely use in successfully interacting with others. First, notice how PD2 (line 1) opens the interaction by stating 'Okay', thus marking off the previous discussion from that which follows. PD2 then identifies the topic of the subsequent interaction and invites a plea from DA3 by asking 'is there an offer in Delaney'. DA3 accepts the request (line 2) by offering the charge of 'Mal Mish' (malicious mischief) and a punishment ('uh uhm modest fine and uh restitution'). PD2 continues to collaborate in the interaction by agreeing to the proposed charge and punishment (line 3). The pause (line 4) might also be understood as a collaborative act. It signals PD2's and DA3's readiness to move to a new topic, which PD2 raises by suggesting $50 as an appropriate amount for the fine (line 5). DA3 then closes the interaction on line 6 by agreeing to the suggested fine.

In sum, conversation analysis is a radically local approach to the study of reality construction. It focuses on the details and contingencies of social interactions, and emphasizes how every social interaction is a distinctive occasion for constructing social reality. Conversation analysts portray the distinctive details and contingencies of particular social interactions as their context-sensitive features (Rawls, 1987). But conversation analysts also analyse social interactions as involving elements that are not distinctive. That is, they include elements that are context-free because they are also evident in other social interactions.

We can see both context-sensitive and context-free aspects of talk-in-interaction in the above exchange between PD2 and DA3. While each move in the interaction is a local and collaborative accomplishment, PD2 and DA3 also orient to more general conversational practices. Most obviously, they orient to the interaction as a set of turn-taking sequences by waiting for, and then taking, their speaking turns in the interaction. They also display general understandings about how conversational topics are proposed, negotiated and terminated through such mundane moves as stating 'Okay' and 'Yeah' at the beginning of their speaking turns, and by using the pause to manage a conversational shift. As Zimmerman and Boden state,

> [W]henever, wherever, and by whomever, turns have to be taken, encounters have to be opened and closed, questions asked and answered, requests made and granted or denied, assessments offered and seconded, and so forth. The organization of talk provides the formal resources to accomplish these interactional tasks, and deploys these resources in a manner that is sensitive to just what circumstances and participants happen to be at hand – which is to say *locally*. The shape of talk found in a specific site thus reflects the context-sensitive (and thus particularized) application of a more general, context-free (and thus anonymous) interactional mechanism. (1991: 8)

Conversation analysts share ethnomethodologists' interest in the distinctive circumstances associated with talk and reality construction in institutional settings. They emphasize how these interactions involve both context-free aspects of ordinary conversations, and how interactants assemble them in distinctive ways to produce social contexts within which some interactional patterns and social relationships are encouraged over others (Atkinson and Drew, 1979; Drew and Heritage, 1992; Jefferson and Lee, 1992; Zimmerman and Boden, 1991). Further, the patterns and relationships associated with institutional settings are unlikely to provide all members with equal opportunities and resources for pursuing their interests in the interactions, thus producing social conditions in which some definitions of social reality are more likely to prevail than others.

For example, this focus is central to Peräkylä and Silverman's (1991) analysis of counselling sessions as communication formats within which setting members take different social roles and positions. The communication formats of most interest to Peräkylä and Silverman (1991) are interviews (in which counsellors ask questions and patients answer them) and the information delivery format (in which patients listen to the information and evaluations conveyed by counsellors). While different, both formats offer counsellors greater opportunities to express and pursue their interests, including their preferred definitions of social reality. Indeed, we might extend this analysis by considering how these communication formats are both contexts of, and sources for, the distinctive professional authority and power exercised by counsellors in their interactions with clients.

Conversation analysts usually study the context-sensitive and context-free organization of social interactions by constructing and analysing transcripts made from audio and video recordings of social interactions. The transcripts are fine-grained representations of the interactions that often include notations indicating the length and placement of pauses, simultaneous talk by interactants, speakers' intonation, words that are stressed or elongated by speakers, and the direction of interactants' gazes. Because interactants might take any of these aspects of social interactions into account in responding to others' utterances or in moving the interactions in new directions, they are relevant to conversation analysts' analyses of how social realities are interactionally constructed, sustained and changed.

Foucauldian concerns and strategies

Foucault uses the term *discourse* to analyse diverse configurations of assumptions, categories, logics, claims and modes of articulation. The configurations provide persons with coherent interpretive frameworks and discursive practices for constructing different social realities within which particular kinds of people reside, relationships prevail and opportunities are likely to emerge. Consider, for example, Merry's analysis of legal discourse as a language

> of property, of rights, of the protection of the self and one's goods, of entitlement, of facts and truth. Legal labels for wrongs, such as 'harassment,' 'assault,' 'breach of contract,' 'malicious damage,' and 'trespass' and concepts such as

> property and contract constitute its core. It includes reference to evidence, to the presentation of documents, written lists, pictures, and witnesses. Solutions to problems in this discourse require weighing evidence and determining the applicable rules. (1990: 112)

We enter into discourses as we go about the practical activities of our lives. The discourses are conditions of possibility that provide us with the resources for constructing a limited array of social realities, and make other possibilities less available to us. We enter into discourses and use the resources that they provide to construct concrete social realities by engaging in discursive practices that are similar to the interpretive methods and conversational procedures analysed by ethnomethodologists and conversation analysts. Realities so produced are reflexive, because the discourses that we enter in order to describe social realities also constitute those realities. We don't simply describe conflicts within the discourse of law, for example. Legal descriptions of conflicts construct and organize them in distinctive ways that make them appropriate for the intervention of legal actors and recourse to legal remedies.

Arney and Bergen (1984) elaborate on this point in their discussion of medical discourse as knowledge, power and truth. They state,

> It is more than just a set of facts known by physicians and embodied in a professional, specialized, inaccessible language. The medical discourse is a set of rules that enables facts to become facts for both physicians and patients. It is a set of rules that covers not only what is important to doctors but also what patients can speak about as important. Knowledge is power precisely because the knowledge embedded in the medical discourse supplies rules by which patients ascertain when they are speaking true about the self and when they are speaking about things that are imaginary. Knowledge tells the person what is important and not fanciful about his or her experience of illness and patienthood. (Arney and Bergen, 1984: 5)

It matters, then, which discourse we enter into to organize and make sense of the practical issues emergent in our lives. The discourse of law is only one of several discourses available in contemporary Western cultures for making sense of, and responding to, interpersonal and intergroup conflicts. Others include moral, mediative and therapeutic discourses, each of which involves assumptions, categories, logics, claims and modes of articulation that differ from those making up legal discourse. While politically consequential, our entrance into discourses is usually experienced as unremarkable because we associate different discourses with different kinds of settings. Thus, discourses might be said to have their own social settings, although it is uncommon for only one discourse to be available in a social setting.

Conley and O'Barr (1990) show, for example, that while small claims courts are dominated by legal discourse, judges and litigants occasionally organize disputes within the discourse of relationships. The latter discourse emphasizes the social histories of disputants, and the distinctive (often extenuating) circumstances associated with their disputes. The discourse of relationships also involves a distinctive arrangement of power and authority within the courtroom. That is, the disputants (not judges and lawyers) possess authoritative knowledge about the social histories and circumstances emphasized in this discourse. Others are restricted to helping the disputants tell their stories, and develop mutually agreeable solutions to their disagreements.

Analysing the availability of multiple discourses in social settings also raises questions about the discontinuities within, and between, the discourses. This concern is perhaps most evident in Foucault's (1970, 1972) approach to historical change, which he analyses as filled with radical disjunctures or ruptures which occur when new discourses emerge and replace old ones. While not directly applicable to qualitative studies of social settings which involve much more limited time spans, this theme in Foucauldian discourse studies is still relevant to qualitative research. At the least, it reminds us of the possibilities for discursive discontinuities in social settings. These discontinuities might be observed, for example, in the ways in which setting members move between different discourses in dealing with the practical issues of everyday life, and when setting members operate within available discourses to produce unanticipated and atypical orientations to practical issues.

While most applications of Foucault's perspective are analyses of historical texts, Merry's (1990) and Conley and O'Barr's (1990) studies show that these issues may also be studied by using interviews, observational techniques and tape-recorded data. Whatever the form of the data, Foucauldian discourse studies involve treating the data as expressions of culturally standardized discourses that are associated with particular social settings. Foucauldian researchers scrutinize their data, looking for related assumptions, categories, logics and claims – the constitutive elements of discourses. They also analyse how different (even competing) discourses are present in social settings, how related social settings may involve different discourses, the political positions of setting members within different discourses, and the discursive practices used by setting members to articulate and apply discourses to concrete issues, persons and events.

Establishing complementarity

Despite its limitations, the above discussion of ethnomethodology, conversation analysis and Foucauldian discourse studies provides us with a beginning for identifying and elaborating on areas of complementarity between the perspectives. These areas are, of course, easier to see in comparing ethnomethodology and conversation analysis because they are informed by the same intellectual traditions, address similar questions and focus on similar aspects of everyday life. They are similar, for example, in their concern for how social realities are 'built up' and sustained. Unlike Foucauldian scholars, who focus on the general categories, practices and logics of historically emergent discourses, conversation analysts emphasize the interpretive and interactional methods (both context-sensitive and context-free) that people in concrete social situations use to construct realities.

In the rest of the chapter, then, I emphasize finding areas of complementarity between ethnomethodology and conversation analysis, on the one hand, and Foucauldian discourse studies, on the other. There are, I believe, at least two major and related strategies which we might use to pursue this goal, and open a dialogue between the perspectives. They involve building theoretical bridges through the collection of data and by asking theoretically informed questions. The strategies are related because qualitative research is a creative process which necessarily involves making choices about methods and data, on the one hand, and asking analytic questions about the data, on the other.

Qualitative methods as analytic bridges

Ethnomethodologists, conversation analysts and Foucauldian scholars orient to, and rely upon, empirical data to develop their perspectives. The data analyzed by these theorists are not merely materials for illustrating aspects of their perspectives. The analyses are theory-constructing activities in which data are a central focus. To be sure, the data that these theorists usually analyse are different, but the differences are at least partly matters of choice, not absolute necessities. Indeed, the literature of qualitative sociology includes several examples of how ethnomethodology, conversation analysis and Foucauldian discourse studies might be done using 'unconventional' methods and data.

Holstein's (1993) study of legal proceedings concerned with the involuntary hospitalization of persons diagnosed as mentally ill, for example, shows how conversation analytic concerns can be successfully addressed by using data collected through observational methods. This analysis was successful because Holstein brought an appreciation of the significance of talk-in-interaction to his fieldwork. While these data are not so richly detailed as those that might be gleaned from audio and video recordings, they are sufficient for his analytic tasks and include contextual information that isn't always present in conversation analytic studies based only on mechanical recordings.

Also, McHoul's (1982) and Silverman's (1975) research illustrates how ethnomethodologists can analyse written texts. Silverman (1975) shows us how readers may use the assumptions and concerns of ethnomethodology in interpreting written texts. He treats such texts as useful venues for entering into a distinctive interpretive community (Fish, 1980, 1989) and reasoning process that assigns ethnomethodological significance to narrative accounts. McHoul's (1982) analysis also challenges the usual ethnomethodological preference for studying social interactions by using the insights of this perspective to analyse how textual realities (including the realities of ethnomethodological texts) are constituted. McHoul's study is also interesting because while he does not cite Foucault, he casts his project in a Foucauldian language when he states,

> The discursive order . . . produces every possible version of 'the social' . . . – and that will be so whether it is ethnomethodological discourse that is in question or one of the discourses that ethnomethodology would preferably take as its 'object'. (1982: x)

Finally, Conley and O'Barr (1990), Merry (1990), Miller (1991) and Silverman (1987) all address Foucauldian issues by using ethnographic and conversational data. While different in their empirical and analytic aims, each of these studies considers how social life is organized within institutional discourses, and how knowledge and power are implicated in them. They advance the Foucauldian project by linking it to qualitative researchers' interests in the social organization of everyday life. In particular, such studies provide analytic and empirical frameworks for simultaneously considering how power moves through the various activities and interactions that constitute everyday life.

Taken together, these developments in qualitative research suggest that data are not always a problem in creating dialogue between ethnomethodology, conversation analysis and Foucauldian discourse studies. The analytic concerns of the perspectives can be successfully addressed by analysing several different kinds of data. Of course, it is easy to take this claim too far, because these perspectives are not compatible with any kind of data. At the very least, conversation analysis requires data that are amenable to sequential analysis, ethnomethodology requires data that might be analyzed as mundane interpretive methods, and Foucauldian analysis requires discursive data. These data can be generated within the same or linked qualitative studies, however, by combining two or more data generating techniques (such as observations, tape recordings of social interactions, and textual analysis), and by asking appropriate questions about one's research sites and data.

Questions as analytic bridges

Sociological analysis is as much about asking questions as providing answers, thus asking questions that address themes that are part of, or implied by, two or more of perspectives is a form of analytic bridging. The questions allow qualitative researchers to focus on aspects of the perspectives that are – at least potentially – compatible. They are, in other words, procedures for identifying the shortest distance between the perspectives. Questions that address themes that are part of, or implied by, multiple perspectives are useful in guiding qualitative researchers' data collection. Different questions may point researchers towards different kinds of social settings and/or may be best addressed through one or two methodological strategies.

Based on the above discussions of ethnomethodology, conversation analysis and Foucauldian discourse studies, we can construct a variety of questions towards which qualitative research and analysis might be directed. For example, the discussion addresses issues that are central to ongoing debates about agency and constraint in social life; that is, the extent to which social realities and actions are products of individual initiative or are shaped by larger social forces. Ethnomethodologists and conversation analysts might be seen as stressing agency over constraint because they focus on the local and artful ways in which setting members assemble and use available interpretive resources in formulating their understandings of, and responses to, practical issues. Foucauldian discourse studies, on the other hand, might be interpreted as stressing constraint over human agency because they focus on the ways in which the assumptions and interpretive procedures used by setting members in constructing social realities are provided by the culturally standardized discourses that predominate in social settings.

This interpretation becomes problematic, however, when we consider ethnomethodologically informed and conversation analytic studies concerned with institutional settings and talk. These studies provide both data and interpretive frameworks for analysing the practical constraints which institutional actors take into account in pursuing their interests in social settings, and for assessing the micro-political advantages enjoyed by some setting members in pursuing their interests in institutional settings. Similarly, agency is an aspect of Foucauldian-inspired qualitative studies – such as Conley and O'Barr's (1990) – which consider how institutional actors ('artfully') enter into available discourses and shift from one discourse to another in dealing with practical issues. Agency and constraint are not mutually exclusive issues in these studies, then, but coterminous aspects of the settings under study and appropriate topics for study in their own right.

Recent conversation analytic studies of calls for emergency ambulance services illustrate how these issues may be simultaneously studied through qualitative research. According to Jefferson and Lee (1992), these calls are organized within a 'cargo syndrome' or communication format (Peräkylä and Silverman, 1991) that is guided by a dispatcher who determines the topics of the interactions by asking questions to which the callers are expected to answer. Jefferson and Lee analyse the format as a cargo syndrome because the dispatchers' questions are concerned with obtaining 'information about the caller and not . . . the sick or injured person who [is] simply the item being transferred' (1992: 538). While one might argue that the dispatchers enjoy a substantial micro-political advantage in these interactions because they regulate the direction and flow of the interactions, they are not free to pursue their interests in any possible way. Rather, like callers, dispatchers orient to the demands of the format provided to them by their work setting.

But these constraints do not preclude all human agency from interactions between callers and dispatchers. As in other social interactions, callers and dispatchers simultaneously attend to a variety of situational concerns and contingencies, even as they organize their conversational activities within a general question–answer format. Whalen et al. (1988) illustrate this point by analysing how unexpected developments may occur within such culturally standardized communication formats. Their analysis focuses on an incident involving a call for ambulance services that became a dispute between the dispatcher and caller. Whalen et al. (1988: 358) characterize the incident as a locally accomplished 'failure of words', and analyse how the misunderstanding involved the caller's placement of attempts at giving requested information in 'sequential positions where they did not work' and the dispatchers' treatment of them as signs of conflict.

Comparative research as analytic bridging

A major theme running through the above discussions involves the ways in which they blend detailed studies of language use in everyday life with analytic concerns that make otherwise discrete research findings theoretically informative. Ethnomethodologists and conversation analysts, for example, blend their interests in the local and artful accomplishment of social realities with an interest in analysing the general interpretive and interactional practices that setting members use to construct diverse, local social realities. Foucauldian analysts are more likely to approach these issues by, first, analysing the general features of the discourses provided by social settings to their members, treating them as conditions of possibility within which setting members may act. These analysts then turn to the ways in which setting members operate within the discourses to construct local social realities and power relations.

This dual concern for the situational and transsituational aspects of discourse and language use distinguishes these approaches from other orientations to qualitative research. It also makes comparative research an especially attractive strategy for pursuing their distinctive projects, and for building bridges between them. In analysing comparative data, these researchers might, for example, distinguish the local from the general features of social settings and processes, and explore other questions that cut across and bridge the perspectives.

One such strategy is to analyse comparatively otherwise discrete case studies that deal with similar topics and settings.[1] The studies of legal settings and processes cited in the course of this chapter, for example, might be analysed to explore issues of shared interest to ethnomethodologists, conversation analysts and Foucauldian scholars. Each study, in its own way, addresses micro-political issues associated with the conditions of possibility provided by legal discourses, and how these conditions are given concrete shape in social interaction. These issues include the distinctive knowledge and power relations provided in legal discourses, and how the relations are enacted in setting members' interactions with one another, including how they sometimes resist typical practices and relationships.

Such comparative analyses also provide an empirical base for asking about assumptions, concerns and practices that are excluded from the power/knowledge relations that predominate in a particular setting, but which are evident in other settings.

Both of these analytic aims can also be achieved within the context of a single research project. Indeed, there are several recent examples of how qualitative researchers have comparatively analysed institutional settings, and addressed analytical issues in the process. Gubrium's (1992) ethnographic studies of two family therapy clinics is an example. While presumably dealing with similar problems, Gubrium's analysis shows how the therapists defined and responded to their clients' troubles in very different ways, in one case treating them as family system problems and in the other as emotional troubles. Further, because Gubrium's fieldwork was informed by the ethnomethodological perspective, his study provides detailed information about the mundane interpretive and interactional practices through which the therapists entered into, and operated within, these discourses to produce organizationally preferred trouble definitions and remedies.

Miller and Silverman's (1995) comparative study of an AIDS counselling centre in London and family therapy clinic in the United States is an example of how a comparative strategy may be implemented to address ethnomethodological, conversation analytic and Foucauldian concerns. In this case, the researchers collected their data independent of one another, and then collaborated by analysing the continuities and discontinuities in the data. The study illustrates how conversation analytic and Foucauldian approaches to troubles talk may be bridged through the use of qualitative data. They pursue the latter goal by treating their data as venues for exploring situational and transsituational aspects of counselling discourse, settings and practices.

Miller and Holstein (1995, 1996) take a different approach to comparative research and analysis in their study of conflict emergence and dispute processing in one human service organization. The study is based on extensive observations of everyday life in the organization and analysis of audio tapes of legal proceedings concerned with dispute resolution. The analysis focuses on the ways in which conflicts and disputes are differently organized as they are considered within different dispute domains which Miller and Holstein analyse as made up of the typical assumptions, concerns, vocabularies and interactional practices associated with different social settings. This study, then, offers a distinctive view of the conditions of possibility associated with the evolution of disputes in one organization. But it is more than a case study of a single organization.

Miller and Holstein consider how organizational settings are linked to form an ecology of knowledge and power, and how outside parties (legal officials associated with a different government agency) sometimes become involved in ongoing disputes. The study might also be seen as a natural history of conflict and disputing in one organization, because it considers the ways in which disagreements are changed as they are configured and reconfigured within the conditions of possibility provided by each dispute domain. While maintaining an interest in Foucauldian issues, Miller and Holstein also stress ethnomethodological themes. For example, they analyse how members of these settings use available interpretive and interactional resources to artfully pursue their interests, and, based on members' actions, how disputes sometimes move in unanticipated directions.

A final comparative research and analytic strategy involves longer term (even longitudinal) studies of one or a few settings. The focus here is on how discourses and their associated interpretive and interactional practices change over time. This strategy might be useful in observing the disjunctures or ruptures that Foucault emphasizes in his historical studies of social change, but they may also provide qualitative researchers with information about the ways in which discourses, settings and related interpretive and interactional practices evolve over time. While less dramatic than studies of radical disjunctures, studies of the evolution of discourses and their related settings and practices provide insights into the potentially unstable and changing character of language, culture and institutions.

Miller (1997), for example, analyses how the discourse and practice of brief family therapy evolved and changed over a twelve-year period in one clinic. Brief therapy is concerned with remedying clients' troubles as quickly as possible by creating positive changes in clients' lives. It may be contrasted with forms of psychotherapy that emphasize finding the deep-rooted causes of clients' troubles. Miller analyzes how the therapists initially implemented the brief therapy model by working within an ecosystemic language that locates clients' troubles in their distinctive social systems. Thus, much of the therapists' professional activity involved asking questions about, assessing and developing strategies for intervening in clients' social systems. Each of these activities might be characterized as therapist-centred because it provided information that assisted the therapists in pursuing their interests in ecosystemic therapy sessions.

Over time, however, the therapists began to develop a new and distinctive orientation to the practice of brief family therapy. It partly involved treating the therapeutic interview as an occasion for clients and therapists to collaboratively define clients' troubles and find solutions to them. While the therapists continued to ask some of the same questions that they had previously asked, the interviews were reconfigured to construct new types of power/knowledge relationships. The new relations repositioned clients' and therapists' roles, responsibilities and options in therapy sessions. In the new arrangement, for example, therapists are not primarily responsible for creating change in clients' lives. Rather, the therapists use their questions to encourage clients to construct their own remedies.

In sum, this study – like the others discussed in this section – reminds us of the complexities of everyday life and how agency and constraint are simultaneously implicated in it. An exclusive focus on either side of this dichotomy is inadequate, since everyday life is lived within culturally standardized discourses and the discourses are changed by the ways in which we use them. While ethnomethodology, conversation analysis and Foucauldian discourse studies are distinctive approaches to these issues, comparative qualitative research that bridges them provides analysts with conditions of possibility for artfully extending and displaying (in concrete detail) the importance of their insights.

Conclusion

This chapter has focused on how qualitative research might be treated as a site for sociological analysis and paradigm bridging. One advantage of the bridging metaphor is that it avoids the imagery of totalizing synthesis in which the distinctive themes and contributions of two or more perspectives are de-emphasized (even lost) in the interest of developing grand theoretical schemes. The bridging approach offered here seeks to make different perspectives mutually informative, not to obscure or deny their distinctive features. To that end, I conclude by discussing three general implications of my approach to paradigm bridging through qualitative research.

The first implication involves the selection of minimally compatible perspectives. All sociological perspectives are not equally amenable to the sort of linkage that I describe here. Thus, an early task of qualitative researchers involves specifying the conditions of compatibility between the perspectives which they wish to link through their research, such as I have done in noting the complementary emphases in ethnomethodology, conversation analysis and Foucauldian discourse studies. How they differ on these issues is also relevant, but discussion of the differences is only possible after areas of compatibility have been specified.

A related implication involves qualitative sociologists' development of the areas of compatibility. As noted above, bridging projects are not about the total synthesis of divergent points of view, but about providing bridge-like structures for intercourse between different theoretical formations. Qualitative sociologists' attention should, then, be focused on those aspects of the perspectives that most profitably contribute to their bridging projects. The projects are strategic enterprises that require that qualitative sociologists be clear about their analytic goals, and how aspects of different perspectives contribute to their goals.

Finally, qualitative sociologists' bridging projects must include the analysis of data about research sites. While the qualitative tradition in sociology includes numerous and significant theoretical contributions, these developments should not be separated from the empirical focus of the tradition. This statement may be a source of controversy for some readers who properly reject past claims by some sociologists that their data are objective facts which 'speak for themselves', and should be treated as authoritative adjudicators of theoretical disagreements about the nature of the 'real' world. This position neglects the ways in which qualitative and other sociological data are themselves social constructions that reflect the assumptions and practices of the researchers who produced them.

Acknowledging that qualitative data are social constructions, however, does not render them theoretically useless or irrelevant. Rather, such an acknowledgement recasts them as aspects of a distinctive discourse that treats the practices of everyday life as worthy topics of analysis. Qualitative data provide sociologists with a shared conversational focus for managing their discussions, whether the data are ethnographic descriptions, transcripts of conversations or written texts. Such an acknowledgement also reminds qualitative sociologists that while theory is – by definition – abstract, it should also speak to issues that are recognizable as features of persons' everyday lives and social worlds.

Notes

I would like to thank David Silverman and Anssi Peräkylä for their helpful comments on an earlier draft of this chapter.

1. For one example of how this might be done, see Dingwall and Strong (1985).

References

Arney, W.R. and Bergen, B.J. (1984) *Medicine and the Management of Living: Taming the Last Great Beast*. Chicago: University of Chicago Press.

Atkinson, J.M. and Drew, P. (1979) *Order in Court: The Organization of Verbal Interaction in Judicial Settings*. Atlantic Highlands, NJ: Humanities Press.

Atkinson, J.M. and Heritage, J. (eds) (1984) *Structures of Social Action: Studies in Conversation Analysis*. Cambridge: Cambridge University Press.

Best, S. and Kellner, D. (1991) *Postmodern Theory: Critical Interrogations*. New York: Guilford Press.

Boden, D. and Zimmerman, D.H. (eds) (1991) *Talk and Social Structure: Studies in Ethnomethodology and Conversation Analysis*. Berkeley: University of California Press.

Button, G. and Lee, J.R.E. (eds) (1987) *Talk and Social Organization*. Clevedon: Multilingual Matters.

Conley, J.M. and O'Barr, W.M. (1990) *Rules Versus Relationships: The Ethnography of Legal Discourse*. Chicago: University of Chicago Press.

Coulon, A. (1995) *Ethnomethodology*. Thousand Oaks, CA: Sage.

Denzin, N.K. (1978) *Sociological Methods: A Sourcebook*. New York: McGraw-Hill.

Dingwall, R. and Strong, P.M. (1985) 'The interactional study of organizations: A critique and reformulation', *Urban Life*, 14 (July): 205–32.

Dingwall, R., Eekelaar, J. and Murray, T. (1983) *The Protection of Children: State Intervention and Family Life*. Oxford: Blackwell.

Drew, P. and Heritage, J. (eds) (1992) *Talk at Work: Interaction in Institutional Settings*. Cambridge: Cambridge University Press.

Dreyfus, H.L. and Rabinow, P. (1982) *Michel Foucault: Beyond Structuralism and Hermeneutics*. Chicago: University of Chicago Press.

Eagleton, T. (1983) *Literary Theory: An Introduction*. Minneapolis: University of Minnesota Press.

Emerson, R.M. (1969) *Judging Delinquents*. Chicago: Aldine.

Emerson, R.M. and Messinger, S.L. (1977) 'The micro-politics of trouble', *Social Problems*, 25: 121–35.

Fish, S. (1980) *Is There a Text in This Class? The Authority of Interpretive Communities*. Cambridge, MA: Harvard University Press.

Fish, S. (1989) *Doing What Comes Naturally: Change, Rhetoric and the Practice of Theory in Literary and Legal Studies*. Durham, NC: Duke University Press.

Foucault, M. (1970) *The Order of Things: An Archaeology of the Human Sciences*. New York: Vintage.

Foucault, M. (1972) *The Archaeology of Knowledge and the Discourse on Language*, trans. A.M. Sheridan Smith. New York: Harper & Row.

Foucault, M. (1980) *Power/Knowledge: Selected Interviews and Other Writings 1972–1977*, ed. C. Gordon. New York: Pantheon.

Garfinkel, H. (1967) *Studies in Ethnomethodology*. Englewood Cliffs, NJ: Prentice Hall.

Giddens, A. (1976) *New Rules of Sociological Method: A Positive Critique of Interpretative Sociologies*. New York: Basic Books.

Gubrium, J.F. (1989) 'Local cultures and service policy', in J.F. Gubrium and D. Silverman (eds), *The Politics of Field Research: Sociology Beyond Enlightenment*. London: Sage. pp. 94–112.

Gubrium, J.F. (1992) *Out of Control: Family Therapy and Domestic Disorder*. Newbury Park, CA: Sage.

Heritage, J. (1984) *Garfinkel and Ethnomethodology*. Cambridge: Polity.

Hilbert, R.A. (1992) *The Classical Roots of Ethnomethodology: Durkheim, Weber, and Garfinkel*. Chapel Hill: University of North Carolina Press.

Holstein, J.A. (1993) *Court-Ordered Insanity: Interpretive Practice and Involuntary Commitment*. New York: Aldine de Gruyter.

Jefferson, G. and Lee, J. (1992) 'The rejection of advice: Managing the problematic convergence of a "troubles-telling" and a "service encounter"', in P. Drew and J. Heritage (eds), *Talk at Work: Interaction in Institutional Settings*. Cambridge: Cambridge University Press. pp. 521–48.

Lindstrom, L. (1990) *Knowledge and Power in a South Pacific Society*. Washington, DC: Smithsonian Institution Press.

McHoul, A.W. (1982) *Telling How Texts Talk: Essays on Reading and Ethnomethodology*. London: Routledge and Kegan Paul.

Maynard, D.W. (1984) *Inside Plea Bargaining: The Language of Negotiation*. New York: Plenum Press.

Mehan, H. and Wood, H. (1975) *The Reality of Ethnomethodology*. New York: Wiley.

Merry, S.E. (1990) *Getting Justice and Getting Even: Legal Consciousness Among Working-Class Americans*. Chicago: University of Chicago Press.

Miller, G. (1991) *Enforcing the Work Ethic: Rhetoric and Everyday Life in a Work Incentive Program*. Albany: SUNY Press.

Miller, G. (1994) 'Toward ethnographies of institutional discourse: Proposal and suggestions', *Journal of Contemporary Ethnography*, 23 (October): 280–306.

Miller, G. (1997) 'Systems and solutions: The discourses of brief therapy', *Family Therapy*, 19 (March): 5–22.

Miller, G. and Holstein, J.A. (1995) 'Dispute domains: organizational contexts and dispute processing', *Sociological Quarterly*, 36 (1): 37–59.

Miller, G. and Holstein, J.A. (1996) *Dispute Domains and Welfare Claims: Conflict and Law in Public Bureaucracies*. Greenwich, CT: JAI Press.

Miller, G. and Silverman, D. (1995) 'Troubles talk and counseling discourse: A comparative study', *Sociological Quarterly*, 36 (4): 725–47.

Peräkylä, A. and Silverman, D. (1991) 'Reinterpreting speech-exchange systems: Communication formats in AIDS counselling', *Sociology*, 25 (4): 627–51.

Rawls, A.W. (1987) 'The interaction order sui generis: Goffman's contribution to social theory', *Sociological Theory*, 5 (Fall): 136–49.

Sacks, H. (1992) *Lectures on Conversation*, Vols I and II, ed. G. Jefferson. Oxford: Blackwell.

Sacks, H., Schegloff, E.A. and Jefferson, G. (1974) 'A simplest systematics for the organization of turn-taking for conversation', *Language*, 50: 696–735.

Schwartz, H. and Jacobs, J. (1979) *Qualitative Sociology: A Method to the Madness*. New York: Free Press.

Shumway, D.R. (1989) *Michel Foucault*. Boston: Twayne Publishers.

Silverman, D. (1975) *Reading Castanada: A Prologue to the Social Sciences*. London: Routledge and Kegan Paul.

Silverman, D. (1987) *Communication and Medical Practice: Social Relations in the Clinic*. London: Sage.

Smith, D.E. (1978) '"K is mentally ill": The anatomy of a factual account', *Sociology*, 12 (1): 23–53.

Unruh, D.R. (1983) *Invisible Lives: Social Worlds of the Aged*. Beverly Hills, CA: Sage.

Whalen, J., Zimmerman, D.H. and Whalen, M.R. (1988) 'When words fail: A single case analysis', *Social Problems*, 35 (October): 335–62.

Zimmerman, D.H. (1969) 'Record-keeping and the intake process in a public welfare agency', in S. Wheeler (ed.), *On Record*. New York: Russell Sage Foundation. pp. 319–54.

Zimmerman, D.H. and Boden, D. (1991) 'Structure-in-action: An introduction', in D. Boden and D.H. Zimmerman (eds), *Talk and Social Structure: Studies in Ethnomethodology and Conversation Analysis*. Berkeley: University of California Press. pp. 3–21.

PART III TEXTS

4 Analysing Documentary Realities

Paul Atkinson and Amanda Coffey

Introduction: Documentary realities

A great deal of ethnographic fieldwork takes place in literate societies, in organizational or other settings in which documents are written, read, stored and circulated. Ethnographic fieldwork was historically conceived and developed for research in exclusively oral settings, not only in non-literate societies, often studied by social anthropologists, but in essentially oral cultures or subcultures in more advanced literate societies. Contemporary ethnographic fieldwork is often conducted in settings that are themselves documented by the indigenous social actors. While such documentary work is rarely 'ethnographic' in itself, it is important to realize the extent to which many cultures and settings are self-documenting. In this chapter, we shall try to spell out some of the consequences of studying documentary societies and cultures. We shall try to indicate some of the ways in which qualitative field researchers can set about the study of documentary realities and the location of documentary work within the fabric of everyday social life. It is important to do so because many researchers continue to produce ethnographic accounts of complex, literate social worlds as if they were entirely without writing. Occupational, professional, organizational and even academic settings are implicitly represented as devoid of written documents and other forms of recording.

Such accounts hardly do justice to the settings they purport to describe, and it is necessary to redress the balance if only for the sake of completeness and fidelity to the settings of social research. Our concerns go rather further than that, however. As we have already hinted, many organizations and settings have ways of representing themselves collectively to themselves and to others. It is, therefore, imperative that our understanding of contemporary society – whether our own near-at-hand, or one to which we are strange and distant – incorporate those processes and products of self-description.

Consider, for instance, an ideal-typical organization. It goes virtually without saying that this quintessentially modern kind of social formation is thoroughly dependent on paperwork. Administrators, accountants, lawyers, civil servants, managers at all levels, and other experts or specialist functionaries are all routinely, often extensively, involved in the production and consumption of written records and other kinds of documents. If we wish to understand how such organizations work and how people work in them, then we cannot afford to ignore their various activities as readers and writers. Moreover, if we wish to understand how organizations function, then we also need to take account of the role of recording, filing, archiving and retrieving information. The collective organization of work is dependent on the collective memory that written and electronic records contain.

In addition to those familiar record-keeping tasks, organizations produce significant documents of other kinds, including a variety of sources concerned with their self-presentation. They involve annual reports, prospectuses, financial accounts, and the like. Many, though by no means all, of those documents are produced for external, even public, consumption. They may be among the methods whereby organizations publicize themselves, compete with others in the same market, justify themselves to clients, shareholders, boards of governors or employees.

Over and above these institutional documents there are the documentary records that embody individual actions and encounters. People-processing professions routinely compile documents and records of professional–client interactions, in the production of medical records, case notes in social work, and so on. These written records inform future action, and are themselves fed into the recording mechanisms of official statistics, performance indicators, efficiency league-tables and similar constructs.

The purpose of these introductory paragraphs is not just to list a few indicative types of documents or to hint at some of their functions. The point is to remind us of the pervasive significance of documentary records, written and otherwise, in contemporary social settings. What follows logically from such an observation is that qualitative field research must pay careful attention to the collection and analysis of documentary reality. Such inquiry is not confined just to the inspection of documents themselves (important though a close scrutiny must be). It must also incorporate a clear understanding of how documents are produced, circulated, read, stored and used for a wide variety of purposes.

Numerous organizations and work settings are concerned with the production and consumption of records and documentary data. Well-known analyses of such processes and products include: school reports (Woods, 1979); medical records (Rees, 1981); classifications of causes of death (Prior, 1985); and health visitors' case records (Dingwall, 1977). There are many research questions and research settings that cannot be investigated adequately without reference to the production and use of textual materials. To give just one example: it would be fruitless to study the everyday work and occupational culture of a profession such as actuaries without addressing the construction and interpretation of artifacts such as the life-table (cf. Prior and Bloor, 1993). Likewise, the ethnographic study of accountants would be jejune without reference to the professional use of accounts, book-keeping techniques, and so on (Coffey, 1994a). In the same way, to ignore the range of texts in circulation within and between modern firms and bureaucracies would seem pointless. As Bloomfield and Vurdabakis (1994) point out, textual communicative practices are a vital way in which organizations constitute 'reality' and the forms of knowledge appropriate to it.

In paying due attention to such materials, however, one must be quite clear about what they can and cannot be used for. They are 'social facts', in that they are produced, shared and used in socially organized ways. They are not, however, transparent representations of organizational routines, decision-making processes or professional diagnoses. They construct particular kinds of representations with their own conventions. We should not use documentary sources as surrogates for other kinds of data. We cannot, for instance, learn through records alone how an organization actually operates day-by-day. Equally, we cannot treat records – however 'official' – as firm evidence of what they report. This observation has been made repeatedly about data from official sources, such as statistics on crime, suicide, death, educational outcomes, and so on (Atkinson, 1978; Cicourel and Kitsuse, 1963; Sudnow, 1967). That strong reservation does not mean that we should ignore or downgrade documentary data. On the contrary, our recognition of their existence as social facts alerts us to the necessity to treat them very seriously indeed. We have to approach them for what they are and what they are used to accomplish. We should examine their place in organizational settings, the cultural values attached to them, their distinctive types and forms. The analysis of such evidence is therefore an important part of many ethnographic studies of organizations, professional work and similar settings. Documentary work may also be the main topic of qualitative research in its own right. In either event it is important to establish a methodological framework for the analysis of documentary reality. In the rest of this chapter we shall outline a number of complementary strategies for such qualitative data analysis. It cannot be entirely comprehensive, and we do not claim to have reviewed all the relevant empirical research. Our intention is to introduce some practical approaches to the systematic analysis of documentary data and the contexts of their use.

It is important to recognize throughout our analysis that we are not – as are many of the social actors we observe – trying to use the documents to support or validate other data. It is tempting, when undertaking ethnographic fieldwork or some similar piece of qualitative research, to treat observational and oral data (such as may be derived from interviews or recorded interaction) as the primary data, and any documentary materials as secondary. If used at all, then the latter would be drawn on to cross-check the oral accounts, to provide a descriptive and historical context. Our view here, on the contrary, is that such attitudes to documentary data are inappropriate and unhelpful. We would urge that documentary materials should be regarded as data in their own right. They often enshrine a distinctively documentary version of social reality. They have their own conventions that inform their production and circulation. They are associated with distinct social occasions and organized activities. This does not mean that there is a documentary level of reality that is divorced from other levels, such as the interactional order. Documents are used and exchanged as part of social interaction, for instance. Nevertheless, it is vital to give documentary data due weight and proper analytic attention.

We shall draw on ideas and examples taken from our own experience, as researchers and practising academics, related to various aspects of *audit*. Audit is an increasingly pervasive feature of late modern societies. Indeed, it is arguable that audit in its various guises is characteristic of what has been called reflexive modernity, or modernization. That is, a distinctive mode of modern social organization in which states, corporations, bureaucracies and other agencies are constrained to scrutinize and account for their own activities and their consequences. Audit includes the most familiar type of accounting scrutiny of balance sheets, published accounts, stock inventory, and the like (Roslender, 1992). It has also come to embrace a much wider range of domains in recent years. For example, academic institutions are now subject to periodic audits and similar inspections; similar types of review are increasingly common in medical settings and among other professional groups. Public agencies and government departments are also subject to audit of various kinds. The possibility of investigation by the Public Accounts Committee (PAC) in the UK is a threat which hangs over many agencies concerned with the use of public funds. In addition to checking financial probity, contemporary forms of audit are also aimed at establishing more general issues such as ensuring value for money and assuring quality. Audit implies compliance to various standards. It also implies the maintenance of documentary records that are open to scrutiny.

There are many ways in which textual data can be analysed and it is not our intention to try to describe them all (see Silverman, 1993: Chap. 4, for an excellent overview). Rather, we shall introduce and exemplify a series of related themes and issues that can be brought to bear on documentary sources. Our general perspective is informed by a broadly ethnographic interest, while our specific analytic approaches derive more from a semiotic perspective. By that we mean an analytic perspective that examines how documents can be examined as systems of conventional signs and modes of representation (cf. Feldman, 1995). The discussion will be informed by ethnographic fieldwork among accountants (Coffey, 1994a, 1994b, 1996), and our experience as academics living and working in an era of accountability and audit. In illustrating a semiotic perspective we shall consider how one needs to take account of the *form* of textual materials, the distinctive uses of language they may display, the relationships between texts and the conventions of genre.

Documentary language and form

Documentary reconstructions of social reality often depend on particular uses of language. Certain document types constitute – to use a literary analogy – *genres*, with distinctive styles and conventions. They are, for instance, often marked by quite distinctive uses of linguistic *registers*. That is, the specialized use of language associated with some particular domain of everyday life. Particular occupations often have distinctive registers, as do particular kinds of organization, cultural activity, and the like. One can often recognize what *sort* of document one is dealing with simply through a recognition of its distinctive use of language. You can, for instance, probably recognize the register of, say, a theatre review, or a wine appreciation, without seeing more than a random extract from it. Each genre has its characteristic vocabulary, for instance, and reviews in general have characteristic form and tone as well. (The register of wine-talk is richly fascinating in its own right, of course! See Lehrer, 1983.)

We know for instance, at a common-sense level, that official documents, reports, and so on, are often couched in language that differs from everyday language use. Indeed, as we shall try to illustrate, that is often one sort of device that is used to construct the distinctive and special mode of documentary representation. It is not necessary to endorse a glib condemnation of 'officialese' or to assume that bureaucracies deliberately confuse or mislead through their special uses of written language. Indeed, it is usually unhelpful to approach the analysis of documentary materials from an initially critical or evaluative stance. It is undoubtedly more helpful to try to adopt – at the outset at least – a more interpretive standpoint. The initial task is to pay close attention to the question of *how* documents are constructed as distinctive kinds of products. It is therefore appropriate to pay close attention to the textual organization of documentary sources.

In order to illustrate this, we can consider the process of audit, as carried out by professional accountants. As part of the preparation for a full financial audit of a business, a statement of source and application of funds needs to be prepared. This indicates the sources of funds which became available during a fixed period, and the manner in which those funds were used during the same period. The statement of source and application of funds makes comparisons between opening and closing balance sheets, explaining the differences in terms of sources and applications of funds. Example 4.1 shows the format for the preparation of such a statement. The format is as prescribed by the Statement of Standard Accounting Practice 10 (SSAP 10). Statements of Standard Accounting Practice are prepared by the professional accountancy bodies and represent examples of good practice. Such codes of practice reflect and prescribe the kinds of assumptions and conventions that are used to generate and interpret such representations.

This is a typical example of the sorts of documentary material which will be prepared and available during a financial audit of a business. At a glance it is clear that it does not textually represent, in any simple sense, the source and application of funds. It does not, for example, *say* to a lay readership where funds come from and where they went. If we ignore for

Example 4.1

Financial Statement: Source and Application of Funds

	This Year			Last Year		
	£'000	£'000	£'000	£'000	£'000	£'000
Source of Funds						
Profit before tax			1,430			440
Adjustment for items not involving the movement of funds:						
Depreciation			380			325
Total generated from operations			1,810			765
Funds from other sources						
Issues of shares for cash			100			80
			1,910			845
Application of Funds						
Dividends paid			(400)			(400)
Tax paid		(690)			(230)	
Purchase of fixed assets		(460)			(236)	
			(1,550)			(866)
			360			(21)
Increase/decrease in working capital						
Increase in stocks		80			114	
Increase in debtors		120			22	
(Increase) decrease in creditors – excluding taxation and proposed dividends		115			(107)	
Movement in net liquid funds:						
Increase (decrease) in:						
Cash balances	(5)			35		
Short-term investments	50			(85)		
		45			(50)	
			360			(21)

our purposes the financial significance of the statement, we can, however, still begin to make sense of it, in terms of the specific characteristics it embodies. As we have mentioned already, the statement is set out in a particular, prescribed way, in accordance with stylistic conventions. It does not contain lengthy, descriptive prose and turgid explanation. It is tabulated in an ordered and structured manner. The source and application of funds statement will look similar, in terms of style and layout, across all businesses and all audits. These stylistic conventions for the preparation of financial statements mean that all businesses – despite size, scope, clientele, funds, nature of work – can still be represented in exactly the same way. The statements in themselves construct a version of documentary reality common to all.

Like the layout, it is also clear that the language used in the statement is particular, 'Adjustment for items not involving the movement of funds', 'purchase of fixed assets', 'movement in net liquid funds', and other expressions like them will be very familiar to accountants, auditors, financial officers, yet they are not part of the everyday language of a lay audience, or indeed most of the employees of a business. They are well-established linguistic tools of the financial auditor and understood by them. It is expected (and statutorily required) that financial statements of this sort will operate with this sort of language, and this sort of format. The finished financial statements give a particular account of the affairs of the organization – which will be read and interpreted by individuals who share an understanding of the language and stylistic conventions.

Faced with a file full of statements like the one above, the financial auditor can read a 'representation' of the organization under review. This sort of documentary reality does not enable a lay reader to find out about the organization in any simple sense. The competent, professional reader can, however, read into the document a great deal more than the lay person. The statements enable all businesses to be similarly represented and compared, yet they do so in very particular, coded and highly stylized ways. In an important way, therefore, such documents and their associated conventions help to define the very idea of an 'organization' itself. In this sense financial audit involves the creation and use of particular documentary artefacts, as a way of constructing and representing an organization.

Of course, many of the documentary sources we find ourselves using are different from the financial representation used by accountants. Many consist primarily of prose text rather than figures. They are equally conventional, and deserve similar attention to matters of *form*. We can illustrate this theme with reference to another kind of audit, that is, 'academic audit'. Most British academics will now be familiar, at least in principle, with various kinds of academic audit, in particular the Teaching Quality Assessment (TQA) process. Many students in the UK will have come across the exercise, preparations for it, or its aftermath in their academic departments. For those who are not familiar with this aspect of contemporary UK higher education, some brief background is needed. All disciplines/departments in British higher education are subject to a rolling programme of external scrutiny and evaluation, by means of which their degree schemes are evaluated. In theory, they are evaluated in accordance with the institution's own stated objectives. The rhetoric of 'fitness for purpose' is used. The assessment is not supposed to be about absolute 'standards' of academic excellence, but the 'quality' of provision. This latter concept relates to the pervasive idea of quality management and quality assurance, which has become a widespread component of organizational culture in service and manufacturing sectors in recent years. This, in turn, is related to the sorts of financial audits usually carried out by chartered accountants and required by statute. Auditors here are required to form a judgement, on the basis of the documentary and other evidence made available to them, that the organization's accounts reflect a true and fair picture of their profitability. Interim and year end financial audits are embedded within the temporality of most organizational structures. Auditors assess the efficiency of the organizational control mechanisms, developing a working knowledge of those systems in operation. At the interim audit stage, auditors are concerned with forming a judgement on the effectiveness and efficiency of the organizational structures and control processes. At the end of the financial year auditors return to verify the organization's account books and balance sheets. The overall aim is for the auditor to be in a position to give an unqualified audit report that can be publicly available and demonstrative of the good standing of the organization. Audit reports are often attached to annual reports of organizations, which are in themselves presenting particular documentary realities (McKinstry, 1996; Preston et al., 1996). The process of TQA and other kinds of parallel exercise (such as internal quality reviews) undertaken by institutions themselves take much from the more traditional notions of audit. By examining documentary evidence, and following 'paper trails' to check monitoring and processing systems, they are also concerned with arriving at a judgement that an academic department is fulfilling its aims/maximizing its objectives and presenting a 'true and fair' assessment of itself. In addition, many academic disciplines in higher education are also subjected to external scrutiny and inspection by professional bodies (such as engineering, law, town planning, social work, pharmacy and accountancy).

While such 'audit' may involve the direct observation of educational experiences by external observers (and we shall have something to say about that aspect of things later, for it also involves documentary work), it relies heavily on the construction of documentary reality. For instance, as part of the TQA, departments must submit a 'self-assessment'. This enshrines statements about the degree schemes, their philosophy and objectives; how those objectives are attained; how courses are intended to impart specific skills and competencies to students; how examinations or other forms of assessment are used to test whether those skills have been acquired. In one sense, therefore, such self-assessments constitute a kind of description of the department or degree scheme in question. There are all sorts of ways in which an educational environment might be described, but it is clear that TQA self-assessments call for very particular kinds of 'description'. At this point we can proceed best with a concrete example. Since these things are sometimes sensitive, we can only use a self-assessment document prepared in our own department. We cannot embark

Example 4.2: A list of key features

Quality in sociology and social policy

In defining quality in our subject areas we stress:

- provision of a core curriculum that incorporates the fundamental theoretical, methodological and substantive issues of the disciplines;
- clear connections between research excellence and the teaching programme;
- ability to allow students to pursue their own areas of interest, within a clear disciplinary framework;
- provision of a well resourced learning environment in which students can develop their analytical skills while acquiring key competencies in the relevant disciplines;
- promoting a working environment in which informal and productive relationships between students and staff are encouraged, within a clear framework of student monitoring.

In order to help students and staff attain these objectives we:

- combine formal lectures with small group teaching;
- offer students opportunities for individual practical work;
- provide student help and guidance through the personal tutor scheme;
- provide formal mechanisms for student consultation and feedback;
- have a comprehensive mechanism for monitoring student progress;
- engage in regular staff development activities, with an in-house scheme as well as participation in College-wide activities.

on a comparative, systematic analysis that would require access to documents relating to other departments. We use the Cardiff department's self-assessment without evaluative intent. For our purposes it does not matter much whether it is a particularly 'good' or 'successful' document of its kind, only that it is of a kind, and displays some characteristic features.

Example 4.2, then, is a fairly representative extract from the Cardiff self-assessment in Sociology and Social Policy, finalized early in 1995. We reproduce its layout as well as its contents. It refers to our department by its acronym (SOCAS), which is short for School of Social and Administrative Studies. As the reader may imagine, other parts of the document seek to justify and amplify the claims made in this extract.

How, then, can we start to make sense of such documentary material? In the first place, we can note that it has some specific characteristics. The layout itself is a valuable clue (and, more generally, the physical, material character of a document is an important feature for detailed attention). As can be seen, it betrays its character through various stylistic conventions. Most notably, the twin characteristics of lists and 'bullet-points' betray its character as an official document, with an essentially practical function. Lists can be analysed in more general terms. They can, of course, be occasional and ephemeral products, like shopping lists, but they often incorporate some implicit idea of order and importance. In singling out these particular features of the department, and in listing them as we have, we *mark* them as special and deserving particular attention. We lift them out of all the many things we might find to say about a department of sociology and social policy. Moreover, while no rank order of importance is implied here, the list of key features is intended to convey a sense of purpose and logic. The authors here are pursuing a familiar set of textual conventions in their attempt to convey a particular sense of order and structure to their self-evaluation.

We can, moreover, examine the kind of language used in this extract. It contains many phrases that will seem awfully familiar to academic readers. For instance: 'core curriculum', 'within a clear disciplinary framework', 'well resourced learning environment', 'student monitoring'. These, and expressions like them, are not necessarily part of the everyday talk even of academics, but they, and phrases like them, are now massively familiar to academics, who find themselves composing and consuming such documents. They are among the linguistic building-blocks of this particular genre of academic management. Indeed, one can think of them as resembling verbal formulae, and their deployment in such documents can be likened to the composition of *oral epic*. It is well documented that bards (such as Homer in pre-classical Greece, and contemporary individuals in the Balkans) can extemporize the composition of lengthy oral verse, celebrating epic themes such as heroes and wars. They can 'compose' line after line, usually in strict metre, on stock themes, peopled with stock characters. It can be demonstrated that this capacity for fluent improvisation is possible because the skilled bard has at his (rarely her) disposal a repertoire of stock phrases for main characters and recurrent actions. These fit the poetic metre in very precise and highly evolved ways. The oral bard, therefore, does not compose verse from scratch, but puts it together from well-established patterns and pre-formed components. These are, in turn, familiar to the audience, who can draw on the same stock and traditions of composition. In much the same way, the writer of official, organizational documents rarely does so from scratch. He or she can often draw upon a stock of well-established and well-understood phrases and expressions. In that sense, such a genre constitutes a kind of *restricted code*, defined in terms of limited possibilities of choice and combination in composition. The notion of a restricted code, with such implications, is derived from the work of Basil Bernstein (1981; see also Atkinson, 1985). It can clearly be applied to written language use as well as oral performance.

In much the same way, the author(s) will have restricted scope in terms of the content of the document. It is not just the language that is restricted. These documents normally follow more-or-less prescribed models and formats. In the case of the TQA self-assessment, the department has some leeway in constructing the account. Yet its author(s) cannot operate with complete freedom. There are written guidelines that indicate the kinds of things that need to be covered. There are, moreover, expectations and understandings about such documents and their use among academics and higher education administrators. As drafts are composed, read and commented upon internally, so relevant individuals bring to bear their shared understandings of such background cultural assumptions.

Most importantly, perhaps, we can now see that this document may be 'about' an academic department at Cardiff, but it is not a transparent description. You certainly cannot take the document and read off from it a picture of the department and its academic programme. That is not because the author(s) lied. The issue is not about honesty, or even about accuracy, in any simple sense. It reflects the extent to which documentary realities constitute distinctive levels of representation, with some degree of autonomy from other social constructions. This is true of the kinds of financial audits carried out by accountants as well. The accountants' audit of a company's books and balance sheets is not intended to authenticate every record of every transaction, and the auditor is not forever comparing the 'books' with some independent level of reality. The audit compares records with records, and checks them for features such as consistency. A key auditing process is the referencing of the audit file; a process whereby an auditor (usually a junior accountant) is charged with the task of checking for consistency and order across the range of balances and documents presented to the audit. Like the TQA, it too is conducted primarily within the domain of documentary reality.

Such a conclusion does not mean that we cannot learn a great deal from such documentary sources. On the contrary, we have already sketched some ways in which an understanding of the TQA document, and others like it, can start to give us valuable data about organizational life in academic institutions and their characteristic cultures. We can, moreover, learn something about the sort of work, and its associated skills, that goes into the creation and use of such an artefact.

What is at stake here is the construction of a distinctive documentary reality. Our TQA self-assessment does not so much report a reality as *construct* a reality. It creates a very particular version of reality. It is, moreover, a distinctively documentary one. It draws on the genre of other documents, and their characteristic language. It is constructed so that other kinds of documentary work can be accomplished with it. This brings us, indeed, to our next analytic issue: documents do not exist in isolation. Documentary reality depends on systematic relationships between documents. Analysis must take account of such relationships. We now turn, therefore, to a discussion of the relationships between documents, or the intertextuality of texts.

Intertextuality

Documents do not stand alone. They do not construct systems or domains of documentary reality as individual, separate activities. Documents refer – however tangentially or at one remove – to other realities and domains. They also refer to *other* documents. This is especially, though not exclusively, true of organizational settings and their systems of record keeping. The analysis of documentary reality must, therefore, look beyond separate texts, and ask how they are related. It is important to recognize that, like any system of signs and messages, documents make sense because they have relationships with other documents. In that sense, therefore, we can examine such artefacts and their significance in just the same way we approach the signs of language itself.

If we start with one of our guiding themes – the topic of audit – then it starts to become quite easy to grasp the point of systematic relations between documents. One of the root metaphors of an audit is that of the *audit trail*. Traditionally defined audits of firms and organizations carried out by accountants place great emphasis on the audit trail. At the beginning of their training, junior accountants are instructed in how to carry out a detailed audit trail. This involves retracing each document and statement presented in the accounts to other documents contained in the audit file (the preparation of papers by the organization for an audit). There is an assumption that reference can and should be made to other documents. An auditor's task is to establish the extent of these relationships and intertextualities. 'Ticking' is a folk-term used by accountants to describe this process of retracing links and establishing an audit trail. (It is parallelled by 'bashing', which refers to the action of signing-off segments of an audit as consistent and fair.)

Academic auditors follow similar procedures. It therefore ought to be possible for an academic auditor to pick an item, such as a transaction or a decision, and follow a 'paper trail' through the appropriate procedures of meetings, minutes, accounts, and so on, in order to trace an orderly and properly authorized procedure which is in turn correctly accounted for. Such investigative procedures are predicated on the assumption that there are and should be regular, identifiable relationships between documentary records. These relationships are based on elementary – but significant – principles. They include principles of *sequence* and *hierarchy*. These in turn are part of the constitutive machinery whereby organizations produce and reproduce themselves. From a general analytic perspective, therefore, we can see that the realm of documentary reality does not rely on particular documents mirroring and reflecting a social reality. Rather, we can think of a semi-autonomous domain of documentary reality, in which documents reflect and refer (often implicitly) to other documents.

When academic auditors and similar external people use documents to scrutinize organizations of higher education, they examine a range of documentary sources. As we have indicated, they undertake an audit trail. In simple terms, that means following an organizational decision, an innovation or a problem through a sequence of documents. Such a trail might, for instance, examine the *minutes* of departmental meetings in order to trace the progress of an item from one meeting to the next and so on. Such organizational records have distinctive characteristics. Again, we can note that such documents have specific, stylized formats. They have particular functions. They do not record everything that was said and done in a meeting, for instance. Indeed, in a sense they precisely are not intended to record what was actually said. They record what was *decided*. In a sense, indeed, they constitute what was decided. Unless challenged and corrected with the agreement of the members, the written record takes precedence over members' own recollections and intentions. Moreover, such documents are written in order to refer to other, equivalent documents. They are constructed and read precisely as part of a documentary domain of interlinked documents. If we pursue the hypothetical example of our academic audit, we can see that an audit trail would pick up on documents such as minutes of staff–student meetings, meetings of the academic staff (or subgroups of them). We can analyse such documentary realities in various ways. We have already referred to the notion of *intertextuality*. This term is derived from contemporary literary criticism, in which context it is used to refer to the fact that literary texts (such as novels) are not free-standing, and that they do not refer just to a fictional world. Rather, they refer, however implicitly, to other texts. They include other texts of the same genre, or other kinds of textual product (such as journalism, biography, movies). We can therefore analyse texts in terms of these intertextual relationships, tracing the dimensions of similarity and difference.

In analysing the documentary realities of an organizational or work setting, therefore, we can explore the intertextual relationships. We can examine how conventional formats are shared between texts, and thus how they construct a uniform, bureaucratic style. We can note how they are linked as series or sequences of documents. Minutes of meetings refer to previous minutes and things like 'matters arising'. Minutes of different meetings will look remarkably similar in construction, language and tone. They thus construct rational sequences of decisions and their consequences, distributed regularly over time, and reported in uniform formats. Therefore we could examine how documentary realities have *temporal* dimensions built into them. Note that this is an organizational or documentary time; it does not describe the passage of time as experienced as an everyday phenomenon by the individual actors concerned. In another sense, documentary sources *suppress* time, by lifting events out of the flow of lived experience, and recording them in the decontextualized language and formats of official records. Intertextuality thus alerts us to the fact that organizational and official documents are part of wider systems of distribution and exchange. Official documents in particular circulate (though often in restricted social spheres) through social networks which in turn help to identify and delineate divisions of labour and official positions.

Documents can circulate and be exchanged partly because they are used to decontextualize events. We transform things by incorporating them into texts. By writing things into a documentary format, we translate them from the specific and the local, and make of them 'facts' and 'records' which take on an independent existence. Some texts become 'official', and can become 'proof' of events and identities. Some can enshrine what are taken for 'facts'. This point is made in relation to the production of scientific facts and findings by Latour and Woolgar (1986), who write about the production of scientific papers, and suggest that they achieve an existence independent of their original site of production – the research group, the laboratory. The accountants' audit of a business organization takes on a similar existence. The audit report becomes the documentary reality, superseding other files, records and memories.

Equally, organizational records are written and read with reference to other occasions of use. They may be referred to in order to warrant or challenge subsequent actions and decisions – possibly long after they were first constructed. They also inscribe positions of hierarchy. Documents report discussions, decisions and events to people or bodies that are superior to the originators. Organizations use expressions like 'parent' committees to express such principles of stratification. The right to construct a document, to challenge it, to receive it and act on it (or not) is part of the formal division of labour within many social settings. One cannot 'read off' such organizational realities from documentary sources, and the attempt to do so would be based on a fundamental misunderstanding. Documentary realities, based on complex inter-linkages between documents, *create* their own versions of hierarchy and legitimate authority. Indeed, the issue of authority raises for us the closely related issue of authorship and readership, to which we now turn.

Authorship and readership

The kinds of documents we have been discussing may have identifiable, individual authors or they may be anonymous, even collective, products. Equally, they may be addressed to specific individuals or they may appear to address an impersonal world at large. In any event it is important to address authorship (actual or implied) and readership (actual or implied) if one is to understand the overall system of production, exchange and consumption of documentary materials.

While it is self-evident that a person or a group of people must actually 'write' documents (since they do not write themselves), that does not always imply a social recognition of 'authorship'. Indeed, it is part of the factiticity of many official and organizational documents that they are not identifiably the work of an individual author. Their very anonymity is part of the official production of documentary reality. There may be an implied 'ownership' of a document – such as the originating administrator or department – but official materials do not normally have visible human agencies expressing 'opinions', 'beliefs', and so on. We can therefore inspect texts for indications of authorship, or its absence. In that sense, too, we can look for how they claim whatever authority may be attributed to them.

Another concrete example may help here. In Example 4.3 we reproduce an extract from the Report on the Teaching Quality Assessment of our own

Example 4.3: The quality of teaching and learning

17. There are considerable strengths in the quality of teaching in SOCAS.
18. The range of teaching methods is imaginative and entirely appropriate to the stated aims. Teaching is consistent with the overall aims of providing a variety of learning opportunities. It succeeds generally in providing students with both the thorough grounding in core areas and the practical and analytical skills that are at the heart of the revised programmes.
19. Course material is of a very high quality. It is evident that the staff put a great deal of effort into devising this material, both in individual initiatives and in small group teams. Generally, the quality of team work in the teaching programme is impressive. At its best, it is exemplary.

department. Once more we reproduce the original format. (The astute reader will realize why we choose to use such an example about our own academic department.)

It is noticeable that the statements in this extract are made without explicit reference to the personal agency that was actually responsible for putting together the report. (The entire document is devoid of named authorship, and is identified solely with the, impersonal, Higher Education Funding Council for Wales. We ourselves know who the assessment team were, but their names appear nowhere.) It is made up of many statements that have a similar form to those reproduced above; not every paragraph is as fulsome in its praise as those, unfortunately. But the report is not identifiable with an authorial 'voice'. We do not read phrases like 'It seemed to us . . .', or 'we felt'. This lack of a personal author is entirely characteristic of many 'official' documents. In this context it is important to keep in mind a distinction that is taken from literary criticism: the contrast between the 'author' as a person (named or not) and the 'implied author'. The latter expression refers to the textual presence (or absence) of an authorial voice in the text. For instance, a paper in a scientific journal will normally be written in an impersonal manner (using devices such as the passive voice), with no personal implied author, even though an author's name, or a collection of names, may be credited as its 'authors'.

The absence of an implied personal author is one rhetorical device that is available for the construction of 'authoritative', 'official' or 'factual' accounts. It implies a reality that exists independently of any individual observer, interpreter or writer. That device is not sufficient in itself to guarantee such status, which also rests on the organizational, professional or bureaucratic contexts in which documents are produced and used. It should also be noted at this point that the report we have just quoted is a response to the self-assessment we cited earlier in this chapter. This sort of dialogue between the documents is a particular kind of intertextual relationship.

Documentary reality construction also involves *implied readers.* Any literate person may actually pick up and read a document, but texts are often aimed at particular classes of reader, and it may be that only a restricted readership, with specific competencies, will be able fully to decode them. This is especially true of organizational documents, where an understanding of the organization and its working assumptions may be a prerequisite to a thoroughly competent reading. This observation reflects the fact that no text, whether literary or official, can determine or constrain precisely how it shall be read. Reading is an activity, not the passive receipt of information. The reader brings to the text his or her stock of cultural knowledge, a knowledge (or ignorance) of similar texts, and his or her unique biography.

The examples we have already given can be understood quite transparently from this perspective. At one level, any reader of English can make sense of them. On the other hand, it takes somebody who knows about academic departments and the evaluation of teaching to grasp much more of the significance of the bland phrases that are contained in the documents of teaching audit. Such people are among the implied readers of such a text. Furthermore, the members of our own academic department, SOCAS, are able to bring to bear their personal knowledge and commitments, and will read the text differently from readers who are not personally involved. They will be able to infer (not always accurately) who is being referred to at particular places in the report.

In some contexts, it takes a highly socialized member of a subculture (such as a professional group) to make any sense at all of a text. The case of the medical record is a classic one on which a number of sociologists have focused. They all conclude that the medical record, or case note, is a partial and cryptic text. Competent medical practitioners can make sense of their own or others' fragmentary notes because they bring to bear a wealth of context-specific, often tacit, knowledge about medical history-taking, clinical examination, interpretation of laboratory test results, diagnosis and treatment. The briefest of notes, often in the form of abbreviation, may have a wealth of routine medical work and interpretation read into it.

Conclusion

In the course of this brief chapter we have not tried to provide a comprehensive account of how to analyse documents and other kinds of textual materials. Rather, we have tried to indicate, by example, just some of the ways in which documentary reality construction can be approached. The kinds of things we have discussed could well be conducted as exercises in their own right. Equally, and probably more frequently, they could form part of a broader ethnographic examination of organizational settings, work practices, professional cultures, and the like.

Here, by way of conclusion, we recapitulate some of the key methodological points we have introduced along the way. First, it is important to realize that documentary reality does not consist of descriptions of the social world that can be used directly as evidence about it. One certainly cannot assume that documentary accounts are 'accurate' portrayals in that sense. Rather, they construct their own kinds of reality. It is, therefore, important to approach them *as texts*. Texts are constructed according to conventions that are themselves part of a documentary reality. Hence, rather than ask whether an account is true, or whether it can be used as 'valid' evidence about a research setting, it is more fruitful to ask ourselves questions about the form and function of texts themselves.

Consequently, one can examine texts for some of their formal properties. We have indicated, very briefly, how one might look at the characteristic language used in such texts. Moreover, one can look at them in terms of their *rhetorical* features. Sociologists and others have come to recognize with increasing force that much can be learned from the discipline of rhetoric. Rhetoric is not just about the ornamentation of speeches, or the effects of speakers like politicians. Rhetoric is, fundamentally, about how texts (spoken and written) *persuade* their readers and hearers. We all use rhetorical devices in order to get a particular point of view across to others. We draw on conventions that are widely shared within our culture. We have touched on some of the ways in which documentary sources can be examined from such a perspective.

It is important to think about documents in relation to their production (authorship) and their consumption (readership), but one should note that in textual terms these are not coterminous with the particular individual social actors who write and read. We need to pay close attention to the implied readers, and to the implied claims of authorship. This becomes particularly interesting when we are examining how a text implicitly claims a special kind of status – as factual, authoritative, objective or scientific. Linking this perspective with that of rhetoric, then, we can ask ourselves what 'claims' a text seems to inscribe, and what devices are brought to bear in order to enter that implied claim. The same would be true – though the rhetorical devices would differ – if the document in question had a different function (such as constructing a complaint, a confession or a personal reminiscence).

We have also drawn on another analytic perspective from literary and rhetorical analysis in emphasizing *intertextuality*. We have stressed that texts do not refer transparently to the social world. Their referential value is often to other texts. In literate, bureaucratized settings in particular, one may identify a semi-autonomous domain of texts and documents that refer primarily to one another. A dense network of cross-referencing, and shared textual formats, creates a powerful version of social reality.

In singling out these particular themes, we have implicitly drawn on the ideas and perspectives of literary theory. This is not the only viewpoint from which to examine textual data. You will find others outlined in other chapters in this volume. We do not claim that these are the best – let alone the only – ways of approaching such sociological analysis. It is, none the less, our contention that the ideas we have outlined can be used and developed to provide analytic frameworks for the examination of documents and similar cultural artefacts.

References

Atkinson, J.M. (1978) *Discovering Suicide: Studies in the Social Organization of Sudden Death.* London: Macmillan.

Atkinson, P.A. (1985) *Language, Structure and Reproduction: An Introduction to the Sociology of Basil Bernstein.* London: Methuen.

Bernstein, B. (1981) 'Codes, modalities and the process of cultural reproduction: A model', *Language in Society*, 10 (3): 327–63.

Bloomfield, B.P. and Vurdabakis, T. (1994) 'Re-presenting technology: IT consultancy reports as textual reality constructions', *Sociology*, 28 (2): 455–78.

Cicourel, A. and Kitsuse, J. (1963) *The Educational Decision-Makers.* New York: Bobbs-Merrill.

Coffey, A. (1994a) 'Timing is everything: Graduate accountants, time and organizational commitment', *Sociology*, 28 (4): 943–56.

Coffey, A. (1994b) 'Collective responsibility and individual success: The early training experiences of graduate accountants', in A. Coffey and P. Atkinson (eds), *Occupational Socialization and Working Lives.* Aldershot: Avebury. pp. 23–40.

Coffey, A. (1996) 'The power of accounts: Authority and authorship in ethnography', *International Journal of Qualitative Studies in Education*, 9 (1): 61–75.

Dingwall, R. (1977) *The Social Organization of Health Visitor Training.* London: Croom Helm.

Feldman, M.S. (1995) *Strategies for Interpreting Qualitative Data.* Thousand Oaks, CA: Sage.

Latour, B. and Woolgar, S. (1986) *Laboratory Life: The Production of Scientific Facts.* Princeton, NJ: Princeton University Press.

Lehrer, A. (1983) *Wine and Conversation.* Bloomington: Indiana University Press.

McKinstry, S. (1996) 'Design of the annual reports of Burton Plc from 1930–1994', *Accounting, Organizations and Society*, 21 (1): 89–111.

Preston, A.M., Wright, C. and Young, J.J. (1996) 'Imag[in]ing annual reports', *Accounting, Organizations and Society*, 21 (1): 113–37.

Prior, L. (1985) 'Making sense of mortality', *Sociology of Health and Illness*, 7 (2): 167–90.

Prior, L. and Bloor, M. (1993) 'Why people die: Social representations of death and its causes', *Science as Culture*, 3 (3): 346–74.

Rees, C. (1981) 'Records and hospital routine', in P. Atkinson and C. Heath (eds), *Medical Work: Realities and Routines.* Farnborough: Gower. pp. 55–70.

Roslender, R.C. (1992) *Sociological Perspectives on Modern Accountancy.* London: Routledge.

Silverman, D. (1993) *Interpreting Qualitative Data: Methods for Analysing Talk, Text and Interaction.* London: Sage.

Sudnow, D. (1967) *Passing On: The Social Organization of Dying.* Englewood Cliffs, NJ: Prentice Hall.

Woods, P. (1979) *The Divided School.* London: Routledge and Kegan Paul.

5 Following in Foucault's Footsteps

Text and Context in Qualitative Research

Lindsay Prior

The domain of the knowing subject

> There are no Lele books of theology or philosophy to state the meaning of the [pangolin] cult. The metaphysical implications have not been expressed to me in so many words by Lele, nor did I even eavesdrop on a conversation between diviners covering this ground. Indeed I have recorded that I started on the cosmic patterning approach to Lele animal symbolism because I was frustrated in my direct inquiries seeking reasons for their food avoidance. (Douglas, 1966: 204)

Pick up almost any text on research design or on the nature of the social research process in general and you will immediately notice that the discussion is predicated on the presence of what we might call a knowing subject. Almost invariably, your chosen research manual will suggest that the knowing subject be questioned, queried, interrogated and enticed into revealing to the investigator some conscious aspect of social life or social behaviour. In order to achieve this aim the manual will probably offer instruction on such things as how to compose questionnaires and scales, how to check for reliability and validity, and how to administer the instruments. Sometimes the intending researcher will be encouraged to become an active participant in the social milieu that she or he has elected to study. In which case the researcher will be instructed in how to enter the 'field', how to find informants and negotiate with gatekeepers, and how, eventually, to analyse the resultant data that the knowing subject divests.

This focus on the knowing subject is characteristic of both quantitative and qualitative research – and it is, perhaps, one of their few points of commonality. Thus, big survey research is just as ready to embrace the knowing subject as is small-scale qualitative research. So the *British Household Panel Survey* (Buck et al., 1994), for example, is built around approximately 10,000 subjects who are closely questioned on such topics as diverse as their attitudes to work, their voting intentions, domestic plans and housing choices. Somewhat surprisingly, however, given the pride of place that the knowing subject is awarded, you will discover that the raw data generated by individual subjects are ultimately of little interest to the researcher. So quantitative researchers, in particular, usually seek to reconstruct the answers they get from individual respondents in terms of a wider mesh, and will therefore aggregate the personal data in a search for such things as class, generational, gender or ethnic 'effects' –none of which can, of course, be attributed to any individual.

In like manner, qualitative researchers also take the knowing subject as their starting point. Indeed, in one of the seminal texts of ethnographic method Malinowski once argued that the guiding theme of anthropological research should be to 'grasp the native's point of view, his relation to life, to realise *his* vision of *his* world' (Malinowski, 1922: 25). And these very same words are often paraphrased in more modern texts on qualitative research. Thus Bogdan and Taylor, for example, talked about the need for the phenomenologically inclined researcher to 'see things from [a participant's] point of view' (1975: 14). Bryman, meanwhile, says that 'the most fundamental characteristic of qualitative research is its express commitment to viewing events, action, norms, values etc. from the perspective of the people who are being studied' (1988: 61). Yet, as with the quantitative researcher, the ultimate goal of the qualitative researcher is rarely, if ever, the mere replication of the 'native's point of view', for usually the ethnographer's eye is focused on a broader target. That target can vary from being something as vast and amorphous as another 'culture' (Malinowski, 1944), or as intricate as a symbol system (Geertz, 1984), to something as localized as a 'moral order' (Garfinkel, 1967a), or as apparently mundane as 'the common-sense world of daily life' (Schütz, 1962).

This dependence of the social sciences on the knowing subject, however, has itself been consistently questioned during the final decades of the twentieth century. Thus, Charles Taylor, for example, in an essay entitled 'Interpretation and the sciences of man', has railed against an epistemology that predicates the source of social scientific knowledge on 'the impressions imprinted on the individual subject' (1987: 61). Taylor's individual subject is, of course, the selfsame one who is randomly sampled and questioned and interrogated and asked to self-report and introspect in the very worthy cause of providing social scientific data. But according to Taylor little of such introspection, self-reporting and questioning touches the core of social life because social life is established on mutual social relations of various kinds. That is to say, it is established on forms of collective activity or praxis, and if that is so then it must follow that social science research has to confront a dimension of human activity that cannot be contained in the consciousness of the isolated subject. In short, it has to look at something that lies beyond the world of atomistic individuals.

This plea for a focus on something other than the thinking subject has also been a marked feature of the work of Michel Foucault –perhaps one of the most influential of all late twentieth-century thinkers. For example, in his Foreword to the English edition of *Les Mots et les Choses*, Foucault argued that his analysis was to be based 'not [on] a theory of the knowing subject, but rather [on] a theory of discursive practice' (1970: xiv). Consequently, one of the guiding themes of Foucault's entire *oeuvre* involved the rejection of the 'author' as the source and origin of textual knowledge, whilst in place of authorial intent and design, Foucault attempted to examine the discursive rules through which knowledge comes to be produced, encoded and displayed. For, according to him, it is only by means of such rules that any 'author' can claim a legitimacy to speak, write and authoritatively pronounce on a given topic in the first instance.

Texts and textual knowledge form the centrepiece of this chapter, and many of the texts to which I shall make reference may be described as texts without authors – such as statistical tables, certificates, records and reports from government departments. That is not to say that such things are other than human creations, but in the same way that it would be erroneous to credit a given performance of a Beethoven symphony solely to Beethoven, or a single performance of *Hamlet* to Shakespeare, then it is equally fallacious to credit textual materials of the type mentioned below to an identifiable creator – a subject. Of course, texts are far from being neglected in qualitative research. Indeed, the role of text is often given pride of place in sociological studies of interaction (see, e.g. Strauss, 1987). What I shall argue for here, however, is that the study of text need not be subordinated to studies of interaction, nor need texts be regarded as a mere adjunct to the empirical analysis of subjects; still less do we need to seek out the 'meaning' or authorial intent of texts. Texts can constitute a starting point for qualitative analysis in their own right, and to expand on this theme I shall begin by describing some ways in which we can study texts as representations.

Text as representation

In 1903 Durkheim, together with his nephew Mauss, published a series of papers entitled *Primitive Classification* (Durkheim and Mauss, 1963). The papers were subtitled 'a contribution to the study of collective representations'. Although the empirical detail contained in *Primitive Classification* is flawed, it remains an interesting and worthwhile publication because it focuses on how human beings think with things. More directly, it focuses on aspects of classification and how concepts of time and space are reflected in and constituted through aspects of social organization. So Durkheim and Mauss, for example, analysed the ways in which the so-called 'clan system' of the Pueblo Indians reflected and constituted their concepts of orientation (namely north, south, east, west, zenith, nadir and centre). In cultural anthropology this basic idea was followed through in numerous and diverse contexts. Hence, the internal layout of domestic dwellings, the layout of a dining table, the order in which food is served, the order of a procession, the ways in which items of personal dress are combined or the ways in which animals are described might all be used to represent the structure of a conceptual, or classificatory, scheme. Some years ago Mary Douglas collected some interesting examples on this elemental theme in her *Rules and Meanings* (1973). More recently, Sahlins (1995) in his study of Captain Cook in Hawaii, has extended this line of discussion to say something about the limits of psychologistic interpretations of intent, as against a structuralist analysis of order in general.

This notion that human beings often choose to think with things (including the sea routes of Captain Cook) rather than with abstract ideas and notions was followed through with particular force in the anthropological work of Claude Lévi-Strauss. So in his study of *Totemism*, for example, he focused not on the personal subjective meaning which statements held for individuals, but on how things are arranged. Thus when the Nuer say that twins are 'one person' or twins are 'birds', we should not, according to Lévi-Strauss (1969: 151–3), take such statements as literal description, nor as reflecting the misunderstandings of some primitive mind, but regard them instead as the concrete representation of a covert classificatory system. In other words there is little point in seeking out the subjective meaning of Nuer statements about twins and birds, but everything to be gained by analysing the rules concerning how such statements are related. This same fascination with classificatory schemes also tended to dominate the work of Foucault during the 1960s. Which is why, perhaps, he opened *The Order of Things* with a discussion of a 'certain Chinese encyclopaedia' (cited by Jorge Luis Borges) which classified animals as (a) belonging to the Emperor . . ., (k) drawn with a very fine camel hairbrush . . ., (n) that from a long way off look like flies, and so on.

As the reference to Borges's encyclopaedia suggests, in most literate cultures the order of things is often displayed and represented in text as well as in artefacts. The classification of flora and fauna in a biological taxonomy, the classification of constellations in a star atlas, the classification of human beings in a text of physical anthropology, or the classification of diseases in a nosology. Often such schemes of classification can appear as bizarre as the Chinese encyclopaedia invented by Borges. Thus, some years ago I recall seeing the causes of insanity listed in the 1901 *Census of Ireland.* A partial list is as follows: 'Disappointment, love and jealousy, terror, grief, reverse of fortune, religious excitement, study, pride, sunstroke, childbirth, . . . seduction'. It is a puzzling mixture by any standards (and the reference to sunstroke in Ireland was a source of considerable and long-lasting hilarity to one of our Guyanese students). Yet in looking at such taxonomies we should not rush to the conclusion that the order of causation is somehow incoherent, incomplete or lacking in rigour. On the contrary we should treat each text as coherent simply because it is there, lying before us as a unified object. The task of the researcher is therefore to investigate 'archaeologically', as Foucault might say, the innumerable accidents and myriad twists and turns of human practice that have brought the text to its present form. Qualitative research in this context, then, is not so much a question of deciding what a given text or textual extract might mean to a thinking subject as a matter of analysing the origins, nature and structure of the discursive themes by means of which the text has been produced.

Textually ordered knowledge packages and stabilizes the order of things as they appear within a wider realm of discourse. Indeed, a text instructs us how to see the world, how to differentiate the parts within it, and thereby provides the means by which we can engage with the world. One might even argue that in many spheres of human practice one can only know the world through the representational orders contained within text. Perhaps I could provide an example. I am looking at *Norton's 2000.0 Star Atlas* (Ridpath, 1989). The atlas represents the shape of the universe as we currently understand it, and it describes that universe mainly by reference to the constellations (Pisces, Orion, Cygnus, and so on). These constellations are very clearly human constructions in the sense that they exist only in the annals of human culture. (Thus, no one, I think, would argue that the stars in Andromeda belong together in anything other than a star atlas made by earthpersons.) More importantly, of course, the atlas informs us how we should 'observe' the night sky. It tells us what to 'see', it structures our observation and our understanding. Moreover, as its maps and projections of the universe change from one edition to another, so do our perceptions of that same universe. In that respect the text takes ontological precedence over what is observed and discovered by an observer.

A star atlas is not the only kind of text that structures observation of course. Lynch and Woolgar (1990) offer many other examples of representations that serve to construct scientific and other objects of human attention. For example, their book includes references to the use of ornithological field guides, and visual images of evolutionary theory. In this section, however, I intend to concentrate on a particularly authoritative representation of the world's diseases – a nosology. I shall begin with a reference to the ninth edition of the World Health Organization's (WHO) nosology on causes of disease – which I shall refer to as the *ICD*, the *International Classification of Diseases* (World Health Organization, 1977). Furthermore, for the purposes of this chapter I shall elect to examine the *ICD* in the context of causes of death.

Table 5.1 provides a summary of causes of death. I have laid out the table in terms of the seventeen separate chapters which appeared in the ninth edition of the *ICD*. I have also added some empirical detail of the death rates appropriate to each category for Belfast 1993 (though any town, region or nation would have sufficed as an example).

It is, of course, interesting to know that causes of death can be classified at all when one considers the myriad things that can precede a death. It is even more interesting to consider what can and what cannot be regarded as a relevant cause of human fatality. Thus we can see at once, for example, how the vision of death expressed herein is, in the main, one predicated on the human body, its biological subsystems and the diseases to which they fall prey. There is thus no reference to ill-luck, malfeasance or misfortune, nor to more mundane ideas such as poverty or old age or exhaustion here.

Now, one way to begin our investigation of this frame would be to ask some questions about its origins. That is to say, to first ask about its

Table 5.1 *The causes of death by World Health Organization nosological categories, Belfast, 1993.*

Chapter	Nosological category	Deaths per 100,000 both sexes, all ages
I	Infectious and parasitic diseases	3.58
II	Neoplasms (sub-classified by anatomical site)	315.14
III	Endocrine, nutritional and metabolic diseases and immunity disorders	5.73
IV	Diseases of the blood and blood forming organs	1.79
V	Mental disorders	6.08
VI	Diseases of the nervous system and sense organs	14.32
VII	Diseases of the circulatory system	541.12
VIII	Diseases of the respiratory system	241.73
IX	Diseases of the digestive system	5.01
X	Diseases of the genitourinary system	2.86
XI	Complications of pregnancy and childbirth	0.0
XII	Diseases of the skin and subcutaneous tissue	2.51
XIII	Diseases of the musculoskeletal system and connective tissue	2.86
XIV	Congenital anomalies	7.88
XV	Conditions originating in the perinatal period	2.51
XVI	Symptoms, signs and ill-defined conditions	2.86
XVII	External causes of injury and poisoning	52.29

Source: Annual Report of the Registrar General, Northern Ireland, 1995

genealogy (to use a term much favoured by Foucault). And at the broadest level one would be drawn to study a system of medicine that sought to describe and understand disease in terms of what might be called anatomical lesions. In his *The Birth of the Clinic*, Foucault examined such a localizing anatomical discourse as historically peculiar and opened his study with the following claim. 'For us, the human body defines, by natural right, the space of origin and of distribution of disease. . . . But this order of the solid, visible body is only one way – in all likelihood neither the first, nor the most fundamental – in which one spatializes disease' (1973: 3). Foucault did not, of course, have the *ICD* taxonomy of disease in mind when he wrote that passage, but his words have a particular resonance when one considers the table of death that lays before us.

For practical research activities of course it would be unrealistic to suggest that qualitative researchers can immediately turn themselves into broad-brush historians of medical discourse or whatever. It is not, however, unrealistic to suggest that qualitative researchers can and should ask questions about the points at which certain terms in a classificatory framework, such as this, appear and disappear. When, for example, did such items as 'old age' and decrepitude as causes of death disappear from the *ICD* list? Was poverty ever regarded as a legitimate cause of death? Which diseases and anatomical subsystems have disappeared from the list during the twentieth century and which disorders and subsystems have newly appeared? (The tenth edition of the *ICD*, for example, has introduced new chapters for diseases of the eye and the ear, and added behavioural disorders to Chapter V [World Health Organization, 1992].) How might the concept of violence (as in deaths from violence) have changed and altered during the mid- or late twentieth century?

It is comparatively easy to discover the answers to such questions by consulting the different editions of the *ICD* – starting with the current, tenth, edition and working backwards as far as is required. (The first *ICD* was published in 1903.) In fact, in relation to most of the questions listed above, I have already provided the answers (Prior, 1989).

If one were to follow through on such a genealogical trek one would also discover, among other things, that until the tenth edition of the *ICD*, each disease and possible cause of death was placed into one of 999.99 categories. So all known causes of death could be numbered in a system from 0.01 to 999.99. (In the most recent edition of the *ICD* [World Health Organization, 1992] the classification has been changed somewhat so that each anatomical category contains causes divided into 99.9 subdivisions, thus enhancing the possibilities for expansion within each anatomical subsystem.) I recall being asked on one occasion what would happen if a new disease were discovered – would there then be 1,000 causes of disease and death? The answer, of course, must be 'no', because the *ICD* classification is no more a mirror image of some independent empirical reality than are the classificatory systems of flora and fauna used by the Nuer or the Tallensi that Lévi-Strauss discusses in his *Totemism*. The *ICD* is simply a grid for organizing things – in this case a grid constructed on and around the human frame. It is not a reflection of some external reality in that sense, but rather a representation of what is assumed to exist. It is, if you like, a simulacrum rather than a reflection.

As well as examining the relationship of one *ICD* chapter to another we can of course zoom in to a different level of detail and ask questions about particular types of disease, such as, say, mental illnesses. The *ICD* naturally contains a subclassification of such illnesses. It is headed by reference to organic diseases and ends with a reference to unspecified mental disorder. As well as examining the order in which these various illnesses are arranged, one of the tasks of the genealogist would be to trace the points at which certain illnesses have been admitted into the nosology and others expelled from it. So, for example, in the *ICD*, mental illnesses used to be classified under the heading of diseases of the nervous system – they are now separated as mental and behavioural disorders – and we can legitimately ask at what point were 'nervous diseases' separated from mental disorders. (For an answer see Prior, 1993.) Or again, we might look at the *Diagnostic and Statistical Manual* (*DSM*) of the American Psychiatric Association (1994), which is perhaps even more influential as a classificatory system in psychiatry than is the *ICD*. In which case we might begin by noting that its classificatory principles concentrate on symptoms rather than 'causes' and it therefore presents us with a somewhat different image of the range of mental disorders from that contained in the *ICD*. In addition, of course, we can also ask questions about the genealogy of specific diagnostic terms and concepts, and investigate the different points at which they appear and disappear in the nosology of the *DSM*. (So we might, for example, be interested to note when 'behaviour' as a category first appears in the *DSM*, or the point at which homosexuality was removed from it.)

These nosological frameworks provide just two examples of a genre of representations – texts without authors. These are not, of course, the only examples of such texts. I could therefore have presented a life table as an example of a textual representation, and asked questions about its categorizations and the genealogy of its conceptual structure. In which case I would have been drawn to examine mathematical (mainly probabilistic) representations against medical ones. Or, again, I could have chosen, say, a textbook discussion of schizophrenia and carried out a similar exercise – looking at how the features of the disorder have changed and altered in different editions of key psychiatric texts. Or had I been interested in sociological representations of class and occupation, I could have set about examining the changing classification of occupations in the UK using, say, the *Classification of Occupations*.

Overall, then, classificatory systems provide a fruitful terrain for the qualitative researcher. For each use of the template and each revision of the score produces a new schema, and with it a new image of the world. By examining the rules of revision and the nature of the new and the discarded components, the qualitative researcher can determine how the world is ordered and reordered. In short, one can discover how people think with things.

Text as product

I suggested, above, that a representation should be understood not as a true and accurate reflection of some aspect of an external world, but as something to be explained and accounted for through the discursive rules and themes that predominate in a particular socio-historical context. The task of the researcher is to disentangle the rules of association by means of which the representation is structured, the genealogy of the various elements contained in the text (such as the points at which new terms and concepts enter the text), and the image of 'reality' which the text projects. Foucault, of course, denied that representations were representations *of* anything in particular, and merely referred to the process of similitude – implying that there were no such things as ultimate reference points (in the external world, say) to which the representations corresponded. For our purposes, however, we can leave that argument in abeyance, and turn instead to the question of how representations are produced.

In his *The Archaeology of Knowledge*, Foucault (1972) pointed out that discourse not only restricts, limits and arranges what can and cannot be said about the phenomena within its domain; it also empowers (and disempowers) certain agents to speak on this or that question of fact. In many respects one might say that discourse empowers certain agents to create representations, and thereby to authoritatively pronounce on the shape and form of the world.

To expand on this theme I would like to examine an issue that has occupied the sociological imagination ever since Durkheim published his infamous study of suicide in 1897. It concerns the nature of suicide statistics as representations. For convenience, I shall structure my discussion in relation to the question of whether such statistics ought to be considered as a resource for sociological study or as a 'topic' for investigation. (The distinction between topic and resource was, I think, first explicated by Zimmerman and Pollner [1971], though not in the context of examining suicide statistics.)

In his *Suicide*, Durkheim (1952), rather like ourselves, was somewhat concerned to sidestep the investigation of a knowing subject. That is to say, he was keen to offer social rather than psychological explanations of suicide, and he wished to avoid referring to the motives and dispositions of victims. (However, it is sometimes argued that in his rush to avoid examining interpretations of 'knowing subjects', Durkheim frequently interjected his own interpretations into the data – but I leave that aside.) In place of the individual and personal, therefore, Durkheim wished to establish the primacy of the collective. Moreover, during his quest for the collective, Durkheim turned to an examination of contemporary suicide statistics – which he called upon as a resource for establishing the presence of 'collective' effects.

Understandably, perhaps, Durkheim took such statistics to offer a fair and accurate representation of events in the world – that is, to offer a reasonably accurate count of suicide events. What he failed to consider and investigate, however, was the manner in which such statistics were produced. It was (and is) a failure regularly compounded during the twentieth century by all kinds of social scientific investigators. As for sociology, it was only during the 1960s that researchers turned with any enthusiasm to the issue of whether suicide statistics should be regarded as a resource for study at all. Subsequently it was argued that such statistics should, perhaps, be more properly treated as a topic for investigation than as a resource for study. In other words, sociologists should turn their attention away from regarding suicide statistics as a mirror on the world and instead examine the ways in which they are assembled and produced.

J.D. Douglas (1967), for example, sought to emphasize how the imputation of suicide demanded a study of situated or contextual meanings. For without such a study how could anyone differentiate between a suicide, an accident or a homicide? (Perhaps I should point out that in most cases of violent death, all that is discovered is a corpse. The cause of death for that corpse always remains a matter to be negotiated – usually and principally, though not entirely, through the procedures of coroners and other legal officials.) Indeed, when later investigators (such as Atkinson, 1978; Taylor, 1982) examined the matter of suicide imputation via their empirical investigations, they brought forth endless examples of the ways in which suicide verdicts are manufactured from all kinds of strange and interesting background expectancies. Thus, in English law, before a decision of suicide is formally arrived at, relatives, pathologists, coroners, witnesses, friends, associates, jurors, and so on, have to impute (to a greater or lesser degree) an intention of self-harm to the deceased. The procedures by means of which they fulfil that task can form a rich seam for sociological research.

To show how difficult it can be to identify a death as a suicide, I have provided below three coroner's summary statements on three 'unnatural' deaths. The written summaries contain details of what the coroner regarded as being relevant to the cases in question. In each case, take care to note the primary cause of death.

CASE ONE

Death of a woman aged sixty-two years. The causes of death were given as:

I(a) Overdose of pentobarbitone
II Hypertension and Chronic Bronchitis.

The coroner's description of what he considered to be the relevant detail is as follows:

> The deceased suffered from her nerves and from angina and was addicted to sleeping tablets. On November 17th, she went to bed at about 5.15 p.m. and at about 7 p.m. her husband gave her something to eat and then left for his club. When he returned at midnight he found the deceased dead on the bedroom floor, leaning against the bed.

CASE TWO

Death of a woman aged fifty-eight years. The causes of death were given as:

I(a) Poisoning by alcohol and chlordiazepoxide (Librium)

The coroner stated of this death:

> The deceased lived alone and was last seen alive by a neighbour on the morning of November 13th. She was found dead by her nephew at about 3.30 p.m. the same day, lying over the television set in her living room.

CASE THREE

Death of a woman aged sixty-two years. The causes of death were given as:

I(a) Poisoning by Maprotiline

The coroner's summary description is as follows:

> The deceased suffered from depression for 5 years for which she had received hospital and out-patient treatment. On October 23rd, her husband was admitted to hospital and she visited him there the following Saturday. At 6.30 p.m. she was visited by her grandson at her home. The next day she failed to pay her customary visit to her daughter who alerted the police. At the request of her daughter, the police made a forced entry into the deceased's house and found her laying dead in bed with several empty packets of Ludiomil nearby.

Each of these texts could, of course, be used as starting points for research in their own right. We might justifiably ask, for example, why the coroner considers reference to such things as 'nerves' and 'depression' as relevant to his 'findings' and not, say, reference to the financial background of the deceased on the day. Or why there is no reference to suicide notes, while there is to visitors. However, just to concentrate on the problems involved in classifying such deaths perhaps you would like to lay your bets now on which, if any, of the three cases were regarded as suicide. I have listed the official decision of each case at the end of the chapter.[1]

The imputation of suicide in cases such as these is important, because in Northern Ireland, where the relevant events occurred, there are no court or coroners' verdicts on such matters as suicide – simply a record of findings. (Sometimes a coroner will scribble in pencil the single word 'suicide', 'accident' or 'homicide' on the back of the certificate. However, he or she is not obliged to do so and it has no legal basis, for 'verdicts' were abolished in 1982.) The ultimate decision about whether a death is a suicide or whatever is therefore a task for a coding clerk, and the coding clerk has no more information on the matter than what is included above. For example, and in terms of the tenth edition of the *ICD*, the coding clerk has to decide whether to code the deaths as cases of, say, X41 (accidental poisoning), or X61 (intentional self-poisoning). What is more, in the event of case two another complication arises – namely the reference to alcohol poisoning – which leaves open the possibility of coding the death as X45 or X65. You can deduce quite easily that statistics on such things as suicide and accident and even such finer distinctions as alcohol-related accidents are very much products of these coding activities, and that when we multiply the coding process by hundreds of cases, the cumulative effects will be significant.

Now, asking questions about how text is produced, under what conditions, according to which rule books and by what kinds of people is therefore fundamental to the analysis of representational products. In terms of the example which I have chosen, I would go further and argue that studying the technical organizational processes by means of which the text is produced is directly related to the representational product which social scientists commonly use as a research resource. To clarify this point perhaps we can turn to consider Figure 5.1.

Figure 5.1 contains at least two representations of the suicide rate in Northern Ireland between 1968 and 1993. The upper trace, which makes the suicide rate look volatile and rising, and the lower trace, which makes it

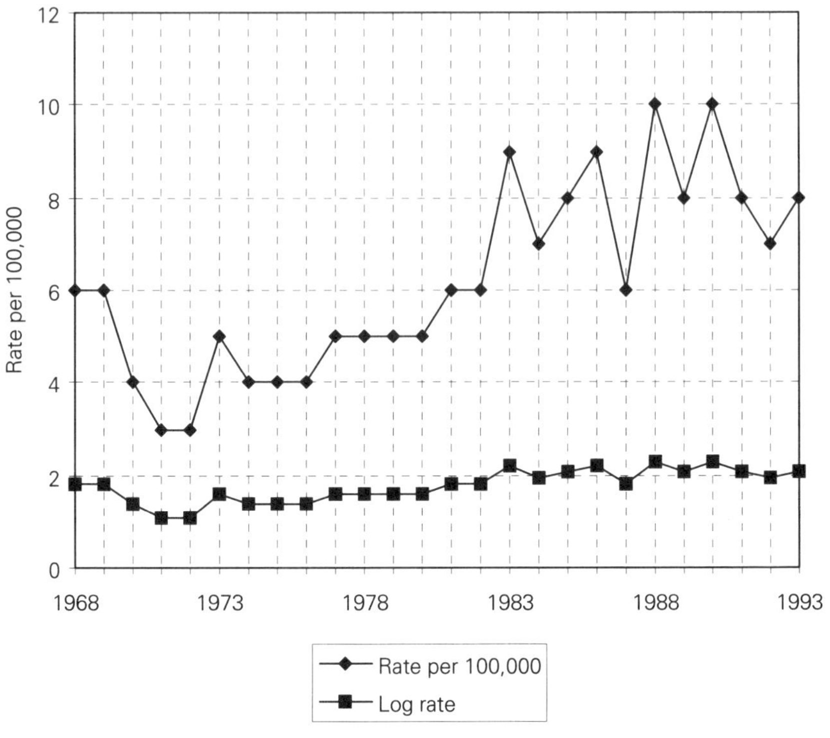

Figure 5.1 *Suicides in Northern Ireland, 1968–1993 per 100,000 at mid-year estimates of population. Annual Reports of Registrar General, Northern Ireland*

look relatively smooth and predictable. (The different effects are achieved merely by using different scales.) By concentrating solely on the upper trace, however, we can see that there was a marked variability in rates after 1982. Indeed, following the abolition of verdicts in 1982, the graphical representation of the suicide rate shows a notable year on year variability and a significant rise over the rate for the 1970s. (There had also been a change in legal practice at the end of the 1960s which, I believe, can be linked to the apparent decrease in the suicide rate during the early 1970s.) In other words changes in the rate are at the very least coincident with changes in the human practices through which the representation has been produced. In fact one might argue that as the agents entitled to pronounce on a death as a 'suicide' change, then so too does the graphical pattern. As researchers, we could probably carry out parallel exercises for crime, economic and all other kinds of statistical product.

Naturally, having produced a representation of suicide, crime, accidents, the movement of prices or whatever, others endow it with meaning. Thus, for almost every fluctuation in a graph or table of events there will be a nascent social theorist waiting in the wings to explain it. In the case of suicides in Northern Ireland, for example, various individuals have attempted to explain the fluctuations by reference to such things as the 'troubles', unemployment, changing roles of masculinity, and moral decline in general. Such a hermeneutics of representation indeed has its place, and to illustrate how that might be followed through I would like to end with a brief consideration of the hermeneutics of the 'subject'.

The subject of text

P: Tell me Freddie. How do you feel in your nerves today?
F: I feel upset.
P: You feel upset Freddie? Why is that tell me?
F: Control of me. I feel like a thick sound from a plate. Dolphin been drove into the cooking room. There must be some kind of connection (. . inaudible).
P: A sound from a plate? What sort of sound is it Freddie?
F: Sound. Teacup. Rattle of a tea cup. Hold on my body (. . inaudible).
P: Tell me Freddie. How do you get on with the other patients?

As the information contained in line 9 might suggest, this extract is taken from an interview between a psychiatric 'patient' and a health professional. The professional was a psychiatrist, and as was explained to the researcher just before the interview took place, the psychiatrist was intending to assess Freddie's 'mental state'. Yet whatever his intentions, there is no doubt that we as sociologists could analyse this interchange in numerous ways. For example, had I given more data on the way in which the interview was structured in relation to time and conversational emphasis, we could have set about analysing the manner in which the patient–doctor relationship is created and constructed in the course of the interview. Or we could have looked at the ways in which, say, the symptoms of psychoses are constructed in and through the interview session. (That is to say, we could examine the ways in which the psychiatrist draws out the 'symptoms' by using a specific and deliberate scheme of questioning.) We might even be tempted to search for the meanings embodied in the interchange and perhaps go on to question the psychiatrist about his interpretation of Freddie's responses. Had we done so he would have referred at some point to such things as 'first-rank symptoms' and the nature of schizophrenic reactions, and so on. Indeed, were we to look at Freddie's 'chart' (medical file) we would see that previous interviews with Freddie have usually been written up and summarized in terms of his expressing reactions considered typical of a schizophrenic condition.

Psychiatric interviews and the records which they have generated have constituted the subject of study for numerous sociological inquiries (e.g.

Byrd, 1981; Garfinkel, 1967b; Hak, 1992). Most of the discussions have been concerned with looking at how such records are assembled and how what has been 'put together' relates to some external point of reference; that is to say, how the records 'fit' with organizational requirements (Byrd, 1981; Garfinkel, 1967b), or how they are composed so as to express instances of some idealized representation of a psychiatric trait (Schegloff, 1963), or even how they relate to the requirements of professional practice (Hak, 1992). Naturally, any one of these routes into the analysis of records has a place in the armoury of the qualitative researcher, and some of them have been discussed elsewhere in this volume. Here, however, I would like to pick up on a Foucauldian theme and show how such records are used to manufacture the 'subjects' of sociological inquiry.

In his later work, such as *Discipline and Punish* (1977), Foucault became fascinated with the exercise of what he called power/knowledge. In particular he focused on how specific forms of power/knowledge (such as medical or juridical discourse) impinged on human beings so as to manufacture docile, pliant and disciplined bodies. That is to say, Foucault was interested, among many other things, in the manner in which discourse and its associated forms of daily human practice combined to manufacture *subjects*. In talking of records, for example, he thereby mentions how 'the carefully collated life of mental patients or delinquents' functioned as a procedure of objectification and subjection (1977: 192).

The carefully collated life of psychiatric patients is of course written in many registers. Thus, as well as being written up in a psychiatric 'chart', Freddie is also written up in nursing care notes and social work records. In each case the discourse that describes him is drawn together from different threads. Thus, the psychiatrist, in large part, draws his threads from the vade-mecum knowledge contained in psychiatric texts. Nurses draw on one of many of their 'models of nursing', and social workers draw their threads from their professional texts. In the case of Freddie, for example, the nurses described him primarily in terms of his 'activities of daily living' (ADL). Indeed, in some respects one could say that he was described as a functioning machine whose communication skills, everyday living skills, hygiene skills, and so on, were graded and scaled. One of the major tasks of the nursing staff involved assessing Freddie in terms of such scales, and having made notes on his 'deficiencies', they subsequently drew plans of nursing action to correct the perceived shortcomings.

In such ways Freddie, as a subject of sociological inquiry, might be said to have been more properly constructed in text than in action. This is so because the text (i.e. the records) has a permanence, combined with an easy possibility of transfer through time and space so as to fix Freddie's identity more firmly than any episodic encounter in, say, a psychiatric ward. Thus Freddie was often referred to as a 'schizophrenic' even during those periods when none of the first-rank (or even lesser) symptoms of schizophrenia were evident. Naturally, his psychiatric notes – which fixed and stabilized his biography – followed him wherever he went.

Researching text

In *The Archaeology of Knowledge* (1972: 138–9) Foucault draws a distinction between document and monument. Archaeology, he says, 'does not treat discourse as *document*, as a sign of something else . . . it is concerned with discourse in its own volume, as a *monument*'. Archaeology, then, is not an interpretive discipline, 'it does not seek, a better-hidden discourse', but instead seeks to analyse the structure of discourse in its own terms. In order to undertake such an analysis, it is not always necessary to interrogate authors or other thinking subjects. (Indeed, such humanism would have been anathema to Foucault.) Instead we are free to focus on such issues as the rules concerning what can and cannot be thought, the ways in which knowledge can be represented, the nature of the grid by means of which thought is expressed and classified, and the rules concerning who is, and who is not, entitled to pronounce on the nature of a given phenomenon.

It is not, of course, always easy to translate Foucault's work into a set of methodological precepts that can be followed by the empirical researcher. Moreover, it may seem to some that I have been curiously selective in my exposition of his work. In reply to that, however, I can do no better than quote Foucault himself. 'All my books', he stated, 'are little tool boxes. If people want to open them, to use a particular sentence, a particular idea, a particular analysis like a screwdriver or a spanner .. so much the better!' (1995: 720). In that generous vein, perhaps I could end by mentioning the work of someone who, although he was not specifically influenced by Foucault, nevertheless might be said to have provided some further clues as to how discursive regimes may be investigated in an empirical manner.

The someone is Phillippe Ariès, who, in his *The Hour of Our Death* (1981) and *Images of Man and Death* (1985), sought to examine Western attitudes towards death from the Middle Ages to the present. In so doing he demonstrated how such varied phenomena as the layout of cemeteries, the nature of a liturgy, the arrangement of human bodies, the style and content of painting, icons and other text intertwined and interconnected to express coherent discourses on death. Unfortunately, and all too frequently, Ariès also interjected himself, as a knowing subject, into the interpretive frame. Despite that, however, his work served to illustrate how qualitative research can not only start with the investigation of things (rather than persons), but can also examine links and connections between objects that cannot speak, yet nevertheless bear messages. In the preceding sections, I hope only that I have gone some way towards showing how the investigation of such connections might begin.

Note

1. The respective verdicts were: accident, accident, suicide.

References

American Psychiatric Association (1994) *Diagnostic and Statistical Manual: Mental Disorders* (4th edn). (*DSM-IV*). Washington, DC: American Psychiatric Association.

Ariès, P. (1981) *The Hour of Our Death*, trans. H. Weaver. New York: Knopf.

Ariès, P. (1985) *Images of Man and Death*, trans. J. Lloyd, Cambridge, MA: Harvard University Press.

Atkinson, J.M. (1978) *Discovering Suicide: Studies in the Social Organization of Death.* London: Macmillan.

Bogdan, R. and Taylor, S.J. (1975) *Introduction to Qualitative Research Methods: A Phenomenological Approach to the Social Sciences.* New York: Wiley.

Bryman, A. (1988) *Quantity and Quality in Social Research.* London: Unwin Hyman.

Buck, N., Gershuny, J., Rose, D. and Scott, J. (eds) (1994) *Changing Households: The British Household Panel Survey 1990–1992.* Colchester, Essex: ESRC Research Centre.

Byrd, D.E. (1981) *Organizational Constraints on Psychiatric Treatment: The Outpatient Clinic.* Greenwich, CT: JAI Press.

Douglas, J.D. (1967) *The Social Meanings of Suicide.* Princeton: Princeton University Press.

Douglas, M. (1966) *Purity and Danger: An Analysis of Concepts of Pollution and Taboo.* London: Routledge and Kegan Paul.

Douglas, M. (ed.) (1973) *Rules and Meanings: The Anthropology of Everyday Knowledge.* Harmondsworth: Penguin.

Durkheim, É. (1952) *Suicide: A Study in Sociology*, trans. J.A. Spaulding and G. Simpson. London: Routledge and Kegan Paul.

Durkheim, É. and Mauss, M. (1963) *Primitive Classification*, trans. R. Needham. London: Cohen and West.

Foucault, M. (1970) *The Order of Things: An Archaeology of the Human Sciences*, trans. A. Sheridan. London: Tavistock.

Foucault, M. (1972) *The Archaeology of Knowledge*, trans. A.M. Sheridan Smith. London: Tavistock.

Foucault, M. (1973) *The Birth of the Clinic*, trans. A. Sheridan. London: Tavistock.

Foucault, M. (1977) *Discipline and Punish*, trans. A. Sheridan. Harmondsworth: Penguin.

Foucault, M. (1995) *Dits et écrits, 1954–88*, Vol. 2, ed. D. Defert and F. Ewald. Paris: Gallimard.

Garfinkel, H. (1967a) 'Studies of the routine grounds of everyday actions', in *Studies in Ethnomethodology*. Englewood Cliffs, NJ: Prentice Hall. pp. 35–75.

Garfinkel, H. (1967b) 'Good organizational reasons for "bad" clinical records', in *Studies in Ethnomethodology*. Englewood Cliffs, NJ: Prentice Hall. pp. 186–207.

Geertz, C. (1984) '"From the native's point of view": On the nature of anthropological understanding', in R.A. Shweder and R.A. LeVine (eds), *Culture Theory*. Cambridge: Cambridge University Press. pp. 123–36.

Hak, T. (1992) 'Psychiatric records as transformations of other texts', in G. Watson and R.M. Seiler (eds), *Text in Context: Contributions to Ethnomethodology*. London: Sage. pp. 138–55.

Lévi-Strauss, C. (1969) *Totemism*, trans. R. Needham. Harmondsworth: Penguin.

Lynch, M. and Woolgar, S. (eds) (1990) *Representation in Scientific Practice.* Cambridge, MA: MIT Press.

Malinowski, B. (1922) *Argonauts of the Western Pacific.* London: Routledge.

Malinowski, B. (1944) *A Scientific Theory of Culture and Other Essays.* Chapel Hill: University of North Carolina Press.

Prior, L. (1989) *The Social Organization of Death: Social Practices and Medical Discourse in Belfast.* Basingstoke: Macmillan.

Prior, L. (1993) *The Social Organization of Mental Illness.* London: Sage.

Ridpath, I. (ed.) (1989) *Norton's 2000.0 Star Atlas and Reference Handbook* (18th edn). Harlow: Longman.

Sahlins, M. (1995) *How 'Natives' Think, about Captain Cook, For Example*. Chicago: University of Chicago Press.

Schegloff, E.A. (1963) 'Toward a reading of psychiatric theory', *Berkeley Journal of Sociology*, 8: 61–91.

Schütz, A. (1962) 'Common-sense and scientific interpretation of human action', in *Collected Papers*, Vol. 1, ed. M. Natanson. The Hague; Martinus Nijhoff. pp. 3–47.

Strauss, A.L. (1987) *Qualitative Analysis for Social Scientists*. Cambridge: Cambridge University Press.

Taylor, C. (1987) 'Interpretation and the sciences of man', in P. Rabinow and M.W. Sullivan (eds), *Interpretive Social Science: A Second Look*. London: University of California Press. pp. 33–81.

Taylor, S. (1982) *Durkheim and the Study of Suicide*. London: Macmillan.

World Health Organization (1977) *Manual of the International Statistical Classification of Diseases, Injuries and Causes of Death*, 2 vols (9th edn). Geneva: WHO.

World Health Organization (1992) *International Statistical Classification of Diseases and Related Health Problems*, 3 vols (10th edn). Geneva: WHO.

Zimmerman, D.H. and Pollner, M. (1971) 'The everyday world as a phenomenon', in J.D. Douglas (ed.), *Understanding Everyday Life*. London: Routledge and Kegan Paul. pp. 80–103.

6 Ethnomethodology and Textual Analysis

Rod Watson

Tattoos, bus tickets, pay slips, street signs, time indications on watch faces, chalked information on blackboards, computer VDU displays, car dashboards, company logos, contracts, railway timetables, television programme titles, teletexts, T-shirt epigrams, 'on'/'off' switches, £10 notes and other bank notes, passports and identity cards, cheques and payslips, the Bible, receipts, newspapers and magazines, road markings, computer keyboards, medical prescriptions, birthday cards, billboard advertisements, maps, Hansard, graffiti on walls, music scores, church liturgies, drivers' licences, birth, marriage and death certificates, voting slips, degree certificates, book-keepers' accounts, stock inventories, cricket scoreboards, credit cards – these and countless other items that involve written language and diagrammatic forms indicate the immensely pervasive, widespread and institutionalized place of texts in our society.

This list also indicates the extraordinary diversity in the work done by texts – contractual commitment, ratifying work, facilitating work, record-keeping, persuasive work, identity-establishing work, and so on. In fact, one might suggest that virtually every recognizable activity in our society has its textual aspects, involving and incorporating people's monitoring of written or other textual 'signs' – texts that, in a wide variety of ways, help us to orientate ourselves to that activity, occasion or setting and to make sense of it.

These observations might, at first glance, seem like news from nowhere, as unutterably banal and unremarkable. However, it must also be observed that there is a relative paucity of studies which deal with texts as mundane phenomena, as a routine part of our everyday activities. A great many textual analyses in the humanities and social sciences concern themselves with the textual phenomena of 'high culture' – novels, academic texts, exegeses of biblical or Talmudic texts or the texts of classical antiquity. These by and large exegetical studies have taken a variety of academic forms or positions – textual interpretations, etymological work, and so on. Whilst valuable in themselves, these analyses tended to address texts that were, at best, of narrowly restricted relevance to everyday, ordinary life as opposed to the *habitus* of a literary or intellectual élite. They tended to divert attention from the myriad mundane textual phenomena in our society and, indeed, to selectively focus on the exotic rather than on the ordinary, the esoteric rather than the commonplace.

However, even these textual exegeses sometimes constituted an advance over the conventional approach in the humanities and social sciences to the written or printed word. This approach is to treat language as a kind of transparent 'window on the world', as a conduit, a direct channel to some 'real thing' in the social world. Thus, the anthropologically inclined historian Alan Macfarlane (1978) used the Rev. Ralph Josselin's journal as providing a 'window' on the family and individualism in sixteenth-century England.[1] Anthropologists treat their field notes as providing and preserving access to (say) the kinship structure of a tribal society.[2] Survey analysts in social science treat their statistical tables and charts as providing access to (say) the income distribution in society, and so on.

The language, numerical constellations, diagrams and other features of these texts are, by and large, regarded by these analysts as unproblematic, as mere conduits to the phenomenon of their analytic interest, be it family, income, individualism or whatever. From the standpoint of these scholars the text operates as a more or less unnoticed and unremarkable means to an end. Texts are placed in service of the examination of 'other', separately conceived phenomena. From this standpoint, the text purportedly comprises a *resource* for accessing these phenomena – phenomena existing 'beyond' the text, as it were, where the text operates as an essentially unexamined conduit, a kind of neutral 'window' or 'channel' to them.

This contrasts in a major way with the work of scholars such as Edward Rose (1960). In his important work, he does not treat 'words' and '(things in) the world' as two separate phenomena. Instead, the world itself is seen as 'worded entity' and ordinary words are seen as inextricable parts of the phenomena they define. There is, from this perspective no 'thing in itself' separate from the word that identifies it. Instead, we common-sensically experience those things in terms of the words for them – be those words oral or textual. Think of how a sign saying 'Parking' serves to define for competent society-members what a particular space '*is*'.

The above is an important point for sociology, particularly because professional sociologists possess their own vocabulary for defining and identifying the (social) world, whether this vocabulary be orally or textually delivered. Typically, these technical words are, as Rose shows, derived from ordinary, common-sense ones. Terms such as 'status', 'role' or 'society' may now be seen as part of the technical vocabulary of society but they were originally part of ordinary, common-sense usage: this usage evolved through time and its evolved forms have worked to shape their professional/analytic determinations.

Rose claims that this stock of ordinary words itself comprises a 'natural sociology', a set of shared common-sense conceptual understandings of society. A major corollary of this is that the professional sociologists' use of a given term, such as 'role' or 'status', is shaped by the common-sense cultural meanings of that term – often, meanings that have evolved since the seventeenth century or earlier. Virtually all the technical expressions used by professional sociologists have their basis in evolved ordinary usage, and that basis sets the terms for the conventional meanings that professional sociologists impute in those expressions. That professional sociologists are, at best, often only dimly aware of this does not change the fact that their discipline, with all its technical vocabulary, is premised upon a natural sociological vocabulary. Rose's argument is that sociology is a natural language pursuit and that sociological analysis is linguistically constructed. This argument gives us our position on sociological texts, whether these be research reports or instructional textbooks. These texts themselves manifest the fact that professional sociology is not only a discipline whose technical vocabulary has a lay or common-sense origin but is *ipso facto* also a discipline that is conducted, whether orally or textually, in some natural language or other – Japanese, English, French, and so on – and depends utterly upon the descriptive and other resources of that language. Sociologists can and do provide analytic descriptions of social order but they are only able to do so because their own ordinary, natural language furnishes the general resources for them to do so. The form, character and development of their academic analyses are, consequently, shaped or fashioned by the conventional properties of the natural language that they *necessarily* employ quite as much as by the methodological constraints of their discipline. Certainly, sociologists and other academics cannot exempt their own work from textual analysis. It would, for instance, be interesting to analyse the ways in which Alan Macfarlane's (1978) historical claims are shaped by the texts he uses as data sources and by his own textual practices in making sense of those texts and in writing them up into a report.

So far as sociology texts are concerned, we might observe that not only do these texts unavoidably partake of the general properties of the natural language that is used, but they will also necessarily be shaped by the ordinary textual conventions employed by that language. These textual conventions vary, of course: in some cultures one does not read from left to right and progressively downward line by line.

An example of this textual structuring of an analysis is to be found in the transcription procedures of some conversation analysts in sociology. Conversation analysts have a highly crafted technical system for transcribing the minute details of communicative interactions, but many of their procedures derive from ordinary, common-sense textual practice – not only their 'left to right, progressively downward' nature, but also their identificatory characterization of utterances and utterance sequences. In other words, verbal or non-verbal actions are characterized in terms of 'the' (or a) category or other identity of the speaker. In this sense, the conversation analyst's transcription formats are derived from broader sources – sources that are familiar in our culture, originating, for instance, in the formatting of the scripts of plays, from courtroom transcripts as presented in court and newspaper reports, and so on. Indeed, some conversation analysts have actually used court or tribunal reports as their 'raw data', where the categorial identifications of 'Counsel' and 'Witness' are provided in the left-hand column (see Atkinson and Drew, 1979). See, for example, the following (for an explanation of transcription conventions see the Appendix to this volume):

(C = Counsel, W = Witness)

C: Aind (4.2 sec.) You knew at that time of course about the trouble that had (1.7) gone on between Mister Rooney an (.) Mister Maclean (1.7)
W: Yih mean pu(h) – ah earlier in the day (stabbing) (starting)
C:
W: earlier in the day =
C: = Yes
W: Yes
((continues))
(Atkinson and Drew, 1979: 64, example 24)[3]

and, from an analysis by Heath on non-spoken/non-verbal aspects of medical interaction:

(Dr = Doctor, P = Patient)

Dr: Do sit dow::n
(5.5 sec.)
Dr: What's up:?
P: I've had a bad eye ::: (in there) =
Dr: = oh yeah
(1.2)
P: an:: it (had) fat flew up
((continues))
(Heath, 1986: 35, Fragment 2:6, Transcript 1)

In our culture we use the 'left to right' reading procedure, so we read the category-identification (e.g. 'counsel', 'doctor') *before* we read the utterance *per se*. Thus, by the time we read the utterance we are *already* predisposed to reading the utterance as (say) distinctively a 'doctor's' or a 'patient's' utterance and thus as understandable in terms of a 'counsel–witness cross-examination'. This predisposition is *textually* established through the apparently innocuous stipulation of the categorial identifications in the left-hand column. We thus operate with a textually (categorially) instructed reading of the interaction, where each utterance is read over a temporal course as (say) 'the doctor's utterance' because that category has been provided as an initial feature of that course.

This might seem quite unexceptionable, even trivial. However, given the fact that (a) as Schegloff (1991) has observed, in (say) telephone calls to the police, there is no guarantee that, in a given utterance, the category 'police officer' is the one that will be, or will become, relevant to the caller, and (b) it is at least arguable that many of the sequences in exchanges between counsel and witness, doctor and patient, police officer and caller, and so on, could without the insertion of these categorial identifications be easily seen as, say, ordinary conversations between, for instance, friends or acquaintances, then we might claim that the textual practice of incorporating categorial identifications in the left-hand column works to select and to privilege *one* sociological characterization of the exchanges over other potential characterizations. This has major analytic consequences for how one describes the interaction: is it ordinary talk or a more specialized interactional system, for example medical interaction? It is clear that the transcription procedures themselves incline us towards one characterization rather than another, and this has major implications for how one proceeds with the analysis and for what kind of analysis eventuates. Nor is this textual practice restricted to conversation analysts: it is widely employed by ethnographers (see, e.g., Atkinson, 1982).[4] We might say that the very transcriptions they produce do persuasive and predisposing work before the ethnographic analysis *per se* really begins, and, indeed, risks introducing an artifactual element into that ethnographic analysis. In a strong sense, the ethnography is done before the transcribed data are analysed: once the categories are provided, a predisposing interpretation is potentiated and it is 'all over bar the shouting'.

This extended illustration is simply to show how the textual practices of professional sociologists shape their data and their analysis and how many of these practices are rooted in lay textual reasoning. Unsurprisingly, professional sociologists unavoidably rely upon these ordinary 'common-sensical' cultural procedures of reading and of making ordinary 'textual sense' of what we read. We have already outlined one such procedure, 'left to right', and how it can be used as a resource. Clearly, finding out about these resources is important, particularly as much remains unknown about them (and, consequently, we do not fully know how these procedures shape the discipline of sociology). Even those procedures that *are* known about tend to be disattended by sociologists: consequently, our discipline of sociology is shaped in more or less unknown or unacknowledged ways by ordinary linguistic (including textual) resources and procedures that are, currently, at best dimly known by its practitioners. Thus *sociological* textual practices rely heavily in tacit ways on ordinary, 'common-sensical' textual practices. We may now turn to an examination of the place of texts in ordinary, everyday cultural reasoning and conduct.

Texts as active social phenomena

As I have indicated earlier, texts of all kinds have typically been employed by conventional sociologists as 'information on something else', as Dorothy E. Smith (1982, 1984) has put it in a series of influential papers. That is, texts have been used to 'convey' the reader to some 'other' phenomenon such as family life four hundred years ago, a train accident, and so on, or something else existing 'beyond' the text. As Smith puts it, we are, quite simply, used to finding out what texts say, what we have learned from them as a resource. Texts have, therefore, often been regarded by sociologists as transparent, as 'windows' giving onto this or that 'other' phenomenon. In this sense, most sociologists have oriented themselves towards texts in the same way as ordinary society-members, that is, they have treated texts as 'conduits' to a reality beyond the text. Texts have seldom been treated as analytically significant phenomena in their own right, as comprising self-contained data in themselves, to be taken as objects of attention on their own behalf.

Linked with this tendency to treat texts as mere conduits to a separately conceived reality is an assumption of what Dorothy E. Smith terms the 'inertia of the text'. That is, the text is typically taken as mere marks on a page, inoperative and inert. However, Smith attempts to replace this notion of the text as a passively transparent 'channel' with a conception of an *active* text, a text that has a structuring effect, that actively organizes a course of social action and that is consequential for that action, directing it in its course. A text may thus be inspected for *how* it actively makes sense of some phenomenon, for example *how* one newspaper report may, in its profile of a train accident, lay the blame on one party and a second newspaper report on another.[5] To use Smith's simile (it is no more than that, and even then has its dangers), the text is akin to 'a crystal which bends the light as it passes through'.

An example: in the journal *Women's Studies International Forum*, John Lee (1984) analyses an actual newspaper headline: GIRL GUIDE AGED 14 RAPED AT HELL'S ANGELS CONVENTION. Lee makes the point that newspaper headlines work actively (a) to attract readers' attention to particular stories; (b) to persuade them to read those stories; and (c) to predispose them towards a particular way of reading the following story, a particular way of making sense of and understanding the contents of the story.

The headline, then, has impetus. Not only does it actively capture readers' attention but, also, it furnishes them with an 'instructed reading' of the story: newspaper headlines may be seen as incorporating 'interpretive practices and schemata' (Smith) which often take the form of instructions for reading what follows. Part of the 'attention-getting' work done by this headline is its puzzle format: what was an incumbent of the category 'Girl Guide' (let alone one categorized as 'aged 14') doing at a get-together of incumbents of the category 'Hell's Angels'? The categories do not seem to go 'naturally' together, as, for instance, might the categories 'Hell's Angel' and 'sidekick'. The headline directs us towards the story in order to find a solution to the puzzle: after all, we might even find the Girl Guide to have been complicit to some degree, looking for 'cheap thrills', and so on. However, the story presents another solution to the puzzle generated by the co-selection of these categories, namely that the Girl Guide had been abducted by the Hell's Angels and that her prior movements were such that it was simply ill-fortune that she was in a certain place when the Hell's Angels arrived.

Puzzle-solution formats abound in newspaper headlines: note another 'puzzle' analysed by Jim Schenkein (1979), from a copy of the *Guardian*: POLICE INQUIRY INTO WHY THEY MISSED THE RADIO RAIDERS. Schenkein reports his initial bafflement on reading the headline: to what did it refer?

To whom did it refer? Hence his characterization of the headline as a *referential* puzzle (and, indeed, we can see that Lee's headline is a similar kind of puzzle). His bafflement induced him to read the story to find a solution. Perhaps the reader of this article has been 'hooked' by the puzzle: I am not going to provide the solution here (but the issue of the *Guardian* was published in autumn 1971). Schenkein's article does, in a way, echo Smith's simile of the text as being like a 'crystal which bends the light as it passes through'. He refers to the way in which the headline begins the task of transforming 'events in the world' into 'stories in the news': again, we have the notion of an active text, a text with impact, impetus.

Part of the active, operational, structuring character of the text is the 'slant' imparted to the story. As Lee records, he once observed a news editor on a local radio station reporting a record football pools win in another area of the country. The story was put out under the heading: LOCAL MAN LOSES RECORD OF LARGEST POOLS WIN. The headline, and the text that followed, gained its impact by presenting the story with a 'slant' derived from the local frame of reference. The text actively effects a particular transformation of the story. As an exercise in determining what texts do, you might like to examine the *activity of implication* as it occurs in this actual (but pseudonymized) US police report of a murder. By 'activity of implication' I intend the way in which the suspect, Stuart Riley, is, through this text, which is a bland, unremarkable police report, potentially implicated in one murder but not (so far as this document is concerned) in another:

FACTORY CITY POLICE DEPARTMENT

INTRA-DEPARTMENTAL CORRESPONDENCE

TO: Lieut. Donald O. Corcoran,
Homicide Bureau - Commanding

FROM: Alan J. Rimsky - Detective
Michael D. Holt - Detective
Evidence Unit Ident. Bur.

DATE: 8.9.83

SUBJECT
Re: Latent print comparison against inked impressions of Stuart Riley.

Sir
On September 3, 1983, and at the direction of Lt. David O. Corcoran, Commander of the Homicide Bureau, a latent print comparison of all the latent prints developed from the following two scenes were compared against the inked impressions of Stuart Riley, Factory City Police Mug no. 96713:

1. 431 Ash St. – Homicide Victim – Herb Morris – 23.8.83
2. 826 Sycamore Ave. – Assault Victim – Hank Stebbins – 31.8.83

From the latent prints of 431 Ash Street a latent print developed from the top of a stereo player was identical in ridge characteristic to the left thumb of the inked impression of Stuart Riley no. 96713.

From the latent prints of 826 Sycamore Ave., no identification was effected.

Comparison effected by Detectives Michael D. Holt and Alan J. Rimsky of the Evidence Unit.

Lt. Corcoran Homicide
File

Respectfully
Alan J. Rimsky – Detective
Evidence Unit

Files no 1216 and no 1217

(Stamp Received)
Sept. 9 1983
Homicide Bureau
Factory City Police Dept

(signed) Donald O. Corcoran

Note that this document is a very small, utterly routine part of an overall investigation, but that nonetheless the statement of evidence – that Riley's fingerprint matched in one respect a print found in the murder victim Morris's home but that there was no such match established in assault victim Hank Stebbins's home – renders inferentially available a putative guilt-implication for Riley in one case rather than in the other. Of course, the rest of the investigation may even, eventually, implicate Riley in the second case and exonerate him in the first, but here we are concerned simply with what *this* text actively brings about *here and now*, however provisionally and inferentially.

Some concerns that you may (or may not!) wish to bear in mind in considering how the implication is actively brought about by and through the report as a text are: (a) the invocation of a method, of systematic procedure; (b) the various and diverse provisions of persons', including the investigators', identities; (c) the formal, 'official' style of the text and the stamps, signatures and ratifications it includes; and (d) the precision of the formulation of the statements in the text (the precise nature, and, by implication, the limits of the comparison effected). These and other textual methods actively bring about an 'implicative placing' of Riley in one scene rather than another, where this 'placing' is also textually authorized as an account. Note that no direct statement of guilt is made: instead, such a judgement is actively potentiated by the text. It is through such undramatic, seemingly straightforward texts that 'guilt-implicativeness' may be actively implied or pointed up: such routine texts are active indeed.

A similar guilt-implicative text – again without any explicit accusation or other guilt-attribution – may be found in the following newspaper headline: WIFE FOUND MURDERED AT HOME – where, given the conventional category-pair 'wife'–'husband' and the setting ('home') being a conventional location for such a pair, the husband may (rightly or wrongly) be deemed by readers the favourite candidate for the additional category 'culprit'.

Of course, the reader of the text plays a crucial role in all this, not simply passively receiving that text but also actively interpreting it (including, sometimes, generating different or divergent versions of a textual account). It is to the act of reading that we now turn.

Reading as activity

Texts, then, in the resources they mobilize and in their fashioning and formatting, are anything but passive, anything but mere inert marks on a page or screen. Texts have their own active structuring effect. However, this effect has to be *activated* or *animated* by the reader(s): when referring to the active text we are always referring to the text-as-read.

Again, reading has often been presented as passive reception of the message of the text. Even the school of thought in textual analysis called reception theory tends to conceive of reading in terms of relatively simple 'responses' – a kind of 'copy process'. In fact, reading a text is an extraordinarily complex interpretive activity employing the wide-ranging, sophisticated sense-making procedures as furnished within the respective culture involved. Thus, as McHoul's (1982) study points out, we may talk about the reader(s) producing a 'culturally competent course of reading'.

A culturally competent course of reading might involve readers' ability to use categories or identities such as 'Girl Guide' and 'Hell's Angel', their ability to understand the serial or sequential aspects of the text (the headline being followed by the story, the story being serially organized as a beginning, middle and end and as, e.g., a series of event-descriptions, etc.) and the able deployment of other culturally based sense-making procedures that s/he brings to the text as part of his/her 'background understandings'.

McHoul (1982: Chap. 2) made up a 'poem' from randomly selected first lines from other actual poems and then recorded readers' attempts to make sense of it: he considered that their efforts in trying to understand this 'strange' poem would make explicit techniques of reading that are usually implicit. He found that readers made sense of these randomly collected lines as lines of a single, meaningful poem, that they relied heavily on following through its temporal sequences in order to gain an understanding of it. Readers also treated each line as an evidence of a single emerging pattern of meaning, a continuing course, but they were also ready to revise their interpretations line by line. They treated the lines as, by and large, fitted to each other and a second line came to be seen as having been projected by a prior line – even if some succeeding line were apparently disjunctive, it was often seen as 'metaphorically related' to the prior one or to the overall pattern evidenced by the prior one.

Some or all of these cultural methods for competent reading can be found in our everyday reading of all documents, for example receipts which record each item purchased and the sequence of purchasing. Of course, some texts such as 'No Parking' may be designed for 'at-a-glance' reading, so there is, for instance, no serially ordered lineage. However, a 'No Parking' sign placed halfway up a wall still requires the readers' active interpretation: for instance, readers will know that the sign does not simply prohibit parking halfway up a wall, but refers to a space in front of the wall, and they will have to try to figure out how far that space extends, and so on.[6] Obvious as this may seem, active interpretive or sense-making work is, clearly, unavoidably involved on the part of the reader.

It is in this sense that the reader 'activates' the text. Whatever active potential a text possesses, this potential has to be activated through its being read. This, clearly, is what Lee has in mind when he says: 'headlines must be so constructed as to allow readers to employ a variety of methods and techniques of sense-assembly which enable them to decode the headings so as to discover the message and instructions which they impart' (1984: 69). Readers' active employment of these sense-assembly methods and techniques are, quite evidently, central to the activation of the properties of the text.

Perhaps one of the clearest examples of activating a text is when lecturers 'animate' a set of notes they have written. Erving Goffman (1981) writes at length about the varied practices involved in animating such a text: among these is what he terms 'text-parenthetical remarks', where a lecturer departs from 'strict adherence' to her/his prepared text *per se* to introduce parenthetical remarks, qualifications, elaborations, clarifications, editorializing, and so on (1981: 176–7). These 'extra' commentaries are often addressed to making oral sense of a written or printed text, drawing out its significance, and so on. In the case of the lecture, the text's author is also its principal (i.e. its advocate) and animator (presenter and interpreter to an audience). The 'animation' of a lecture-text involves its transformation into a 'spoken-aloud' form designed for a particular type of social occasion or face-to-face encounter.

Reading a text, then, has two aspects which are only analytically distinguishable. When one is reading a text, as a practical matter, one is, in all likelihood, unaware of the distinction. The first aspect is the way in which the text is organized so as to potentially predispose readers towards a given set of relevances, and the second is the way that the actual practices of reading the text actualize those relevances.

Indeed, texts are often designed to engage with a specific set of presumed relevances amongst readers – hence we get texts slanted towards particular categories of person – *Woman's Own*, *Men Only*, *Motoring News*, *The Dalesman*, *The Jewish Chronicle*, *The British Journal of Sociology*, and so on. These texts are slanted or designed so as to address the putative relevances of what has been called the 'implied' (or 'intended') 'reader'. Many texts are designed for readers from groups characterized by special distributions of knowledge – lawyers, doctors, clergy, engineers, and so on. Each of these groups may be termed 'interpretive communities' since their members bring special (or specialist) interpretive resources to their particular class of text – legal, medical, religious and engineering texts, respectively.

Readers, then, actively interpret texts but cannot interpret them in just any way they wish. The texts themselves contain 'instructions' which yield strongly preferred readings. There is a dialectical, back-and-forth process in operation. The text makes available various interpretive schemata and the reader activates these schemata in particular instances by bringing his/her interpretive work into alignment. As Lee's (1984) article suggests, readers must be able to employ congruent interpretive schemata in order to identify the message and instructions projected by the text. One might say that in effecting this alignment the act of reading establishes a presumed reciprocity of perspectives – that potentiated by the text and that deployed by the reader. This does not necessarily mean that readers always agree with the 'message' of what they read, only that they can, initially, understand that message. The matter of agreement, disagreement or neutrality is a further, and crucial, aspect of the act of reading. One thing seems sure: we cannot have anything approaching an adequate textual analysis without including an intricately interwoven consideration *both* of textual organization *and* of reading as an activity.

Textually mediated social action: Professional and everyday

Let us return to the opening paragraph of this chapter, to the list of examples of textual items. Most of these examples derive from the situations and settings of everyday life, the scenes of everyday activity. However, there is also a branch of textual analysis which focuses upon social scientific (and particularly anthropological) practices. This tendency in textual analysis addresses issues concerning so-called 'high culture' – novels, drama scripts, poetry, religious or academic texts, and the like. Textual analysis was, in part, devised as a way of analysing these 'high-status' textual artefacts – perhaps for the purposes of biblical or Talmudic exegesis, the literary criticism of novels or drama scripts, and so on. As such, there was an 'in-group' or élitist element to this exercise: it was, typically, one segment of a literary, cultural or academic élite commenting on the work of another segment of that élite as part of a debate with that segment – or, even more pleasurable, one segment of that élite talking about itself.

This strand of textual analysis, and the, arguably, élitist, literally self-regarding features that it has always possessed are still pursued by various academic schools of thought. One of the major schools of this kind in social science is the 'writing culture' school, whose best-known representatives are James Clifford and George E. Marcus (1986).

For Clifford and Marcus, the anthropologist's taking of field notes based on her/his observations, conversations, and so on, and the subsequent writing-up of a 'final report' based, to a great extent, upon these field notes comprises the anthropologist's 'inscribing of culture', that is, the transformation of one culture – often a non-literate one – into written/printed textual terms and, very often, into the textual conventions of another culture and of a specific professional group within it.

For Clifford and Marcus, ethnographic field notes are active parts of the circumstances they describe – they define those circumstances, making them available to readers who have no direct or independent access to them. Furthermore, they argue that ethnographic field notes and reports contain literary or textual conventions that not only construct but also work to privilege and authorize anthropological accounts, thus legitimating the discipline of anthropology itself. Often, however, these accounts are highly contestable. Clifford and Marcus argue, for instance, that the textual conventions for writing anthropology actually suppress the native's point of view whilst claiming to represent it. Often, such texts present a society or social setting as internally unitary or clearly bounded, unambiguously patterned, where 'in fact' that representation may be arguable: were anthropological writing conventions other than what they are, those societies might be presented as internally varied, composed of the diverse perspectives and discourses of varying parties and groups within the society ('polyphony'), such that the society may be presented as fragmented, open-ended, in flux, ambivalent and ambiguous. Often, argue Clifford and Marcus, anthropologists' reports effectively take sides with one or other of these groups or perspectives and – along with the anthropologists' textual techniques for self-privileging their discipline, their Western culture and intellectual tradition – this amounts to a 'politics' of anthropology.[7] For a critique of such claims see Watson, 1991.

In other words, these analysts ask: who is to be the trusted advocate of the 'native's point of view', and what textual form should this advocacy take? All this is part of the textual production of what symbolic interactionists of the Everett Hughes school have called the 'segmentation' of a profession – in this case, that of anthropology. For an analysis of the textual production of the segmentation of that profession, see G. Watson's (1984) paper on the construction of the boundaries between social and cultural anthropology.

The 'writing culture' school of thought do not examine or focalize textual procedures in so explicit or detailed a way as, for instance, do Lee, Smith or McHoul.[8] Nor is there much of a theory of reading in the work of the 'writing culture' school. Indeed, much of the effort of Clifford, Marcus and their associates is to subvert conventionally constructed anthropological textual accounts by, for instance, pointing out the ways in which such accounts partake of the same literary devices used by writers of fiction. This approach, which is often called 'analytic irony', contrasts with the approach of Lee and similar analysts who see their task as the analytic explication or 'explicitation' of texts, treating them as topics rather than setting up in 'competition' with them.

However, the above approach refers largely to scholarly or research practices and texts (although, secondarily, there is some concern with socio-political context). The most pervasive level of social practice is, though, that of everyday life and of society-members' culturally based sense-making and reasoning. Newspaper articles, road signs, shopping lists, and so on, are all, clearly, of the 'everyday' rather than the scholarly or professional kind of text. Their everyday or common-sense status does not mean they are of any less significance: quite the contrary. This is the most generic level of 'textual work' and it is the scholarly/professional one which is in many respects derivative, as was indicated earlier in our discussion of Rose's work.

Texts may be seen as 'mediating' in a variety of ways, for example an anthropology or sociology text may be regarded as mediating between its author (including, indeed, focalizing, that author's definition of the circumstances s/he reports) and the reader. However, there is perhaps a more directly apparent mediating effect, and this becomes most evident when we move away from professional/academic texts and turn towards ordinary, everyday textual items.

Consider some initial, basic observations for further analysis that John Lee and I made of some video recordings (with soundtrack) as part of a broader range of analytic projects of a research team investigating the social organization of public space in urban areas. Lee and I collected and examined (*inter alia*) some data on bus stops and shelters in an inner suburb of Paris.[9]

People formed a cluster in and around the shelter. A bus came with the sign '16' on its side. On the front was another '16' plus the name of the destination. Some people in the cluster self-selected for the bus and formed a queue in order to board it. Others 'disqualified' themselves for this bus, often pulling back to let past those visibly wishing to board. The bus route (and destination) sign served to 'partial out' or partition those passengers wishing to board that particular bus and those wanting a bus for another destination. In addition, there were some young people hanging around the outside of the shelter for a considerable time with no apparent intention of boarding any bus, and it is arguable too that the sign on the bus helped to 'partial out' waiting passengers' as opposed to 'non-passengers'.

In other words, the reading of the bus sign(s) worked to activate a variety of courses of action amongst parties to the shelter: the self-inclusion and subsequent queuing of passengers for this bus, the self-exclusion of passengers waiting for other buses on different routes but who still manifested 'waiting behaviour', and those whose activities were those of a non-travelling spectatorship, including the researchers. This list is not exhaustive of those with an interest in the bus stop or shelter. These courses of action resulted in the re-formatting of the configuration of persons in and around the bus shelter in somewhat the same way as a kaleidoscope re-formats patterns – something like a change of *gestalt* in interactional patterning.

Here, we can observe that the common-sensical 'textual work' of the sign(s) comprises a 'duplex action'. The first 'moment' of this is parties' monitoring of the sign(s), and the second 'moment' is the incorporation of the sign into a 'further' action, for example self-inclusion, self-exclusion, meeting someone alighting from bus no. 16, and those simply watching such scenes. The monitoring of the no. 16 sign is an integral feature of such sorting activities, so the two 'moments' are, in a certain sense, only strongly distinguishable for the purposes of analysis. It is in the practical, everyday world, however, that the careful observer can, perhaps, discern the operation of this duplex action most clearly.

The course of action of (say) boarding the no. 16 bus is a *textually mediated* one: that is what imparts to it its specifically duplex character. The text is highly consequential in how people act, there and then. If this example seems trivial and all too obvious, let us also note that, as we observed, the self-selection activities were far from 'automatic'. The bus number or destination notice still left an interpretive problem for some passengers: 'does the bus go to that destination where *I* want to get off?' 'What is the *precise* route of this bus?', and so on. Thus, the text had to be interactionally disambiguated through questions put to the driver, to other passengers getting onto the bus, and so on, or, perhaps, through the consultation of another text, the route description-cum-timetable. Thus, the incorporation of the reading of the bus sign into an overall project of action (e.g. 'going to the Latin Quarter' in Paris) was by no means always so simple as it appears at face value.

Actions and interactions produce (more or less) organized social settings and what we have in this example is not just a set of textually mediated actions but also a textually mediated social organization[10] – a system of action (both oriented towards and administered by the parties to the shelter themselves) which we might gloss as a system of triage: a textually mediated, self-administered sorting system. That is, the reconfiguration of the people at the shelter, for example the formation of some of them into a queue upon the arrival of the bus, where before there had simply been a cluster of waiting persons, was their own collaborative, textually mediated accomplishment. Thus, we may speak of 'textually mediated social actions *and* social organizations', such organization being a product of action.

Furthermore, textually mediated action clearly plays a focal part in studies of what has, perhaps misleadingly, come to be termed 'human–computer interaction' (HCI). It is evident that on-screen operating and processing instructions, textually formatted data retrieval, the textual potential of CD-ROMs, and so on, are all very highly relevant to the concerns outlined in this chapter. It must be said, however, that such studies vary greatly on the degree to which they see the concerns of textual analysis as figuring in HCI analysis as such. Some HCI studies treat the displayed texts as having the same unproblematic 'transparency' as did the orthodox studies that I described at the beginning of this chapter.

I must confess some unease at the term 'textual mediation' since it is all too easily interpreted as though the text, somehow or to some extent, stood apart from the course of action into which it is incorporated. I suspect that a more ethnomethodological view might eventually supplant the notion 'textual mediation', perhaps through the employment of one of its core concepts, namely 'reflexivity'.

The ethnomethodological version of this concept is that descriptions or definitions are constituent features of the circumstances they describe. Descriptions or definitions elaborate those circumstances and are elaborated by them: they are integral to, and non-extractable from, those circumstances (see Garfinkel and Sacks, 1970). Since texts furnish descriptive resources, they may be said to fall squarely within the ambit of this definition. However, the notion of 'textually mediated' social action and organization has performed an important service in 'bringing texts in from the cold' and showing their relevance to everyday social life. To pirate some of Wittgenstein's imagery, the term 'textually mediated' social action/organization has served, and continues to serve, as a ladder to get us to a higher level, after which we shall be able to throw the ladder away.

Perhaps one of the most perspicuous examples of the reflexive or constitutive conception of texts in relation to courses of action is Psathas's (1979) analysis of 'occasioned' direction maps. These are maps drawn by people to help others specifically for the purpose of finding a particular place – sketch maps are perhaps the most prevalent example, but such things as the linear route maps for racing cyclists and rally drivers' pace notes give us more formal counterparts.

Psathas bids us consider how remarkable it is that people can interpret a number of lines on paper as being about a world they have in common. He observes that such readings do not occur 'automatically' but are methodically accomplished through readers' active deployment of sense-making practices (although in all likelihood they are not engaged in a self-reflection on how they make such textual sense). This accomplishment renders the direction maps readable/interpretable to others (to users), as displays of a world known in common – it displays the world in an accountable, readable, comprehensible way as being an understandable phenomenon. Part of this jointly known world is the 'how' of that world, that is, the methods of cultural reasoning for making, reading and using the map.

Psathas shows how direction maps are read as an eminently practical solution to a practical problem, that of finding the desired destination. They contain a set of sequentially organized instructions, arranged as being before, after, next to, and so on, some intermediate point, such that actually travelling the route covered by the map presents itself as a 'discovery' of the features designated in the map. Thus, we all know streets 'go' from A to B, that points or places are arranged along (say) streets, at cross-roads, and so on, that destinations may be reached by following a designated series of those points or places, that some of these points may be critical, may be important landmarks for the route, and so on: occasioned maps count on all that common-sense cultural knowledge, and more. Reading the direction map, using it to find a destination, may require all kinds of 'extra' interpretive work in order to 'operate' the map – maybe, for instance, asking someone *en route* if a place actually *is* the one designated on the map, enquiring about distances, and so on. Often, the person drawing the map will attempt to provide in advance for this interpretive problem by amplifying the drawn instructions through oral elaboration. Again, we see reading and writing/drawing as *activities*. Elaborating on Psathas's analysis, we can see that the use of a direction map is very much a constituent feature of the actual project of finding a given destination. It is part of the selfsame project that it describes. This very well exemplifies the reflexive properties of the map.

The map describes a project of action that is realized through its, the map's, actual use. The descriptive resources of the map will serve to define or to 'foreground' points along the route, and as these points are found, they will, reciprocally, impart sense to the map as 'descriptively adequate' (at least in that particular respect). Finding the features symbolized in the map gives sense to it as recognizable, readable and usable for the next phase of finding a given destination.

Thus, whilst the direction map describes the points on the route, the order in which they will be found, and so on, the route-finder's sense of the map is itself specified, amplified, revised, respecified, and so on, in view of how, when (and if) those points are found. Particularly where some descriptive ambiguity is found on the map, actually locating a point may serve to disambiguate that ambiguity. Thus the map-as-used may be said to exhibit reflexive properties in that it describes (e.g. 'foregrounds') various points *en route* to a destination but is, in turn, described (specified, revised, etc.) by those points as they are found.

Concluding comments

In this chapter I have tried to make a connected series of points which textual analyses might take into account. First, I noted that texts pervade our everyday life to such an extent that they are often difficult to notice. Then I pointed out that texts of all kinds depend greatly upon the ordinary, common-sense properties of the language in general. This point was exemplified by reference to sociology texts, where it was argued that sociological analysis is itself profoundly shaped by the generic properties of ordinary language and also by the properties of ordinary textual organization in that culture.

I then turned to these properties, arguing that texts are active rather than inert in that they predispose readers to a given interpretation of a text.

Reading, too, was seen as an active, interpretive process rather than one of passive reception. Readers were conceived as 'activating' the properties of the text. This led to the notion of 'textually mediated' social action – social action whose character and course involves the incorporation of some text. Finally, I tried to indicate ways in which we might hope to move beyond the notion of the 'textual mediation' of action by bringing into play the ethnomethodological concept of 'reflexivity'.

It is, surely, about time that texts became a central topic for sociology, rather than being tacitly accepted by very many social scientists as being unproblematic.

Notes

This chapter was written while I was Francqui Professor of the Human Sciences, Belgium. I should like to thank the Francqui Foundation and, in particular, its Executive Administrator, Professor Luc Eyckmans, for their support.

1. Macfarlane uses many other textual sources too, of course. He examines parish registers and other records, land rental and sale records, and so on. The attitude he adopts towards these texts does not vary, however: he treats them simply as mere conduits to the phenomena they 'report'.

2. For analytic commentaries on this, see Clifford and Marcus (1986).

3. The example is taken from a selection on the distinctive features of counsel–witness cross-examination.

4. It might be added that the comments above on transcription procedures in conversation analysis, and the ethnography of communication are not (entirely) critical. My primary interest is in turning the work of transcription into data to be analysed in its own right in order to show the basis of professional sociology in mundane cultural (in this case textual) reasoning and sense-making. It is not at all easy to see how such transcription practices could be avoided in this kind of analysis. The only sociological studies that analyse (inter alia) conversational interaction without stipulating identities in the left-hand column tend to be highly formalistic and behaviouristic in character. An inventive, detailed and fascinating example of such a study which does not count on the imputation of categorial or other identities to interactants is that of Collins and Collins (1973). See, for instance, their sequential analysis of conversations in Example 9, pp. 124–6 and Example 10, pp. 127–31.

5. Thus, blame-allocation is one of many *specific* and *consequential* activities the text may bring about just as 'signing a contract' brings about a commitment, 'signing a death warrant' works to facilitate an execution, 'signing a marriage contract' brings about a married state, and so on. In this respect, texts draw heavily upon the conventional properties of the natural language as such, e.g. in its oral form, too, 'saying' things can be 'doing' things, e.g. 'promising', 'threatening', 'condemning' and the like. All these and very many other activities can be textually as well as orally transacted by anyone having a competent mastery of a natural language in both oral and written forms.

6. I owe this point, and this example, to Sharrock (n.d.).

7. One important example of an analysis of cultural politics and advocacy is to be found in Papastergiadis (1994). See also Sanjek (1990) and Watson (1991).

8. For example, see Dorothy E. Smith's closely analysed work on authorization procedures in a written text (Smith, 1978: 33–7).

9. Other members of the overall research team, funded by the French Government's *Plan Urbain* programme, were Kenneth L. Brown, Isabelle Haumont, Michèle Jolé and Georges Knaebel. We should like to thank them for their valued input into our analysis. Our thanks

also to Programme Director Isaac Joseph. The team's report was titled *Comment trouver sa place*? (Plan Urbain, 1993) and the document of that report for which Dr Lee and I were primarily responsible was *Final Report: The Interactional Organization of Public Space.*

10. For a specification of this term, see Smith (1984).

References

Atkinson, J.M. and Drew, P. (1979) *Order in Court: The Organization of Verbal Interaction in Judicial Settings.* London: Macmillan.

Atkinson, P. (1982) 'Talk and identity: Some convergences in micro-sociology', in H.J. Helle and S.N. Eisenstadt (eds), *Micro-sociological Theory: Perspectives on Sociological Theory*, Vol. 2. London: Sage Studies in International Sociology, No. 34 (Proceedings of the International Sociological Association's World Congress of Sociology, Mexico City). pp. 117–32.

Clifford, J. and Marcus, G.E. (eds) (1986) *Writing Culture: The Poetics and Politics of Ethnography.* Berkeley: University of California Press.

Collins, O. and Collins, J.M. (1973) *Interaction and Social Structure.* The Hague and Paris: Mouton.

Garfinkel, H. and Sacks, H. (1970) 'On formal structures of practical actions', in J. McKinney and E.A. Tiryakian (eds), *Theoretical Sociology: Perspectives and Developments.* New York: Appleton-Century-Crofts. pp. 337–66.

Goffman, E. (1981) 'The lecture', in *Forms of Talk.* Oxford: Blackwell. pp. 160–96.

Heath, C. (1986) *Body Movement and Speech in Medical Interaction.* Cambridge: Cambridge University Press.

Lee, J. (1984) 'Innocent victims and evil-doers', *Women's Studies International Forum*, 7 (1): 69–73.

Macfarlane, A. (1978) *The Origins of English Individualism.* Oxford: Blackwell.

McHoul, A.W. (1982) *Telling How Texts Talk.* London: Routledge and Kegan Paul.

Papastergiadis, N. (1994) *The Complicities of Culture.* Manchester: Cornerhouse Publications.

Plan Urbain (1993) *Comment trouver sa place*? Paris: Plan Urbain.

Psathas, G. (1979) 'Organizational features of direction maps', in G. Psathas (ed.), *Everyday Language: Studies in Ethnomethodology.* New York: Irvington (Halsted-Wiley). pp. 203–26.

Rose, E. (1960) 'The English record of a natural sociology', *American Sociological Review*, XXV (April): 193–208.

Sanjek, R. (ed.) (1990) *Fieldnotes: The Making of Anthropology.* Ithaca, NY: Cornell University Press.

Schegloff, E.A. (1991) 'Reflections on talk and social structure', in D. Boden and D.H. Zimmerman (eds), *Talk and Social Structure: Studies in Ethnomethodology and Conversation Analysis.* Cambridge: Polity. pp. 44–70.

Schenkein, J. (1979) 'The radio raiders story', in G. Psathas (ed.), *Everyday Language: Studies in Ethnomethodology.* New York: Irvington. pp. 187–201.

Sharrock, W. (n.d.) 'Rules'. Unpublished manuscript. Department of Sociology, University of Manchester, Manchester M13 9PL.

Smith, D.E. (1978) '"K is mentally ill": The anatomy of a factual account', *Sociology*, 12 (1): 23–53. (Reprinted in *Texts, Facts and Femininity.* Boston: Northeastern University Press, 1986. pp. 12–51.)

Smith, D.E. (1982) 'The active text: Texts as constituents of social relations'. Paper delivered to the World Congress of Sociology, Mexico City (section on Language and Formal Organization). (Reprinted in D.E. Smith: *Texts, Facts and Femininity.* Boston: Northeastern University Press, 1986. pp. 120–58.)

Smith, D.E. (1984) 'Textually-mediated social organization', *International Journal of Social Science*, 36 (1): 59–75.

Watson, G. (1984) 'The social construction of boundaries between social and cultural anthropology in Britain and North America', *Journal of Anthropological Research*, 40: 351–66.

Watson, G. (1991) 'Rewriting culture', in R.G. Fox (ed.), *Recapturing Anthropology: Writing in the Present.* Santa Fé, NM: School of American Research Press/University of Washington Press Distributors. pp. 73–92.

PART IV INTERVIEWS

7 The 'Inside' and the 'Outside'

Finding Realities in Interviews

Jody Miller and Barry Glassner

In his *Interpreting Qualitative Data*, Silverman (1993) highlights the dilemmas facing interview researchers concerning what to make of their data. On the one hand, positivists have as a goal the creation of the 'pure' interview – enacted in a sterilized context, in such a way that it comes as close as possible to providing a 'mirror reflection' of the reality that exists in the social world. This position has been thoroughly critiqued over the years in terms of both its feasibility and its desirability. On the other hand, radical social constructionists suggest that no knowledge about a reality that is 'out there' in the social world can be obtained from the interview, because the interview is obviously and exclusively an interaction between the interviewer and interview subject in which both participants create and construct narrative versions of the social world. The problem with looking at these narratives as representative of some 'truth' in the world, according to these scholars, is that they are context-specific, invented, if you will, to fit the demands of the interactive context of the interview, and representative of nothing more or less.

For those of us who hope to learn about the social world, and, in particular, hope to contribute knowledge that can be beneficial in expanding understanding and useful for fostering social change, the proposition that our interviews are meaningless beyond the context in which they occur is a daunting one. This is not to say that we accept the positivist view of the possibility of untouched data available through standardized interviewing, but rather to suggest that we are not willing to discount entirely the possibility of learning about the social world beyond the interview in our analyses of interview data.

In this chapter, we try to identify a position that is outside of this objectivist–constructivist continuum yet takes seriously the goals and critiques of researchers at both of its poles. We will argue that information about social worlds is achievable through in-depth interviewing. The position we are attempting to put forward is inspired by authors such as Harding (e.g. 1987) and Latour (e.g. 1993), who posit explicitly anti-dualistic options for methodological and theorizing practices in media studies and science studies – options which recognize that both emulation and rejection of dominant discourses such as positivism miss something critically important. Dominant discourses are totalizing only for those who view them as such; they are replete with fissures and uncolonized spaces within which people engage in highly satisfying and even resistant practices of knowledge-making.

We concur with Sanders that while

> [w]e would do well to heed the cautions offered by postmodern ethnographers . . . [t]here is a considerable difference between being skeptical about the bases of truth claims while carefully examining the grounds upon with these claims are founded (a conventional interactionist enterprise) and denying that truth – as a utilitarian and liberating orientation – exists at all. (1995: 93, 97)

Narratives and worlds

As Silverman notes, for interviewers in the interactionist tradition, interview subjects construct not just narratives, but social worlds. For researchers in this tradition, 'the primary issue is to generate data which give an authentic insight into people's experiences' (Silverman, 1993: 91). While interactionists do not suggest that there is

> 'a singular objective or absolute world out-there' . . . [they] do recognize 'objectified worlds.' Indeed, they contend that some objectification is essential if human conduct is to be accomplished. Objectivity exists, thus, not as an absolute or inherently meaningful condition to which humans react but as an accomplished aspect of human lived experience. (Dawson and Prus, 1995: 113)

Research cannot provide the mirror reflection of the social world that positivists strive for, but it may provide access to the meanings people attribute to their experiences and social worlds. While the interview is itself a symbolic interaction, this does not discount the possibility that knowledge of the social world beyond the interaction can be obtained. In fact, it is only in the context of non-positivistic interviews, which recognize and build on their interactive components (rather than trying to control and reduce them), that 'intersubjective depth' and 'deep-mutual understanding' can be achieved (and, with these, the achievement of knowledge of social worlds).

Those of us who aim to understand and document others' understandings choose qualitative interviewing because it provides us with a means for exploring the points of view of our research subjects, while granting these points of view the culturally honoured status of reality. As Charmaz explains:

> We start with the experiencing person and try to share his or her subjective view. Our task is objective in the sense that we try to describe it with depth and detail. In doing so, we try to represent the person's view fairly and to portray it as consistent with his or her meanings. (1995: 54)

Silverman and others accurately suggest that this portrayal of what we do is in some ways romanticized. We will address below some of the problems that make this the case. But the proposition that romanticizing negates, in itself, the objectivity Charmaz defines, or the subjectivities with which we work, does not follow.

We have no trouble acknowledging, for instance, that interviewees sometimes respond to interviewers through the use of familiar narrative constructs, rather than by providing meaningful insights into their subjective view. Indeed, as Denzin notes:

> The subject is more than can be contained in a text, and a text is only a reproduction of what the subject has told us. What the subject tells us is itself something that has been shaped by prior cultural understandings. Most important, language, which is our window into the subject's world (and our world), plays tricks. It displaces the very thing it is supposed to represent, so that what is always given is a trace of other things, not the thing – lived experience – itself. (1991: 68)

In addition to this displacing, the language of interviewing (like all other telling) fractures the stories being told. This occurs inevitably within a storyteller's narrative, which must be partial because it cannot be infinite in length, and all the more partial if it is not to be unbearably boring. In the qualitative interview process, the research commits further fractures as well. The coding, categorization and typologizing of stories result in telling only parts of stories, rather than presenting them in their 'wholeness' (Charmaz, 1995: 60). Numerous levels of representation occur from the moment of 'primary experience' to the reading of researchers' textual presentation of findings, including the level of attending to the experience, telling it to the researcher, transcribing and analysing what is told, and the reading.

Qualitative interviewers recognize these fissures from the ideal text (i.e. interviewees' subjective view as experienced by the interviewees themselves). Interviewers note, for example, that '[t]he story is being told to particular people; it might have taken a different form if someone else were the listener' (Riessman, 1993: 11). The issue of how interviewees respond to us based on who we are – in their lives, as well as the social categories to which we belong, such as age, gender, class and race – is a practical concern as well as an epistemological or theoretical one. The issue may be exacerbated, for example, when we study groups with whom we do not share membership. Particularly as a result of social distances, interviewees may not trust us, they may not understand our questions, or they may purposely mislead us in their responses. Likewise, given a lack of membership in their primary groups, we may not know enough about the phenomenon under study to ask the right questions.

Studying adolescents, as we have done in our own research, presents unique concerns along these lines. On the one hand, the meaning systems of adolescents are different from those of adults, and adult researchers must exercise caution in assuming they have an understanding of adolescent cultures because they've 'been there'. On the other hand, adolescents are in a transitional period of life, becoming increasingly oriented to adult worlds, though with 'rough edges' (Fine and Sandstrom, 1988: 60). As a consequence, 'age begins to decrease in importance as a means of differentiating oneself, and other dimensions of cultural differentiation, such as gender and class [and race], become more crucial' (Fine and Sandstrom, 1988: 66). These dimensions are thus of critical importance in establishing research relationships, rapport and trust, and in evaluating both the information obtained, and the interaction that occurs, within in-depth interviews.

To treat a young person's age as the determinant or predictor of his or her experiences or ways of talking is to neglect another key point about age-ordering as well:

> The idea of an ending of childhood is predicated upon a normative system wherein childhood itself is taken for granted. But childhood may also be 'ended' by narratives of personal or societal 'deviance' or by new stories reconstituting the modelling of childhood itself. (Rogers and Rogers, 1992: 153)

In our experience, much of what adolescents talk about in open-ended interviews is precisely how their acts seem wayward, delinquent, premature or otherwise not befitting proper youthful behaviour. Their discourse towards and with us (and *for* themselves) is much about where and who they are. It is about trying out social locations and identities:

> Our approach is to treat the adolescents' reports as situated elements in social worlds. On the one hand they are ways of making sense to oneself and to another (cf. Mills, 1940). One cannot read the transcripts and fail to recognize that much of what goes on is two persons trying to understand topics that neither would consider in quite this manner or detail except in such special circumstances. The interviewees typically seem to enjoy the chance to 'think aloud' about such matters, and often they say this to the interviewer. Much of that thinking is directed at a major project of their present lives – figuring out what type of person they are and what type they want to be. The interview offers an opportunity to try out various possibilities on this older student who is asking questions, and with reference to how it fits with one's self-image or might work out if directed at other audiences. On the other hand, these ways of viewing self and world come from and build into the social world itself. Ways of thinking and talking derive from daily experiences and are also used in these. (Glassner and Loughlin, 1987: 34–5)

Life outside the interview

Interactionist research starts from a belief that people create and maintain meaningful worlds. As interactionist research with adolescents illustrates, this belief can be accepted 'without assuming the existence of a single, encompassing obdurate reality' (Charmaz, 1995: 62). To assume that realities beyond the interview context cannot be tapped into and explored is to grant narrative omnipotence. The roots of these realities are 'more fundamental and pervasive' (Dawson and Prus, 1995: 121; see also Dawson and Prus, 1993; Schmitt, 1993) than such a view can account for. A vivid illustration of this is to be found in Charmaz's work on the chronically ill, who, she notes, experience sickness regardless of whether they participate in her interviews (1995: 50). We note that the adolescents in our studies experience their age-, gender- and ethnic-based identities and fluidity of identity whether or not we interview them – and within our interviews with them.

Language shapes meanings but also permits intersubjectivity and the ability of willful persons to create and maintain meaningful worlds (Dawson and Prus, 1993: 166). Recognizing this, we cannot accept the proposition that interviews do not yield information about social worlds. Rather, 'we take it that two persons can communicate their perceptions to one another. Knowing full well that there are both structures and pollutants in any discussion, we choose to study what is said in that discussion' (Glassner and Loughlin, 1987: 33). While certainly 'there is no way to stuff a real-live person between the two covers of a text', as Denzin (in Schmitt, 1993: 130) puts it, we can describe truthfully, delimited segments of real-live persons' lives. Indeed, in so delimiting, we may get *closer* to people's lived experience. As Charmaz (1995) notes, many people do not want themselves revealed in their totality. Recognizing this and responding accordingly may result in deeper, fuller conceptualizations of those aspects of our subjects' lives we are most interested in understanding.

Much the same deserves to be said about the interactionist researcher concerning the place and fullness of his or her life within the interview context. On the one hand, scholarship should preserve 'in it the presence, concerns, and the experience of the [researcher] as knower and discoverer' (Smith, 1987: 92; see also Harding, 1987) so that the subjectivity that exists in all social research will be a visible part of the project, and thus available to the reader for examination. As Harding (1987: 9) notes, when 'the researcher appears to us not as an invisible, anonymous voice of authority, but as a real, historical individual with concrete, specific desires and interests' the research process can be scrutinized.

Yet on the other hand, these dictates do not necessitate, as some excessively revealing authors have taken them to mean, engaging in confessionals either with one's interviewees or with one's readers, or boring them with excessive details about oneself. It is precisely the 'concrete, specific desires and interests' that merit airing, not everything that might be aired.

In our experience, interviewees will tell us, if given the chance, which of our interests and formulations make sense and non-sense to them. Glassner and Loughlin (1987: 36) describe instances in their study in which the interviewer brought up a topic that was seen by the subject as irrelevant or misinterpretation, and they offered correction. Moreover, as Charmaz points out, 'creating these observations at all assumes that we share enough experience with our subjects and our readers to define things similarly' (1995: 64).

Of paramount importance regarding how (and how much) we present ourselves is the influence this presentation has on interviewees' ability and willingness to tell various sorts of stories. Richardson notes, 'People organize their personal biographies and understand them through the stories they create to explain and justify their life experiences' (1990: 23; see also Lempert, 1994; Mishler, 1986; Riessman, 1993). Highlighting two types of stories of particular relevance, Richardson first describes the 'cultural story' – 'Participation in a culture includes participation in the narratives of that culture, a general understanding of the stock of meanings and their relationships to each other' (Richardson, 1990: 24). These narratives represent the basis on which individuals create cultural stories, or stories about social phenomena that are typically 'told from the point of view of the ruling interests and the normative order' (Richardson, 1990: 25). An interviewer who presents him- or herself as either too deeply committed to those interests and that order, or as clearly outside of them, restricts which cultural stories interviewees may tell and how these will be told.

Cultural stories are based in part on stereotypes. Richardson dubs an alternative to these the 'collective story'. Collective stories take the point of view of the interview subjects, and 'give voice to those who are silenced or marginalized in the cultural [story]' (Richardson, 1990: 25). They challenge popular stereotypes by 'resist[ing] the cultural narratives about groups of people and tell[ing] alternative stories' (Richardson, 1990: 25). A strength of qualitative interviewing is precisely its capacity to access self-reflexivity among interview subjects, leading to the greater likelihood of the telling of collective stories:

> Respondents may reveal feelings, beliefs, and private doubts that contradict or conflict with 'what everyone thinks,' including sentiments that break the dominant feeling rules. . . . In other cases, interviewers will discover the anxiety, ambivalence, and uncertainty that lie behind respondents' conformity. (Kleinman et al., 1994: 43)

Here again, to be a candidate for 'good listener', the interviewer does best to present him- or herself as someone who is neither firmly entrenched in the mainstream nor too far at any particular margin. Ultimately, though, it is not where the interviewer locates him- or herself that is of greatest relevance to interviewees. In our experience, interviewees' principal concerns focus upon what will become of the interview. Those concerns extend beyond matters such as the protection of confidentiality. Interviewees want to know that what they have to say matters. They want to know what will become of their words. A researcher who interviewed AIDS patients observed:

> Many of my respondents explicitly refer to their interviews as 'legacies.' They are participating in this project despite the pain it might cause them because they believe I will use their stories to help others. Thus they shoulder me with the responsibility of giving meaning to their lives and their deaths. (Weitz, 1987: 21)

More often, the upshot for both interviewer and interviewee is less monumental, if no less important. In interviews with adolescents we have found, for example, that to be taken seriously and regarded as a teacher by someone whose societal role is that of 'teacher' is a defining and highly valued characteristic of the interview situation.

An illustration

We have suggested that narratives which emerge in interview contexts are situated in social worlds, they come out of worlds that exist outside of the interview itself. We argue not only for the existence of these worlds, but also for our ability as researchers to capture elements of these worlds in our scholarship. To illustrate some of the interactionist strategies for achieving that access we turn to a research effort one of us has recently completed (Miller, 1996).

The study involves in-depth, open-ended interviews with young women (ages 13 to 18) who claim affiliation with youth gangs in their communities. These interviews follow the completion of a survey interview administered by the same researcher. While the survey interview gathers information about a wide range of topics, including the individual, her school, friends, family, neighbourhood, delinquent involvement, arrest history, sexual history and victimization, in addition to information about the gang, the in-depth interview is concerned exclusively with the roles and activities of young women in youth gangs, and the meanings they describe as emerging from their gang affiliation.

Compared to the interviewees, the interviewer is ten to fifteen years older (although typically perceived as younger by the interviewees), of the same gender, but often of a different race (Miller is white, the majority of the interviewees are African American) and class background (upper middle versus middle, lower-middle, working class and poor). Some scholars have argued that researchers should be members of the groups we study, in order to have the subjective knowledge necessary to truly understand their life experiences. For example, Collins argues that in order to make legitimate knowledge claims, researchers should 'have lived or experienced their material in some fashion' (1990: 232).

We suggest, however, that the existence of social differences between the interviewer and interviewees does not mean that the interviews are devoid of information about social worlds. In fact, the interviews can be accomplished in ways that put these social differences to use in providing opportunities for individuals to articulate their feelings about their life experiences. As noted above, one potential benefit of social distances in research of this nature is that the interviewee can recognize him- or herself as an expert on a topic of interest to someone typically in a more powerful position vis-à-vis the social structure (in this case, particularly in terms of age, race and education). To find oneself placed in this position can be both empowering and illuminating because one can reflect on and speak about one's life in ways not often available. When individuals are members of groups that have been stereotyped and devalued by the larger culture, and whose perspectives have been ignored (as in the case of female gang members), the promise of this approach is all the more apparent.

We have suggested that knowledge of social worlds emerges from the achievement of intersubjective depth and mutual understanding. For these to be present, however, there must be a level of trust between the interviewer and interviewee. Social distances that include differences in relative power can result in suspicion and lack of trust, both of which the researcher must actively seek to overcome. Rapport building is a key to this process. Establishing trust and familiarity, showing genuine interest, assuring confidentiality and not being judgemental are some important elements of building rapport (Glassner and Loughlin, 1987: 35). Miller has found that the last of these is particularly important when interviewing adolescent female gang members. These young women are members of a group frequently stigmatized by the social groups to which Miller herself belongs, a reality known to both the interviewees and the interviewer. Fortunately, Miller's research design proved useful in alleviating tensions that could result from this schism. Her administration of a survey interview with detailed questions about histories of delinquent involvement and arrest provided an opportunity to exhibit a neutral demeanour that neither condemned nor praised interviewees' responses, even on occasions when individuals reported brutal acts of violence. The benefit of administering a survey first (in addition to its value in providing collaborative evidence or 'triangulation') was that this layer of understanding was already in place when the in-depth interviews occurred.

The assurance of confidentiality is achieved as much by implicit assurances as by explicit guarantees. There were often opportunities for Miller to convey her concern about protecting the subjects' privacy. For example, when interviewing in open areas (such as the visiting room at a juvenile detention centre), she remained aware of the surroundings to ensure against eavesdropping, temporarily stopped the interview when others came within clear hearing range, and moved to more secluded areas when necessary. Likewise, when interviewees accidentally disclosed names, Miller immediately offered to erase these slips from the tape recording and did so in the interviewee's presence before continuing with the interview.

Cultural stories

Rapport involves more, however, than provisions of confidentiality, non-judgemental responses and other offerings from the interviewer. It involves the interviewee feeling comfortable and competent enough in the interaction to 'talk back' (Blumer, 1969: 22). When respondents talk back they provide insights into the narratives they use to describe the meanings of their social worlds and into their experience of the worlds of which they are a part. One way in which Miller's interviewees talked back – both to her and to the audiences for her works about them – was by weaving their personal narratives into larger cultural stories about gangs. In describing their gangs, explaining their gang involvement and attributing personal meanings to being in gangs, they situated these topics in pre-existing narratives about gangs (i.e. cultural stories) both by embracing these stories and by challenging them. They gain at least part of their understanding, and convey their understanding to the interviewer, by drawing on the narratives which come out of the social worlds around them.

Scholars have noted 'the impact of "already established cultural standards" on individuals' (Schmitt, 1993: 126). In Miller's interviews, two somewhat divergent stories of the gang emerged – the 'bad' gang, which fits larger cultural stereotypes, and the 'good' gang, which is in some ways a challenge to larger cultural stereotypes. The description of the 'bad' gang was in many ways in keeping with the cultural story of the gang, with depictions of the gang as tough, brutally violent and, by definition, criminally active. This is the gang of cultural stories, circulated both among gang members and among the public in their images of gang violence. Although the young women were sometimes critical of this aspect of the gang life, more often, they adopted these narratives in order to describe a group from which they derived status. On one level they were adopting a cultural story of the gang as bad, a story told from the point of view of those in power (see Richardson, 1990: 25). On another level, they were attributing meanings that contrast with the negative connotations typically associated with this cultural story. These narratives challenge public views of gangs as evildoers by ascribing positive ('good') meanings to their being such.

Miller's interviewees also spoke of how the gang does good for them personally, describing the positive personal meanings they attributed to being affiliated with gangs. In doing so, they drew on alternative cultural stories of gang membership, stories that, rather than resisting the negative connotations associated with gangs in some cultural stories, instead provided sympathetic accounts of young people in gangs as having turned to the gang to fill voids in their lives.

Describing why she joined her gang, one young women told Miller, 'well, I didn't get any respect at home. I wanted to get some love and respect from somebody somewhere else, so.' Another explained, 'I didn't have *no* family. . . . I had nothin' else.' Another young woman, when asked to speculate on why young people join gangs, suggested:

> Some of 'em are like me, don't have, don't really have a basic home or steady home to go to, you know, and they don't have as much love and respect in the home so they want to get it elsewhere. And, and, like we get, have family members in gangs or that were in gangs, stuff like that.

These narratives, which are variations on familiar cultural stories, do not attempt to challenge public views of gangs as bad, but they do challenge the notion that the interviewee herself is bad. The interviewees deploy these narratives to make their actions explainable and understandable to those who otherwise may not understand. Another way in which interviewees can break clear of a dominant cultural story about their groups or themselves is by locating themselves and their narratives within *another* cultural story (cf. Goffman, 1974, on breaking frame). Adolescents have available to them, for example, cultural stories about adolescence as a life stage.

Stories about adolescence are about the transition from youth to adulthood, or becoming who/what one is not. Miller's interviewees spoke of their transitional status between youthful gang membership and adulthood, the time to 'do something' with one's life. One young woman explained that in some ways joining her gang 'was just weird, cause, I mean I don't know, I guess it's just not the right picture of my life would be to be part of a gang'. When asked to think about what she would be like in the future, one young woman said, 'I'll look back in the past and see what I did and how I changed and all that and I'll wonder why I acted like that and why I joined the gangs and all that.' A young woman who was an ex-gang member reflected back on both the positive and negative aspects of gang membership for her, including how it helped her grow up but also kept her from maturing:

> Being in that gang gave me, now that I left, I still have that backbone of my own. But, before I didn't have that. I would, somebody could just cuss me and I start cryin' and run, 'I'm tellin' my mom and my dad,' and all this. But, now it's like I handle my own. I can handle it by myself. I don't, I mean, I need them for some things. But, then again I don't need 'em for others. But before I needed 'em for everything. . . . [The downside:] I started gettin' real mean and angry. I wasn't the same [person] that I was before. I was Miss Bad Ass. That's what they called me. I mean, I didn't, I didn't take, I disrespected people. I lost all manners. I mean, I just lost everything. It was like I was turnin' in, turnin' into somebody that I really wasn't. And, then I started seein' it for myself. And, how it was affectin' my family 'n stuff. So, that's why I said, 'No, I can't do this. I gotta get, gotta get outta this.'

There were also elements of the interviews that reflected the adolescent part of their personalities as well, in their present-orientedness and the seriousness with which they took some elements of gang lore. The gang was described by some young women as a permanent part of their lives, whether they wanted it or not, that once membership was established, there was no changing that status. For example, one young woman who planned to disassociate herself from her gang after she was raped by one of the members explained that she could stop spending time with them, but could never leave: 'I can change my whole life but I'll still be in the gang.' She told Miller she had gotten herself into something she couldn't get herself out of. Others described not wanting to get pregnant because it would mean that their babies would 'belong' to the gang from birth to death.

Collective stories

Some of the young women go further and describe their gang involvement in ways that directly challenge prevailing stereotypes about gangs as groups that are inherently bad or antisocial and about females' roles within gangs.

Sometimes this involves responding to cultural stories of the 'bad' gang in a manner that explicitly challenges what the interviewees know to be popular beliefs about youth gangs. In such cases, they attempt to convey the normalcy of their activities: 'It was really, it was just normal life, the only difference was, is, that we had meetings.' Another young woman pointed out: '[We] play cards, smoke bud, play dominoes, play video games. That's basically all we do is play. You would be surprised. This is a bunch of big kids. It's a bunch of big old kids in my set.' These narratives directly challenge cultural stories of the gang. As such, they are collective stories.

A proposition of this chapter is that interviews have the capacity to be interactional contexts within which social worlds come to be better understood. One way in which this is achieved is through interviewees' re-visions of cultural stories, as we have just suggested. We have proposed that another sort of story can be told as well, one that privileges the social world under discussion and its stories over the stories of the larger society. Miller's interviews illustrate this possibility particularly in those places where the young women described the ordinariness of their daily lives within gangs. The gang activities thus described provide a vivid contrast to images of gangs as dangerous criminal enterprises; they reveal that the social worlds of young women in gangs are much more routine than cultural stories usually reveal. For example, when asked to describe a typical day, one girl explained:

> A typical day would be sittin' back at the park or somethin' like that or one of our friend's houses, or a gang member's house, gettin' drunk, gettin' high and, you know, watchin' TV, listenin' to the radio. Actually, we listen to tapes and stuff, stackin' and all this stuff.

Another described:

> Sometimes, sometimes we sit on the porch and just sit there and we just be watchin' the cars go back and forth. Just relaxin' in a chair. The guys'd have their forties and then they'd have their blunts or whatever, or weed. And be sittin' there smokin' on the porch. And, that's a typical day, just hangin' out.

The young women also broke away from the cultural stories about gangs by reframing their relationship with others in the gang in terms that fail to support notions of gang membership as all-encompassing or definitional. Here they were not necessarily trying to make their actions understandable to outsiders, but were expressing the value of their relationships on their own terms. Describing someone she admired in her gang, one girl explained:

> We're, we're just, we're close. I mean, we show respect towards one another. She helps me out when I'm down. I mean, cause, even though we may have that title as a gang, I mean, we're still there for one another. I mean, we still have feelings. And I'm there for her, she's there for me.

Another young woman, describing what she values in her gang, told Miller:

> I like the fact that if I decided to leave here [a placement facility] right now I would always have somewhere to stay. And I wouldn't have to worry about wealth, what am I going to have to wear tomorrow. What am I going to put on

> or what's gonna happen or nothin' like that because I would have, I would have clean clothes, a place to sleep that's warm, food to eat. I mean, stuff like that. Havin', it's like, the best thing to me is like I have a back-up system. Like, if I, if I ever got tired of stayin' with my grandmother then I could go stay somewhere else and wouldn't have to worry about wealth or if their parents will let me stay here. I would just go knock on the door and they would say, 'Come on. Are you spendin' the night, or what?'

Another type of collective story that emerged from the interviews was specifically a story about the place of girls in gangs. Collective stories challenge stereotypes, and one common stereotype about girls in gangs is that their primary function is as sexual outlets for the male members. One young woman expressed her frustration that people outside of gangs often assume that she was sexed into the gang (an initiation that involves the girl having sex with some of the male members):

> They be showin' these little movies on TV, like, well, the females have to get sexed in and the males have to get jumped in and like that. You know, you seen 'em on TV. And they, they just figure, well, if you a girl gang member then you got sexed in. And I, I really didn't. I wasn't even down for nothin' like that.

The young women Miller spoke to instead described their place in the gang as comparable to the male members in terms of activities, toughness and willingness to fight. Describing her initiation, one young woman explained:

> I got my respect off the bat because instead of takin' six from the girls I took six from four guys. I took six hits to the head from four guys. I got my respect off the bat. So the girls, they had nothin' to say about me bein' a punk, neither did the guys.

They characterized themselves as tougher than most other girls. Describing which females wouldn't make good members, many referred to 'sissy girls', girls who 'don't want to mess up their nails or their hair or whatever'. One young woman explained:

> I think some girls, they're just scared of that type of stuff. They're scared of fighting. They're scared of violence. . . . [But] I mean, even when I wasn't in it, I fought all the time. I never backed down from anybody. I didn't care, either.

According to this collective story, the gang is an arena in which they receive status and esteem from being strong and being willing to stand up for themselves, exhibiting traits much more commonly associated with males than females.

Conclusion

Silverman argues in *Interpreting Qualitative Data* that 'while "open-ended" interviews can be useful, we need to justify departing from the naturally occurring data that surrounds us and to be cautious about the "romantic" impulse which identifies "experience" with "authenticity"' (1993: ix). We agree, but with different words in scare quotes.

On the one hand, we have tried to suggest in this chapter some strategies by which interviews can be less-than-problematically open-ended, and that interviewers need not resort to romanticism, or to identifying experience with authenticity, in order to call upon interviewees' experiences and produce authentic accounts of social worlds. On the other hand, we would put in scare quotes 'naturally occurring data', because we question the grounds for any neat distinction between the natural and cultural, in sociological data as elsewhere (cf. Douglas, 1986).

All we sociologists have are stories. Some come from other people, some from us, some from our interactions with others. What matters is to understand how and where the stories are produced, which sort of stories they are, and how we can put them to honest and intelligent use in theorizing about social life.

References

Blumer, H. (1969) *Symbolic Interactionism: Perspective and Method.* Berkeley: University of California Press.

Charmaz, K. (1995) 'Between positivism and postmodernism: Implications for methods', *Studies in Symbolic Interaction*, 17: 43–72.

Collins, P.H. (1990) *Black Feminist Thought.* Boston: Unwin Hyman.

Dawson, L.L. and Prus, R.C. (1993) 'Interactionist ethnography and postmodern discourse: Affinities and disjunctures in approaching human lived experience', *Studies in Symbolic Interaction*, 15: 147–77.

Dawson, L.L. and Prus, R.C. (1995) 'Postmodernism and linguistic reality versus symbolic interactionism and obdurate reality', *Studies in Symbolic Interaction*, 17: 105–24.

Denzin, N.K. (1991) 'Representing lived experiences in ethnographic texts', *Studies in Symbolic Interaction*, 12: 59–70.

Douglas, M. (1986) *Risk Acceptability According to the Social Sciences.* New York: Russell Sage Foundation.

Fine, G.A. and Sandstrom, K.L. (1988) *Knowing Children: Participant Observation with Minors.* Newbury Park, CA: Sage.

Glassner, B. and Loughlin, J. (1987) *Drugs in Adolescent Worlds: Burnouts to Straights.* New York: St Martin's Press.

Goffman, E. (1974) *Frame Analysis.* New York: Harper & Row.

Harding, S. (1987) *Feminism and Methodology.* Bloomington: Indiana University Press.

Kleinman, S., Stenross, B. and McMahon, M. (1994) 'Privileging fieldwork over interviews: Consequences for identity and practice', *Symbolic Interaction*, 17 (1): 37–50.

Latour, B. (1993) *We Have Never Been Modern.* Cambridge, MA: Harvard University Press.

Lempert, L.B. (1994) 'A narrative analysis of abuse: Connecting the personal, the rhetorical, and the structural', *Journal of Contemporary Ethnography*, 22 (4): 411–41.

Lofland, J. and Lofland, L.H. (1984) *Analyzing Social Settings: A Guide to Qualitative Observations and Analysis.* Belmont, CA: Wadsworth.

Miller, J. (1996) 'Female gang involvement in a Midwestern City: Correlates, nature and meanings'. Doctoral dissertation, Department of Sociology, University of Southern California.

Mills, C.W. (1940) 'Situated actions and vocabularies of motives', *American Sociological Review*, 5: 904–13.

Mishler, E.G. (1986) *Research Interviewing: Context and Narrative.* Cambridge, MA: Harvard University Press.

Richardson, L. (1990) *Writing Strategies: Reaching Diverse Audiences.* Newbury Park, CA: Sage.

Riessman, C.K. (1993) *Narrative Analysis.* Newbury Park, CA: Sage.

Rogers, R.S. and Rogers, W.S. (1992) *Stories of Childhood.* Toronto: University of Toronto Press.

Sanders, C.R. (1995) 'Stranger than fiction: Insights and pitfalls in post-modern ethnography', *Studies in Symbolic Interaction*, 17: 89–104.

Schmitt, R.L. (1993) 'Cornerville as obdurate reality: Retooling the research act through postmodernism', *Studies in Symbolic Interaction*, 15: 121–45.

Silverman, D. (1993) *Interpreting Qualitative Data: Methods for Analysing Talk, Text and Interaction.* London: Sage.

Smith, D.E. (1987) 'Women's perspective as a radical critique of sociology', in S. Harding (ed.), *Feminism and Methodology.* Bloomington: Indiana University Press. pp. 84–96.

Weitz, R. (1987) 'The interview as legacy', *Hastings Center Report*, 17: 21–3.

8 Active Interviewing

James A. Holstein and Jaber F. Gubrium

In our 'interview society' (Silverman, 1993), the mass media, human service providers and researchers increasingly generate information by interviewing. The number of television news programmes, daytime talk-shows and newspaper articles that provide us with the results of interviews is virtually incalculable. Looking at more methodical forms of information collection, it has been estimated that 90 per cent of all social science investigations use interviews in one way or another (Briggs, 1986). Interviewing is undoubtedly the most widely applied technique for conducting systematic social inquiry, as sociologists, psychologists, anthropologists, psychiatrists, clinicians, administrators, politicians and pollsters treat interviews as their 'windows on the world' (Hyman et al., 1975).

Interviewing provides a way of generating empirical data about the social world by asking people to talk about their lives. In this respect, interviews are special forms of conversation. While these conversations may vary from highly structured, standardized, quantitatively oriented survey interviews, to semi-formal guided conversations and free-flowing informational exchanges, all interviews are interactional. The narratives that are produced may be as truncated as forced-choice survey answers or as elaborate as oral life histories, but they are all constructed *in situ*, as a product of the talk between interview participants.

While most researchers acknowledge the interactional character of the interview, the technical literature on interviewing stresses the need to keep that interaction strictly in check. Guides to interviewing – especially those oriented to standardized surveys – are primarily concerned with maximizing the flow of valid, reliable information while minimizing distortions of what the respondent knows (Gorden, 1987). The interview conversation is thus framed as a potential source of bias, error, misunderstanding or misdirection, a persistent set of problems to be controlled. The corrective is simple: if the interviewer asks questions properly, the respondent will give out the desired information.

In this conventional view, the interview conversation is a pipeline for transmitting knowledge. A recently heightened sensitivity to representational matters (see Gubrium and Holstein, 1997) – characteristic of poststructuralist, postmodernist, constructionist and ethnomethodological inquiry – has raised a number of questions about the very possibility of collecting knowledge in the manner the conventional approach presupposes. In varied ways, these alternate perspectives hold that meaning is socially constituted; all knowledge is created from the actions undertaken to obtain it (see e.g., Cicourel, 1964, 1974; Garfinkel, 1967). Treating interviewing as a social encounter in which knowledge is constructed suggests the possibility that the interview is not merely a neutral conduit or source of distortion, but is instead a site of, and occasion for, producing reportable knowledge itself.

Sociolinguist Charles Briggs (1986) argues that the social circumstances of interviews are more than obstacles to respondents' articulation of their particular truths. Briggs notes that, like all other speech events, interviews fundamentally, not incidentally, shape the form and content of what is said. Aaron Cicourel (1974) goes further, maintaining that interviews virtually impose particular ways of understanding reality upon subjects' responses. The point is that interviewers are deeply and unavoidably implicated in creating meanings that ostensibly reside within respondents (also see Manning, 1967; Mishler, 1986, 1991; Silverman, 1993). Both parties to the interview are necessarily and ineluctably *active*. Meaning is not merely elicited by apt questioning, nor simply transported through respondent replies; it is actively and communicatively assembled in the interview encounter. Respondents are not so much repositories of knowledge – treasuries of information awaiting excavation, so to speak – as they are constructors of knowledge in collaboration with interviewers. Participation in an interview involves meaning-making work (Holstein and Gubrium, 1995).

If interviews are interpretively active, meaning-making occasions, interview data are unavoidably collaborative (see Alasuutari, 1995; Holstein and Staples, 1992). Therefore, any technical attempts to strip interviews of their interactional ingredients will be futile. Instead of refining the long list of methodological constraints under which 'standardized' interviews should be conducted, we suggest that researchers take a more 'active' perspective, begin to acknowledge, and capitalize upon, interviewers' and respondents' constitutive contributions to the production of interview data. This means consciously and conscientiously attending to the interview process and its product in ways that are more sensitive to the social construction of knowledge.

Conceiving of the interview as active means attending more to the ways in which knowledge is assembled than is usually the case in traditional approaches. In other words, understanding *how* the meaning-making process unfolds in the interview is as critical as apprehending *what* is substantively asked and conveyed. The *hows* of interviewing, of course, refer to the interactional, narrative procedures of knowledge production, not merely to interview techniques. The *whats* pertain to the issues guiding the interview, the content of questions, and the substantive information communicated by the respondent. A dual interest in the *hows* and *whats* of meaning production goes hand in hand with an appreciation of the constitutive activeness of the interview process.

This appreciation derives from an ethnomethodologically informed social constructionist approach that considers the process of meaning production to be as important for social research as the meaning that is produced (cf. Berger and Luckmann, 1967; Blumer, 1969; Garfinkel, 1967; Heritage, 1984; Pollner, 1987). In many significant ways, this also resonates with methodological critiques and reformulations offered by an array of feminist scholars (see DeVault, 1990; Harding, 1987; Reinharz, 1992; Smith, 1987). In their distinct fashions, ethnomethodology, constructionism, poststructuralism, postmodernism and some versions of feminism are all interested in issues relating to subjectivity, complexity, perspective and meaning-construction. Still, as valuable and insightful as this is, these 'linguistically attuned' approaches can emphasize the *hows* of social process at the expense of the *whats* of lived experience. We want to strike a balance between these *hows* and *whats* as a way of reappropriating the significance of substance and content to studies of the social construction process. The aim is not to obviate interview material by deconstructing it, but to harvest it and its transactions for narrative analysis. While the emphasis on process has sharpened concern with, and debate over, the epistemological status of interview data, it is important not to lose track of *what* is being asked about in interviews and, in turn, *what* is being conveyed by respondents. A narrow focus on *how* tends to displace the significant *whats* – the meanings – that serve as the relevant grounds for asking and answering questions.

Taking the meaning-making activity of all interviewing as our point of departure, we will discuss how the interview cultivates its data. We begin by locating the active view in relation to more traditional conceptions of interviewing, contrasting alternate images of the subject behind the interview respondent.

Traditional images of interviewing

Typically, those who want to find out about another person's feelings, thoughts or actions believe that they merely have to ask the right questions and the other's 'reality' will be theirs. Studs Terkel, the consummate journalistic and sociological interviewer, says he simply turns on his tape recorder and invites people to talk. Writing of the interviews he did for his brilliant study of *Working*, Terkel notes:

> There were questions, of course. But they were casual in nature . . . the kind you would ask while having a drink with someone; the kind he would ask you. . . . In short, it was conversation. In time, the sluice gates of dammed up hurts and dreams were opened. (1972: xxv)

As unpretentious as it is, Terkel's image of interviewing permeates the social sciences; interviewing is generally likened to 'prospecting' for the true facts and feelings residing within the respondent. Of course there is a highly sophisticated technology that informs researchers about how to ask questions, what sorts of questions not to ask, the order in which to ask them, and the ways to avoid saying things that might spoil, contaminate or otherwise bias the data (Fowler and Mangione, 1990; Hyman et al., 1975).

The basic model, however, remains similar to the one Terkel exploits so adroitly.

The image of the social scientific prospector casts the interview as a search-and-discovery mission, with the interviewer intent on detecting what is already there inside variably cooperative respondents. The challenge lies in extracting information as directly as possible. Highly refined interview techniques streamline, systematize and sanitize the process. This can involve varying degrees of standardization (see Maccoby and Maccoby, 1954), ranging from interviews organized around structured, specially worded questions and an orientation to measurement, to flexibly organized interviews guided by more general questions aimed at uncovering subjective meanings. John Madge contrasts what he calls 'formative' with 'mass' interviews, categorizing them according to whether the respondent 'is given some sort of freedom to choose the topics to be discussed and the way in which they are discussed' (1965: 165). Formative interviews include the non-directive interviews favoured in Rogerian counselling (see Rogers, 1945), informal interviews and life histories. Most large-scale surveys fall into the mass interview category. Mainly, classification centres on the characteristics and aims of the interview process, with little attention paid to how interviews differ as occasions for knowledge production.

The subject behind the respondent

Regardless of the type of interview, there is always an image of the research *subject* lurking behind persons placed in the role of interview respondent (Holstein and Gubrium, 1995). Projecting a subject behind the respondent confers a sense of epistemological agency, which bears on our understanding of the relative validity of the information that is reported. In traditional approaches, subjects are basically conceived as passive *vessels of answers* for experiential questions put to respondents by interviewers. They are repositories of facts and the related details of experience. Occasionally, such as with especially sensitive interview topics or with recalcitrant respondents, researchers acknowledge that it may be difficult to obtain accurate experiential information. None the less, the information is viewed, in principle, as held uncontaminated by the subject's vessel of answers. The trick is to formulate questions and provide an atmosphere conducive to open and undistorted communication between the interviewer and respondent.

Much of the methodological literature on interviewing deals with the nuances of these intricate matters. The vessel-of-answers view cautions interviewers to be careful in how they ask questions, lest their manner of inquiry bias what lies within the subject. The literature offers myriad procedures for obtaining unadulterated facts and details, most of which rely upon interviewer and question neutrality. For example, it is assumed that the interviewer who poses questions that acknowledge alternative sides of an issue is being more 'neutral' than the interviewer who does not. The successful implementation of neutral practices elicits truths held in the vessel of answers behind the respondent. Validity results from the successful application of the procedures.

In the vessel-of-answers approach, the image of the subject is epistemologically passive, not engaged in the production of knowledge. If the interviewing process goes 'by the book' and is non-directional and unbiased, respondents will validly give out what subjects are presumed to merely retain within them – the unadulterated facts and details of experience. Contamination emanates from the interview setting, its participants and their interaction, not the subject, who, under ideal conditions, serves up authentic reports when beckoned to do so.

What happens, however, if we enliven the image of the subject behind the respondent? Construed as active, the subject behind the respondent not only holds facts and details of experience, but, in the very process of offering them up for response, constructively adds to, takes away from and transforms the facts and details. The respondent can hardly 'spoil' what he or she is, in effect, subjectively creating.

This activated subject pieces experiences together, before, during and after assuming the respondent role. As a member of society, he or she mediates and alters the knowledge that is conveyed to the interviewer; he or she is 'always already' an active maker of meaning. As a result, the respondent's answers are continually being assembled and modified and the answers' truth value cannot be judged simply in terms of whether they match what lies in a vessel of objective knowledge.

From a more traditional standpoint, the objectivity or truth of interview responses might be assessed in terms of reliability, the extent to which questioning yields the same answers whenever and wherever it is carried out, and validity, that is, the extent to which inquiry yields the 'correct' answers (Kirk and Miller, 1986). When the interview is seen as a dynamic, meaning-making occasion, however, different criteria apply. The focus is on how meaning is constructed, the circumstances of construction, and the meaningful linkages that are made for the occasion. While interest in the content of answers persists, it is primarily in how and what the active subject/respondent, in collaboration with an equally active interviewer, produces and conveys about the active subject/respondent's experience under the interpretive circumstances at hand. One cannot simply expect answers on one occasion to replicate those on another because they emerge from different circumstances of production. Similarly, the validity of answers derives not from their correspondence to meanings held within the respondent, but from their ability to convey situated experiential realities in terms that are locally comprehensible.

This active image of the interview is best put in perspective by contrasting it with specific traditional approaches. The two approaches we have selected differ considerably in their orientations to the experiential truths held by the passive subject. The first orients to the rational, factual value of what is communicated. Typical of survey interviewing, it focuses on the substantive statements, explanations and reasons with which the respondent articulates experience. We use Jean Converse and Howard Schuman's candid book *Conversations at Random* (1974) as an exemplary text. The second approach orients to the purportedly deeper and more authentic value of the subject's feelings. It emphasizes sentiment and emotion, the ostensible core of human experience. We use Jack Douglas's book *Creative Interviewing* (1985) to illustrate this approach.

Survey interviewing

While Converse and Schuman attempt to elaborate upon the most standardized of interviewing techniques, their book also considers the survey interview 'as interviewers see it' and richly illustrates how interpretively engaging and, relatedly, how difficult and exasperating the survey respondent can be. It describes the interesting and complex personalities and meanings that interviewers encounter while interviewing, depicting them, respectively, as 'the pleasure of persons' and 'connoisseurs of the particular'. But the authors caution the reader that, even though it will be evident throughout the book that the respondent can be quite interpretively active, this does not work against the pursuit of objective information. This information, the reader eventually learns, is derived from the repository of knowledge that lies passively behind the respondent. The authors do not believe that the respondent's conduct implicates his or her subject in the construction of meaning. As lively, uninhibited, entertaining and difficult as the respondent might be at times, his or her passive subject ultimately holds the answers sought in the research.

Converse and Schuman's book is filled with anecdotal reminders of what interviewers must learn in order to keep the subject's vessel of answers in view and the respondent on target. In part, it is a matter of controlling oneself as an interviewer so that one does not interfere with what the passive subject is only too willing to disclose. The interviewer must shake off self-consciousness, suppress personal opinion and avoid stereotyping the respondent. Learning the interviewer role is also a matter of controlling the interview situation to facilitate the candid expression of opinions and sentiments. Ideally, the interview should be conducted in private. This helps assure that respondents will speak directly from their vessels of answers, not in response to the presence of others. The seasoned interviewer learns that the so-called 'pull of conversation', which might have an interpretive dynamic of its own fuelled by the active subjectivity of both the respondent and the interviewer, must be managed so that the 'push of inquiry' (p. 26) is kept in focus. Ideally, the cross-pressures of conducting inquiry that will produce 'good hard data' are managed by means of 'soft' conversation (p. 22).

Throughout, Converse and Schuman's book provides glimpses of how problematic the image of the passive subject is in practice. The illustrations repeatedly tell us that interviews are conversations where meanings are not only conveyed, but cooperatively built up, received, interpreted and recorded by the interviewer. While the veteran interviewer learns to manage the pressures of conversation for the purposes of inquiry, orienting to an active, meaning-making occasion seems to be a mere epistemological step away.

Creative interviewing

This is different from the approach exemplified in Douglas's book *Creative Interviewing*, but there are some marked similarities that borrow from traditional images. The word 'creative' in Douglas's title refers primarily to the interviewer, not the respondent, and, according to Douglas, derives from the difficulties he encountered attempting to probe respondents' 'deep experience'. Douglas writes that in his many empirical studies, he repeatedly discovered how shallow the standard recommendations were for conducting research interviews. Canons of rational neutrality, such as those Converse and Schuman espouse, failed to capture what Douglas calls his respondents' 'emotional wellsprings' and called for a methodology for deep disclosure.

Douglas's difficulties relate as much to his image of the passive subject as they do to shortcomings of standard interviewing technique. Like the image of the subject behind the survey respondent, Douglas also imagines his subjects to be repositories of answers, but in his case, they are well-guarded vessels of feelings. The respondent authentically communicates from an emotional wellspring, at the behest of an interviewer who knows that mere words cannot draw out or convey what experience ultimately is all about. Standard survey questions and answers touch only the surface of experience. Douglas aims more deeply by creatively 'getting to know' the real subject behind the respondent.

Creative interviewing is a set of techniques for moving past the mere words and sentences exchanged in the interview process. To achieve this, the interviewer must establish a climate for *mutual* disclosure. The interview should be an occasion that displays the interviewer's willingness to share his or her own feelings and deepest thoughts. This is done to assure respondents that they can, in turn, share their own thoughts and feelings. The interviewers' deep disclosure both occasions and legitimizes the respondent's reciprocal revelations. This, Douglas suggests, is thoroughly suppressed by the cultivated neutrality of the standard survey interview. As if to state a cardinal rule, he writes:

> Creative interviewing, as we shall see throughout, involves the use of many strategies and tactics of interaction, largely based on an understanding of friendly feelings and intimacy, to optimize *cooperative, mutual disclosure and a creative search for mutual understanding*. (1985: 25)

Douglas offers a set of guidelines for creative interviewing. One is to figure that, as he puts it, 'genius in creative interviewing involves 99 percent perspiration' (1985: 27); getting the respondent to deeply disclose requires much more work than obtaining mere opinions. A second admonition for engaging in 'deep-deep probes into the human soul' is 'researcher, know thyself' (1985: 51). Continual self-analysis on the part of the interviewer, who usually is also the researcher, is necessary, lest the creative interviewer's own defence mechanisms work against mutual disclosure and understanding. A third guideline is to show a commitment to disclosure by expressing an abiding interest in feelings. Referring to a neophyte creative interviewer who 'has done some wondrously revealing life studies', Douglas writes that the creative interviewer is 'driven by . . . friendly, caring, and adoring feelings, but adds to those an endearing, wide-eyed sense of wonderment at the mysteries unveiled before her' (1985: 29).

The wellsprings tapped by creative interviewing are said to be emotional, in distinct contrast with the preferred rational image of facts that filters through Converse and Schuman's book. As Douglas puts it, knowledge and wisdom are '*partially* the product of creative interactions – of mutual searches for understanding, of soul communions' (p. 55). While Douglas's imagined subject is basically emotional, this subject, in the role of respondent, actively cooperates with the interviewer to create mutually recognizable meanings, paralleling what interviewers' accounts in Converse and Schuman's book suggest. In this regard, the mutuality of disclosure – the 'creative' thrust of creative interviewing – mediates, adds to and shapes what is said in its own right. What Douglas does not recognize, however, is that this ideally cooperative subject could alternatively constitute the wellsprings of experience in rational or other terms, not necessarily emotional ones. Thus, the subject behind Douglas's respondent remains an essentially passive, if concertedly emotional, fount of experience, not unlike the respondent who 'opens up' while having a drink with Studs Terkel.

The active interview

Ithiel de Sola Pool (1957), a prominent critic of public opinion polling, once argued that the dynamic, communicative contingencies of the interview literally activate respondents' opinions. Every interview, he suggests, is an 'interpersonal drama with a developing plot' (1957: 193). This metaphor conveys a far more active sense of interviewing than is traditionally conceived, an image of the interview as an occasion for constructing, not merely discovering or conveying, information. As Pool writes:

> [T]he social milieu in which communication takes place [during interviews] modifies not only what a person dares to say but even what he thinks he chooses to say. And these variations in expression cannot be viewed as mere deviations from some underlying 'true' opinion, for there is no neutral, non-social, uninfluenced situation to provide that baseline. (1957: 192)

The active interview and interpretive practice

Conceiving of the interview as an interpersonal drama with a developing plot is part of a broader image of reality as an ongoing, interpretive accomplishment. From this perspective, interview participants are practitioners of everyday life, constantly working to discern and communicate the recognizable and orderly features of experience. But meaning-making is not merely artful (Garfinkel, 1967); meaning is not built 'from scratch' on each interpretive occasion. Rather, interpretation orients to, and is conditioned by, the substantive resources and contingencies of interaction.

Meaning is constituted at the nexus of the *hows* and the *whats* of experience, by way of *interpretive practice* – the procedures and resources used to apprehend, organize and represent reality (Holstein, 1993; Holstein and Gubrium, 1994). Active interviewing is a form of interpretive practice involving respondent and interviewer as they articulate ongoing interpretive structures, resources and orientations with what Garfinkel (1967) calls 'practical reasoning'. Linking artfulness to substantive contingencies implies that while reality is continually 'under construction', it is assembled using the interpretive resources at hand. Meaning reflects relatively enduring interpretive conditions, such as the research topics of the interviewer, biographical particulars and local ways of orienting to those topics (Gubrium, 1988, 1989, 1994; Holstein and Gubrium, 1994, 1995). Those resources are astutely and adroitly crafted to the demands of the occasion, so that meaning is neither predetermined nor absolutely unique.

An active subject

The image of the *active interview* transforms the subject behind the respondent from a repository of opinions and reasons or a wellspring of emotions into a productive source of knowledge. From the time one identifies a research topic, to respondent selection, questioning and answering, and, finally, to the interpretation of responses, interviewing itself is a concerted project for producing meaning. The imagined subject behind the respondent emerges as part of the project, not beforehand. Within the interview itself, the subject is fleshed out – rationally, emotionally, in combination, or otherwise – in relation to the give-and-take of the interview process and the interview's broader research purposes. The interview *and* its participants are constantly developing.

Two communicative contingencies influence the construction of the active subject behind the respondent. One kind involves the substantive *whats* of the interview enterprise. The focus and emerging data of the research project provide interpretive resources for developing both the subject and his or her responses. For example, a project might centre on the quality of care and quality of life of nursing home residents (see Gubrium, 1993). This might be part of a study relating to national debates about the organization of home and institutional care. If interviews are employed, participants draw out the substantiality of these topics, linking the topics to biographical particulars in the interview process, and thus producing a subject who responds to, or is affected by, the matters under discussion. For instance, a nursing home resident might speak animatedly during an interview about the quality of care in her facility, asserting that, 'for a woman, it ultimately gets down to feelings', echoing Douglas's emotional subject and articulating a recognizable linkage between affect and gender. Another resident might coolly and methodically list her facility's qualities of care, never once mentioning her feelings about them. Offering her own take on the matter, the respondent might state that 'getting emotional' over 'these things' clouds clear judgement, implicating a different kind of subject, more like the rational respondent portrayed in Converse and Schuman's text. Particular substantive resources – such as the common cultural link between women and feelings or the traditional cultural opposition of clear thought and emotionality – are used to form the subject.

A second communicative contingency of interviewing directs us to the *hows* of the process. The standpoint from which information is offered is continually developed in relation to ongoing interview interaction. In speaking of the quality of care, for example, nursing home residents, as interview respondents, not only offer substantive thoughts and feelings pertinent to the topic under consideration, but simultaneously and continuously monitor who they are in relation to the person questioning them. For example, prefacing her remarks about the quality of life in her facility with the statement 'speaking as a woman', a nursing home resident informs the interviewer that she is to be heard as a woman, not as someone else – not a mere resident, cancer patient or abandoned mother. If and when she subsequently comments, 'If I were a man in this place', the resident frames her thoughts and feelings about the quality of life differently, producing an alternative subject. The respondent is clearly working at how the interview unfolds.

Narrative incitement, positional shifts and resource activation

Interviews, of course, hold no monopoly over interpretive practice. Nor are they the only occasions upon which subjects and their opinions, emotions and reports are interpretively constituted. Why, then, is interviewing an especially useful mode of systematic social inquiry? One answer lies in the interview situation's ability to incite the production of meanings that address issues relating to particular research concerns. In the traditional view of interviewing, the passive subject engages in a 'minimalist' version of interpretive practice, perceiving, storing and reporting experience when properly asked. Our active conception of the interview, however, invests the subject with a substantial repertoire of interpretive methods and stock of experiential materials. The active view eschews the image of the vessel waiting to be tapped in favour of the notion that the subject's interpretive capabilities must be activated, stimulated and cultivated. The interview is a commonly recognized occasion for formally and systematically doing so.

This is not to say that active interviewers merely coax their respondents into preferred answers to their questions. Rather, they converse with respondents in such a way that alternate considerations are brought into play. They may suggest orientations to, and linkages between, diverse aspects of respondents' experience, adumbrating – even inviting – interpretations that make use of particular resources, connections and outlooks. Interviewers may explore incompletely articulated aspects of experience, encouraging respondents to develop topics in ways relevant to their own everyday lives (DeVault, 1990). The objective is not to dictate interpretation, but to provide an environment conducive to the production of the range and complexity of meanings that address relevant issues, and not be confined by predetermined agendas.

Pool's dramaturgic metaphor is apt because it conveys both the structuring conditions and the artfulness of the interview. As a drama of sorts, its narrative is scripted in that it has a topic or topics, distinguishable roles and a format for conversation. But it also has a *developing* plot, in which topics, roles and format are fashioned in the give-and-take of the interview. This active interview is a kind of limited 'improvisational' performance. The production is spontaneous, yet structured – focused within loose parameters provided by the interviewer, who is also an active participant.

While the respondent actively constructs and assembles answers, he or she does not simply 'break out' talking. Neither elaborate narratives nor one-word replies emerge without provocation. The active interviewer's role is to incite respondents' answers, virtually *activating narrative production.* Where standardized approaches to interviewing attempt to strip the interview of all but the most neutral, impersonal stimuli (but see Holstein and Gubrium, 1995, for a discussion of the inevitable failure of these attempts), the consciously active interviewer intentionally provokes responses by indicating – even suggesting – narrative positions, resources, orientations and precedents. In the broadest sense, the interviewer attempts to activate the respondent's stock of knowledge (Schütz, 1967) and bring it to bear on the discussion at hand in ways that are appropriate to the research agenda.

Consider, for example, the ways in which diverse aspects of a respondent's knowledge, perspectives, roles and orientations are activated and implicated in an interview involving an adult daughter who is caring for her mother – a victim of senile dementia – at home. The daughter is employed part-time, and shares the household with her employed husband and their two sons, one a part-time college student and the other a full-time security guard. The extract begins when the interviewer (I) asks the adult daughter (R) to describe her feelings about having to juggle so many needs and schedules. This relates to the so-called 'sandwich generation', which is said to be caught between having to raise its own children and seeing to the needs of frail elderly parents. Note how, after the interviewer asks the respondent what she means by saying that she had mixed feelings, the respondent makes explicit reference to various ways of thinking about the matter, as if to suggest that more than one narrative resource (with contradictory responses) might be brought to bear on the matter. The respondent displays considerable narrative control: she not only references possible *whats* of caregiving and family life, but, in the process, informs the interviewer of *how* she could construct her answer.

I: We were talking about, you said you were a member of the, what did you call it?
R: They say that I'm in the sandwich generation. You know, like we're sandwiched between having to care for my mother . . . and my grown kids and my husband. People are living longer now and you've got different generations at home and, I tell ya, it's a mixed blessing.
I: How do you feel about it in your situation?
R: Oh, I don't know. Sometimes I think I'm being a bit selfish because I gripe about having to keep an eye on Mother all the time. If you let down your guard, she wanders off into the back yard or goes out the door and down the street. That's no fun when your hubby wants your attention too. Norm works the second shift and he's home during the day a lot. I manage to get in a few hours of work, but he doesn't like it. I have pretty mixed feelings about it.
I: What do you mean?
R: Well, I'd say that as a daughter, I feel pretty guilty about how I feel sometimes. It can get pretty bad, like wishing that Mother were just gone, you know what I mean? She's been a wonderful mother and I love her very much, but if you ask me how I feel as a wife and mother, that's another matter. I feel like she's [the mother], well, intruding on our lives and just making hell out of raising a family. Sometimes I put myself in my husband's shoes and I just know how he feels. He doesn't say much, but I know that he misses my company, and I miss his of course. [*Pause*] So how do you answer that?

The interviewer goes on to explain that the respondent can answer in the way she believes best represents her thoughts and feelings. But as the exchange unfolds, it is evident that 'best' misrepresents the narrative complexity of the respondent's thoughts and feelings. In the following extract, notice how the respondent struggles to sort her opinions to accord with categorically distinct identities. At one point, she explains that she knows how a wife could and should feel because she gathers from the way her husband and sons act that 'men don't feel things the same way'. This suggests that her own thoughts and feelings are drawn from a fund of gendered knowledge as well. Note, too, how at several points the interviewer collaborates with the respondent to define her identity as a respondent. At the very end of the extract, the respondent suggests that other respondents' answers might serve to clarify the way she herself has organized her responses, indicating that further narrative contextualizing might encourage even more interpretations of her own experience.

R: I try to put myself in their [husband and sons'] shoes, try to look at it from their point of view, you know, from a man's way of thinking. I ask myself how it feels to have a part-time wife and mama. I ask myself how I'd feel. Believe me, I know he [husband] feels pretty rotten about it. Men get that way; they want what they want and the rest of the time, well, they're quiet, like nothing's the matter. I used to think I was going crazy with all the stuff on my mind and having to think about everything all at once and not being able to finish with one thing and get on to the other. You know how it gets –

doing one thing and feeling bad about how you did something else and wanting to redo what you did or what you said. The way a woman does, I guess. I think I've learned that about myself. I don't know. It's pretty complicated thinking about it. [*Pause*] Let's see, how do I really feel?

I: Well, I was just wondering, you mentioned being sandwiched earlier and what a woman feels?

R: Yeah, I guess I wasn't all that sure what women like me feel until I figured out how Norm and the boys felt. I figured pretty quick that men are pretty good at sorting things out and that, well, I just couldn't do it, 'cause, well, men don't feel things the same way. I just wouldn't want to do that way anyway. Wouldn't feel right about it as a woman, you know what I mean? So, like they say, live and let live, I guess.

I: But as a daughter?

R: Yeah, that too. So if you ask me how I feel having Mother under foot all the time, I'd say that I remember not so far back that I was under foot a lot when I was a little girl and Mother never complained, and she'd help Dad out in the store, too. So I guess I could tell you that I'm glad I'm healthy and around to take care of her and, honestly, I'd do it all over again if I had to. I don't know. You've talked to other women about it. What do they say?

I: Well, uh

R: Naw, I don't want to put you on the spot. I was just thinking that maybe if I knew how others in my shoes felt, I might be able to sort things out better than I did for ya.

The respondent's comments about both the subject matter under consideration and how one does or should formulate responses show that the respondent, in collaboration with the interviewer, activates diverse narrative resources as an integral part of exchanging questions and answers. Treating the interview as active allows the interviewer to encourage the respondent to shift positions in the interview so as to explore alternate perspectives and stocks of knowledge. Rather than searching for the best or most authentic answer, the aim is to systematically activate applicable ways of knowing – the possible answers – that respondents can reveal, as diverse and contradictory as they might be. The active interviewer sets the general parameters for responses, constraining as well as provoking answers that are germane to the researcher's interest. He or she does not tell respondents what to say, but offers them pertinent ways of conceptualizing issues and making connections – that is, suggests possible horizons of meaning and narrative linkages that coalesce into the emerging responses (Gubrium, 1993). The pertinence of what is discussed is partly defined by the research topic and partly by the substantive horizons of ongoing responses. While the active respondent may selectively exploit a vast range of narrative resources, it is the active interviewer's job to direct and harness the respondent's constructive storytelling to the research task at hand.

Implications for analysis

Compared to more conventional perspectives on interviewing, the active approach seems to invite unacceptable forms of bias. After all, far more is going on that simply retrieving the information from respondents' repositories of knowledge. 'Contamination' is everywhere. This criticism only holds, however, if one takes a narrow view of interpretive practice and meaning construction. Bias is a meaningful concept only if the subject is a preformed, purely informational commodity that the interview process might somehow taint. But if interview responses are seen as products of interpretive practice, they are neither preformed, nor ever pure. Any interview situation – no matter how formalized, restricted or standardized – relies upon the interaction between participants. Because meaning construction is unavoidably collaborative (Garfinkel, 1967; Sacks et al., 1974), it is virtually impossible to free any interaction from those factors that could be construed as contaminants. All participants in an interview are inevitably implicated in making meaning.

While naturally occurring talk and interaction may appear to be more spontaneous, less 'staged' than an interview, this is true only in the sense that such interaction is staged by persons other than an interviewer. Resulting conversations are not necessarily more 'realistic' or 'authentic'. They simply take place in what have been recognized as indigenous settings. With the development of the interview society, and the increasing deprivatization of personal experience (see Gubrium and Holstein, 1995a, 1995b, 1995c; Gubrium et al., 1994), the interview is becoming more and more commonplace, also making it a 'naturally occurring' occasion for articulating experience.

Nevertheless, discussion of some topics, while being deeply significant, may none the less be relatively rare in the normal course of everyday life, even in the interview society. For example, as seemingly ubiquitous as is talk about family and domestic life, we have found it useful to study 'family discourse' in a relatively circumscribed range of settings, most of which intentionally provoke talk about family as an integral part of conducting routine business, such as in a family therapy agency, for example (see Gubrium, 1992; Gubrium and Holstein, 1990). Active interviews can thus be used to gain purchase on interpretive practice relating to matters that may not be casually topical, yet which are socially relevant. By inciting narrative production, the interviewer may provoke interpretive developments that might emerge too rarely to be effectively captured 'in their natural habitat', so to speak.

Given the unconventional nature of active interviewing, how does one make sense of its data? Analysing data concerning interpretive practice is something of an 'artful' matter in its own right. This does not mean that analysis is any less rigorous than that applied to traditional interview data; on the contrary, active interview data require disciplined sensitivity to both process and substance.

Interviews are traditionally analysed as more or less accurate descriptions of experience, as reports or representations (literally, re-presentations) of reality. Analysis entails systematically coding, grouping or summarizing the descriptions, and providing a coherent organizing framework that encapsulates and explains aspects of the social world that respondents portray. Respondents' interpretive activity is subordinated to the substance of what they report; the *whats* of experience overwhelm the *hows*.

In contrast, active interview data can be analysed to show the dynamic interrelatedness of the *whats* and the *hows*. Respondents' answers and comments are not viewed as reality reports delivered from a fixed repository. Instead, they are considered for the ways that they construct aspects of reality in collaboration with the interviewer. The focus is as much on the assembly process as on what is assembled. Using sociologically oriented forms of narrative and discourse analysis, conversational records of interpretive practice are examined to reveal reality-constructing practices as well as the subjective meanings that are circumstantially conveyed (see DeVault, 1990; Gubrium and Holstein, 1994; Holstein and Gubrium, 1994; Propp, 1968; Riessman, 1993; Silverman, 1993). The goal is to show how interview responses are produced in the interaction between interviewer and respondent, without losing sight of the meanings produced or the circumstances that condition the meaning-making process. The analytic objective is not merely to describe the situated production of talk, but to show how what is being said relates to the experiences and lives being studied.

Writing up findings from interview data is itself an analytically active enterprise. Rather than adhering to the ideal of letting the data 'speak for themselves', the active analyst empirically documents the meaning-making process. With ample illustration and reference to records of talk, the analyst describes the complex discursive activities through which respondents produce meaning. The goal is to explicate how meanings, their linkages and horizons, are constituted both in relation to, and within, the interview environment. The analyst's reports do not summarize and organize what interview participants have said, as much as they 'deconstruct' participants' talk to show the reader both the *hows* and the *whats* of the narrative dramas conveyed, which increasingly mirrors an interview society.

References

Alasuutari, P. (1995) *Researching Culture: Qualitative Method and Cultural Studies*. London: Sage.

Berger, P.L. and Luckmann, T. (1967) *The Social Construction of Reality*. New York: Doubleday.

Blumer, H. (1969) *Symbolic Interactionism*. New York: Prentice Hall.

Briggs, C. (1986) *Learning How to Ask: A Sociolinguistic Appraisal of the Role of the Interviewer in Social Science Research*. Cambridge: Cambridge University Press.

Cicourel, A.V. (1964) *Method and Measurement in Sociology*. New York: Free Press.

Cicourel, A.V. (1974) *Theory and Method in a Study of Argentine Fertility*. New York: Wiley.

Converse, J.M. and Schuman, H. (1974) *Conversations at Random: Survey Research as Interviewers See It*. New York: Wiley.

DeVault, M. (1990) 'Talking and listening from women's standpoint: Feminist strategies for interviewing and analysis', *Social Problems*, 37: 96–117.

Douglas, J.D. (1985) *Creative Interviewing*. Beverly Hills, CA: Sage.

Fowler, F.J. and Mangione, T.W. (1990) *Standardized Survey Interviewing*. Newbury Park, CA: Sage.

Garfinkel, H. (1967) *Studies in Ethnomethodology*. Englewood Cliffs, NJ: Prentice Hall.

Gorden, R.L. (1987) *Interviewing: Strategy, Techniques, and Tactics*. Homewood, IL: Dorsey.

Gubrium, J.F. (1988) *Analyzing Field Reality*. Beverly Hills, CA: Sage.

Gubrium, J.F. (1989) 'Local cultures and service policy', in J.F. Gubrium and D. Silverman (eds), *The Politics of Field Research*. London: Sage. pp. 94–112.

Gubrium, J.F. (1992) *Out of Control*. Newbury Park, CA: Sage.

Gubrium, J.F. (1993) *Speaking of Life: Horizons of Meaning for Nursing Home Residents*. Hawthorne, NY: Aldine de Gruyter.

Gubrium, J.F. (1994) 'Interviewing', in *Exploring Collaborative Research in Primary Care*. Thousand Oaks, CA: Sage. pp. 65–76.

Gubrium, J.F. and Holstein, J.A. (1990) *What is Family*? Mountain View, CA: Mayfield.

Gubrium, J.F. and Holstein, J.A. (1994) 'Analyzing talk and interaction', in J.F. Gubrium and A. Sankar (eds), *Qualitative Methods in Aging Research*. Newbury Park, CA: Sage. pp. 173–88.

Gubrium, J.F. and Holstein, J.A. (1995a) 'Biographical work and new ethnography', in R. Josselson and A. Lieblich (eds), *The Narrative Study of Lives*, Vol. 3. Newbury Park, CA: Sage. pp. 45–58.

Gubrium, J.F. and Holstein, J.A. (1995b) 'Life course malleability: Biographical work and deprivatization', *Sociological Inquiry*, 65: 207–23.

Gubrium, J.F. and Holstein, J.A. (1995c) 'Qualitative inquiry and the deprivatization of experience', *Qualitative Inquiry*, 1: 204–22.

Gubrium, J.F. and Holstein, J.A. (1997) *The New Language of Qualitative Method*. New York: Oxford University Press.

Gubrium, J.F., Holstein, J.A. and Buckholdt, D.R. (1994) *Constructing the Life Course*. Dix Hills, NY: General Hall.

Harding, S. (ed.) (1987) *Feminism and Methodology*. Bloomington: Indiana University Press.

Heritage, J. (1984) *Garfinkel and Ethnomethodology*. Cambridge: Polity.

Holstein, J.A. (1993) *Court-Ordered Insanity: Interpretive Practice and Involuntary Commitment*. Hawthorne, NY: Aldine de Gruyter.

Holstein, J.A. and Gubrium, J.F. (1994) 'Phenomenology, ethnomethodology, and interpretive practice', in N.K. Denzin and Y. Lincoln (eds), *Handbook of Qualitative Research*. Newbury Park, CA: Sage. pp. 262–72.

Holstein, J.A. and Gubrium, J.F. (1995) *The Active Interview*. Thousand Oaks, CA: Sage.

Holstein, J.A. and Staples, W.G. (1992) 'Producing evaluative knowledge: The interactional bases of social science findings', *Sociological Inquiry*, 62: 11–35.

Hyman, H.H., Cobb, W.J., Feldman, J.J., Hart, C.W. and Stember, C.H. (1975) *Interviewing in Social Research*. Chicago: University of Chicago Press.

Kirk, J. and Miller, M.L. (1986) *Reliability and Validity in Qualitative Research*. Beverly Hills, CA: Sage.

Maccoby, E.E. and Maccoby, N. (1954) 'The interview: A tool of social science', in G. Lindzey (ed.), *Handbook of Social Psychology*. Reading, MA: Addison-Wesley. pp. 449–87.

Madge, J. (1965) *The Tools of Social Science*. Garden City, NY: Anchor Books.

Manning, P.L. (1967) 'Problems in interpreting interview data', *Sociology and Social Research*, 51: 301–16.

Mishler, E.G. (1986) *Research Interviewing*. Cambridge, MA: Harvard University Press.

Mishler, E.G. (1991) 'Representing discourse: The rhetoric of transcription', *Journal of Narrative and Life History*, 1: 255–80.

Pollner, M. (1987) *Mundane Reason*. Cambridge: Cambridge University Press.

Pool, I. de S. (1957) 'A critique of the twentieth anniversary issue', *Public Opinion Quarterly*, 21: 190–8.

Propp, V.I. (1968) *The Morphology of the Folktale*. Austin: University of Texas Press.

Reinharz, S. (1992) *Feminist Methods of Social Research*. New York: Oxford University Press.

Riessman, C.K. (1993) *Narrative Analysis*. Newbury Park, CA: Sage.

Rogers, C.R. (1945) 'The non-directive method as a technique for social research', *American Journal of Sociology*, 50: 279–83.

Sacks, H., Schegloff, E.A. and Jefferson, G. (1994) 'A simplest systematics for the organization of turn-taking for conversation', *Language*, 50: 696–735.

Schütz, A. (1967) *The Phenomenology of the Social World*. Evanston, IL: Northwestern University Press.

Silverman, D. (1993) *Interpreting Qualitative Data: Methods for Analysing Talk, Text and Interaction*. London: Sage.

Smith, D.E. (1987) *The Everyday World as Problematic: A Feminist Sociology*. Boston: Northeastern University Press.

Terkel, S. (1972) *Working*. New York: Avon.

9 Membership Categorization and Interview Accounts

Carolyn Baker

Interviews are among the most widely used methods of data generation in the social sciences. While a great deal has been written for decades about the procedures for generating such data (how to ask questions, how to relate), rather less attention has been given until relatively recently to the analysis of such data. A focus on *analysis*, a focus on the researcher's expertise in the analysis of the *interactional* data as much as in the generation of it, changes significantly how interviewing may be understood and pursued within the social sciences.

Investigating interiors and exteriors

From many conventional social science perspectives, the relevant researcher expertise is in the getting of the data, and criteria of success at interviewing include such matters as whether there was good 'rapport', whether the respondent talked a lot, and what they talked about, whether and how they divulged what the interviewer was after. All such criteria of success rely on the assumption that there is pre-existing information of some sort (e.g. beliefs, attitudes, knowledge, perspectives) to extract from the respondent. The interviewer attempts to position herself or himself as colleague, friend or confessor in order that the respondent speaks openly, authentically or truthfully, to produce valid reporting on some interior or exterior state of affairs. From within this romantic notion of special connection between interviewer and respondent, an interview can be found to be good or not, successful or not.

The analysis which follows from this conventional perspective typically seeks 'themes' in the content of what is said by the respondent. This perspective on interview data might be captured by the phrase 'from thought through language to themes'. That is, the contents of the respondents' thoughts (beliefs etc.) are expressed in the medium of language (the interviewer's task is to encourage this expression) and then this content is rethematized by the analyst, who typically chunks the data, categorizes it, moves it around and rearranges it into a different formation. The words spoken by the respondents and the ideas they are heard to represent are 'the data'. This is a common-sense view of interviewing in which the interviewer, and later the analyst, investigate 'interiors' (states of mind) or 'exteriors' (descriptions of social settings) through a representational view of language.

Investigating talk as social action

Another way of approaching the analysis of interview data brackets this common-sense perspective, and brings into play a different set of assumptions about language and social action. Drawing on earlier work in which I analysed interview talk between an adult researcher and adolescent subjects (see Baker, 1984; Silverman, 1993), I will explicate further how the use of 'membership categorization devices' is a key to treating interview data differently. In this perspective, (1) interviewing is understood as an interactional event in which members draw on their cultural knowledge, including their knowledge about how members of categories routinely speak; (2) questions are a central part of the data and cannot be viewed as neutral invitations to speak – rather, they shape how and as a member of which categories the respondents should speak; (3) interview responses are treated as accounts more than reports – that is, they are understood as the work of accounting by a member of a category for activities attached to that category. This accounting work is the core of the analysis of data. In this accounting work, we look for the use of membership categorization devices by the interviewer and respondent, and show how both are involved in the generation of versions of social reality built around categories and activities. Further, in the work done with categories and activities, we see the local production in each case of versions of a moral order.

It is helpful to understand that from this perspective the process of interviewing is better described not as data 'collection', but rather as data 'making' or data 'generation'. The analysis of interview data from talk or transcripts of the talk is organized not to locate interior beliefs or knowledges or to seek actual descriptions of social settings. Rather it is organized to identify the speakers' methods of using categories and activities in accounts. This is a round-about way (but the only one possible) of identifying cultural knowledge and logic *in use*. Cultural knowledge is audible and visible in how people account to one another, whatever might be inside their heads. This approach draws also on Sacks's introduction of the possibilities of using conversational data to do sociology, and on Silverman's many analyses of interview data. It sets up the interviewer and respondent as ordinary competent members of the culture and the analyst as *post hoc* ethnomethodologist, looking for the social-organizational work being done by interviewer and respondent. The speakers are viewed as competent observer-analysts of the interaction they are involved in. It is their artful use of talk we look for in analysis. In this approach, it is not interviews that are good or bad, successful or unsuccessful in themselves. The criterion of success is the ability of the analyst to explicate the routine grounds of the work that interviewer and respondent do together to assign sense and meaning to the interiors or exteriors they talk about.

Members' analytic resources

Members have analytic resources that they put to work as they engage in any kind of talk, including interview talk. One of those resources is the use of membership categorization devices as introduced by Sacks (1992). Talk, further, is not simply expressive of interior states or contents. Talk is social action: people achieve identities, realities, social order and social relationships through talk. How people describe things and how they reason about them are pragmatic selections from a range of possibilities. Even 'simple' describing is always a social and moral activity (Jayyusi, 1984, 1991; Schegloff, 1988) turning on category identifications. Imagine the differences in being approached to speak as 'a mother of three' and being approached to speak as 'a professor'. Both may be correct identifiers, but the selection made calls on very different domains of knowledge and reason. To account for oneself 'as a mother' calls into play other related categories (such as 'children') and activities or properties associated with those categories (e.g. 'needs' of children, caringness, guilt). Speaking 'as a professor' invokes a different set of category relevances and activities (e.g. 'students', teaching, theorizing or researching). When we are asked to speak in some situation, as in an interview for example, we mobilize the resources of available membership categorization devices. These devices are collections of categories and associated activities (such as mother + father + children = nuclear family).

An anecdote will make more striking the point about members' uses of membership categorizations to assign social identities and achieve social order. Recently I observed the following scene. A woman, a young male child holding a screwdriver, and a man entered a bakery. The woman behind the counter greeted them and then addressed the child as follows: '*Have you been helping Daddy*?' There was a pause that I distinctly remember because, as an observer-analyst of the scene, I had time to consider the gender assumption being made: that *Daddy* was being helped rather than the mother. The woman customer then spoke: '*This is not Daddy*'. What resources had the woman behind the counter used to generate her 'mistake'? Should we take it that the woman customer is the child's mother? *Is this Mommy?* How do we hear her that way?

Category incumbencies are 'made to happen', are produced (and sometimes corrected) in talk. We routinely and pre-reflectively use membership categorization devices to organize our characterizations of what we see or hear. Membership categorization is a pervasive resource for sense-making through utterances. Tracing members' use of these categories and devices in any settings, including interview settings, is a means of showing how identities, social relationships and even institutions are produced.

Interview talk as accounting

The first segment from interview talk to be studied here comes from an interview that took place as part of routine institutional practice but was recorded for research purposes. The following interview extract shows the opening turns of an audio-recorded parent–teacher interview (Baker and Keogh, 1995). Right from the beginning, participants immediately go to work with their own and the other's membership categories relevant to this encounter (see Appendix to this volume for transcription key).

Teacher (T): Ellen
Student: Donna
Parent(s): Mother (M) and Father (F)

1 *T:* Ok all right we'll just forget it I should cover it up or something I hate tape recorders! (hh) Right um Donna um I just took over Mister Jay's class um four weeks ago so, I don't really know a lot about Donna's work I've had a quick look at her work in her folder, and from her marks she um, you seem to have, passed in the first part of the year and then really gone down in last two um,pieces of work which was a poetry oral? and a um a novel (2.0) a novel in another form that was putting part of the novel into another style of writing. Now um (2.0) in class (1.0) Donna's a little bit distracted? often? down the back there, with um the girls that she sits with, though she does give in class when she's asked to, she does do all her work, um I'm (1.0) would you like to- do you work with Donna at home with her schoolwork at all? do you see it at all or?
2 *F:* Not really no=
3 *M:* =(We very rarely) see her schoolwork
4 *F:* they generally disappear off to their bedrooms with their homework and um=
5 *T:* =Ye:es (2.0) Well um
6 *F:* We don't see much of (it)
7 *T:* Let me see yes I didn't mark this this was all Mr Jay's (1.0) This is a summary, they had to summarize um this (1.0) um let's see where her, mistakes seem to lie. (3.0) Oh it seems alright. (3.0) Why did she only get four and a half for that. Hmmm. [. . .]

In the teacher's long first turn, she describes her work in considerable detail and accounts for possible shortcomings in that work prior to turning the talk over to the parents or Donna. The turn combines information segments (how Donna is doing, how she is in class) with apology segments (how the teacher is herself doing in the interview). The combination can be seen as depicting the category of 'teacher' as one who: has first-hand and long-term knowledge of the student; can read other teachers' notations and make sense of them; observes what is going on, where, in the classroom; knows who the student's friends in class are; and knows what the parents want to know. The prefacing of the turn with the information that she is not Donna's long-time teacher and then turning directly to Donna's marks is also a characterization in her talk of the category 'parents' as those who want to know about Donna's academic achievement in the first instance and want to know about her behaviour in class. The teacher's first turn can be heard as an elaborate version of 'who I am/what I know/what my relevancies are, and who you are/what you know/what your relevancies are, and what we want of each other': a way of connecting the two institutional categories, teacher and parents. Donna, the subject of the talk, is present but silent. The teacher's work here can be seen as identifying, colouring in and connecting the two institutional categories of parent and teacher. In Silverman's (1993: 114) terms, she is assembling connections between cultural particulars.

The teacher also calls on unnamed but alluded-to student categories in scenic descriptions such as 'down the back there, with um the girls that she sits with'. These describings are forms of social action done through talk (cf. Schegloff, 1988).

At the end of the first turn the teacher changes the topic to what the parents do at home concerning schoolwork. The teacher's question to the parents,

> would you like to- do you work with Donna at home with her schoolwork at all? do you see it at all or?

begins like a perspective display series (cf. Maynard, 1991) asking for the clients' view of matters but then introduces what looks like an information question. This is information-seeking, but in terms of interaction in the interview it is more than that. It is a further elaboration of the category 'parents' – done by adding to 'parenting' as already established, the category-related attribute of possibly working with Donna or seeing what she does at home or something else. The question gives three options of descending involvement for what parents might do: work with Donna's schoolwork (at all = ever? sometimes?), see Donna's schoolwork (at all = ever? sometimes?), or? (hearably, something even less?).

Interview talk as category elaboration

Before the parents have had a single turn at the formal business of the interview, the teacher has, using her knowledge of category memberships and related activities, presented a complex social landscape that connects the interests, territories and activities of parents and teachers. The landscape is also a moral one now in several respects, including the descending order of parental help to Donna laid out as the teacher asks the parents to speak.

As member-analysts of this scene, the parents can take it that the teacher wants to know what happens at home and where it fits in her descending order. 'Not really no' and 'we very rarely see her schoolwork' are heavily mitigated answers to the information question. The sense these turns produce is that something interferes with this legitimate parental task, and that is that 'they generally disappear off to their bedrooms with their homework'. This is an artfully constructed account. Who 'they' is is not clear, but it is *more than just Donna*. Donna has now been placed in an unnamed category of people who 'disappear off . . . with their homework'. It could be as if Donna cannot wait to get at her homework, she disappears off so fast, and that is why the parents do not see it or work with her. The teacher is called upon to recognize this scenic description of home life.

We now have at least two Donnas produced in this talk: distracted school Donna who sits with the girls at the back (but nevertheless does do her work in class), and keen home Donna who disappears off to do homework. Both are moral constructions of Donna at the same time that they are moral constructions of the speakers themselves as observant parents and teacher.

This analysis suggests a way of beginning a membership categorization device analysis of interview talk. We have in this talk a topic which is 'Donna and her school achievement'. This topic is introduced explicitly, then elaborated through various proposed descriptors of Donna's activities. These descriptors can be seen as 'activities' in terms of the notion of 'category-bound activities' which imply membership in categories. In this case, the descriptors do not all get 'bound' to the category Donna, nor even 'attached' very firmly, since the speakers go on to delve further into Donna's activities. These descriptions of Donna, then, are candidate descriptions, which may or may not turn out to be 'attached' to Donna in the end. The descriptions variously state or imply Donna's membership in possible categories such as distracted student, keen student, and so on. The talk is a display of speakers' knowledge of how such statements and implications might be heard by the other: they use what might be termed social-structural and cultural knowledge. It is certainly at least inter-institutional knowledge that they draw on to do these descriptions of Donna. It is in this sense that the talk provides us with an insight into what they know. What they know is how to do descriptions and how to do accounts in precisely this inter-institutional setting. Remember that their descriptions of Donna are reflexively descriptions of themselves: 'they disappear off to their bedrooms', placed just where it was in the talk, is effectively a scenic description of a parent who could not possibly help with homework, not by his own choice.

In this interview, then, there is much more than the asking for or getting of information or perspectives about Donna and her work. The interview itself is a site for displaying the cultural knowledges that can be used to account for oneself as a competent parent or teacher. These cultural knowledges turn on the naming of or sometimes merely alluding to category, category-relations or category-bound activities.

What this recommends for the analysis of interview data is the identification of the category-knowledges at work in the talk of the participants. These need not be contained in elaborated turns, but can be sketched – spoken in shorthand – with the same effects. As seen above, a single utterance can call on and convey a great deal of cultural knowledge through its design and placement in talk.

The parent–teacher interviews from which this extract was drawn are thick with accounting on both sides. They are 'inter-views' in the original sense of 'entrevoir' – 'see each other' – perhaps more than are most research interviews. The talk is not symmetrical but questioning is done by both parties, and there is often a practical outcome in the form of resolutions or advice towards which the participants continue to talk. The interview is often conducted or organized, by at least two parties, and three where the student is present and both student and parent(s) are involved in raising topics or responding to them. In one interview with the teacher, father and student present, the interview became an extended speech by the father, with the teacher positioned as audience and the student mostly silent. These parent–teacher interviews have family resemblances to many health, clinical and other institutional encounters and consultations where problems concerning one of the parties to the talk (the client) are discussed. The approach to analysis represented here is interested in the pragmatics of the interactional setting. How people do things with words, and what they do with them, are the focus of interest.

Membership categorization work in research interviews

Another category of interviews are those which are conducted for research purposes only, which would not have taken place had the research not been undertaken. Unlike the interview described above, research interviews are designed and conducted in order that respondents will speak about some topic of interest to the researcher. In such interviews a more asymmetrical organization of talk is usually seen, with the interviewer asking questions or making probes, while the interviewee talks at more length to supply the information sought.

Such interviews are typically conducted under the traditional social science stand which asks respondents to reveal, describe, report on their interiors or on their external world as they know it. The respondent is positioned essentially as a witness of their own interiors and exterior circumstances who gives testimony to their experience of events. In this mode of doing social science, the sticky problems of bias (on the interviewer's part) and truth-telling (on the witness's part) come to the fore.

These problems were encountered in analyses of research interviews conducted with 'young adolescents' (Baker, 1984). These interviews were saturated with category-talk in the form of powerful assumptions about activities attaching to the category 'adolescent' (see Silverman, 1993: 90–114 for extracts and discussion). These assumptions were lodged right inside the interviewer's questions, for example 'when do you think you'll be an adult?' The resulting talk by the interviewees to questions such as this was rife with talk about responsibilities, the end of carefree living, and other cultural icons of conventional adulthood. The way out of this incestuous relation between interviewer categories and interviewee categories was to treat the interview data as displays of membership categorization work by interviewees as well as interviewer. What this resulted in was in the end not about 'adolescents' or these particular individuals at all, but about how the people positioned as 'adolescents' in the interview used membership categorization analysis in answering the questions. Especially in their use of category-bound or category-implied activities attached to each of the life stages that the interviewer had presented as given, the respondents produced accounts which displayed their cultural knowledge about *adult* constructions of adolescence. If we take this one step further, they displayed their knowledge of culture as framed up through the adult lens of life-stage folk psychology. This is the particular cultural knowledge they activated in order to take part in the interview, on the interviewer's terms. It is cultural knowledge in three senses: first, it is knowledge about the culture; secondly, it is not specific to individual respondents but reappears in different people's accounts; and thirdly, it demonstrated a 'successful' reading of the particular interview situation: how does this person want me to speak? Which of the many possible ways of characterizing my membership is in play here?

Letting go the presumption that (good) interviews give us some kind of privileged insight into what people really think, believe or do is the first step to seeing interview data as the production of situated 'accountings-for' whatever is the topic the interviewer presents. In Silverman's terms, '[b]y analysing how people talk to one another, one is directly gaining access to a cultural universe and its content of moral assumptions' (1993: 108).

Membership categorization and cultural logics

A very large proportion of research interviews would be conducted for the purpose of finding out some specific information, perspectives or beliefs. Such interviews are typically characterized by a very asymmetrical organization of talk, in which the interviewer asks the questions but talks much less than the respondent. In such circumstances, the material for analysis is in large part the talk done by the respondent to make available to the interviewer whatever information is asked for.

In a study undertaken of a school's 'welfare system', I was interested to capture the sense and logic behind the system. The system in question was an elaborate system of teacher-assigned 'tickets' to students for good or poor behaviour. Tickets were physically issued to students, either yellow ones for good achievement or behaviour, or white for misbehaviour of some kind.

My knowledge of the system came from visiting the school on several occasions and attending a staff meeting in which changes to the rules were being discussed at considerable length (see Baker, 1997, for an analysis of the staff meeting talk).

A talk was later arranged with the Chair of the welfare committee. I invited the Chair to give his view of the system, a 'perspective display'.

1 *I:* Um. What's what's your view (.) of of the system [is it

2 *C:* [It's great. It's um (1.0) the good kids it it kind of recognizes what their their efforts ( ) they get. The kids who it is hard for (1.0) who don't get the yellow (.) tickets um ( ) kids who just plod along and they usually don't, mighn't get a yellow ticket for because they haven't done anything extra great (.) but they still go up the system because, if they don't get a ticket, don't get a white ticket for ten weeks they go up anyway. Um (2.0) they're the ones that, you know, you try to encourage (staff), if you look for the plodders who are just plodding along but who are probably putting as much effort in as the (.) people who are getting, you know, the best marks in the class, we try and encourage that.

3 *I:* It is now possible for the plodders as you say to get up to plus four?

4 *C:* No. They can still only, still only get to (.) to negative er positive two. ((Sound of paper rustling. 4.0)) Let's see. (10.0) That's basically the state of the nation, that's, the issues. (1.5)

The Chair's view is reported directly and minimally in his first answer: 'It's great'. What follows is an account of how the system is working well, and how it isn't. This account turns on the early production of two contrasting categories of students: the 'good kids', whom the system rewards, and the 'plodders'. Thus a membership categorization device of the form [good kids, plodders] is produced, to which further categories could later be added. There are activities attached to the main contrast pair [good kids, plodders] as these categories are produced. The system works well for good kids who have their efforts recognized, but it does not work so well for plodders who 'just plod along' and never get a yellow ticket because they don't do anything 'extra great'. On the other hand, the Chair remarks, the plodders don't get white tickets either and are 'probably putting as much effort in' as the 'people . . . getting . . . the best marks in the class' – a category who may or may not be the same as the 'good kids' he began with.

The interviewer has heard a problem being stated, and asks whether the plodders can now get up to the top of the scale. This question is an acknowledgement of the problem and of the categorization device [good kids, plodders]. It perfectly matches the Chair's concern about how high up the system the plodders can get, and shows the interviewer entering into the problematic. Both interviewer and interviewee characterize the plodders as ambitious in this respect, and the system as autonomously constraining their ascent. This organization of empathy with the plodders confirms their reality in the social world of the school.

The design of the Chair's answer is as important as the contents of it. There may or may not really be good kids and plodders; these may or may not be the same descriptors used elsewhere in discussing the system. The production of the two categories is part of an account which elaborates what we could call a local morality. Looking at the beginning of the Chair's response, we hear that the system is at once 'great', it rewards the efforts of 'good kids', but is hard on 'all the other kids that just plod along'. From this it would appear that a minority of students is benefiting and a majority is not.

As the account proceeds there are some revisions made to the problem and a form of response to the problem is described. The Chair remarks that staff are encouraged to 'look for the plodders', although it is not clear what is supposed to be done differently for plodders except to recognize them. Here 'plodders' are produced as types of students any teacher could recognize. The category device now connects staff and students [good kids, plodders, teachers] – the cast of characters so far – and we can note that they are connected through attributions of empathy and care. Describing plodders now as 'probably putting in as much effort' effects a reorganization of 'plodder' character (earlier, twice, they 'just plod along'). Talk about the distribution of tickets (giving or not giving) seems to refer to an underlying organization of sympathy. Whether or not staff are in fact encouraged to 'look out for plodders', in this interview at least this response to the problem brings forward a version of a duty of care that teachers have towards plodders. This duty of care was not attached to these students when they were (earlier in the answer) 'just plodding along'. At that earlier point they were described as not getting tickets and this was represented as a natural consequence of their (plodding) behaviour, although it was acknowledged that the system is 'hard' for them.

Far from being merely a 'report' about the operation of the ticketing system, this account displays a version of the local practical reasoning that members could use to describe the system. The account is designed to convey the speaker's recognition of the categorizations, motivations and morality that attach to teachers' work with the system. That is, the social world of the school (the 'exterior' being talked about here) is assembled as a complex of categories and motivations which produce a moral order as well as a setting of practical reasoning and action.

Each move in the interview serves to add to and elaborate on the categories and activities proposed in the initial description. Such categories and activities are woven into a set of relationships and values, including justifications and evaluations, in the course of the telling. In effect a moral ordering of this aspect of the work of the school is being done while the Chair provides his views.

The interview continues:

5 *I:* Could I get a copy of that?
6 *C:* Yeah you can have that copy.
7 *I:* Thank you.
(1.0)
8 *C:* Um, we've also got a wel- welfare policy that [principal] a draft one that we put together. I'll give you a copy of that too.

9 *I:* Thanks.
(1.0)
10 *C:* Er, we chang- this is different to last year's (.) in that after three white tickets they get a warning letter (.) home, and then five white tickets they go on to negative one and then another three (1.0) they get to er another warning letter, and from here to there is only three so from (.) negative level two to negative level four (.) is going to be, very quick (.) progression if they continue on (.) on like this.
11 *I:* Mmm
12 (3.0)

In turn 10 the Chair offers the topic of how the system was changed from last year's. In this turn another category of student is implied through a description of descent to lower levels of the system. This additional category implied through talk about tickets and warning letters sent home is the poorly behaved student who did not appear in the initial description. Such students are ones who could, hypothetically, 'continue on like this' (getting more and more white tickets) and who would, in fact, have a quick progression to the bottom of the levels system. A downward descent is the *only* direction implied in the organization of the Chair's description, although presumably not everyone who gets to negative level two does in fact travel down to negative level four, and the system is elsewhere said to be designed to catch and stop such descents. The downward descent is accounted for by the possible activity attached to students in this category, 'if they continue on like this', which assigns the agency involved to the students persisting in their inappropriate behaviour. The Chair's concluding formulation 'so from two to four is going to be a very quick progression if they continue on like this' is first treated as a description and appears soon after to be heard *as a problem.*

The interviewer, as recipient of the Chair's description, first provides a weak agreement with the assessment made by the Chair. After a pause, the Chair starts to speak again, at which point the interviewer provides a stronger agreement, returning the upshot that progression downward will be quick:

11 *I:* Mmm
12 (3.0)
13 *C:* ([ )
14 *I:* [Quick, yeah.

The design of the Chair's next turn suggests that the interviewer's appreciation of the upshot has not been strong enough, that she is still hearing it as a description rather than as a problem.

14 *I:* [Quick, yeah.
15 *C:* So it's only an extra from negative level two which is ten white tickets, it's only another three and then negative level three (.) and (.) another another three after that and they can be (.) it's up to suspension sort of stage so it's um (2.0) that's where all the kind of er (.) er counsellor and er (2.0) all the work with the parents etcetera has to be done (.) fairly quickly. Because a kid can get to this stage in the matter of a week, you

know, well kids have. I- and (.) what we also look at is now is (.) that (.) three white tickets if it's within a (.) um (1.0) from one teacher we try to kind of counsel the teacher more than (2.0) so (.) so one teacher hasn't got that effect on one kid, so one one theoretically one teacher can put someone on negative level (.) two in a matter of a couple of weeks if they're having a run-in with them. So now we're trying to, looking at, if one teacher's giving out three or five white tickets we try to kind of (1.0) find out what the problem is with the teacher as well, more so than (1.0) just the student.

15 *I:* Do you cancel the ticket?

16 *C:* Well it can be yeah I (mean) we can't cancel them but we can cancel them we ask the teacher [. . . . . .]

In turn 14, the Chair embellishes the point he made earlier about quick descent, that it is 'only' another three tickets that drives the student down the levels. This was the change from last year's policy introduced in turn 10, and it is a change that he, and not the interviewer, has made accountable. In making it accountable in this way, he has underscored its status as a problem. Retrospectively, it seems the interviewer's earlier appreciation of what it means was not stated strongly enough, she was not grasping the moral point.

The Chair's turn in 14 can be seen as having three parts, beginning with the elaboration of the speed of descent and its consequentiality, that is, serious trouble for those students. At the centre of the turn is a central fact that holds the whole turn, and the whole logic, together: '*Because a kid can get to this stage in the matter of a week you know, well kids have*', of which more below. In the latter part of the turn, a new category of problem actor in the system is described: teachers who give out too many white tickets to one kid. This category is generated as another account of how a kid could get to this stage so fast. In contrast to the kid 'continuing on like this' in turn 10, now we have teachers having run-ins with kids and needing counselling themselves. The description of these teachers appears to be something of a trouble source for the Chair, given the pauses surrounding the delivery.

Within the third part of this turn, the Chair begins by describing the Committee's solution ('and (.) what we also look at is now is') before naming the problem ('three white tickets if it's within a (.) um (.) from one teacher'). What this does is to assign alertness to the Committee, another category of actors within the school, on whose behalf the Chair is accountably speaking. In the course of this elaboration, a different version of the kid on the decline has been produced, one who is at least in part possibly a victim of run-ins with teachers.

There are different possible upshots that could have been produced in relation to this turn. For example one could be that run-ins with kids should not happen and that this problem in teacher–student relations is important to discuss further. Another upshot could be that the run-ins are taken for granted but they should not skew the ticketing system. The second hearing is produced by the interviewer in her question 'do you cancel the ticket?' This formulation by the interviewer seems to ignore the Chair's description of the Committee's counselling work and attends to the Committee's moral action in relation to the practical outcome for the kid understood now as a member of the category 'victim of teacher run-in'.

It appears that the interviewer has by now heard the central problem as : '*Because a kid can get to this stage in the matter of a week, you know, well kids have*', and not as the problem of teachers and run-ins. The Chair's turn is designed around this central point, first leading up to it, and then moving sideways, producing an account for it. In producing the account for it, what is underscored is the moral issue of 'How can this happen in the matter of a week?', backed up by the adjacent point that it has actually happened. What the Chair is presenting here is an Extreme Case Formulation (Pomerantz, 1986) whose design and placement may achieve up to three things at this point in the interview. First it may be produced as a correction to the interviewer's failure to appreciate the matter of speeds of descent sufficiently. Second, it underscores the alertness of the Committee to the complexities of the system, the Committee's competence. Finally, it produces the kid/kids in question as the ultimate subjects of the Committee's duty of care.

What we see here is the conversational product of the identity, 'Chair of the Welfare Committee', which is the speaking identity he was asked to assume. The interviewer's uptakes and their absences appear to have been oriented to by the Chair in his work of moral description and accounting. By examining the membership categorization and other resources the Chair draws on in his accounts, the cultural particulars he produces for this listener, and by noticing how the interviewer's hearing of the talk itself evidences membership categorization work, we are able to see how deeply interactional this interview is, despite apparently minimal input from the interviewer.

Conclusion: Assembling possible worlds

In the preceding sections of this chapter I have demonstrated some procedures for beginning a membership categorization device analysis of interview talk. Essentially the search is for how *participants in the interview* make use of the resources of membership categorization. The first step is to locate the central categories (of people, or places, or things) that underpin the talk, including any standard relational pairs such as parents–teacher or contrast pairs such as plodders and good kids. These categories are sometimes named and sometimes implied through the 'activities' that are attached to them. A second step is to work through the activities associated with each of the categories in order to fill out the attributions that are made to each of the categories. The attributions that are hinted at are as important as any stated in so many words: hinted-at categories or activities or connections between them indicate the subtlety and delicacy of much implicit membership categorization work. A third step is to look at the categories + attributions connections that members produce (connections between 'cultural particulars'), to find the courses of social action that are implied: descriptions of how categories of actors do, could or should behave.

As in the examples I have presented here, when speakers 'do describing', they assemble a social world in which their categories have a central place. These categories are in a sense the speakers' 'puppets', which they can dress up in different ways and make behave in various ways (category-associated activities). These are powerful statements about *what could be the case*, how the social order *might be arranged*, whether or not it really is. The artful production of plausible versions using recognizable membership categorization devices is a profoundly important form of cultural competence. What we hear and attend to in these interview accounts are members' methods for putting together a world that is recognizably familiar, orderly and moral.

References

Baker, C.D. (1984) 'The search for adultness: Membership work in adolescent–adult talk', *Human Studies*, 7: 301–23.

Baker, C.D. (1997) 'Ticketing rules: Categorization and moral ordering in a school staff meeting', in S. Hester and P. Eglin (eds), *Culture in Action: Studies in Membership Categorization Analysis*. Lanham, MD: University Press of America. pp. 79–102.

Baker, C.D. and Keogh, J. (1995) 'Accounting for achievement in parent–teacher interviews', *Human Studies*, 18 (2): 263–300.

Jayyusi, L. (1984) *Categorization and the Moral Order*. London: Routledge and Kegan Paul.

Jayyusi, L. (1991) 'Values and moral judgement: Communicative praxis as moral order', in G. Button (ed.), *Ethnomethodology and the Human Sciences*. Cambridge: Cambridge University Press. pp. 227–51.

Maynard, D. (1991) 'The perspective-display series and the delivery of diagnostic news', in D. Boden and D.H. Zimmerman (eds), *Talk and Social Structure: Studies in Ethnomethodology and Conversation Analysis*. Cambridge: Polity. pp. 164–92.

Pomerantz, A. (1986) 'Extreme case formulations: A way of legitimizing claims', *Human Studies*, 9 (2/3): 219–99.

Sacks, H. (1992) *Lectures on Conversation*, Vols I and II, ed. G. Jefferson. Oxford: Blackwell.

Schegloff, E.A. (1988) 'Description in the social sciences I: Talk-in-interaction', *IpRA Papers in Pragmatics*, 2 (1/2): 1–24.

Silverman, D. (1993) *Interpreting Qualitative Data: Methods for Analysing Talk, Text and Interaction*. London: Sage.

PART V AUDIO AND VIDEO

10 Discourse Analysis as a Way of Analysing Naturally Occurring Talk

Jonathan Potter

This chapter will focus on the way discourse analysis can be used to study naturally occurring talk. This may seem to be a straightforward task, and in the course of this chapter I will do my best to make it so. Yet I also want to explore some complexities that may seem like diversions, but which, if they do not get explored, are likely to remain as traps for analysts to get caught in at later times.

So what complexities are there here? First, and most immediately, there are a whole range of things that have been called discourse analysis. Secondly, the kind of discourse analysis I will be describing is a broad approach to social life which combines meta-theoretical assumptions, theoretical ideas, analytic orientations and bodies of work. Thirdly, it is quite misleading to think of discourse analysis as a method in the way that social psychologists and many sociologists would conceive of that term. Fourthly, the status of naturally occurring talk as a topic is itself far from unproblematic.

In the first part of the chapter I will discuss these four issues as a way of introducing some of the central features of a discourse analytic perspective. I will then move on in the second half of the chapter to discuss an extended example which is intended to illustrate something of the analytic mentality involved in doing discourse analysis.

Issues in the discourse analysis of naturally occurring talk

Stories of discourse

What is discourse analysis? This is a tricky question and its answers are changing rather quickly. One way of thinking about some of the species of discourse analysis is to consider them as having evolved in the different disciplinary environments of linguistics, cognitive psychology, sociolinguistics and poststructuralism.

In the past, the name 'discourse analysis' has been applied to a range of rather different approaches to social science. In linguistics it has been applied to work on the way sentences or utterances cohere into discourse.

For example, it has examined the way words such as 'however' and 'but' operate, along with different kinds of references that occur between sentences. One of the aims of this work was to duplicate on a wider canvas the success of linguistic analyses on units such as sentences (Brown and Yule, 1983). In cognitive psychology the focus has been on the way mental scripts and schemata are used to make sense of narrative. Do people work with story grammars to understand narratives in the way they use sentence grammars to understand sentences (Van Dijk and Kintch, 1983)? Again, the hope was to duplicate some of the (perceived) success of work on grammar in the psychological domain.

Another distinctive style of discourse analysis developed in linguistics through work on classroom interaction. Sinclair and Coulthard (1975) attempted to provide a systematic model to describe typical interaction patterns in teaching based around 'initiation–response–feedback' structures. For example,

Teacher:	What is keeping the mercury up?	(*Initiation*)
Pupil:	The vacuum sucking.	(*Response*)
Teacher:	Not really, Peter. Susan?	(*Feedback*)

The goal here was to produce a model that would make sense of discourse structure in a whole range of different settings (Coulthard and Montgomery, 1981).

In poststructuralism and literary theory a very different tradition developed, sometimes called continental discourse analysis to differentiate it from its rather more strait-laced Anglo-Saxon counterparts. This is most associated with Michel Foucault, and is less concerned with discourse in terms of specific interaction as with how a discourse, or a set of 'statements', comes to constitute objects and subjects. For example, medical discourse may come to constitute particular objects as distinct and factual ('vapours', 'HIV+') and the doctor as a particular individual with knowledge and authority. (For an accessible discussion of Foucault's notion of discourse, see McHoul and Grace, 1993.)

There are, then, at least these four somewhat independent forms of discourse analysis with different disciplinary homes. To make things even more complicated, discourse analysis is sometimes used as an inclusive label for some or all of these approaches combined with speech act work, Gricean pragmatics, linguistic presupposition, critical linguistics and conversation analysis (Stubbs, 1983; Van Dijk, 1985). The rough logic of inclusion here is an emphasis on language function and/or a concern with language outside of the restricted categories of grammar, phonetics and phonemics.

The rest of this chapter will concentrate on yet another variant of discourse analysis. This developed initially in the field of sociology and more recently in social psychology and communications (Billig, 1992; Edwards and Potter, 1992; Gilbert and Mulkay, 1984; Potter and Wetherell, 1987). This is distinctive in various ways. Discourse analysts in this tradition reject the cognitivism of the work in linguistics and cognitive psychology because it makes it very difficult to properly address the way discourse is oriented to action (Edwards, 1997). They treat the interactional analysis of Sinclair and Coulthard (1975) as overly based on rather mechanistic linguistic analysis and inattentive to the complex social practices that take place in classrooms and similar locations. They have expressed similar doubts about Foucauldian approaches to discourse, while being impressed by, and influenced by, some of their insights.

Discourse analysis

Discourse analysis of this latter kind (henceforth DA) is characterized by a meta-theoretical emphasis on anti-realism and constructionism. That is, DA emphasizes the way versions of the world, of society, events and inner psychological worlds are produced in discourse. On the one hand, this leads to a concern with participants' constructions and how they are accomplished and undermined; and, on the other, it leads to a recognition of the constructed and contingent nature of researchers' own versions of the world. Indeed, it treats realism, whether developed by participants or researchers, as a rhetorical production that can itself be decomposed and studied (Edwards et al., 1995; Gergen, 1994; Potter, 1992).

As a complement to this, there is an emphasis on reflexivity: for example, what are the implications from the conclusions of discourse analytic research for the practice of DA and for its literary forms, including this very text? Note the way I have introduced this chapter using the conventional homogenizing categorizations of research specialities and the familiar rhetoric of progress. Reflexivity encourages us to consider the way a text such as this is a version, selectively working up coherence and incoherence, telling historical stories, presenting and, indeed, constituting an objective, out-there reality (Ashmore, 1989; Atkinson, 1990; Potter, 1996a).

DA has an analytic commitment to studying discourse as *texts and talk in social practices*. That is, the focus is not on language as an abstract entity such as a lexicon and set of grammatical rules (in linguistics), a system of differences (in structuralism), a set of rules for transforming statements (in Foucauldian genealogies). Instead, it is the medium for interaction; analysis of discourse becomes, then, analysis of what people do. One theme that is particularly emphasized here is the rhetorical or argumentative organization of talk and texts; claims and versions are constructed to undermine alternatives (Billig, 1987, 1991).

This conception of the focus of DA may make it seem to be pitched at a level of analysis somewhere between studies of individual psychology and studies of structural sociology. On this reading it would be an approach falling within the traditional remit of social psychology or micro-sociology. However, these kinds of distinctions have been made problematic by DA. On the one hand, DA has eaten away at traditional psychological notions by reformulating them in discursive terms. For example, a classic psychological notion such as a cognitive script can be reworked by considering the sorts of business that people do by 'script formulating' descriptions of their own or others' behaviour (Edwards, 1994). The suggestion is that there is a whole field of discursive psychology which is amenable to systematic study and has hardly been touched in mainstream psychology (Edwards, 1997; Edwards and Potter, 1992).

On the other hand, the micro–macro distinction has also been made problematic. It has been blurred by two kinds of work. First, there are now a range of conversation analytic studies which are concerned with the way in which the institutionally specific properties of a setting such as a news interview, a doctor–patient consultation or an award ceremony are constituted in talk rather than being structurally determined in any simple way (Boden and Zimmerman, 1991; Drew and Heritage, 1992). For example, pedagogic interaction certainly happens in school classrooms, and yet much of what happens in classrooms is not pedagogic (playing around, chatting) while much recognizably pedagogic interaction ('test' questions, encouraging discovery) happens over family breakfast tables or with a partner in front of the television. Secondly, there is work on the way people produce stories of social organization in their talk. For example, Wetherell and Potter (1992) studied the way particular constructions of social groups, processes of conflict and influence, histories, and so on, were drawn on as practical resources for blaming minority groups for their own disadvantaged social position. That is, social structure becomes part of interaction as it is worked up, invoked and reworked (Potter, 1996a).

Typical discourse analytic studies focus on transcripts of talk from everyday or institutional settings, on transcripts of open-ended interviews, or on documents of some kind. Sometimes these different materials are combined together in the same study. DA is overwhelmingly qualitative, although the principled argument is not against quantification *per se*, but against the way counting and coding often obscures the activities being done with talk and text (see Heritage, Chapter 11 this volume; Potter and Wetherell, 1987; Schegloff, 1993).

Discourse analysis and method

In much traditional social research, method is understood as something that can be codified with specific guidelines which, if not guaranteeing good research, are a necessary condition for its conduct. Indeed, it is often the case that the research conclusions are justified by reference to the correct and complete following of procedures such as operationalizing variables, getting high levels of inter-rater reliability for codings, and so on. Discourse analysis is not like this. The analytic procedure used to arrive at claims is often quite different from the way those claims are justified.

A large part of doing discourse analysis is a craft skill, more like bike riding or chicken sexing than following the recipe for a mild chicken rogan josh. Conversation analysts sometimes talk of developing an *analytic mentality*, which captures what is involved rather nicely (Psathas, 1990). This makes it hard to describe and learn. But that does not mean that the claims are necessarily hard to evaluate – if you cannot easily say precisely how someone has learned to ride a bike, you do not have so much difficulty saying whether they have fallen off or not. Likewise, there are a range of ways in which the adequacy of discourse analytic studies can be evaluated, including a focus on deviant cases, checking that participants' themselves orient to claimed phenomena, coherence with other discourse analytic studies, and, most importantly, the evaluation that readers themselves can make when they are presented with a transcript along side of its analytic interpretations (Potter, 1996b).

In traditional stories of method in social research you have a question and then you search for a method to answer that question. For example, you may be interested in the 'factors' that lead to condom use in sexual encounters, and ponder whether to use an experiment with vignettes, some open-ended interviews, or DA to check them out. DA is not like that. Some questions are simply not coherent from a discourse analytic perspective. For example, the kinds of assumptions about factors and outcomes that underpin a lot of thinking in traditional social psychology and survey research do not mesh with its rhetorical and normative logic. Rather than conceiving of a world of discrete variables with discrete effects, in DA there are constructions and versions that may be adopted, responded to or undermined. Thus a categorization, say, may be undermined by a particularization; no upshot is guaranteed (Billig, 1991). Norms are *oriented to*; that is, they are not templates for action but provide a way of interpreting deviations. The absence of a return greeting does not disconfirm a regularity; rather it is the basis for inference: the recipient is rude, sad or deaf perhaps (Heritage, 1988).

So what kinds of questions are coherent within DA? Given the general focus is on texts and talk as social practices, there has been a dual focus on the practices themselves and on the resources that are drawn on in those practices. Take gender inequalities for example. Studies have considered both the way in which such inequalities are constructed, made factual and justified in talk, and the resources ('interpretive repertoires', identities, category systems) that are used to manufacture coherent and persuasive justifications that work to sustain those inequalities (Gill, 1993; Marshall and Wetherell, 1989; Wetherell et al., 1987).

Naturally occurring talk as topic

I am going to focus here on DA specifically as applied to naturally occurring talk. However, it is important to note that this topic is not as simple as it might appear. Naturally occurring talk can be relatively straightforwardly defined as spoken language produced entirely independently of the actions of the researcher, whether it is everyday conversation over the telephone, the records of a company board meeting, or the interaction between doctor and patient in a surgery. It is natural in the specific sense that it is not 'got up' by the researcher using an interview schedule, a questionnaire, an experimental protocol or some such social research technology.

Although this is useful in highlighting how far traditional researchers are implicated in the production of 'data', it also implies a hierarchy moving from somewhat ephemeral interaction in the laboratory to more real interaction happening naturally out in the world. A better conceptualization treats naturally occurring talk not as a straightforward discovered object, but as a theoretical and analytic stance on conversational interaction. This may seem rather abstruse but it has two advantages. On the one hand, it differentiates DA from other work on records of interaction such as content analysis which involves the kinds of coding and counting that obscures the subtly contexted nature of conversational interaction as well as the sorts of turn by turn displays of understanding and repair that have been effectively used in conversation analysis (Psathas, 1995). On the other hand, it provides a different perspective on research procedures such as interviews. Instead of treating these as a machinery for harvesting data from respondents, they can be viewed as an arena for interaction in its own right; that is natural-interaction-in-interview. What I am suggesting, then, is that it is properly the analytic and theoretical stance that constitutes its object as naturally occurring talk, and we should be wary of accepting too readily assumptions about what kinds of talk are natural and what are not.

This point is particularly important for showing what is distinctive about the considerable body of discourse analytic work which has used open-ended interviews. When interviews are treated as a machinery for harvesting psychologically and linguistically interesting responses, the research is inevitably focused on those elements of interviews contributed by the participant rather than those from the researcher. However, it is possible to conceptualize interviews as arenas for interaction between two or more parties. That is, we can treat them as a form of natural conversational interaction, by analysing them the same way that we might a telephone conversation between friends or the cross-examination in a courtroom. Widdicombe and Wooffitt (1995) provide one of the most thoroughgoing attempts to use interviews in this way, treating materials originally collected for a study of social identity as examples of unfolding conversational interaction where the sense of social categories is refined and reworked. Furthermore, once this perspective on interviews is adopted, the standard methodology textbook injunctions to be as neutral and uninvolved as possible become highly problematic. It only makes sense as part of the fiction that the researcher can somehow disappear from the interaction if only they can make themselves passive enough – in DA it has been productive to be actively engaged and even argumentative during interviews (Wetherell and Potter, 1992).

Having resisted a too simple distinction between natural and artificial talk I do not want to diminish the difficulties of working with interview talk. It is contrived; it is subject to powerful expectations about social science research fielded by participants; and there are particular difficulties in extrapolating from interview talk to activities in other settings. Discourse analysts are increasingly turning away from interviews to focus on materials less affected by the formulations and assumptions of the researcher.

In this discussion I have addressed a number of background issues for discourse analytic research. There are a range of other concerns to do with transcription, interview conduct, coding, forms of validation, writing up discourse research that there is no space to discuss. (For a more detailed discussion of these, see Coyle, 1995; Gill, 1996; Potter, 1996b; Potter and Wetherell, 1987, 1994, 1995; Wetherell and Potter, 1992; Widdicombe and Wooffitt, 1995; Wooffitt, 1990, 1993.) For the rest of this chapter I will focus on a particular example, with the aim of highlighting something of the analytic mentality involved in doing discourse analytic research on talk. In addition, I hope to illustrate some of the recurring themes in such work as well as exploring some of the similarities and differences between conversation and discourse analysis.

Discourse analysis of naturally occurring talk

There are a wide range of different ways of analysing discourse. It is useful, for example, to make a broad distinction between a focus on the kinds of resources drawn on in discourse and the practices in which those resources are used. The emphasis here will be on the latter kind of study. What I hope to do is highlight some of the concerns that analysis works with, and one of the best ways of doing this is to work with some specific materials. I will try to avoid the common goal in writing about method which is to provide justifications to other academics rather than assist in the conduct of analysis itself.

Princess Diana and 'I dunno'

I have chosen to start with a piece of talk that is interesting, and probably familiar, at least in its broad outline, to many readers. It comes from a BBC television interview; the interviewer is Martin Bashir and the interviewee is Princess Diana.

(1) *Bashir:* The Queen described nineteen ninety two as
her (.) annus horribilis, .hh and it was in that year that
Andrew Morton's book about you was published.
Princess: Um hm. ((nods))
Bashir: .hh Did you ↑ever (.) meet Andrew Morton or
personally (.) help him with the book?

Princess: In never- I never met him, no.
(1.0)
Bashir: Did you ever (.) personally assist him with
the writing of his book.
(0.8)
Princess: A lot of people .hhh ((clears throat))
saw the distress that my life was in. (.)
And they felt (.) felt it was a supportive thing
to help (0.2) in the way that they did.
Bashir: Did you (.) allow your ↑friends, >your close friends,<
to speak to Andrew °Morton°?
Princess: Yes I did. Y[es, I did
Bashir: [°Why°?
Princess: I was (.) at the end of my tether (.)
I was (.) desperate (.)
>I think I was so fed up with being< (.)
seen as someone who was a ba:sket case (.)
because I am a very strong person (.)
and I know (.) that causes complications, (.)
in the system (.) that I live in.
(1.0) ((smiles and purses lips))
Bashir: How would a book change that.
→ *Princess:* I ↑dunno. ((raises eyebrows, looks away))
Maybe people have a better understanding (.)
maybe there's a lot of women out there
who suffer (.) on the same level
but in a different environment (.)
who are unable to: (.) stand up for themselves (.)
because (.) their self-esteem is (.) cut into two.
→ I dunno ((shakes head))
Bashir: .hh What effect do you think the book had on (.)
your husband and the Royal Family?
Princess: I think they were (.) shocked,
and horrified,
and very disappointed.
(0.8)
Bashir: Can you understand why?
Princess: (Well) I think Mr Dimbleby's book (0.2)
was a shock to a lot of people,
and disappointment as well.
(*Panorama*, BBC1, 20 November 1995 – see Appendix for transcript conventions)

The first thing to note here is that even a short sequence of interaction of this kind is enormously rich, and could be the stimulus for a very wide range of different discourse analytic studies. I am going to focus principally on just the two lines that have been arrowed; the two 'I dunno's'. Why these? There are three reasons, all of which illustrate different facets of doing work of this kind.

First, as will become increasingly clear, these fragments of talk relate to broader and established analytic concerns with fact construction and the role of descriptions in interaction. The point, then, is that although I have not come to this material with a pre-set hypothesis of the kind that a social psychologist might have when designing an experiment, my way into it is related to a wide range of prior interests, knowledge and concerns. However, there is nothing particularly special about the topic of fact construction; a range of different established interests could be bought to bear on this same material.

Secondly, these fragments are easily treated as the trivial details of interaction. If we were to make a précis of the interaction we would probably not draw attention to them. On the video they sound almost throwaway. However, one of the features of talk that has been strongly emphasized by Harvey Sacks (1992) and other conversation analysts is that what seem to be its details are fundamental. Social scientists often treat talk as a conduit for information between speakers: there is a message and it is passed from one person to another. When we use this picture it is easy to imagine that what is important is some basic package of information, and then there is a lot of rather unimportant noise added to the signal: hesitations, pauses, overlaps, choice of specific words, and so on. For conversation analysts this view is fundamentally misguided. Rather than treating these features of talk as simply a blurred edge on the pure message, these features are treated as determining precisely what action is being performed as well as providing a rich analytic resource for understanding what that activity is.

It is for this reason that talk is carefully transcribed as it is delivered rather than being rendered into a conventional 'playscript' that is common in some kinds of qualitative work. Note that it is sometimes complained that such transcription is unnecessary, unhelpful or even – sin of sins – positivistic! However, it is important to remember that the potential playscript that often passes for transcript is itself highly conventionalized and buys into a whole set of more or less implicit assumptions about interaction.

The third reason for focusing on 'I dunno' is that it provides a neat way of contrasting DA with a cognitive psychological approach to talk. What might a cognitive psychologist make of 'I dunno's'? There are all sorts of possibilities, but one approach that might be taken is to treat such utterances as 'uncertainty tokens'; that is, words or expressions that people use to report states of uncertainty. This would be in line with the general cognitive psychological approach of relating language use to individuals' cognitive processes and representations (Edwards, 1997). Considering 'I dunno's' therefore has the virtue of allowing us to compare and contrast a cognitive and discursive approach to talk.

One of the notable features of discourse analytic work is that the best way into some materials like this may be to consider *other* materials or *other* sorts of findings. At its most basic, a good feel for some of the standard features of everyday and institutional talk is particularly useful for producing high-quality analyses (Nofsinger, 1991, provides a basic introduction and overview). In this case, I suggest that one of the ways into Princess Diana's 'I dunno's' is to consider the way issues of stake and interest have been conceptualized in discursive psychology.

Stake as a participants' concern

Work in the ethnomethodological and conversation analytic tradition has long highlighted the importance of accountability as a general concern. More recently, discourse analysts dealing with psychological issues – discursive psychologists – have emphasized the significance that participants place on issues of stake and interest (Edwards and Potter, 1992). People treat each other as entities with desires, motives, institutional allegiances and so on, as having a stake in their actions. Referencing stake is one principal way of discounting the significance of an action or reworking its nature. For example, a blaming can be discounted as merely a product of spite; an offer may be discounted as an attempt to influence.

Here is a explicit and familiar example where the speaker invokes an interest to undercut a (reported) claim. The extract is from a current affairs programme in which the author Salman Rushdie is being interviewed by David Frost. Frost is asking about the fatwah – the religious death sentence on Rushdie.

(2) *Frost:* And how could they cancel it now? Can they cancel it – they say they can't.
→ *Rushdie:* Yeah, but you know, they would, wouldn't they, as somebody once said. The thing is, without going into the kind of arcana of theology, there is no technical problem. The problem is not technical. The problem is that they don't want to.
(Public Broadcasting Service, 26 November 1993, transcription by newscaster)

Rushdie's response to the claim that the fatwah cannot be cancelled is to discount the claim as obviously motivated. The familiar phrase 'they would, wouldn't they' treats the Iranians' claim as something to be expected: it is the sort of thing that people with that background, those interests, that set of attitudes *would* say; and it formulates that predictability as shared knowledge. This extract illustrates the potential for invoking stake and interest to discount claims.

Both discourse and conversation analysts have stressed that where some difficulty or issue is widespread there are likely to be some well-developed procedures for dealing with it. For example, given the established procedures that exist for managing turn-taking we would expect there to be some procedures to exist for terminating conversations, and this is what is found (Levinson, 1983; Schegloff and Sacks, 1973). Or, to take a more discourse analytic example, given that scientists tend to keep separate the inconsistent repertoires of terms they use for justifying their own claims and undermining those of opponents, we would expect that some devices would be developed for dealing with situations where those repertoires come together; and this is what is found (Gilbert and Mulkay, 1984). Following this logic, we might expect to find procedures that people use to resist the kind of discounting seen in Extract 2.

All kinds of possibilities exist. Here is a candidate discursive technique for undermining discounting. It was not the product of a systematic search; rather I came across it while reading the newspaper and thinking about this issue. It comes from an article in the *Guardian* newspaper headlined 'Psychiatrist Reveals the Agony and the Lunacy of Great Artists'.

(3) The stereotype of the tortured genius suffering for his art and losing his mind in a sea of depression, sexual problems and drink turns out to be largely true, a psychiatrist says today.

While scientists, philosophers and politicians can all suffer from the odd personality defect, for real mental instability you need to look at writers and painters, says Felix Post.

→ Dr Post was initially sceptical, but having looked at the lives of nearly 300 famous men he believes exceptional creativity and psychiatric problems are intertwined. In some way, mental ill health may fuel some forms of creativity, he concludes. (*Guardian*, 30 June 1994)

The feature of the article that struck me was: 'Dr Post was initially sceptical . . .' Following the idea that all features of talk and texts are potentially there to do some kind of business, we can ask why this particular feature is there. What it seems to do is counter the potential criticism that Dr Post is perpetrating stereotypes about madness and creativity. His initial scepticism encourages us to treat his conclusions as factual because they are counter to his original interests.

I have suggested that such features of discourse can be understood by a medical analogy. People can avoid catching a disease such as tuberculosis by being inoculated against it. Perhaps in the same way conversationalists and writers can limit the ease with which their talk and texts can be undermined by doing a *stake inoculation* (Potter, 1996a). Just as you have a jab to prevent the disease, perhaps you can inject a piece of discourse to prevent undermining.

Let me now stand back and highlight two features of the kind of thinking I am using here, two features of the analytic mentality I am working with. First, in common with conversation analysis, discourse analysts are concerned to use evidence from the materials as far as possible rather than basing interpretations on their own prior assumptions about people, society or whatever. In this case, note that the idea that there is a stereotype about madness and creativity is not my own, it is introduced in the text itself. Moreover, the analysis does not depend on this stereotype actually existing, merely that it is invoked as an issue in this text. Note that this does not mean that the analyst expects to be able to free themselves of all their preconceptions, rather it is that analysis is, to an important extent, an interrogation of those expectations (Potter, 1988).

Secondly, note the way I have moved in this analysis between conversational and textual material. Discourse analysts have been much more willing than conversation analysts to combine such materials and have tried to avoid making *a priori* assumptions about differences between the two.

Both talk and texts are treated as oriented to action; *both* orient to issues of stake and may be inoculated against discounting.

'I dunno' as a stake inoculation

So far, then, I have emphasized some background considerations that might help us understand what the 'I dunno' in Extract 1 is doing. One helpful way to continue the analysis is to collect some more examples of a similar kind. More formally, we might think of this as building a corpus for study or even coding of a set of data. Whatever we call it, the goal is to help the analyst see patterns and to highlight different properties of particular constructions. Although some of the initial procedures are superficially similar, the goal is not the content analytic one of providing counts of occurrences of particular kinds of talk within categories.

A brief search for 'I don't know's' through a set of materials taken from relationship counselling sessions provided Extract 4. The extract comes from the start of a long story in which the speaker, Jimmy, is describing a difficult evening in a pub with his wife, Connie. As well as Connie and Jimmy there is a counsellor present. One of the themes in the session is a series of complaints by Jimmy that Connie flirts with other men. At the same time Connie has made a number of suggestions that he is pathologically jealous and prone to seeing harmless sociability as sexual suggestion (for more detail see Edwards, 1995).

(4) *Jimmy:* This ↑one particular night, (0.2)
anyway (0.2) there was uh: (1.2) I didn't-
Connie had made arrangements to ↑meet people.
(1.8)
And I didn't want to. (0.6)
It wasn't any other thing.
(1.6)
A:nd (0.8) we sat in the pub and
we (.) started to discuss =
= >we had a little bit of a row.< (2.0)
in the pub. (0.6)
And arguing about the time. (0.8)
U:m (.) whe:n these people came in. (.)
>It was:< (.) John and Caroline. (1.0)
And then they had- (.)
this other fella Dave.
°With them as well.°
[6 lines omitted]
they all came in the pub anyway. (1.0)
Well (.) Connie sat beside (0.6) Caroline.
And I sat (further back).
So you was (.) you was split between us.
They sat in- on the other side.
(1.0)
[16 lines omitted]
And uh:: (1.0)

1→ Connie had a short skirt on
2→ I don't know. (1.0)
And I knew this- (0.6)
uh ah- maybe I had met him. (1.0) Ye:h. (.)
I musta met Da:ve before. (0.8)
But I'd heard he was a bit of a la:d ( ).
He didn't care: (1.0) who he (0.2) chatted up or (.)
who was in Ireland (.) y'know
those were (unavailable) to chat up with.
(1.0)
So Connie stood up (0.8)
pulled her skirt right up her side (0.6)
and she was looking straight at Da:ve (.)
>°like that°< (0.6)
(DE–JF:C2:S1:10–11)

Let us start by considering Jimmy's description of Connie's skirt length (arrow 1). The description is an especially delicate one, where Jimmy's stake in it is likely to be a particular concern. The problem for Jimmy is that the description could be turned round and used as evidence that he is *precisely* the sort of pathologically jealous guy who can remember every detail of his partner's skirt length. That is, his description might generate problems for him as much as for Connie.

It is immediately after the description of the skirt length that Jimmy produces the 'I don't know' (arrow 2). What might this be doing here? We could treat it as a straightforward report of uncertainty about this feature of the narrative. This would be in line with the cognitive psychological account of such utterances as 'uncertainty markers'. However, another way of interpreting it might consider how the 'I don't know' operates in the interaction. Could a display of uncertainty just at this point head off the potential counter (which has already been raised at length, but in general terms, earlier in the session) that Jimmy was jealously inspecting Connie's clothing, that he was already concerned about it even before the evening was under way? This latter interpretation is consistent with the detail of the sequence. Jimmy provides the description of Connie's skirt length which is part of the picture of *her* flirtatious behaviour, which, in turn, makes *his* own strong reaction more accountable. At the same time the expression of uncertainty works against the idea that *he* is saying this, noticing this, because *he* is pathologically jealous.

Are there any other ways in which we can help adjudicate between different interpretations of 'I don't know'? One approach that discourse analysts have found particularly fruitful has been to look for variability between different versions. Variability is to be expected where people are constructing their talk in different ways to perform different actions – variability in versions can be an important clue to understanding the actions being done. In this case, for example, we can search the materials for other references to Connie's skirt length. If we do that we find the following exchange on the very next page of transcript.

(5) *Connie:* My skirt probably went up to about there. ((gestures with hand on thigh))
Jimmy: ((a sharp intake of breath))
Connie: Maybe a bit shorter. It was done for no- I never looked at that particular bloke when I did it it was my friend commented Oh you're showing o:ff a lot o' leg tonight.
(DE–JF:C2:S1:11)

What is notable is this extract is that Jimmy does not seem to be in any doubt about the precise length of Connie's skirt. I take his sharp, deliberately audible, inbreath as a display of disagreement with Connie's claim about her skirt length; and this is certainly how Connie interprets his breath, for it occasions a modification to the claim. The point, then, is that there is no evidence of Jimmy's cloudy memory – no 'I dunnoness' – here; precision in skirt length now seems to be the order of the day. I suggest that variability of this kind supports the account I have been offering in terms of stake inoculation and is rather hard to fit with a plain vanilla cognitive account where the speaker is merely reporting lack of certainty about their claim.

Let us return now to Martin Bashir's interview with Princess Diana. Can we offer an interpretation of the 'I dunno's' in this passage of talk on the basis of the general considerations about management of stake and interest and the specific examples we have considered so far? Can we see these 'I dunno's' as stake inoculations?

The first question to ask is: do the participants orient to a potential issue of stake? It is not hard to find such an issue. A claim widely made in newspaper reports was that the Princess used Andrew Morton's book as a device to get back at Prince Charles, her husband. This issue was raised again in much of the newspaper coverage of the royal interview, and it is alluded to elsewhere in the interview itself. More directly, the very fact that Bashir chooses to focus upon a number of questions on her motives for cooperating with Andrew Morton, and the nature of that cooperation, shows this to be considered to be consequential.

The second question to ask is: can 'I dunno' potentially act as a stake inoculation? I suggest that the placement of the 'I dunno's' in the Princess's talk is precisely where the issue of motive is most acute. For the Princess to accept that the book was part of a planned and strategic campaign to present a particular view of the royal marriage and her role in it would be potentially culpable. The 'I dunno's' present her as not sure of the role of the book, perhaps thinking it fully over for the first time. This is combined with the answer that displays her motive as not a selfish or small-minded one, but one of (rather vaguely) promoting sisterly solidarity. The vagueness here is rather neatly in tune with both the 'on the hoof' quality presented by the 'I dunno's'; and the non-verbal finessing of the phrase with a look into the distance as though searching for the answer (in the first instance), and then shaking her head as though it is a difficult question which she did not have a ready or clear answer for (in the second instance).

This is by no means a definitive account of the role of 'I dunno' in Extract 1. However, what I have tried to do is show some of the procedures that can help build an interpretation of a piece of discourse, and the mentality that goes with such analysis. Let me list some of these features.

Themes in the analysis of discourse

This chapter has attempted to overview some of the issues that arise when analysing discourse. Developing skills in such analysis is best characterized as developing a particular mentality rather than following a preformed recipe. DA is more inductive than hypothetico-deductive; generally work starts with a setting or particular discursive phenomenon rather than a preformulated hypothesis. The focus is on texts and talk as social practices in their own right. Part of DA may involve coding a set of materials, but this is an analytic preliminary used to make the quantity of materials more manageable rather than a procedure that performs the analysis itself. There is nothing sacred about such codings and extracts are often freely excluded and included in the course of some research.

DA follows the conversation analytic assumption that any order of detail in talk and text is potentially consequential for interaction, and for that reason high-quality transcripts are used in conjunction with tape recordings. In addition, discourse analytic research generally avoids trading on analysts' prior assumptions about what might be called ethnographic particulars (e.g. participants' status, the nature of the context, the goals of the participants), preferring to see these as things that are worked up, attended to and made relevant in interaction rather than being external determinants.

DA does not use talk and texts as a pathway to underlying cognitions; indeed, DA resolutely steers clear of cognitive reduction, instead treating purportedly cognitive phenomena as parts of social practices. Such discursive psychology has focused on the way participants invoke stake and interest to understand and undercut accounts, and how such undercutting may be resisted by performing actions via accounts that are constructed as factual.

In this chapter I attempted to illustrate these themes by way of a discussion of 'I dunno' and 'I don't know'. I have considered only a small number of examples. However, I hope that the insights might be more general. Let me end with an extract from the US comedy sitcom *Friends*. Even with my minimal, cleaned-up transcription I think we can start to see the way the humour in the sequence depends on the sorts of features of 'I don't know' discussed above. The sequence starts with Ross talking to a psychologist, Rodge, about his ex wife.

(6) *Ross:* You see that's where you're wrong! Why would
I marry her if I thought on any level that
she was a lesbian?

→ *Rodge:* I don't know. ((shrugs)) Maybe you wanted your marriage to fail. ((laughs))
Ross: Why, why, why would I, why, why, why.
→ *Rodge:* I don't know. Maybe . . . Maybe low self esteem, maybe to compensate for overshadowing a sibling. Maybe you w-
Monica: W- w- wait. Go back to that sibling thing.
→ *Rodge:* I don't know. ((shrugs)) It's conceivable that you wanted to sabotage your marriage so the sibling would feel less like a failure in the eyes of the parents.
Ross: Tchow! That's, that's ridiculous. I don't feel guilty for her failures.

(*The One with the Boobies*, Channel 4, 27 June 1996 – Ross is Monica's brother, Rodge is a psychologist boyfriend of Ross and Monica's friend.

References

Ashmore, M. (1989) *The Reflexive Thesis: Wrighting Sociology of Scientific Knowledge.* Chicago: University of Chicago Press.

Atkinson, P. (1990) *The Ethnographic Imagination: The Textual Construction of Reality.* London: Routledge.

Billig, M. (1987) *Arguing and Thinking: A Rhetorical Approach to Social Psychology.* Cambridge: Cambridge University Press.

Billig, M. (1991) *Ideologies and Beliefs.* London: Sage.

Billig, M. (1992) *Talking of the Royal Family.* London: Routledge.

Boden, D. and Zimmerman, D. (eds) (1991) *Talk and Social Structure: Studies in Ethnomethodology and Conversation Analysis.* Cambridge: Polity.

Brown, G. and Yule, G. (1983) *Discourse Analysis.* Cambridge: Cambridge University Press.

Coulthard, M. and Montgomery, M. (eds) (1981) *Studies in Discourse Analysis.* London: Routledge.

Coyle, A. (1995) 'Discourse analysis', in G.M. Breakwell, S. Hammond and C. Fife-Schaw (eds), *Research Methods in Psychology.* London: Sage. pp. 243–58.

Drew, P. and Heritage, J.C. (eds) (1992) *Talk at Work: Interaction in Institutional Settings.* Cambridge: University of Cambridge Press.

Edwards, D. (1994) 'Script formulations: A study of event descriptions in conversation', *Journal of Language and Social Psychology*, 13 (3): 211–47.

Edwards, D. (1995) 'Two to tango: Script formulations, dispositions, and rhetorical symmetry in relationship troubles talk', *Research on Language and Social Interaction*, 28: 319–50.

Edwards, D. (1997) *Discourse and Cognition.* London: Sage.

Edwards, D. and Potter, J. (1992) *Discursive Psychology.* London: Sage.

Edwards, D., Ashmore, M. and Potter, J. (1995) 'Death and furniture: The rhetoric, politics and theology of bottom line arguments against relativism', *History of the Human Sciences*, 8: 25–49.

Gergen, K.J. (1994) *Realities and Relationships: Soundings in Social Construction.* Cambridge, MA: Harvard University Press.

Gilbert, G.N. and Mulkay, M. (1984) *Opening Pandora's Box: A Sociological Analysis of Scientists' Discourse.* Cambridge: Cambridge University Press.

Gill, R. (1993) 'Justifying injustice: Broadcasters' accounts on inequality in radio', in E. Burman and I. Parker (eds), *Discourse Analytic Research: Repertoires and Readings of Texts in Action.* London: Routledge. pp. 75–93.

Gill, R. (1996) 'Discourse analysis: Practical implementation', in J.T.E. Richardson (ed.),

Handbook of Qualitative Research Methods for Psychology and the Social Sciences. Leicester: British Psychological Society. pp. 141–56.

Heritage, J.C. (1988) 'Explanations as accounts: A conversation analytic perspective', in C. Antaki (ed.), *Analysing Everyday Explanation: A Casebook of Methods.* London: Sage. pp. 127–44.

Levinson, S.C. (1983) *Pragmatics.* Cambridge: Cambridge University Press.

McHoul, A.W. and Grace, A. (1993) *A Foucault Primer: Discourse, Power, and the Subject.* Melbourne: Melbourne University Press.

Marshall, H. and Wetherell, M. (1989) 'Talking about career and gender identities: A discourse analysis perspective', in S. Skevington and D. Baker (eds), *The Social Identity of Women.* London: Sage. pp. 106–29.

Nofsinger, R.E. (1991) *Everyday Conversation.* London: Sage.

Potter, J. (1988) 'What is reflexive about discourse analysis? The case of reading readings', in S. Woolgar (ed.), *Knowledge and Reflexivity: New Frontiers in the Sociology of Knowledge.* London and Beverly Hills, CA: Sage. pp. 37–54.

Potter, J. (1992) 'Constructing realism: Seven moves (plus or minus a couple)', *Theory & Psychology*, 2: 167–73.

Potter, J. (1996a) *Representing Reality: Discourse, Rhetoric and Social Construction.* London: Sage.

Potter, J. (1996b) 'Discourse analysis and constructionist approaches: Theoretical background', in J.T.E. Richardson (ed.), *Handbook of Qualitative Research Methods for Psychology and the Social Sciences.* Leicester: British Psychological Society. pp. 125–40.

Potter, J. and Wetherell, M. (1987) *Discourse and Social Psychology: Beyond Attitudes and Behaviour.* London: Sage.

Potter, J. and Wetherell, M. (1994) 'Analyzing discourse', in A. Bryman and B. Burgess (eds), *Analyzing Qualitative Data.* London: Routledge. pp. 47–56.

Potter, J. and Wetherell, M. (1995) 'Discourse analysis', in J. Smith, R. Harré and L. van Langenhove (eds), *Rethinking Methods in Psychology.* London: Sage. pp. 80–92.

Psathas, G. (1990) 'Introduction', in G. Psathas (ed.), *Interactional Competence.* Washington, DC: University Press of America. pp. 1–29.

Psathas, G. (1995) *Conversation Analysis: The Study of Talk-in-Interaction.* London: Sage.

Sacks, H. (1992) *Lectures on Conversation*, Vols I and II, ed. G. Jefferson. Oxford: Blackwell.

Schegloff, E.A. (1993) 'Reflections on quantification in the study of conversation', *Research on Language and Social Interaction*, 26: 99–128.

Schegloff, E.A. and Sacks, H. (1973) 'Opening up closings', *Semiotica*, 7: 289–327.

Sinclair, J. McH. and Coulthard, R.M. (1975) *Towards an Analysis of Discourse: The English Used by Teachers and Pupils.* London: Oxford University Press.

Stubbs, M. (1983) *Discourse Analysis.* Oxford: Blackwell.

Van Dijk, T.A. (ed.) (1985) *Handbook of Discourse Analysis*, Vols 1–4. London: Academic Press.

Van Dijk, T.A. and Kintch, W. (1983) *Strategies of Discourse Comprehension.* London: Academic Press.

Wetherell, M. and Potter, J. (1992) *Mapping the Language of Racism: Discourse and the Legitimation of Exploitation.* Hemel Hempstead: Harvester; New York: Columbia University Press.

Wetherell, M., Stiven, H. and Potter, J. (1987) 'Unequal egalitarianism: A preliminary study of discourses concerning gender and employment opportunities', *British Journal of Social Psychology*, 26: 59–71.

Widdicombe, S. and Wooffitt, R. (1995) *The Language of Youth Subcultures: Social Identity in Action.* Hemel Hempstead: Harvester Wheatsheaf.

Wooffitt, R.C. (1990) 'On the analysis of interaction: An introduction to conversation analysis', in P. Luff, D. Frohlich and G.N. Gilbert (eds), *Computers and Conversation.* New York: Academic Press. pp. 7–38.

Wooffitt, R.C. (1993) 'Analysing accounts', in N. Gilbert (ed.), *Researching Social Life.* London: Sage. pp. 287–305.

11 Conversation Analysis and Institutional Talk

Analysing Data

John Heritage

In a long series of writings, Erving Goffman (1955, 1983) established that social interaction embodies a distinct moral and institutional order that can be treated like other social institutions, such as the family, education, religion, and so on. This 'interaction order', he argued, comprises a complex set of interactional rights and obligations which are linked both to face and personal identity, and also to large-scale macro-social institutions. Further, the institutional order *of* interaction has a particular social significance. It underlies the operations of all the other institutions in society, and it mediates the business that they transact. The political, economic, educational and legal conduct of societies is all unavoidably transacted by means of the practices that make up the institution of social interaction.

Goffman's idea of an 'institutional order *of* interaction' was pursued by conversation analysts who study the practices that make up this institution as a topic in its own right. Conversation analysis (CA) has established that these practices – which are complex and intricate and, in many cases, acquired early in life – make social action and interaction, mutual sense-making and social reality construction possible. These practices are special and significant because they are basic to human sociality (Schegloff, 1992). Conversation analytic studies of these practices describe how people take turns at talk in ordinary conversation and negotiate overlaps and interruptions; how various kinds of basic action sequences are organized and different options are activated inside those sequences; how various kinds of failures in interaction – for example, of hearing and understanding – are dealt with; how conversations are opened and closed; how gaze and body posture are related to talk; how laughter is organized; how grammatical form and discourse particles are related to turn-taking and other interactional issues, and so on.

However, there are also social and institutional orders *in* interaction. The social worlds of the corporation and the classroom, of medicine, law, and so on, are evoked and made actionable in and through talk. But though their reality is invoked in talk – 'talked into being' (Heritage, 1984) in interaction – their reality is not confined to talk. These institutional realities also exist in and as documents, buildings, legal arrangements, and so on.

The conversation analytic study of institutional talk is concerned with how these institutional realities are evoked, manipulated and even transformed in interaction.

There are, therefore, at least two kinds of conversation analytic research going on today, and, though they overlap in various ways, they are distinct in focus. The first examines the social institution *of* interaction as an entity in its own right; the second studies the management of social institutions *in* interaction. The aim of this chapter is to describe some ways to go about the second task, and specifically to identify ways of cutting into the data to gain access for analysis. To keep things simple, I'll illustrate the chapter mainly with observations about a single 'institutional' conversation which is typical of the 'professional–lay' interaction that many sociologists are interested in. But the relevance of the entry points I describe is not confined to this interaction. In fact, I believe that there is a reasonable chance that they are useful in gaining access to most kinds of 'institutional' data, including the new 'workplace' studies (Goodwin and Goodwin, 1997; Goodwin, 1996; Heath et al., forthcoming) that are now emerging.

Conversation analysis and interactional sequences

CA is a field that focuses heavily on issues of meaning and context in interaction. It does so by linking both meaning and context to the idea of sequence. In fact, CA embodies a theory which argues that sequences of actions are a major part of what we mean by context, that the meaning of an action is heavily shaped by the sequence of previous actions from which it emerges, and that social context is a dynamically created thing that is expressed in and through the sequential organization of interaction.

Underlying this approach is a fundamental theory about how participants orient to interaction. This theory involves three interrelated claims:

1 In constructing their talk, participants normally address themselves to preceding talk and, most commonly, the immediately preceding talk (Sacks, 1987, 1992; Schegloff, 1984; Schegloff and Sacks, 1973). In this simple and direct sense, their talk is *context-shaped.*
2 In doing some current action, participants normally project (empirically) and require (normatively) that some 'next action' (or one of a range of possible 'next actions') should be done by a subsequent participant (Schegloff, 1972). They thus *create* (or *maintain* or *renew*) a context for the next person's talk.
3 By producing their next actions, participants show an understanding of a prior action and do so at a multiplicity of levels – for example, by an 'acceptance', someone can show an understanding that the prior turn was complete, that it was addressed to them, that it was an action of a particular type (e.g. an invitation), and so on. These understandings are (tacitly) confirmed or can become the objects of repair at any third turn

in an ongoing sequence (Schegloff, 1992). Through this process they become 'mutual understandings' created through a sequential '*architecture of intersubjectivity*' (Heritage, 1984).

CA starts from the view that all three of these features – the responsiveness to context by producing a 'next' action that a current projects, the creation of context by the production of that next action, and the showing of understanding by these means – are the products of a common set of socially shared and structured procedures. Conversation analyses are thus simultaneously analyses of action, context management and intersubjectivity because all three of these features are simultaneously, but not always consciously, the objects of the participants' actions. Finally, the procedures that inform these activities are normative in that participants can be held morally accountable both for departures from their use and for the inferences which their use, or departures from their use, may engender.

Conversation analysis and institutional interaction

As CA turned to the study of talk in institutions, it began with the same assumptions that had proved successful in studying ordinary conversation. Rather than starting with a 'bucket' theory of context (Heritage, 1987) in which pre-existing institutional circumstances are seen as enclosing interaction, CA starts with the view that 'context' is both a project and a product of the participants' actions. The assumption is that it is fundamentally through interaction that context is built, invoked and managed, and that it is through interaction that institutional imperatives originating from outside the interaction are evidenced and made real and enforceable for the participants. We want to find out how that works. Empirically, this means showing that the participants build the context of their talk *in and through* their talk. For example, if we analyse emergency calls to the police, we want to be able to show the ways in which the participants are managing their interaction *as* an 'emergency call' on a 'policeable matter'. We want to see how the participants co-construct it as an emergency call, incrementally advance it turn by turn as an emergency call, and finally bring it off as having been an emergency call.

Now how are we going to go about this business of digging into institutional talk to see the ways in which participants are addressing themselves to these specialized and particular tasks? In general, we can look at three main types of features (Drew and Heritage, 1992):

1 Institutional interaction normally involves the participants in specific goal orientations which are tied to their institution relevant identities: doctor and patient, teacher and pupil, and so on.
2 Institutional interaction involves special constraints on what will be treated as allowable contributions to the business at hand.

3 Institutional talk is associated with inferential frameworks and procedures that are particular to specific institutional contexts.

These special features create a unique 'fingerprint' (Heritage and Greatbatch, 1991: 95–6) for each kind of institutional interaction – the fingerprint being made up of specific tasks, identities, constraints on conduct and relevant inferential procedures that the participants deploy and are oriented to in their interactions with one another.

Implicit in this way of thinking is the idea that institutional interaction generally involves a reduction in the range of interactional practices deployed by the participants and in the sites they are deployed at, and a specialization and respecification of the practices that remain (Drew and Heritage, 1992). These reductions and respecifications are often experienced as constraining and irksome – especially by the lay participants (Atkinson, 1982). And underlying these ideas is the further assumption that, relative to the institution of conversation, the law courts, schools, news interviews, doctor–patient interactions, and so on, are relatively recent inventions that have undergone a great deal of social change. The institution of mundane conversation, by contrast, exists, and is experienced as, prior to institutional interaction both in the life of the individual and in the life of the society.

Where would someone go in the data to look for these and other related features of institutional interaction? The short answer to this question, of course, is 'everywhere'. But we need to start somewhere, and I will describe six basic places to probe the 'institutionality' of interaction. These are:

1 Turn-taking organization.
2 Overall structural organization of the interaction.
3 Sequence organization.
4 Turn design.
5 Lexical choice.
6 Epistemological and other forms of asymmetry.

I'll deal with each one in turn.

(1) Turn-taking organization

A first thing to consider is whether the interaction you are looking at involves the use of a special turn-taking organization. All interactions involve the use of some kind of turn-taking organization (Sacks et al., 1974), and many kinds of institutional interaction use the same turn-taking organization as ordinary conversation. Some, however, involve very specific and systematic transformations in conversational turn-taking procedures. These special turn-taking systems can be very important in studying institutional interaction because they have the potential to alter the parties' opportunities for action, and to recalibrate the interpretation of almost every aspect of the activities that they structure. Think, for example, of how the opportunities for action, what the actions mean and how they will be interpreted can be shaped by the turn-taking rules for interaction in a 'formal' classroom (McHoul, 1978).

In conversation, very little of what we say, the actions we perform or the order in which we do things is determined in advance (Sacks et al., 1974). In this sense, conversations are unpredictable. In some forms of interaction – debates, ceremonies and many kinds of meetings – the topics, contributions and order of speakership is organized from the outset in an explicit and predictable way. This kind of organization involves special turn-taking procedures.

The decisive feature of a special turn-taking organization is that departures from it – for example, departures from the order of speakership, or the types of contributions individuals are expected to make – can be explicitly sanctioned. This happens in meetings when speakers are ruled 'out of order', in the courts when persons are sanctioned for answering when they should not, or failing to answer appropriately, or when children in classrooms are punished for 'shouting out' answers, or talking when the teacher is talking. These explicit sanctions are very important analytically. They tell us that the turn-taking organization is being oriented to normatively *in its own right*. Many of these turn-taking organizations work by specifically restricting one party to asking questions and another to answering them. Interactions organized by this kind of Q–A turn-taking organization are distinct from those, like many professional–client interactions, in which one party tends to do most of the question asking and the other does most of the answering. Here the imbalance between the two parties is normally a product of the task the parties are engaged in or some other feature of the interaction, and is *not* the result of a special – and sanctionable – turn-taking organization (Heritage and Greatbatch, 1991).

The most intensively studied institutional turn-taking organizations have been those that obtain in the courts (Atkinson and Drew, 1979), news interviews (Greatbatch, 1988; Heritage and Greatbatch, 1991) and classrooms (McHoul, 1978; Mehan, 1985). As these examples – courts, news interviews, classrooms – suggest, special turn-taking organizations tend to be present in large-scale 'formal' environments when (a) there are a large number of potential participants in the interaction, whose contributions must be 'rationed' in some kind of formal way, and/or (b) when the talk is designed for an 'overhearing' audience. However, special turn-taking systems can be found in other contexts. For example, Peräkylä (1995: Chap. 2) has described turn-taking practices within counselling contexts that are designed to implement special therapeutic processes. Similarly Garcia (1991) has shown that mediation can involve special turn-taking practices as a means of limiting conflict between the participants. Finally, there are other turn-taking organizations that order speakership by age, rank or other criteria of seniority (Albert, 1964; Duranti, 1994), though, perhaps because European and North American societies are less hierarchical than others in the world, these systems have so far been less studied.

(2) Overall structural organization

Once you have determined whether (or not) some special turn-taking organization is in operation in your data, the next thing to do is to build an overall 'map' of the interaction in terms of its typical 'phases' or 'sections'. This will help you to look at the task orientation which is normally central in the kinds of interaction we are looking at. While institutional interactions cannot always successfully be described in terms of a phase structure, it is always worth making an attempt to do so.

This is a convenient moment to introduce the piece of data that we'll look at during the rest of this chapter. It is a short telephone conversation in which a school employee telephones a mother whose son may be a truant from school. This conversation is drawn from a small collection, and many of the observations I'll make are confirmed by other cases in the set. In general, the more conversations you collect, the more sure you can be that what you are studying is representative (see Peräkylä, Chapter 13, this volume). As we turn to the data, you'll see right away that this conversation is very 'institutional' in the sense of being task-focused, but it will also be obvious that no special turn-taking organization is involved in the conversation. To preserve the participants' anonymity, all names in this conversation have been changed. The Appendix to this volume outlines the transcription conventions.

1 *Mom:* Hello.
2 (0.5)
3 *Sch:* Hello Mister Wilson?
4 (0.8)
5 *Mom:* Uh: this is Missus Wilson.
6 *Sch:* Uh Missus Wilson I'm sorry. This is Miss Matalin
7 from Arroyo High School calling?
8 *Mom:* Mm [hm
End of Section 1
9 *Sch:* [.hhhhh Was Martin home from school ill today?=
10 *Mom:* =U:::h yes he was in fact I'm sorry I- I didn' ca:ll
11 because uh::h I slept in late I (.) haven' been feeling
12 well either. .hhhh And uh .hhh (0.5) u::h he had uh yih
13 know, uh fever:
14 (0.2)
15 *Mom:* this morning.
16 *Sch:* U::h hu:h,
17 *( ):* .hhh=
18 *Mom:* =And uh I don' know y'know if he'll be (.) in
19 tomorrow fer sure er no:t, He's kinna j'st bin laying
20 arou:nd j(hh)uhkno:w,=
End of Section 2
21 *Sch:* =Okay well I'll [go ahead en:' u:hm
22 *Mom:* [( )
23 *Sch:* I won' call you tomorrow night if we don' see 'im
24 tomorrow we'll just assume he was home ill.
25 (.)

26 *Mom:* nnRig [ht ( )
27 *Sch:* [A:n-
28 *Sch:* Send a note with him when he does return.
29 *Mom:* I will.

End of Section 3

30 *Sch:* O:kay.
31 *Mom:* Okay=
32 *Sch:* =Thank you
33 *Mom:* Uh huh Bye [bye
34 *Sch:* [B'bye

End Call

In this phone call Ms Matalin, who has been notified by teachers that Martin did not attend school on the day of this call, calls Martin's home to check on his whereabouts. Martin's mother picks up the phone (it could have been another relative or even Martin himself) and the call proceeds. I have divided this phone call into four sections because, although Ms Matalin has only one piece of business to transact with this mother, it takes four distinct clusters of activity to achieve:

1 *Opening:* The first section (lines 1–8) is an 'opening' section in which the parties enter into a state of interaction and establish their identities for one another (Schegloff, 1986).
2 *Problem initiation:* In the second section (lines 9–20), Ms Matalin gets to the 'business' of the call by raising the question of Martin's absence and the mother explains it. I have termed this the 'problem initiation' section, because although Martin's mother resolves the problem in this call, simple resolutions of this kind don't always happen.
3 *Disposal:* In the 'disposal' section (lines 21–9), Ms Matalin details the bureaucratic action she will take towards Martin's absence in the light of the mother's account, and describes the action that the mother should take. In other calls, she describes what the child should do as well.
4 *Closing:* The final section of the call (lines 30–4) is devoted to managing a coordinated exit from the conversation (Schegloff and Sacks, 1973).

Now that we have identified these four sections, we can see that each of them involves the pursuit of a specific sub-goal. Each section is *jointly* oriented to – indeed co-*constructed* – by both participants as involving a task to be achieved. In this call, all tasks are fulfilled to the apparent satisfaction of both parties, but this does not always happen and it is not essential to identifying sections of institutional talk. What we are identifying here are goal- or task-oriented sections, which the parties co-construct and identify as somehow relevant to the completion of their business together.

Identifying these main sections of the call allows us to notice other features as well:

(i) Doing the sectional analysis forces us to see that the call is focused on a single topic – 'dealing with Martin's absence from school.' Other interactions may have more than one 'item' of business to transact: a patient, for example, may have several ailments to be dealt with, or a family may have several difficulties that require social worker support. This distinction can be important in analysing institutional interactions.

(ii) The sectional analysis allows us to see significant stages in the *parties*' co-construction of the tasks and goals of the conversations, and that for the parties, these are incremental moves towards the completion of the business of the call. This is significant: there are institutional interactions where the goals and tasks of the encounter can be unclear, opaque or even suspicious to one or both of the participants (Baldock and Prior, 1981; Heritage and Sefi, 1992). In these interactions, the 'sections' are shapeless or non-existent for the parties and, correspondingly, difficult or impossible to identify analytically.

(iii) Within each section, we can examine how the parties progressively develop (or not) a joint sense of the task that is to be accomplished and look at the roles each party plays in this process.

(iv) We can look at whether the parties agree about 'where the boundaries are' as they shift from one section to another. In this call, the parties make very 'clean' transitions from one section (and one component of their 'business') to the 'next'. But confusion and foot-dragging are also possible: one party may want to move on the next issue while the other party is reluctant to quit the current one. Or one party may not recognize that a 'next issue' is now relevant, while another is trying to press on with it. Different interests (and clear conflicts of interest) may be involved in these clashes.

Using this four section framework, it is relatively easy to identify the same sections, occurring in the same order, in most of the phone calls Ms Matalin makes. However the purpose of identifying these sections is not to exhaustively classify every piece of every one of Ms Matalin's interactions in these terms. Still less is it to assert that these sections will always occur in her conversations in this order, or even that they will always occur (cf. Byrne and Long, 1984). In other cases of these school calls, we can find the participants *reopening* sections and *reinstating* task orientations that they had previously treated as complete. So we are not trying to find invariance or even statistical regularity in the presence or ordering of these sections. The purpose of describing these sections is to identify task-orientations which the *participants* routinely co-construct in routine ways. *Overall structural organization, in short, is not a framework – fixed once and for all – to fit data into. Rather it is something that we're looking for and looking at only to the extent that the parties orient to it in organizing their talk.*

(3) Sequence organization

With the third level of analysis – sequence organization – we come to a very central aspect of conversation analytic work. It is by means of specific actions that are organized in sequences that the participants initiate, develop and conclude the business they have together, and generally manage their encounters. In analysing sequences, we essentially look at how particular courses of action are initiated and progressed and, as part of this, how particular action opportunities are opened up and activated, or withheld from and occluded. All of these possibilities, while explicitly analysed by us, are also implicitly grasped – to a greater or lesser extent – by the participants who may use what transpires as a basis for inferences about the character and situation of their co-interactants.

Ms Matalin's phone call is a rich source for sequence analysis, but here we'll just focus on one aspect of the conversation: the fact that after Ms Matalin's question at line 9, the mother's reply seems to go on and on and on. This is an accomplishment. If we look at the structure of the reply, we can see right away that the mother answers Ms Matalin's question in the very first line of her response with 'U:::h yes he was':

9 *Sch:* [.hhhhh Was Martin home from school ill today?=
10 *Mom:* =U:::h yes he was * in fact * I'm sorry I- I didn' ca:ll *
11 because uh::h I slept in late * I (.) haven' been feeling
12 well either. .hhhh And uh .hhh (0.5) u::h he had uh yih
13 know, uh fever:
14 (0.2)
15 *Mom:* this morning.
16 *Sch:* U::h hu:h,
17 *( ):* .hhh=
18 *Mom:* =And uh I don' know y'know if he'll be (.) in
19 tomorrow fer sure er no:t, He's kinna j'st bin laying
20 arou:nd j(hh)uhkno:w,=

However, the mother then continues with an apology for not 'calling' (to notify the school), and then with an elaborate series of explanations for the situation. A noticeable feature of her turn from line 10 to line 12 is that she is careful to avoid pausing at sentence boundaries. At all the points where her sentences are grammatically complete (marked with a * in this transcript), she (a) is careful to avoid a falling ('final') intonation (which would be marked with a period – see the transcript conventions in the Appendix), and (b) moves straight to the next sentence without a break. It is also noticeable, looking at line 11, that she only pauses at grammatical places where she is unlikely to be interrupted – most significantly after she starts a new sentence with the word 'I' (also in line 11). All of this is significant because, given the turn-taking system for conversation (which is in play in this interaction), a sentence boundary is a place where Ms Matalin could intervene with a question or a new observation, and thus disrupt the explanation that the mother is piecing together. It seems clear that the mother talks in the way she does so as to avoid creating these opportunities, and that she does this so that she can conclude her explanation for why she hasn't called the school without being interrupted. Thus it is only *after* she has completed her explanation that she hasn't been feeling well 'either', that she takes a breath at a sentence boundary (and it's a big breath, as indicated by the four h's)!

If the mother's talk to this point is managed so as to retain the turn in progress, her subsequent elaboration seems to emerge because she is unable to relinquish it. Extending her turn at lines 12–13 with a description of the child's illness, she pauses at line 14, only to find no uptake from Ms Matalin. In response to this, she recompletes her turn with an incremental (and redundant) time specification ('this morning'), and then encounters a response from Ms Matalin ('uh huh') that is prototypically used to indicate an understanding that the previous speaker (in this case, the mother) is not yet finished. In the face of this response, the mother continues with a prognosis of her son's condition (lines 18–20), finally coming to a halt at line 20.

Thus in this exchange of question and answer-plus-elaboration, we can see that the mother treats Ms Matalin's question as implicitly pointing to a fault in her conduct, a fault for which she is accountable, and for which she is at pains to supply an explanation (for some parallels in medical encounters, see Heritage and Lindström, forthcoming; Heritage and Sefi, 1992; Silverman, 1987: 233–64). Her treatment of the question is not as a 'casual enquiry', but rather embodies a particular – and specifically 'institutional' – understanding of its relevance. Subsequently we can see the further extension of her account as the product of an implicit sequential negotiation over who will make the conversational running. The detailed internal structure of the mother's rather lengthy turn is thus the product of a complex sequential negotiation. There are many other aspects of the sequences making up this exchange that merit analysis of the 'institutional' relevances that inform their production. We will catch some of these aspects as we move on to the fourth area where initial analysis might proceed: turn design.

(4) Turn design

Turn design is an important place to examine the 'institutionality' of interaction. When we talk about a turn being 'designed,' we are pointing to two distinct selections that a person's speech embodies: (1) the action that the talk is designed to perform and (2) the means that are selected to perform the action (Drew and Heritage, 1992).

(1) One sense in which a turn is 'designed' concerns the selection of the action which someone wants to accomplish in a turn at talk. In work with Sue Sefi on health visitors' home visits to mothers of newborns, I came across the following sequence in the health visitor's opening visit. The father and mother respond to what looks like a casual observation by the health visitor by performing quite different actions:

HV: He's enjoying that [isn't he.
→ *F:* [°Yes, he certainly is=°

→ *M:* =He's not hungry 'cuz (h)he's ju(h)st (h)had
'iz bo:ttle .hhh
(0.5)
HV: You're feeding him on (.) Cow and Gate Premium.=
(HV:4A1:1) (Heritage and Sefi, 1992: 367)

The health visitor's remark 'He's enjoying that' notices the baby sucking or chewing on something. (Unfortunately, we don't have a videotape, but certainly this is how the mother understands the word 'enjoy' when she responds 'He's not hungry . . .' [lines 3–4].) In replying that way, the mother treats the health visitor's remark as implying that the baby is 'enjoying' whatever he's sucking or chewing because he's hungry – an implication which she rejects by observing that the baby has just been fed. The mother's response, then, is 'defensive' in rejecting an unstated implication which she treats the health visitor's remark as having. The father, by contrast, simply agrees with the health visitor.

Thus, in 'constructing' their responses (quite apart from the particular designs of their turns), the mother and father have elected to perform alternative activities. Both activities, of course, have a 'logic' as relevant next actions. The father treats the health visitor's remark as innocent while the mother finds in it an implied criticism regarding the proper care of her baby. They thus construct their responses differently by selecting different 'next' actions. These two actions may well reflect a 'division of labour' in the family, in which the mother is treated as having the primary responsibility for her baby (reflected in her defensiveness), while the father, with less responsibility, can take a more relaxed and 'innocent' view of things.

(2) The second aspect of turn design is that speakers also select among alternative ways of saying something or performing the same action. The following extract – from the same health visitor interaction as the previous one – illustrates this clearly. In this extract, the mother and father each perform a broadly similar activity – agreeing with the health visitor's suggestion that they'll be 'amazed' at the child's progress (in physical development), and they do so nearly simultaneously (lines 5 and 6). But they design their agreements rather differently. While the mother's agreement refers to the development of children in general ('They learn so quick don't they'), the father refers to their experience of their own child's progress ('We have noticed hav'n't w-'). While the father's utterance exhibits a commitment to noticing their own child's behaviour and development, the mother's response does not.

HV: It's amazing, there's no stopping him now, you'll be
amazed at all the di[fferent things he'll start doing.
F: [(hnh hn)
(1.0)
→ *M:* Yeh. They [learn so quick don't they.
→ *F:* [We have noticed hav'n't w-
HV: That's right.

→ 8 *F:* We have noticed (0.8) making a grab for your bottles.
9 (1.0)
10 *F:* Hm[::.
11 *HV:* [Does he: (.) How often does he go between his feeds?
(HV:4A1:2) (Drew and Heritage, 1992: 34)

Significantly, the mother's response avoids the 'expert–novice' stance that the health visitor's remark might be seen as expressing, while the father's agreement(s) (at lines 6 and 8) seem designed to prove to the health visitor that they are observant and alert about their new baby. The different ways in which they design their actions may also point to the same underlying division of labour in the family that we suggested earlier. The father, who is putatively the junior partner in the family's child care arrangements, appears eager to prove their competence in noticing the details of their child's behaviour. The mother's agreement, by contrast, seems to avoid taking the 'inferior' and 'inexpert' position of 'proving' anything to the health visitor, but rather asserts an agreement in bland and general terms.

The alternatives that may be involved in turn design are rarely as explicitly contrasted as they are here where different speakers employ different designs in the same responsive position. More usually, we analyse turn design by looking at the details of a turn's component features, and by determining their interactional purpose or significance.

To illustrate this, I want to go back to Ms Matalin's telephone call and look at line 9: 'Was Martin home from school ill today='. Ms Matalin very frequently begins her enquiries to the families she calls with this question. In an important sense, it is a 'highly designed' turn that is repeated exactly (or nearly exactly) over and over again.

One way of analysing a highly designed turn of this kind is to think of the interactional contingencies it might be addressing. In the context of Ms Matalin's calls, there are two main possibilities that her question might turn up:

1 The child is away from school sick and the parent knows it. Sickness, of course, is bad news in its own right for the child (who may be in pain) and the parent (who may be worried and losing pay by being away from work). But Ms Matalin's call is also bad news for the parent at another level. The parent of a sick child is normally supposed to call in to notify the school of the situation. There is, if you like, a kind of informal contract between home and school such that the school tells the parent if they have reason to believe the child is missing, but the parents equally have the obligation to tell the school if they suppose that the child will not be coming to school. The fact that Ms Matalin has had to call in the first place may be the product of a little 'breach of contract' on the parent's part. It's just that breach of contract which the mother's defensive explanation, which we looked at earlier, seems designed to address.

2 The child is away from school and the parent does not know it – that is, the child is truant. For this possibility, Ms Matalin's call may involve a very serious piece of information for parents who, up to now, may have no idea that their child is not attending school.

It's in this context that we can begin to see that how Ms Matalin opens up the topic of this call matters a lot, and that her opening utterance involves quite a bit of caution.

Consider the turn itself: (1) it indicates that the child has not been at school 'today' (i.e. on the day of the call), but does not assert it as a fact: that the child has not been at the school is presupposed in the design of the question rather than stated as such (Pomerantz, 1988). (2) It offers as an account for the child's presupposed absence the most *commonplace* and the most *legitimate* reason for the child to be away from school – sickness. (3) The question is designed so that the easiest response for the parent will be an affirmative 'yes' response to the possibility of sickness. In conversation analytic terminology, the question 'prefers' a 'yes' response. (4) Even if the child is, in fact, a truant, the enquiry avoids any implication of this and particularly avoids any accusation of truancy. (5) The question does not in any way directly thematize the parent's responsibility to inform the school. Instead, it leaves it open for the parent, where relevant, to *assume* that responsibility – as our mother in fact does. This, then, is a highly judicious, cautious and 'institutional' piece of question design (see Section 6 below).

Now in recognizing that this is so, you don't have to assume that Ms Matalin is a very tricky, Machiavellian type of person. You just have to remember that she makes dozens, even hundreds, of these calls every week. She has learned the range of possible responses that mothers make to her question, and she has also learned that certain ways of asking this question can attract resistance or cause arguments. So, for Ms Matalin, recurrently raising this topic is like a 'wind tunnel' experiment: the 'wind tunnel' of repetition leads her to a question design that evokes the least resistance. You can see this wind tunnel effect in many other kinds of institutional talk – in medicine, social security offices, emergency calls to the police and fire brigade and others – where the institutional representative has a repetitive set of tasks to be worked through.

Thus, the second sense in which one can say that a turn is 'designed' is that there are always alternative ways of saying something from which speakers, unavoidably, make a selection. The syntactic, lexical and other (e.g. prosodic) selections by a speaker are aspects of a turn that articulate with the performance of organizational tasks and, very often, are shaped into 'least resistant' forms by the repetition of those tasks. An important component of turn design is our next topic: lexical choice.

(5) Lexical choice

A clear way in which speakers orient to institutional tasks and contexts is through their selection of descriptive terms. For instance, while someone might use 'cop' in ordinary conversation, when giving evidence in court they are likely to select 'police officer' instead (Sacks, 1979). The fact that this can involve selection is evident when speakers – as in Jefferson's (1974) data – cut off the beginning of 'cop' ('kuh-') in favour of the word 'police'. Many studies that have dealt with the context-sensitivity of descriptions show that speakers select descriptive terms which are fitted to the institutional setting, or their role within it (Drew and Heritage, 1992). A dramatically clear illustration – first noted by Sacks (1992) – is the way that, when speaking as a member of an organization, persons may refer to themselves as 'we', not 'I' (Drew and Heritage, 1992). There is a clear case in our data (lines 23–4). Here Ms Matalin initially describes a course of action as her own decision ('I won' call you tomorrow night'), but then adds the inference that will be made if Martin is not at school tomorrow: 'if we don' see 'im tomorrow we'll just assume he was home ill.' Here the 'we' referred to as making this inference is evidently the school as an institution.

Another systematic type of lexical selection involves what might be termed 'institutional euphemism'. Here issues that may for some reason be problematic for the institution's representatives to address are downplayed. In the *New York Times* (5 November 1995) it is reported that Microsoft – the giant software corporation – no longer likes to talk of 'industry dominance' but rather of 'industry leadership'. In medicine, references to pain are often euphemistic – a patient will be asked 'Is it sore?' rather than 'Is it painful?' (Heritage and Sorjonen, 1994). In other phone calls like the one we are looking at, when Ms Matalin doesn't get an adequate explanation for a child's absence, she often says 'We need him/her to come into the office to clear this up.' While this seems to indicate just a matter of bureaucratic record keeping, it leaves open the broader question of the child's accountability for the absence and what kind of punishment might be involved in 'clearing up' his or her record.

Lexical selections can shape whole sequences and, with them, the overall pattern of the interaction. For example, the beginning of Ms Matalin's phone call runs as follows:

Mom: Hello
(0.5)
Sch: Hello Mister Wilson?
(0.8)
Mom: Uh: this is Missus Wilson
Sch: Uh Missus Wilson I'm sorry. This is Miss Matalin
from Arroyo High School calling?
Mom: Mm hm

At line 8, the mother, rather than greeting Ms Matalin by saying 'hello' – which is the kind of action that normally occurs at this point (Schegloff, 1986) – just says 'mm hm', a prototypically non-committal 'continuer' (Schegloff, 1982) that invites Ms Matalin to proceed with the conversation. Now one could imagine that this is an unfriendly, even a hostile, action from someone who doesn't like talking to school officials. But if we look back up the sequence, we can see an alternative basis for the mother's action. In particular, we can see that Ms Matalin identifies herself using a particular lexical choice – a formal 'last name plus organizational id' identification. By using this identification, rather than, for example, 'Nancy Matalin' or just 'Nancy', she identifies the phone call as a 'business call' and, specifically, a 'call about school business'. (In fact, that process begins to emerge even earlier when, trying to identify whom she's talking to, Ms Matalin names the mother using 'Mister Wilson' rather than a more informal identification – the mistaken identification [Mister for Missus] seems to arise because the mother's voice sounds rather deep on the phone.) So, when the mother responds to Ms Matalin's formal, business-oriented self-identification with 'mm hm' at line 8, she is in fact inviting Ms Matalin to proceed with the business-based 'reason for the call' that Ms Matalin has clearly projected right from the start. That clear projection – and, because of it, the very brevity and economy of this opening sequence – arises from the lexical selections made at the earliest stages of this telephone call.

(6) Interactional asymmetries

Finally, interactional asymmetries are a place at which to begin examining the specific institutionality of interactions. Here, I'll briefly mention four types of asymmetry that involve: (a) participation; (b) 'knowhow' about the interaction and the institution in which it is embedded; (c) knowledge; and (d) rights to knowledge.

(a) Asymmetries of participation Many studies of institutional interaction document asymmetries of participation in institutional interactions, and in particular that institutional participants in lay–professional encounters – for example, involving doctors, teachers, social workers, and so on – take and retain the initiative in these interactions (Frankel, 1990; Linell et al., 1988; Mishler, 1984). Underlying these observations is an implicit contrast with a standard of 'equal participation' between speakers in ordinary conversation. As Linell and Luckmann (1991) have commented, we need to be cautious about this. This dichotomy between the symmetries of conversation and the asymmetries of institutional discourse can oversimplify the nature of asymmetry and overlook the ways in which talking in ordinary conversation can be asymmetrical. As they observe: 'if there were no asymmetries at all between people, i.e. if communicatively relevant inequalities of knowledge were non-existing, there would be little or no need for most kinds of communication!' (Linell and Luckmann, 1991: 4). Viewed from a perspective that asks which persons participate in talk and to what effect, it is apparent that ordinary conversation can embody several kinds of asymmetry – between the speaker and the hearer of a turn at talk; between the initiator and the respondent in a sequence of interaction; between those who, more broadly, are active in shaping topics and those who are not; and between those whose interventions are decisive for the

outcomes of conversations and those whose interventions are not (Linell, 1990; Linell and Luckmann, 1991). From this standpoint, the contrast between the symmetry of ordinary conversation and the asymmetry of institutional discourse is indeed oversimplified: all social interaction must inevitably be asymmetric on a moment to moment basis and many interactions are likely to embody substantial asymmetry when moment to moment participation is aggregated over the course of one or more encounters.

Yet at a more general level, it is clear that there is a fundamental distinction between the symmetry of ordinary conversation and the asymmetries of institutional interaction. The general operation of ordinary conversation is not tied to any particular set of social roles, identities or tasks. If it were, conversation would be a much less flexible, varied and sophisticated institution. In many forms of institutional discourse, by contrast, there is a direct relationship between institutional roles and tasks, on the one hand, and discursive rights and obligations, on the other. For example, institutional representatives commonly ask questions and require of lay participants that they answer them. In this way, they may secure the initiative in determining (i) when a topic is satisfactorily concluded, (ii) what the next topic will be and, (iii) through the design of their questions, how that new topic will be shaped (Drew and Heritage, 1992; Mishler, 1984). Thus institutional representatives can often direct the interaction in ways that are not found in ordinary conversation.

(b) Asymmetries of interactional and institutional 'knowhow' An important dimension of asymmetry between the participants in institutional interaction arises from the difference, and often tension, between the organizational perspective that treats the individual as a 'routine case', and the client for whom the case is personal and unique. Ms Matalin's phone call to the mother in our data was one of around a dozen she made that day and, for her, it was absolutely routine. For the mother, however, it was an unusual and morally threatening occasion. The parties, therefore, brought asymmetrical experience and reasoning to the encounter. All agencies have procedures for the routine management of multiple cases, for 'processing' cases by assigning them to routine categories, and so on. However, the clients – whose enquiries, troubles, illnesses, claims and the like constitute an organization's routine cases – may not be really aware of, or concerned with, the pattern into which their individual cases fit. The client's perspective often arises out of the particular circumstances which bring him or her into contact with the organization, perhaps for the first or only time, or at least not frequently enough to have developed a self-conception as a routine case. In doctor–patient encounters, this gap between routine institutional 'knowhow' and singular experience can be extraordinarily stressful (Zola, 1987) and can emerge in behaviour that can be experienced as very callous (Maynard, 1996). This gap can exist, and be significant, in all forms of institutional talk. In some psychiatric and social

service encounters, the 'client' may have only a dim awareness of the professional objectives being pursued across the entire encounter (Baldock and Prior, 1981; Heritage and Sefi, 1992; Peräkylä, 1995). In others, the lay caller may have an exact idea of the purpose of the conversation, but may be unable to grasp the point of a particular action. For example, in a notorious call for emergency assistance (Whalen et al., 1988: 337), the following episode occurs. The caller (B) has just given his address and then is asked, using a 'fixed choice' question design, whether the address is a house or an apartment. As the data show, he responds with a lexical selection drawn not from the choices he is given, but rather from the language of real estate. He replies: 'it is a home':

A: Okay iz this uh house or n' apartmen'?
B: It- it is a ho:me

Here, probably under the pressure of the emergency (the caller's mother is dying), the caller simply fails to grasp the relevance of the distinction between a house and an apartment to an ambulance crew looking for an address and a way to enter the location.

Routine organizational contingencies which are taken for granted by one party but are unknown to the other can be the source of many other kinds of difficulty and confusion. In the case of '911' emergency calls, Whalen (1995) has argued that such contingencies as the current position of the cursor on a menu-driven computer screen can influence the order in which questions are asked, and sometimes make them seem confusing or irrelevant to callers. Similar asymmetries in organizational and interactional 'knowhow' often strongly influence police and courtroom interrogations, and other interactions in which organizational resources and routines are used to evaluate the truth of lay claims (Boyd, forthcoming; Drew, 1992; Watson, 1990).

(c) Epistemological caution and asymmetries of knowledge A notable feature of many kinds of institutional interaction is a kind of epistemological 'cautiousness' in which the professionals avoid committing themselves to taking firm positions. This cautiousness is mandatory in certain institutional interactions such as the news interview (Clayman, 1988, 1992; Heritage, 1985; Heritage and Greatbatch, 1991) or the courts (Atkinson, 1992; Atkinson and Drew, 1979). In other contexts, such as medical diagnosis, it is quite common. Even in Ms Matalin's calls a kind of epistemological caution is evident. For example, when a parent seems unaware that their child is away from school, Ms Matalin normally tells them about the absence in this way:

Sch: Was William home from school ill today?
. . . ((conversation off the phone in which Mom asks another person if William was home))
Mom: No he wasn't

Sch: .hhh Well he was reported absent from his thir:d and his fifth period cla:sses today.

Here Ms Matalin doesn't say 'he was absent from . . .'; instead she says 'he was reported absent from . . .'. By including 'reported', Ms Matalin invokes an (unnamed) source for the information and thus portrays herself as *relaying* the information she is giving. She thus avoids underwriting the information as a *fact* and, because 'reports' need to be confirmed before becoming 'facts', she also avoids committing the school to an 'official' position on the issue.

At the same time as professionals and institutional representatives are often cautious about making claims, they also deploy distinctive, functionally specialized and superior knowledge bases that can impart a specific expert authority to claims made within the relevant knowledge domain. The epistemological superiority of expert knowledge is something that is recurrently renewed in talk and in many different ways (Jacoby and Gonzales, 1991; Peräkylä, 1996; Raymond, 1995; Silverman, 1987). Medicine provides numerous examples. Patients may orient to the authority of medical knowledge by their lexical choices, for example the tentative or uncertain use of medical terminology (Drew, 1991; Maynard, 1991; Silverman, 1987), or by failing to raise questions about important problems and concerns (Frankel, 1990; Todd, 1993), or by permitting 'medical' definitions of their problems to prevail over their lifeworld concerns (Mishler, 1984). Moreover, lack of medical knowledge may mean that patients may not know or understand the purposes lying behind particular questions, and they may not grasp the line of inquiry which the doctor is pursuing in questions on what seem to be unconnected topics. This lack of access to the 'hidden agenda' of doctors' questioning represents another avenue of analysis into asymmetry in medical interaction (Fisher, 1983; Silverman, 1987).

(d) Rights of access to knowledge Asymmetry of knowledge arises when people – usually lay people – have limited resources with which to answer the questions 'what do I know?' and 'how do I know it?' But these same people may also have limited resources with which to answer the questions 'what am I entitled to know?' and 'how am I entitled to know it?' Limitation in this regard is an asymmetry in rights of access to knowledge. Here lay people are sometimes in a position analogous to the gossips described by Bergmann (1993): they have information that is relevant or significant, but they don't have *rights* to know it or they have come to know it in a 'morally contaminated' way. Thus a person calling to inform the emergency services about an incident may be at pains to show that they are calling from a sense of duty about an event that imposed itself on them, and not because they are 'nosey' or 'looking for trouble' (Whalen and Zimmerman, 1990). A patient who is concerned about a possible illness may be similarly at pains to show that they are not excessively preoccupied

with minor bodily changes (Halkowski, 1996). Strong (1979) documents the fact that doctors accompanying their children on pediatric consultations suspend their medical expertise and act 'like parents' when dealing with the attending physician. In this last case, persons with every 'right' to medical expertise voluntarily suspend those rights in the limited environment of a medical consultation with another person qualified as expert. In institutional interaction, then, knowledge may not be enough; one must also be entitled to the knowledge, and have come to it in an appropriate way.

Conclusion

By now, you will have seen that these different dimensions or levels of 'institutionality' in talk are thoroughly interrelated. Rather like Russian dolls that fit inside one another, each of these elements is a part of the next higher level: lexical choice is a part of turn design; turn design is a part of sequence organization; sequence organization is a part of overall structural organization.

There are two 'wild cards' in the pack. Turn-taking is one, because where a distinct turn-taking system is in place, it has major effects at many levels of an interaction's organization. Asymmetry is the other, because it is embodied at all other levels of the organization of interaction in institutional settings – lexical choice, turn design, sequence organization, overall structure organization and turn-taking. Indeed conversation analysis may end up with an affinity with a rather Foucauldian conception of power, advocated by other contributors to this volume. The view that power inheres in institutional knowledge, classifications, knowhow and normative arrangements is compatible with the conversation analytic view that it is created, renewed and operationalized in many disparate but interlocking facets of the organization of interaction. Both perspectives converge in the idea that this power inheres both in the knowledge, classificatory and interactional practices of institutions and their incumbents, and in the discretionary freedoms which those practices permit for the incumbents of institutional roles.

References

Albert, E. (1964) '"Rhetoric," 'logic," and "poetics" in Burundi: Culture patterning of speech behavior', *American Anthropologist* 66, pt 2 (6): 35–54.

Atkinson, J.M. (1982) 'Understanding formality: Notes on the categorisation and production of "formal" interaction', *British Journal of Sociology*, 33: 86–117.

Atkinson, J.M. (1992) 'Displaying neutrality: Formal aspects of informal court proceedings', in P. Drew and J. Heritage (eds), *Talk at Work: Interaction in Institutional Settings*. Cambridge: Cambridge University Press. pp. 199–211.

Atkinson, J.M. and Drew, P. (1979) *Order in Court: The Organization of Verbal Interaction in Judicial Settings*. London: Macmillan.

Atkinson, J.M. and Heritage, J. (eds) (1984) *Structures of Social Action: Studies in Conversation Analysis*. Cambridge: Cambridge University Press.

Baldock, J. and Prior, D. (1981) 'Social workers talking to clients: A study of verbal behaviour', *British Journal of Social Work*, 11: 19–38.

Bergmann, J.R. (1993) *Discreet Indiscretions: The Social Organization of Gossip*. Chicago: Aldine.

Boyd, E. (forthcoming) 'Bureaucratic authority in the "company of equals": Initiating discussion during medical peer review', *American Sociological Review*.

Byrne, P.S. and Long, B.E.L. (1984) *Doctors Talking to Patients: A Study of the Verbal Behaviours of Doctors in the Consultation*. Exeter: Royal College of General Practitioners.

Clayman, S. (1988) 'Displaying neutrality in television news interviews', *Social Problems*, 35 (4): 474–92.

Clayman, S. (1992) 'Footing in the achievement of neutrality: The case of news interview discourse', in P. Drew and J. Heritage (eds), *Talk at Work: Interaction in Institutional Settings*. Cambridge: Cambridge University Press. pp. 163–98.

Drew, P. (1991) 'Asymmetries of knowledge in conversational interactions', in I. Markova and K. Foppa (eds), *Asymmetries in Dialogue*. Hemel Hempstead: Harvester Wheatsheaf. pp. 29–48.

Drew, P. (1992) 'Contested evidence in a courtroom cross-examination: The case of a trial for rape', in P. Drew and J. Heritage (eds), *Talk at Work: Interaction in Institutional Settings*. Cambridge: Cambridge University Press. pp. 470–520.

Drew, P. and Heritage, J. (1992) 'Analyzing talk at work: An introduction', in P. Drew and J. Heritage (eds), *Talk at Work: Interaction in Institutional Settings*. Cambridge: Cambridge University Press. pp. 3–65.

Duranti, A. (1994) *From Grammar to Politics*. Berkeley: University of California Press.

Fisher, S. (1983) 'Doctor talk/patient talk: How treatment decisions are negotiated in doctor/patient communication', in S. Fisher and A. Todd (eds), *The Social Organization of Doctor–Patient Communication*. Washington, DC: Center for Applied Linguistics. pp. 135–57.

Frankel, R. (1990) 'Talking in interviews: A dispreference for patient initiated questions in physician–patient encounters', in G. Psathas (ed.), *Interaction Competence*. Lanham, MD: University Press of America. pp. 231–62.

Garcia, A. (1991) 'Dispute resolution without disputing: How the interactional organization of mediation hearings minimizes argumentative talk', *American Sociological Review*, 56: 818–35.

Goffman, E. (1955) 'On face work', *Psychiatry*, 18: 213–31.

Goffman, E. (1983) 'The interaction order', *American Sociological Review*, 48: 1–17.

Goodwin, C. and Goodwin, M.H. (1997) 'Formulating planes: Seeing as a situated activity', in D. Middleton and Y. Engestrom (eds), *Cognition and Communication at Work: Distributed Cognition in the Workplace*. Cambridge: Cambridge University Press.

Goodwin, M.H. (1996) 'Announcements in their environment: Prosody within a multi-activity work setting', in E. Couper-Kuhlen and M. Selting (eds), *Prosody in Conversation: Interactional Studies*. Cambridge: Cambridge University Press. pp. 436–61.

Greatbatch, D. (1988) 'A turn-taking system for British news interviews', *Language in Society*, 17 (3): 401–30.

Halkowski, T. (1996) 'Realizing the illness: Patients' narratives of symptom discovery'. Paper presented at the Annual Meetings of the American Association of Applied Linguistics, Chicago, IL, March 1996.

Heath, C., Luff, P. and Greatbatch, D. (forthcoming) *Technology in Action*. Cambridge: Cambridge University Press.

Heritage, J. (1984) *Garfinkel and Ethnomethodology*. Cambridge: Polity.

Heritage, J. (1985) 'Analyzing news interviews: Aspects of the production of talk for an overhearing audience', in T.A. Van Dijk (ed.), *Handbook of Discourse Analysis*, Vol. 3. New York: Academic Press. pp. 95–119.

Heritage, J. (1987) 'Ethnomethodology', in A. Giddens and J. Turner (eds), *Social Theory Today*. Cambridge: Polity. pp. 224–72.

Heritage, J. and Greatbatch, D. (1991) 'On the institutional character of institutional talk: The case of news interviews', in D. Boden and D.H. Zimmerman (eds), *Talk and Social Structure: Studies in Ethnomethodology and Conversation Analysis*. Berkeley: University of California Press. pp. 93–137.

Heritage, J. and Lindström, A. (forthcoming) 'Motherhood, medicine and morality: Scenes from a medical encounter', in J. Bergmann and P. Linell (eds), *Morality in Discourse*. Hemel Hempstead: Harvester Wheatsheaf.

Heritage, J. and Sefi, S. (1992) 'Dilemmas of advice: Aspects of the delivery and reception of advice in interactions between health visitors and first time mothers', in P. Drew and J. Heritage (eds), *Talk at Work: Interaction in Institutional Settings*. Cambridge: Cambridge University Press. pp. 359–417.

Heritage, J. and Sorjonen, M.-L. (1994) 'Constituting and maintaining activities across sequences: And-prefacing as a feature of question design', *Language in Society*, 23: 1–29.

Jacoby, S. and Gonzales, P. (1991) 'The constitution of expert–novice in scientific discourse', *Issues in Applied Linguistics*, 2 (2): 149–81.

Jefferson, G. (1974) 'Error correction as an interactional resource', *Language in Society*, 2: 181–99.

Linell, P. (1990) 'The power of dialogue dynamics', in I. Markova and K. Foppa (eds), *The Dynamics of Dialogue*. Hemel Hempstead: Harvester Wheatsheaf. pp. 147–77.

Linell, P. and Luckmann, T. (1991) 'Asymmetries in dialogue: Some conceptual preliminaries', in I. Markova and K. Foppa (eds), *Asymmetries in Dialogue*. Hemel Hempstead: Harvester Wheatsheaf. pp. 1–20.

Linell, P., Gustavsson, L. and Juvonen, P. (1988) 'Interactional dominance in dyadic communication: A presentation of initiative–response analysis', *Linguistics*, 26: 415–42.

McHoul, A. (1978) 'The organization of turns at formal talk in the classroom', *Language in Society*, 7: 183–213.

Maynard, D. (1991) 'On the interactional and institutional bases of asymmetry in clinical discourse', *American Journal of Sociology*, 92 (2): 448–95.

Maynard, D. (1996) 'On "realization" in everyday life', *American Sociological Review*, 60 (1): 109–32.

Mehan, H. (1985) 'The structure of classroom discourse', in T.A. Van Dijk (ed.), *Handbook of Discourse Analysis*, Vol. 3. New York: Academic Press. pp. 120–31.

Mishler, E. (1984) *The Discourse of Medicine: Dialectics of Medical Interviews*. Norwood, NJ: Ablex.

Peräkylä, A. (1995) *AIDS Counselling: Institutional Interaction and Clinical Practice*. Cambridge: Cambridge University Press.

Peräkylä, A. (1996) 'Authority and intersubjectivity: The delivery of diagnosis in primary health care'. Unpublished ms., University of Helsinki.

Pomerantz, A. (1988) 'Offering a candidate answer: An information seeking strategy', *Communication Monographs*, 55: 360–73.

Raymond, G. (1995) 'The voice of authority: Turn and sequence design in live news broadcasts'. Paper presented at the Georgetown Linguistics Society Conference on Discourse Analysis, February.

Sacks, H. (1979) 'Hotrodder: A revolutionary category', in G. Psathas (ed.), *Everyday Language: Studies in Ethnomethodology*. New York: Irvington. pp. 7–14.

Sacks, H. (1987) 'On the preferences for agreement and contiguity in sequences in conversation', in G. Button and J.R.E. Lee (eds), *Talk and Social Organization*. Clevedon: Multilingual Matters. pp. 54–69.

Sacks, H. (1992) *Lectures on Conversation*, Vols I and II, ed. G. Jefferson. Oxford: Blackwell.

Sacks, H., Schegloff, E.A. and Jefferson, G. (1974) 'A simplest systematics for the organization of turn-taking for conversation', *Language*, 50: 696–735.

Schegloff, E.A. (1972) 'Notes on a conversational practice: Formulating place', in D. Sudnow (ed.), *Studies in Social Interaction*. New York: Free Press. pp. 75–119.

Schegloff, E.A. (1982) 'Discourse as an interactional achievement: Some uses of "uh huh" and other things that come between sentences', in D. Tannen (ed.), *Analyzing Discourse* (Georgetown University Roundtable on Languages and Linguistics 1981). Washington, DC: Georgetown University Press. pp. 71–93.

Schegloff, E.A. (1984) 'On some questions and ambiguities in conversation', in J.M. Atkinson and J. Heritage (eds), *Structures of Social Action*. Cambridge: Cambridge University Press. pp. 28–52.

Schegloff, E.A. (1986) 'The routine as achievement', *Human Studies*, 9: 111–51.

Schegloff, E.A. (1992) 'Repair after next turn: The last structurally provided for place for the defense of intersubjectivity in conversation', *American Journal of Sociology*, 95 (5): 1295–345.

Schegloff, E.A. and Sacks, H. (1973) 'Opening up closings', *Semiotica*, 8: 289–327.

Silverman, D. (1987) *Communication and Medical Practice*. London: Sage.

Strong, P. (1979) *The Ceremonial Order of the Clinic*. London: Routledge.

Todd, A. (1993) 'Exploring women's experiences: Power and resistance in medical discourse', in S. Fisher and A. Todd (eds), *The Social Organization of Doctor–Patient Communication* (2nd edn). Norwood, NJ: Ablex. pp. 267–86.

Watson, D.R. (1990) 'Some features of the elicitation of confessions in murder interrogations', in G. Psathas (ed.), *Interactional Competence*. Lanham, MD: University Press of America. pp. 263–96.

Whalen, J. (1995) 'A technology of order production: Computer-aided dispatch in public safety communications', in P. ten Have and G. Psathas (eds), *Situated Order: Studies in the Social Organization of Talk and Embodied Activities*. Washington, DC: University Press of America. pp. 187–230.

Whalen, J., Zimmerman, D.H. and Whalen, M.R. (1988) 'When words fail: A single case analysis', *Social Problems*, 35 (4): 335–62.

Whalen, M. and Zimmerman, D. (1990) 'Describing trouble: Practical epistemology in citizen calls to the police', *Language in Society*, 19: 465–92.

Zola, I.K. (1987) 'Structural constraints in the doctor–patient relationship: The case of non-compliance', in H. Schwartz (ed.), *Dominant Issues in Medical Sociology*. New York: Random House. pp. 203–9.

12 The Analysis of Activities in Face to Face Interaction Using Video

Christian Heath

One of the most impressive developments in sociology over the past couple of decades has been the growing body of research concerned with the social organization of talk and discourse. Ethnomethodology and conversation analysis have, in particular, made a profound contribution to our understanding of the social organization of talk and the ways in which it features in the accomplishment of social actions and activities (see, e.g., Atkinson and Heritage, 1984; Boden and Zimmerman, 1991; Drew and Heritage, 1992). The visual aspects of human conduct have received less attention in sociology, and indeed our understanding of the body in social action and interaction is still largely dominated by the substantial tradition of work in psychology concerned with 'non-verbal behaviour'. However, the increasing availability of cheap and reliable video equipment, coupled with the emergence of a suitable methodological framework, is leading to a growing interest in the social organization of the actions and activities accomplished through the body and physical artefacts, as well as talk, in face to face interaction.

In this chapter, I wish to consider the ways in which we can use video recordings of naturally occurring settings to analyse the interactional organization of social actions and activities. In particular, I wish to suggest that ethnomethodology and conversation analysis, whilst providing important resources for the analysis of talk, can also provide a methodological foundation for investigating the visual as well as vocal aspects of human conduct. In this way, the chapter will suggest that sociology can begin to develop a distinctive approach to the ways in which bodily comportment and physical artefacts feature in human activities, and thereby not only contribute to our understanding of face to face interaction, but also cast light on more substantive issues such as organizational conduct.

Before considering some basic methodological issues, it is worth briefly mentioning that whilst sociology has been relatively slow to exploit the opportunities afforded by video, there is a longstanding, though largely disregarded, tradition in social anthropology of 'interaction analysis' using recorded data of naturalistic activities. It emerged in the early 1950s in Palo Alto through the pioneering work of Bateson and Mead and others including McQuown, Hockett and Ruesch, and led to extraordinary studies undertaken by Birdwhistell (1970), Scheflen (1964) and others. Coupled with the wide-ranging essays by Goffman (1959, 1963, 1967), the tradition also influenced Kendon's (1990) impressive work on bodily comportment in interaction and the more ethological studies by Cosnier (1978) and others.

These studies have some parallels with a very different tradition which has led to the emergence of a distinctive body of sociological research concerned with the ways in which talk and bodily conduct feature in social interaction. In particular, ethnomethodology and conversation analysis have provided the methodological resources which have informed the development of a growing body of sociological research which uses video recordings to examine the *in situ* organization of social actions and activities in face to face interaction. For example, in a pioneering series of essays, Goodwin (1979, 1980, 1981) examined the ways in which the production of a turn at talk, a speaker's utterance, is coordinated with the gaze of the recipient, and went on to identify various devices employed by speakers to establish mutual orientation. Related research examined the organization of gesture, and in particular the ways in which various forms of bodily conduct are used by speakers to shape the co-participation of the person(s) with whom they are speaking (see, e.g., C. Goodwin, 1980, 1981; M. Goodwin, 1980; Heath, 1982, 1986). Since these beginnings we have witnessed the emergence of a wide-ranging body of research which has used video recordings of 'naturally occurring events' to examine visual and vocal aspects of a range of activities in both conversational and institutional environments.

Analytic considerations

Ethnomethodology and conversation analysis, therefore, have provided the resources through which it has been possible to exploit video for sociological purposes. Before presenting an example, it might be helpful to provide a brief overview of the analytic issues which informed the research. In general, I wish to suggest that the analysis has been informed by two general issues. First, it has been directed towards investigating the methodological resources used by participants themselves in the production of social actions and activities (through talk, bodily comportment, artefacts, and the like). Secondly, it has exploited the sequential organization of interaction in order to examine how participants themselves are orienting to each other's conduct and to help identify the resources on which they rely.

Ethnomethodology emerged through the pioneering studies of Harold Garfinkel and rapidly led to the development of conversation analysis through the innovative research of Sacks and his colleagues, Schegloff and Jefferson. Unlike other forms of social science inquiry, ethnomethodology and conversation analysis do not provide a 'method', in the sense of clear-cut set of procedures that if followed will generate scientifically valid results or findings. However, they do involve a number of critical analytic commitments which have provided a foundation to a substantial body of empirical studies.

In *Studies in Ethnomethodology* Garfinkel (1967) develops a radical approach to the understanding of human practical activity. He argues that we should place the situated production of social actions and activities at the forefront of the analytic agenda and treat mundane events, even physical and biological phenomena, as the 'artful accomplishments' of the participants in the settings in which they arise. Garfinkel suggests that we should 'bracket' events and ask of any phenomenon what the methodological resources are which inform the production and intelligibility of the event or activity in question. At one point, he contrasts his recommendations to those suggested by Durkheim:

> Thereby, in contrast to certain versions of Durkheim that teach that the objective reality of social facts is sociology's fundamental principle, the lesson is taken instead and used as a study policy, that the objective reality of social facts as an ongoing accomplishment of the concerted activities of daily life, with the ordinary artful ways of that accomplishment being my members known, used, and taken for granted, is for members doing sociology, a fundamental phenomena. (Garfinkel, 1967: vii)

So, for example, in their different studies of 'suicide problem', both Garfinkel (1967) and Atkinson (1978) do not take the official category 'suicide' for granted and examine the variables which explain patterns in the rates of suicide amongst particular classes of individuals. Rather, they examine the practices and practical reasoning on which those responsible for the investigation of equivocal deaths rely in warrantably ascribing the category 'suicide' in a particular case. In this way, analytic attention is directed towards the *in situ* accomplishment of particular events and activities, and in particular the resources on which individuals rely in the production of social actions and activities. Moreover, it is argued that we take for granted or gloss the systematic ways in which we accomplish social actions and activities, the 'objective order to social facts', so that we encounter the 'normal appearances' of everyday life, whilst we concertedly accomplish the very scenes and events we confront. This reflexivity is an integral feature of our activities and the settings in which they arise.

It can be argued that conversation analysis shares these analytic commitments with ethnomethodology and in particular treats 'conversation' and its methodological foundations as a realm of sociological inquiry. Whilst his *Lectures on Conversation* embody a diverse range of observations and analytic insights, it is perhaps the work of Sacks (1992) and his colleagues Schegloff and Jefferson on the sequential organisation of talk which has provided one of the most wide-ranging and fruitful contributions to ethnomethodological studies. It is certainly these studies, reflected perhaps most explicitly in a classic paper on the organization of turn-taking in conversation (Sacks et al., 1974), which have had a profound influence on the analysis of talk both in sociology and in a range of other disciplines. It should be said however, that conversation analysis is not concerned with language *per se*, but rather derives from the recognition that talk is a principal means through which we produce and recognize social actions and activities. Schegloff and Sacks (1974) argued, for example, that their original interest in talk derived from the recognition that it provided the possibility of developing a 'naturalistic discipline which could deal with the details of social action(s) rigorously, empirically and formally'. Using audio recordings and transcriptions of naturally occurring talk, conversation analysis has developed a substantial corpus of empirical studies which delineate the practices and reasoning, the competencies, which inform the accomplishment of a diverse range of conversation activities. In recent years, the original focus on conversation has been increasingly replaced by a growing interest in institutional talk and a rich body of work has emerged concerned with the interactional organization of events such as news interviews, medical consultations and political speeches (see, e.g., Boden and Zimmerman, 1991; Drew and Heritage, 1992).

For Garfinkel, the 'indexicality of practical actions' is a fundamental concern. Indexicality points to the uniqueness of any activity or event, and draws our attention towards the ways in which participants accomplish the rational, routine and mundane character of practical action. The uniqueness of practical activities which informs ethnomethodology and conversation analysis is more radical than the notion of context that is found elsewhere in the social sciences. All too often 'context' is treated as realm of local variables which can be invoked to explain the specific character of practical activity within some particular occasion or circumstance. Indeed, even more radical forms of sociological inquiry, for example symbolic interactionism and perhaps recent developments in cognitive science such as distributed cognition, retain a model of human conduct which, whilst emphasizing the temporal organization of practical action, presupposes that shared meanings or definitions, common frames of reference, and the like, remain stable, if only for brief moments of interaction within social life. By contrast, in ethnomethodology and conversation analysis, social actions and activities are inseparable from, or, better, part and parcel of, the 'context at hand'. The intelligibility of a scene, the character of the event, the 'objective order of social facts', are ongoingly accomplished in and through the practical and concerted actions of the participants themselves; there is 'no time out' from the moment by moment production of the 'objective order of social facts'. The reflexive character of practical action therefore is a central concern and directs analytic attention to the methodological foundations of practical actions and activities and the achieved character of ordinary events.

For conversation analysis, with its principal focus on interaction, the turn by turn, sequential organization of talk has provided an important resource for the analytic depiction of context and the 'indexical properties of practical action'. Heritage, for example, suggests that talk in interaction is both 'context shaped and context renewing'; 'a speaker's contribution is both designed with regard to the local configuration of activity and in particular the immediately preceding actions, and itself inevitably contributes to the framework in terms of which the next action will be understood' (1984: 242). This step by step, sequential organization of talk-in-interaction, whereby each subsequent turn both displays an understanding of prior and is recognized with regard to the immediately preceding action(s) (unless otherwise indicated), provides an important analytic resource. Rather than simply stipulate the meaning or significance of particular utterances in the light of their own personal intuition, researchers can inspect subsequent actions in order to determine how the participants themselves are responding to, and displaying their understanding of, each other's conduct.

The double-edged element whereby sequential organization is both an integral feature of the social organization of talk and a methodological resource for its analysis remains a central and powerful tenet of conversation analytic research. As Sacks et al. suggest, for example:

> [It] is a systematic consequence of the turn taking organization of conversation that it obliges its participants to display to each other, in a turn's talk, their understanding of the other turn's talk. More generally, a turn's talk will be heard as directed to a prior turn's talk, unless special techniques are used to locate some other talk to which it is directed. . . . But while understandings of other turns' talk are displayed to co-participants, they are available as well to professional analysts, who are thereby provided a proof criterion (and a search procedure) for the analysis of what a turn's talk is occupied with. Since it is the parties' understandings of prior turns' talk that is relevant to their construction of next turns, it is their understandings that are wanted for analysis. The display of those understandings in the talk in subsequent turns affords a resource for the analysis of prior turns, and a proof procedure for professional analyses of prior turns, resources intrinsic to the data themselves. (1974: 728–9)

The emergent and sequential organization of interaction is also relevant to how we might consider the contextual or *in situ* significance of visual conduct and the physical properties of human environments. Gestures and other forms of bodily conduct arise in interaction, people not infrequently use artefacts when talking to each other, and it is not unusual for aspects of the physical environment to become relevant within the course of social activities. Unfortunately, however, there has been a widespread tendency amongst research on non-verbal communication to assume that the meaning of a gesture is inextricably tied to its physical form rather than the context in which it arises. This is an assumption which is not unlike the idea that an utterance gains its meaning by virtue of its lexicon or syntax, rather than its sequential location. We might also suggest the physical environment in which actions and activities take place does not have a stable and overarching influence on the interaction, but rather its relevance is assembled in particular ways at certain moments in time with regard to the conduct of the participants. In consequence, we need to consider the ways in which visual conduct features in interaction, with and within talk, and to draw on the sequential organization of conduct as a resource for the analysis of *in situ* social actions and activities.

Visual and tactile elements of human conduct, features of the local environment, and the like, do not reflect the turn by turn, speaker by speaker organization characteristic of talk-in-interaction. Whilst it is speakers who ordinarily gesticulate, even a single turn at talk may involve a complex array of actions produced by various participants, both speaker and listeners and others, which may stand 'within some perceptual range of the event' (cf. Goffman, 1981). For example, as suggested earlier, a single utterance may be coordinated in the course of its production with the visual actions of the person(s) to whom it is addressed, and the speaker may employ various gestures and the like to shape the forms of co-participation he or she requires at different junctures within the turn's development. The actual utterance and the way in which it is understood sequentially, in next turn, is, therefore, the outcome of a complex interaction which includes both visual and vocal contributions by various participants during the very course of its production. Hence, when considering both visual and vocal aspects of activities in interaction, it is useful to consider the ways in which participants' actions may be sequentially related to each other, even though next actions may occur prior to next turn. As in the example below, it is found that the reorientation by a potential recipient to the speaker within an utterance may be engendered sequentially by a particular gesture produced by the speaker; the first action eliciting the second. Or, for example, a co-participant may inspect some feature of the local milieu, like a line of text on a computer screen, by virtue of the actions of another which sequentially encourage the looking at a particular moment in time; moreover, the looking can sequentially implicate a course of action. So whilst visual conduct with and within talk is not necessarily organized on a turn by turn basis, we can inspect the ways in which the participants respond to each other's actions as a way of investigating how their activities may be organized. The sequential and interactional organization of the participants' conduct remains an important analytic resource for investigating how they themselves are orienting to each others' conduct and accomplishing their activities.

However, whilst the sequential organization of interaction remains an important resource for studies of visual and vocal aspects of *in situ* activities using video, it is recognized that it is not always possible to build a strong sequential case for the organization of particular visual actions. For example, whilst a movement such as an iconic or illustrative gesture may appear to be an important aspect of a turn at talk, there may be little evidence either in next turn, or during the course of the utterance's production, that it is relevant, sequentially, to the accomplishment of the activity at hand. Similarly, studies of the use of objects and artefacts in interaction have tended to focus on instances where there is an explicit orientation by the participants themselves to the phenomenon in question rather than the more vague, less apparent ways in which they might feature in the production of particular actions. Moreover, there is an increasing interest in using video to examine the organization of activities which do not occur within 'focused communication', for example people in offices in a 'state of incipient talk' or individuals walking through public space, where it can be very difficult to demonstrate a strong sequential orientation by the participants to each other's conduct, even where their actions appear intimately interrelated. Finally, it also recognized that in settings where activities require extensive specialized knowledge, such as control rooms or trading rooms in the City of London, that analysis necessitates extensive fieldwork and local expertise in order to begin to delineate the organization of the particpants' activities. Despite these difficulties, however, an important part of the richness and rigour of video-based studies of *in situ* social actions and activities derives from their continuing commitment to demonstrate how participants themselves are orienting to the organization of activities described in the analyses. Building an analysis with regard to the sequential and interactional character of social action and activities remains a critical resource in the contributions of these studies and their concern to examine the resources used by participants themselves in organising their conduct.

Observing cases

The situated character of practical action, and the interest in the methodological resources used by the participants themselves, inevitably drives analytic attention towards the investigation of activities and events within the contexts in which they occur. Detailed and repeated inspection of the accomplishment of actual activities, coupled with the analytic orientations briefly discussed above, provide the resources through which researchers can begin to identify the practices and reasoning through which particular events are produced and rendered intelligible.

As some ethnomethodological and conversation analytic researchers become increasingly concerned with talk and interaction, it has been found that audio and audio-visual recordings provide useful resources with which to subject *in situ* practical actions and activities to detailed analysis. Originally the use of recorded data consisted principally of telephone conversations (see, e.g., Sacks, 1992, or Sacks et al., 1974). However, with the increasing interest in the visual as well as vocal aspects of human activity, the use of video has become increasingly common (see, e.g., Goodwin, 1981; Heath, 1986). It has been recognized that recordings of human activities and interaction, despite their limitations, provide researchers with unparalleled access to social action, allowing the aspects of the complexity of particular events to be subjected to detailed and repeated scrutiny. Unlike other forms of qualitative and quantitative 'data', recordings of naturally occurring human activities not only provide the other researchers and the 'scientific community' at large with access to the raw materials on which the investigations are based, but provide a corpus of data which can serve a range of theoretical and analytic interests. As Atkinson and Heritage suggest:

> In sum, the use of recorded data serves as a control on the limitations and fallibilities of intuition and recollection; it exposes the observer to a wide range of interactional materials and circumstances and also provides some guarantee that analytic considerations will not arise as artefacts of intuitive idiosyncrasy, selective attention or recollection, or experimental design. (1984: 4)

Notwithstanding the limitations and constraints of video, it is surprising that there has been such relatively little interest within sociology, and in particular perhaps in field studies and ethnography, in exploiting the possibilities it provides. In anthropology, film and more recently video has received more attention, and yet, even there, it has been increasingly used as a medium of representation and documentation rather than a resource for the analysis of social actions and activities. Marks (1995) has recently argued that ethnographic film has been influenced by successive shifts in anthropological theory since the beginning of the century, and that the absence of a suitable methodological and conceptual framework undermined the early attempts to examine the details of human conduct and locomotion originally initiated by Meybridge and others in the late nineteenth century. Similarly, in sociology the conceptual and theoretical resources which have informed a substantial corpus of rich ethnographic work since the 1950s (e.g. Hughes, 1958) do not readily lend themselves to the analysis of the details of social actions and activities captured on video. In contrast, however, ethnomethodology and conversation analysis, with their commitment to the local *in situ* organization of human conduct, and their interest in taking talk and interaction seriously as topics in their own right, provide an analytic orientation which can take advantage of the opportunities afforded through video.

As studies of talk and interaction have become increasingly interested in more specialized forms of human activities, often arising within particular organizational or institutional domains, it has been recognized that it is necessary to augment recorded materials with extensive fieldwork. So, for example, our own studies of general practice involved a long period of non-participant observation before any recording took place in order to begin to assemble a sense of the organization of certain specialized tasks such as diagnosis, treatment and using medical records (Heath, 1984b, 1986). With the emergence of more wide-ranging studies of workplace interaction, especially those concerned with the use of tools and artefacts in complex technological environments such as control rooms and emergency centres, we have witnessed an increasing commitment to undertaking wide-ranging fieldwork alongside more focused interaction analyses (Whalen, 1995). The necessity to undertake observation and even interviews, does not simply derive from the complexity of the specialized forms of activities under scrutiny, but is a consequence of the range of often distributed activities which feature, if only momentarily, in the accomplishment of the work and tasks in question. It is not unusual in such studies to delay gathering recorded materials until researchers have a passing understanding of the activities in question and the various tools and technologies which feature in the accomplishment of even the more mundane activities in such settings.

The body in action

As a way of illustrating how we might begin to unpack aspects of the organization of an activity, it is perhaps useful to consider the following fragment. It is drawn from a medical consultation and arises towards the end of the consultation as the doctor begins to prepare a prescription. As he starts to write, the patient, who is still standing following the physical examination, begins to tell a story:

Fragment 1.

Dr: (Begins to write a prescription)
(1.4)
P: When I went down into Debenhams I an I felt so aw::ful (eh) I wen (.) I was coming up the steps li:ke this all the way up I felt, (0.4) terribly
(0.3)
P: terrib [ly (.) really you know
Dr: [yeh yes
(0.2)
Dr: No::: (.) it's the knee itself (.) you've go some rheumatism there.

The fragment is transcribed using the orthography developed by Gail Jefferson and which is widely used within ethnomethodology and conversation analysis. The talk is laid out turn by turn, speaker by speaker. The numbers in brackets consist of either pauses or silences measured in tenths of a second, the single stop in brackets referring to a mini-pause of say one tenth of a second. The colons capture the ways in which a sound is elongated, for example 'No:::' in the doctor's reply. Brackets between speakers' utterances indicate that the talk is co-occurring, in overlap. Underlinings capture an emphasis. (For further details concerning the transcription system, see the Appendix to this volume, and e.g., Atkinson and Heritage, 1984; Boden and Zimmerman, 1991; or Drew and Heritage, 1992.)

The patient's story appears to provide an example of the complaint with which she has contacted the doctor. It recounts the events that occurred as she walked up the steps at Debenhams, a local department store, and in particular describes the suffering she incurred. It is interesting to note how the doctor responds to the story sequentially. Whilst he acknowledges the suffering the patient experienced with 'yeh' and 'yes' in overlap with the expression of its 'terribleness', his subsequent turn does not develop or encourage further discussion concerning the patient's feelings. For example, the doctor does not align towards the story as a friend who might show sympathy and encourage discussion concerning the patient's experiences and suffering. Rather, he adopts what we might refer to as a 'diagnostic' or 'analytic standpoint'. He takes the opportunity of the telling of the story to reaffirm the location of the difficulty and his medical assessment of the troubles. Treating the story 'diagnostically' in this way not only allows the doctor to reiterate his assessment of the trouble, but also allows him to avoid further discussion of the patient's experience of her troubles, a discussion which might well have arisen if he had produced a more sympathetic response.

The fragment therefore points to some potentially interesting features of how troubles are managed in interaction in medical consultations and in particular the ways in which doctors align sequentially towards patient's descriptions of their suffering and thereby preserve a diagnostic standpoint. Elsewhere Jefferson and Lee (1981) have powerfully demonstrated the interactional problems which can emerge when professionals conflate different alignments towards the telling of troubles.

The observations thus far ignore some potentially interesting issues. For example, despite the doctor's response, the patient does not actually describe the difficulties she encountered walking up the steps at Debenhams. Moreover, the story co-occurs with the doctor's attempt to write the prescription, but how the patient manages to encourage him to listen and respond to the story remains opaque. Finally, the way in which the story is articulated and achieves its interactional and sequential relevance remains unexplored. A consideration of the participants' visual conduct, as well as their talk, may help illuminate some of these issues.

As the patient begins to describe the difficulties she had walking up the stairs at Debenhams, she starts to walk up and down on the spot, illustrating the problems she experienced. More particularly she places her hand on the doctor's desk and, balancing her weight, shows the way in which she distorted her hip and leg movement to climb the stairs. The movements give sense to the talk they accompany. They lucidly reveal the problems she experienced and provide a vivid picture of the suffering that she incurred. The utterance itself points to the difficulties and provides a framework in which the movements embody, literally, the patient's difficulties and suffering.

To make sense of the story, and for it to achieve its local sequential and interactional significance, the doctor needs to both hear and see what the patient says and does.

A transcript which includes some details concerning the visual conduct of the participants might be useful. The participants' conduct is transcribed across the page with aspects of the visual conduct indicated above and below the talk. A few illustrations which consist of frame-grabbed images from the original data might also be useful (see Figure 12.1). The images have been degraded to conceal the identity of the participants.

Fragment 1, Transcript 2 and Figure 12.1

```
      walks
      up        down        up    down up   down     up    down
      ˘         ˘           ˘     ˘    ˘    ˘        ˘     ˘
P:    I was coming up the steps li:ke this all the way up I felt,
      ^
Dr:   writes
      prescription
```

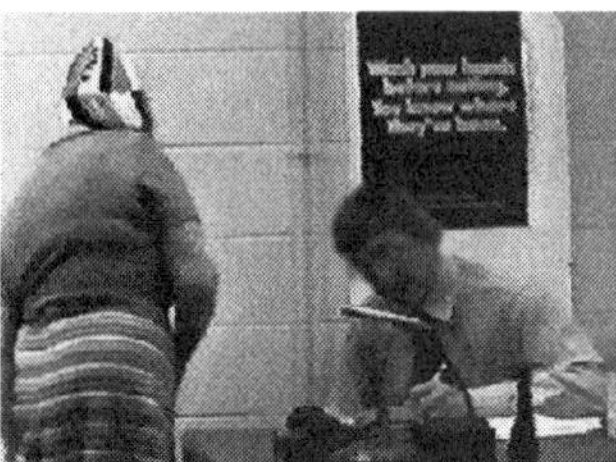

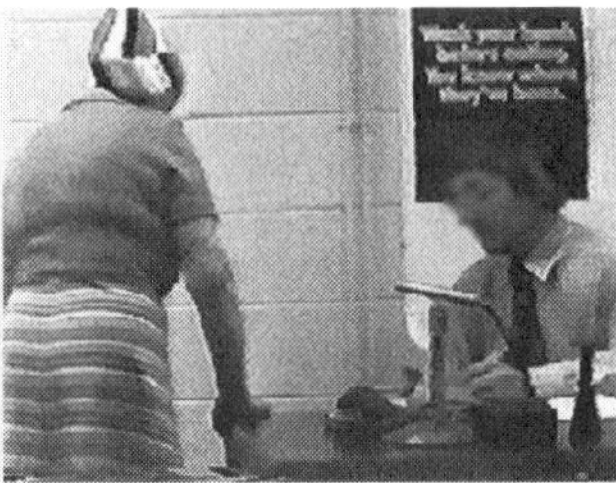

Figure 12.1

The patient assembles an activity, a story which illustrates the problems she has suffered which renders her body relevant in a particular way to her communication with the doctor. In face to face interaction the body of course is always in one sense there, and yet may not be specifically relevant to a particular course of action or activity. In the case at hand, the patient attempts to foreground aspects of her bodily conduct, to have the body itself feature, then and there, as an interactionally relevant and regarded feature of the participants' activities. In this manner the patient attempts to (mutually) constitute her body and its movements in a particular way for the practical purposes of illustrating her suffering; to have the other attend in a particular way to what might ordinarily be disattended.

What is curious perhaps is that the patient tells a story that requires the potential recipient to both listen and look when he shows little interest in temporarily abandoning the activity in which he is engaged. The doctor does not look up during the first part of the story where the patient sets the scene, and indeed even as she begins to walk up and down leaning on his desk, he continues doggedly to write the prescription. And yet, unless the patient can encourage the doctor not only to listen, but also to look and watch her performance, then the gist of the story and its potential sequential significance is lost. In the way in which the story is told, the patient's activity requires the doctor to transform the way in which he is engaged in the interaction.

There are aspects of the earlier part of the patient's story which might be concerned with her sensitivity with regard to the alignment of the recipient. For example, the restart and repair 'I wen (.) I was' may itself be an attempt to encourage the practitioner to turn towards the patient (cf. Goodwin, 1981) and the sentence 'I an I felt so aw::ful' coupled with the restart and emphasis on 'so awful' may be an attempt to delay the gist of the story while encouraging the doctor to temporarily abandon writing the prescription. If so they fail, and deep into the turn the patient constructs the story so that it requires a visually attentive as well as listening recipient. Despite the risk however, the patient not only illustrates her experience and suffering but successfully encourages the doctor to abandon writing the prescription and watch the significant part of the performance (see Figure 12.2). In this way the story achieves its local interactional significance; and receives appreciation and response from the doctor.

Fragment 1, Transcript 3 and Figure 12.2

```
     walks
     up         down        up      down up down      up    down
     ˘          ˘           ˘       ˘    ˘  ˘         ˘     ˘
P:   I was coming up the steps li:ke this all the way up I felt,
     ^                          ^     ^               ^
Dr:  writes                 turns to   turns to       nods &
     prescription             P's face    P's legs    smiles
```

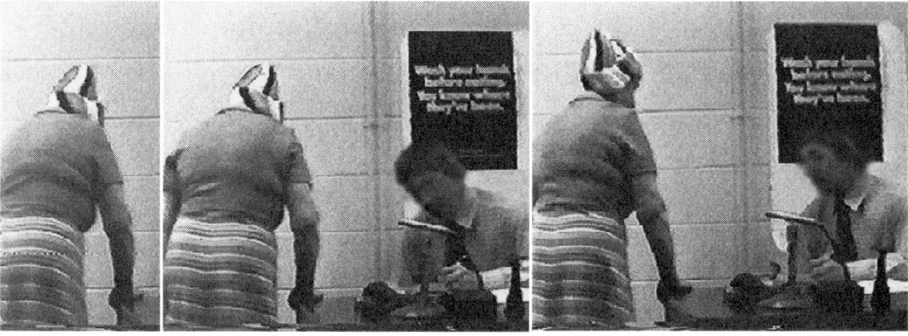

Figure 12.2

The patient's success in encouraging the doctor to watch the performance and thereby achieving the sequential relevance of the story derives from the ways in which she designs her bodily conduct.

As she begins to step up for the second time, she swings her hips towards the doctor and in particular the area between the document and his face. As the hips move towards the doctor he looks up, turning to the face of the patient. It is as if the patient's movement elicits the reorientation by the doctor, encouraging him to temporarily abandon writing the prescription and transform the ways in which he is participating in the delivery of the story (cf. Heath, 1986).

On turning to the patient's face, he finds her looking at her own legs as she utters 'like this'. He immediately turns and watches the performance as she steps up and down. And, as she brings the performance to completion with 'terribly', and the doctor utters 'yeh', 'yes' and nods, she has successfully established a recipient who has not only heard the tale, but witnessed the difficulties experienced by the patient as she walked up the steps at Debenhams.

The story, its sequential relevance and the doctor's ability to respond are therefore the outcome of interaction between patient and doctor. The story itself involves and invokes the bodily portrayal of an event which itself illustrates the patient's difficulties and to which the doctor responds with an appreciation and a diagnostic assessment. In this way the doctor's professional assessment serves to discourage perhaps any further elaboration by the patient concerning her experience of her problems. But even before the patient begins to describe the events which arose in walking up the steps at Debenhams, she is sensitive to the concurrent conduct of the doctor and appears to make various attempts to encourage him to transform the way in which he is participating in the talk. Indeed, the very enactment of the events may even arise in the light of the patient facing a potentially recalcitrant recipient; a recipient who is looking at a notepad and writing as she begins to tell of her 'awful' suffering.

The illustration which reveals the events in Debenhams not only serves to provide a sense of the experience to which the doctor responds following the completion of the story, but simultaneously and systematically establishes an audience for its own performance. Whilst embodying the story in the illustration, the patient designs an action within the developing course of performance which serves to encourage the doctor to turn towards her. The swing of the hips stands out from the surrounding bodily conduct, and, by projecting an object towards the field of vision of the doctor, successfully draws his gaze.

In their own way, therefore, the patient's bodily movements are remarkable. They not only serve to illustrate the difficulties she once experiences, but simultaneously establish an audience for the performance and thereby the sequential relevance of the story. The patient's bodily conduct engenders different, but interrelated sequential trajectories. It forms an integral part of the story to which the doctor responds following its completion. It also, as part of the story, encourages the doctor to transform the ways in which he is participating in the talk and in particular to watch the performance. In a sense therefore we might speak of the bodily movement being a 'double duty' gesture: sequentially implicating specific actions from the recipient at different locations during the course of the movements' articulation (see Heath, 1986; Turner, 1974). And yet such a characterization hardly catches the complexity of the activity; not only is the relevance of the story as an illustration as a whole contingent on establishing within its course a 'seeing' recipient, but the activity is accomplished in and through both talk and bodily conduct.

In this way, therefore, we can begin to disassemble aspects of the social and interactional organization which feature in the accomplishment of a particular event and provide for its character and uniqueness. Even this cursory glance at the fragment begins to reveal the complexity of the participants' activity and the remarkable resources which are brought to bear in the production and intelligibility of the story. In particular, it reveals the emergent character of the participants' actions and the ways in which they are interactionally organized and accomplished. In the case at hand, it can be seen that whilst visual aspects of the participants' conduct are not organized on the turn by turn basis characteristic of talk, nonetheless the sequential relations between visual and vocal actions remain a critical property of their organization. For example, the elicitation of the doctor's gaze is sequentially responsive to an action by the patient, and the doctor's reorientation forms the foundation to the intelligibility of the story and the sequentially appropriate reply. In turning to consider the methodological resources used by the participants in the activity's production and intelligibility, therefore, attention inevitably turns to consider the ways in which actions are interactionally coordinated moment by moment, step by step. In this sense, the context and intelligibility of the activity are unavoidably and continuously emergent, assembled from within its production.

Activities in interaction

The growing body of video-based research within ethnomethodology and conversation analysis concerned with the visual as well as vocal aspects of human conduct stands in marked contrast to more traditional contributions to the understanding of non-verbal behaviour. Non-verbal behaviour is no longer treated as a distinct channel of communication, in isolation from talk and other aspects of human interaction. Rather attention is directed towards the various resources that participants bring to bear in the *in situ* accomplishment of social actions and activities. Given the 'situated' character of human activity and the uniqueness of particular events, studies are naturalistic rather than experimental and deliberately avoid the *a priori* theorizing and the development of hypotheses characteristic of the more variable-centred approaches found within many psychological and social psychological studies of non-verbal communication. Most importantly perhaps, analysis is directed towards developing observations which characterize aspects of the indigenous reasoning and practices that participants themselves use in the production and intelligibility of particular social actions and activities. So, for example, in the data at hand, the analysis is concerned with building a characterization of the methodological resources on which the participants rely in accomplishment of the activity, with regard to the ways in which they produce and coordinate their actions with each other during the developing course of their articulation. The interactional and sequential foundations of the activity's accomplishment provide an important resource in the identification and description of the actions, and the practices and reasoning upon which the participants rely in their production and intelligibility.

The analytic commitment to describing the methodological resources on which participants rely in the accomplishment of ordinary activities has also led to a growing interest in exploring the ways in which objects and the physical environment feature in social action and interaction. In contrast to certain approaches in sociology and cognate disciplines which treat objects and the physical environment as shaping social actions and activities, studies are examining the ways in which the local ecology is constituted in and through the actions and interaction of the participants. A motivation of these studies is to demonstrate how the participants themselves orientate, moment by moment, to aspects of their physical environment, and thereby accomplish the particular and momentary sense of objects, artefacts, and the like. So, for example, studies have explored the ways in which conversationalists over the dinner table orient to and manipulate objects with talk during the developing course of particular activities (Goodwin, 1984), or how patients manipulate their body and present themselves as objects for inspection to medical practitioners during the physical examination (Heath, 1986). More recently, a range of studies have explored ways in which objects are handled, exchanged and referred to in interaction within the accomplishment of a range of activities (e.g. Hindmarsh and Heath, 1995; LeBaron, forthcoming; Streeck, forthcoming; Whalen, 1995; Wootton, 1994).

The growing interest in using video augmented by fieldwork to explore the ways in which participants accomplish activities using talk, body movement, objects, artefacts and the physical environment is perhaps best reflected in the emergence of a corpus of research commonly known as 'workplace studies'. The provenance of such studies is complex, evolving in part through Suchman's (1987) powerful critique of artificial intelligence and HCI (human–computer interaction). In general the studies are directed to exploring the interactional organization of work in complex technological environments and involve detailed analysis of the ways in which participants produce and coordinate a wide range of actions and activities through various systems, tools and artefacts. So, for example, in a recent study of communication and control on London Underground, we have explored the collaborative management of problems and emergencies and the ways in which personnel participate in, and coordinate, simultaneously, multiple activities using various tools and technologies (cf. Heath and Luff, 1992, 1997). In a separate study of an airport operations centre, research has examined, amongst a wide variety of other issues, how personnel mutually constitute a scene in common using various information displays and develop a coordinated and distributed response to problems which arise in unloading aircraft (Goodwin and Goodwin, 1997; Suchman, 1993). Video recordings, often using multiple cameras, augmented by extensive fieldwork, provide unprecedented access to such complex tasks, and ethnomethodology and conversation analysis provide resources through which we can begin to unpack the interactional organization of social actions and activities in these technological settings. Such studies are not only beginning to provide a distinctive contribution to our understanding of organisational activities, but also changing the ways in which social and cognitive scientists conceive of the interaction between human beings and technologies such as computers.

Summary

Ethnomethodology and conversation analysis provide an analytic orientation through which we can begin to exploit the opportunities provided through video. Whilst video itself will be soon superseded by digital cameras and recorders, the possibility of capturing aspects of the audible and visual elements of *in situ* human conduct as it arises within its natural habitats provides researchers with unprecedented access to social actions and activities. With ethnomethodology and conversation analysis, the technology opens up the possibility of developing a sociology which begins to take visual as well as vocal aspects of human interaction and the physical environment seriously, as important topics for investigation and analysis. Such studies not only complement the extraordinarily rich body of work concerned with talk-in-interaction, but further enhance our understanding of how the body and physical objects feature with talk in the production and intelligibility of everyday social actions and activities. In order to develop a sociology which addresses the detail of the body and objects in interaction, it is important that we abandon some of the traditional distinctions which have informed our understanding of 'non-verbal behaviour' and consider the ways in which visual and vocal conduct feature in the *in situ* accomplishment of particular social actions and activities. In this way we can move away from psychological and cognitive characterizations of visual conduct, and begin to develop insights into the social and interactional organization of activities and the range of resources on which they rely in their accomplishment. By turning analytic attention towards the methodological and reflexive foundations of social action, we can develop a distinctive understanding of the organization of human activity in all its intelligence and passing glory.

References

Atkinson, J.M. (1978) *Discovering Suicide: The Social Organization of Sudden Death*. London: Macmillan.

Atkinson, J.M. and Heritage, J. (eds) (1984) *Structures of Social Action: Studies in Conversation Analysis*. Cambridge: Cambridge University Press.

Birdwhistell, R.L. (1970) *Kinesics and Context: Essay in Body-Motion Research*. Philadelphia: University of Pennsylvania Press.

Boden, D. and Zimmerman, D.H. (eds) (1991) *Talk and Social Structure: Studies in Ethnomethodology and Conversation Analysis*. Cambridge: Polity.

Cosnier, J. (1978) 'Specificité de l'attitude ethologique dans l'étude du comportement humain', *Psychologie Française*, 23 (1): 19–26.

Drew, P. and Heritage, J. (eds) (1992) *Talk at Work: Interaction in Institutional Settings*. Cambridge: Cambridge University Press.

Garfinkel, H. (1967) *Studies in Ethnomethodology*. Englewood Cliffs, NJ: Prentice Hall.

Goffman, E. (1959) *The Presentation of Self in Everyday Life*. New York: Doubleday Anchor.

Goffman, E. (1963) *Behavior in Public Places: Notes on the Social Organization of Gatherings*. New York: Free Press.

Goffman, E. (1967) *Interaction Ritual*. New York: Doubleday.

Goffman, E. (1981) *Forms of Talk*. Oxford: Blackwell.

Goodwin, C. (1979) 'An interactional construction of turn at talk in natural conversation', in G. Psathas (ed.), *Everyday Language: Studies in Ethnomethodology*. New York: Irvington.

Goodwin, C. (1980) 'Restarts, pauses and the achievement of mutual gaze at turn-beginning', *Sociological Inquiry*, 50: 272–302.

Goodwin, C. (1981) *Conversational Organization: Interaction between a Speaker and Hearer*. London: Academic Press.

Goodwin, C. (1984) 'Notes on story structure and the organization of participation', in J.M. Atkinson and J. Heritage (eds), *Structures of Social Action: Studies in Conversation Analysis*. Cambridge: Cambridge University Press. pp. 272–302.

Goodwin, C. (1986) 'Gesture as a resource for the organization of mutual orientation', *Semiotica*, 62 (1/2): 29–49.

Goodwin, C. (1995) 'Seeing in depth', *Social Studies of Science*, 25 (2): 237–74.

Goodwin, C. and Goodwin, M.H. (1997) 'Formulating planes: Seeing as a situated activity', in D. Middleton and Y. Engestrom (eds), *Cognition and Communication at Work: Distributed Cognition in the Workplace*. Cambridge: Cambridge University Press.

Goodwin, M. (1980) 'Processes of mutual monitoring implicated in the production of description sequences', *Sociological Inquiry*, 50: 303–17.

Heath, C. (1982) 'Preserving the consultation: Medical record cards and professional conduct', *Journal of the Sociology of Health and Illness*, 5 (2): 36–74.

Heath, C.C. (1984a) 'Interactional participation: The coordination of gesture, speech and gaze', in P. Leonardie and V. d'Orso (eds), *Discourse Analysis and Natural Rhetoric*. Padua: Cleap Edition. pp. 78–92.

Heath, C.C. (1984b) 'Participation in the medical consultation: The coordination of verbal and nonverbal behaviour', *Journal of the Sociology of Health and Illness*, 6 (3): 311–38.

Heath, C.C. (1986) *Body Movement and Speech in Medical Interaction*. Cambridge: Cambridge University Press (Paris: Éditions de la Maison des Science de l'Homme).

Heath, C.C. and Luff, P. (1992) 'Collaboration and control: Crisis management and multimedia technology in London Underground Line Control Rooms', *Journal of Computer Supported Cooperative Work*, 1 (1–2): 69–94.

Heath, C. and Luff, P. (1997) 'Convergent activities: Collaborative work and multimedia technology in London Underground Line Control Rooms', in D. Middleton and Y. Engestrom (eds), *Cognition and Communication at Work: Distributed Cognition in the Workplace*. Cambridge: Cambridge University Press.

Heritage, J. (1984) *Garfinkel and Ethnomethodology*. Cambridge: Polity Press.

Hindmarsh, J. and Heath, C. (1995) 'Constituting objects and mutual experience'. Paper presented at the American Sociological Association Annual Meeting.

Hughes, E.C. (1958) *Men and their Work*. Glencoe, IL: Free Press.

Jefferson, G. and Lee, J.R.E. (1981) 'The rejection of advice: Managing the problematic convergence of a "troubles telling" and a "service encounter"', *Journal of Pragmatics*, 5: 399–522.

Kendon, A. (1990) *Conducting Interaction: Patterns of Behaviour in Focussed Encounters*. Cambridge: Cambridge University Press.

LeBaron, C.D. (forthcoming) 'Gestures made meaningful: A micro-ethnographic study of communication processes in a classroom', *Research on Language and Social Interaction*.

Marks, D. (1995) 'Ethnographic film: From Flaberty to Asch and after', *American Anthropologist*, 97 (2): 337–47.

Sacks, H. (1992) *Lectures on Conversation*, Vols I and II, ed. G. Jefferson. Oxford: Blackwell.

Sacks, H., Schegloff, E.A. and Jefferson, G. (1974) 'A simplest systematics for the organization of turn-taking for conversation', *Language*, 50: 696–735.

Scheflen, A.E. (1964) 'The significance of posture in communication systems', *Psychiatry*, 27: 316–31.

Schegloff, E. and Sacks, H. (1974) 'Opening up closings', in R. Turner (ed.), *Ethnomethodology*. Harmondsworth: Penguin. pp. 233–64.

Streeck, J. (forthcoming) 'How to do things with things: *Objets trouvés* and symbolization', *Human Studies*.

Suchman, L. (1987) *Plans and Situated Actions: The Problem of Human–Machine Interaction*. Cambridge: Cambridge University Press.

Suchman, L. (1993) 'Technologies of accountability: On lizards and aeroplanes', in G. Button (ed.), *Technology and the Working Order*. London: Routledge. pp. 113–26.

Turner, R. (1974) 'Words, utterances and activities', in R. Turner (ed.), *Ethnomethodology*. Harmondsworth: Penguin. pp. 197–215.

Whalen, J. (1995) 'A technology of order production: Computer-aided dispatch in public safety communications', in P. ten Have and G. Psathas (eds), *Situated Order: Studies in the Social Organization of Talk and Embodied Activities*. Washington, DC: University Press of America. pp. 187–230.

Wootton, A.J. (1994) 'Object transfer, intersubjectivity and third position repair: Early developmental observations of one child', *Journal of Child Language*, 21: 543–64.

PART VI VALIDITY

13 Reliability and Validity in Research Based on Tapes and Transcripts

Anssi Peräkylä

As Kirk and Miller (1986: 11) and Silverman (1993: 144) point out, the issues of reliability and validity are important, because in them the *objectivity* of (social scientific) research is at stake. The aim of social science is to produce descriptions of a social world – not just any descriptions, but descriptions that in some controllable way correspond to the social world that is being described. Even though all descriptions are bound to a particular perspective and therefore represent the reality rather than reproduce it (Hammersley, 1992), it is possible to describe social interaction in ways that can be subjected to empirical testing.

There is no single, coherent set of 'qualitative methods' applicable in all analysis of texts, talk and interaction. Rather, there are a number of different sets of methods: different ways of recording and analysing human activity and the use of symbols. Insofar as these various methods claim an epistemic status different from mere common sense, insofar they claim to report more than the research subjects' own descriptions of their circumstances, the question of objectivity is relevant for all these methods.

In research practice, enhancing objectivity is a very concrete activity. It involves efforts to assure the accuracy and inclusiveness of recordings that the research is based on as well as efforts to test the truthfulness of the analytic claims that are being made about those recordings. These concrete efforts, however, take different shapes according to the type of recordings on which the research is based. Questions that arise in the context of ethnographic field notes, for example, are different from questions that arise in the context of written texts. Field notes can be produced so as to be focused on particular issues or, alternatively, they can be produced so as to include as wide a range of events as possible (Hammersley and Atkinson, 1983: 150–1). In the analysis of written texts such a question does not arise: the researcher cannot control the focus of a given text that is used as data. (But the researcher can, of course, select the range of texts that he or she uses.)

This chapter will deal with issues of reliability and validity in research based on tapes and transcripts, and, in particular, in conversation analysis (CA). I will focus this discussion on one specific type of qualitative research only mainly because, as it was just pointed out, the questions of reliability and validity take a different form in different qualitative methods. The second reason for focusing on this specific variant of qualitative research is the fact that there are no accessible discussions available on issues of validity and reliability in conversation analytic studies.[1] This does not mean, however, that questions of validity and reliability have been addressed in conversation analytic research practice. In fact they are addressed more there than in many other types of qualitative research. But what has been lacking is a general student-oriented discussion about validity and reliability in conversation analytic research. The purpose of this chapter is to make a contribution in that direction.

Although the discussion in this chapter focuses on a specific type of qualitative research (conversation analysis), the basic issues raised here are relevant in the context of any qualitative method. Therefore, readers who are not primarily interested in conversation analysis are encouraged to treat this chapter as an *example* of the kinds of considerations that need to be addressed by any qualitative researcher. Even though the specific questions and answers concerning validity and reliability are different in other qualitative methods, the basic concerns are the same.

The argumentation presented in this chapter concerns primarily conversation analytic research *on institutional interaction* (Drew and Heritage, 1992; Drew and Sorjonen, 1997). As John Heritage points out in his contribution to this volume, there are two different kinds of conversation analysis going on today: 'The first examines the social institution *of* interaction as an entity in its own right; the second studies the management of social institutions [such as corporation, classroom, medicine etc.] *in* interaction' (p. 162). The first type of conversation analysis focuses on what is called 'ordinary conversation': informal talking among friends, family members, or the like. The latter one focuses on verbal interaction between professionals and clients or amongst professionals.

The methodological constraints facing these two types of conversation analysis are partially overlapping and partially different. In this chapter, the primary focus is on the latter type of conversation analysis. Hence, I will discuss issues such as the use of written documents along with the conversational data, and the criteria for validating claims about the relevance of an institutional context of interaction. These issues concern the analysis of institutional interaction, not the study of ordinary conversation. Some other issues that I will discuss, however (such as deviant case analysis), are also applicable to the analysis of ordinary conversations.

The aim of all conversation analytic studies (both on ordinary conversation and on institutional interaction) is to produce descriptions of recurrent patterns of social interaction and language use. CA is particularly rigorous in its requirement of an empirical grounding for any descriptions to be accepted as valid. In this respect, CA differs from some other forms of discourse analysis (Fairclough, 1992; Jokinen et al., 1993; Parker, 1992) and social constructionism (Gergen, 1994) which emphasize more the 'openness' of any language use to different interpretations and hence underline more the active contribution of the researcher in 'constructing' the descriptions that she or he produces about language use.

Reliability

Kirk and Miller define reliability as 'the degree to which the finding is independent of accidental circumstances of the research' (1986: 20). In ethnographic research, the reliability of research results entails 'whether or not (or under what conditions) the ethnographer would expect to obtain the same finding if he or she tried again in the same way' (1986: 69).

In the context of ethnography, as Silverman (1993: 146–8) also points out, checking the reliability is closely related to assuring the quality of field notes and guaranteeing the public access to the process of their production (cf. also Hammersley and Atkinson, 1983: 144–61). In conversation analytic research, tapes and transcripts are the 'raw material' comparable to ethnographers' field notes. Accordingly, the quality of tapes and transcripts has important implications for the reliability of conversation analytic research.

Concerns of reliability as a reason for working with tapes and transcripts

Working with tapes and transcripts eliminates at one stroke many of the problems that ethnographers have with the unspecified accuracy of field notes and with the limited public access to them. According to Harvey Sacks, realizing the potential of tape-recorded materials actually gave a crucial impetus to the creation of conversation analysis:

> It was not from any large interest in language or from some theoretical formulation of what should be studied that I started with tape-recorded conversation, but simply because I could get my hands on it and I could study it again and again, and also, consequentially, because others could look at what I had studied and make of it what they could, if, for example, they wanted to be able to disagree with me. (1984: 26)

Tape recordings and transcripts based on them can provide for highly detailed and publicly accessible representations of social interaction. Therefore, Kirk and Miller's suggestion that in qualitative research 'issues of reliability have received little attention' (1986: 42) does not apply to conversation analytic research. CA claims part of its justification on the basis of being free of many shortcomings in reliability characteristic of other forms of qualitative research, especially ethnography.

Securing maximum inclusiveness of tape-recorded data

Although tape-recorded data have intrinsic strength in terms of accuracy and public access, special attention needs to be paid to the *inclusiveness* of such data. Video or audio recordings of specific events (such as telephone conversations, medical consultations or public meetings) may entail a loss of some aspects of social interaction, including (a) medium- and long-span temporal processes, (b) ambulatory events and (c) impact of texts and other 'non-conversational' modalities of action. The potential loss can be prevented with appropriate arrangements in the data collection.

Temporal processes Conversation analytic research has brought a new kind of temporality into the central focus of sociological analysis: sequential organization of interaction operates in and through the relative timing of actions. As ethnographic research has repeatedly shown, however, local social worlds are also organized in terms of longer temporal spans (let alone the historical time focused on in the classical macro-sociological works of Durkheim, Weber and Marx). In hospitals, for example, management of chronically ill or dying patients involves complex trajectories shaped in and through the evolving daily actions of staff and patients (Glaser and Strauss, 1968; Strauss et al., 1985; Sudnow, 1967). Similarly, in social services, the recognition of events such as child mistreatment involves long-span processes with a multitude of agents and their negotiations at different sites (see Dingwall et al., 1983).

In the research based on tape recordings of single encounters, there is a risk that some of these longer-term temporal processes will be lost from sight. To prevent this from happening, longitudinal study designs can be used. Heritage and Lindström (1996), for example, report research based on recordings of six consecutive visits by a health visitor to a mother who had recently given birth. Their analysis focuses on the ways in which the mother progressively discloses morally problematic material, and the ways in which the health visitor manages these disclosures.[2]

Ambulatory events People move about in doing things. In Goffman's terms, the participants in any face to face interaction are 'vehicular entities, that is, human ambulatory units' (1983: 7). For anyone who has acted as a participant or as an observer in a hospital setting, this must be obvious. The ward round, for example, is, from the professionals' point of view, a single event with a number of alternating sub-groups of patient participants; this event moves about in patients' rooms and in the corridors of the ward.

The whole richness of ambulatory interaction can hardly be encapsulated using a stationary video camera, say, in one patient room. By collecting ethnographic data along with the tape recordings, the researcher can capture some aspects of ambulatory events. A good example of the fruitful combination of ethnographic and tape-recorded data is provided by Goodwin (1994, 1995; for a more abstract discussion, see Silverman, 1994). Moreover, by the use of multiple cameras, recordings can be made that are both comprehensive and accurate. Multiple cameras also need to be used when the interaction involves multiple sites which are connected using technical means, such as monitors or telephones. Charles and Marjorie Goodwin, for example, have used multiple cameras in recording the work of the crew in an oceanic research vessel (Goodwin, 1995) and the activities of air-traffic controllers (Goodwin and Goodwin, 1997). Similarly, Heath and Luff (1997) have analysed convergent activities in London Underground Line Control Rooms.

Documentary realities Written documents (and their production and use) are important for social life, as a domain of signification of its own, or, as Dorothy Smith (1974, 1990) puts it, as a 'textual reality'. Written documents also constitute a domain which is in contact with the domain of spoken interaction and which in some events organizes some aspects of it. As Firth (1995: 205–11) has recently shown, in international business communication, written messages (communicated through telex and fax) relate in many ways to the organization of the telephone conversations between the trade partners. Therefore, full understanding of some of the institutional activities conducted by telephone is not possible without the analysis of the prior written messages that inform their production. Similarly, in medical settings the content and the ordering of some of the questions that the professionals pose to the clients can be strongly influenced by clinical forms that the professionals need to fill in. Thus, even though every question has its local interactional management which can be observed in the tape recording, the logic of the questioning as a whole may not be derivable from the vocal events only. Therefore, it is important that the conversation analyst carefully collects and uses all the relevant written documents, along with the collection of tape recordings (for further examples of this, see Maynard, 1996; Whalen, 1995).

Different aspects of social organization In sum, by appropriate research design, conversation analytic studies of institutional interaction can be made more inclusive in terms of different layers of the organization of action. However, it also needs to be pointed out that *conversation analytic studies do not aim at describing all aspects of social organization*. (This is, of course, true concerning any other methodology as well.) The organization of verbal interaction in face to face encounters and telephone conversations is the domain in which adequate conversation analytic studies can rightly claim superior reliability, and this is indeed the home base of CA methodology. In studies that focus primarily on other aspects of social organization (such as textual, pictorial or technological realities) other methods may be more suitable.

Improving the reliability of CA in its own field

The claim of superior reliability in studies of face to face interaction needs to be justified, however, in each single piece of conversation analytic research. The key aspects of reliability involve *selection of what is recorded, the technical quality of recordings* and *the adequacy of transcripts.*

Basic *selection of what is recorded* arises, of course, from the research problem. But after this has been done (i.e. when the researcher has decided to tape-record encounters in a specific setting such as classroom, doctor's surgery, educational counsellor's office, or the like) the researcher still has to make some very consequential choices. The most important choice is *how much to record.*

There is a limit to how much data a single researcher or a research team can transcribe and analyse. But on the other hand, a large database has definite advantages. As the analysis of data in conversation analytic studies usually progresses inductively, the researcher normally does not know at the outset of the research what exactly the phenomena are that he or she is going to focus on. Therefore, it may turn out that she or he wants to analyse events that do not occur very many times in each single recording. For example, delivery of the diagnosis in medical consultations is such an event: there are consultations where no diagnosis is delivered, and in many consultations, it is done only once (cf. Heath, 1992; Peräkylä, 1995b). In order to be able to achieve a position where he or she can observe *the variation of the phenomenon* (such as the delivery of the diagnosis) in any reliable way, the researcher needs a large enough collection of cases. Therefore, he or she may need to have access to a relatively large database. In practice, a large portion of the data can be kept as a resource that is used only when the analysis has progressed so far that the phenomena under study have been specified. At that later stage, short sections from the data in reserve can be transcribed, and, thereby, the full variation of the phenomenon can be observed.

The technical quality of recordings is a decisive issue: if something is lost from sight or remains inaudible in the tapes, there is no way of recovering it. It may be extremely frustrating to have some badly recorded sections of events that at a later stage of the research turn out to be of primary importance for the analysis. This kind of frustration can be minimized by already at the planning stage of the research paying enough attention both to the quality of the equipment and to the arrangements of recording. The crucial aspects of quality include the sound (quality and location of microphones) and the inclusiveness of the video picture (the location and the type of the lens of the camera(s)). (For further details, readers are advised to consult Goodwin's [1992a] thorough treatment of the topic.)

The adequacy of transcripts is equally important: even though in a proper analysis of data the tapes need to be listened to and watched, at least the selection of what is analysed in detail is usually done on the basis of the transcripts only. The quality of transcripts in research on naturally occurring interaction seems to vary greatly. Not only are the details of intonation and prosody sometimes omitted, but what is more problematic, whole utterances (especially in multi-party situations) can be missing from transcripts in studies that otherwise have been seriously and adequately designed and conducted.

Transcription is a skill that can only be acquired through long enough training. It is extremely useful if an experienced transcriber can supervise a beginner. This is most easily done by the more experienced one correcting some of the beginner's transcripts. In fact, the correction of transcripts is useful for anybody preparing transcripts: another researcher can always hear some of the things that one has not noticed. Correction by colleagues also enhances a culture of shared practices in measuring pauses, intonation, and so on.

It is advisable to include many aspects of vocal expression in the initial transcripts (for conversation analytic transcription conventions developed by Gail Jefferson, see the Appendix to this volume and Atkinson and Heritage, 1984: ix–xvi). A rich transcript is a resource of analysis; at the time of transcribing, the researcher cannot know which of the details will turn out to be important for the analysis. After the analysis has been accomplished and the results are published, however, some of the special notation not used in the analysis can be left out. 'Simplified' transcripts can make the reception of the analysis easier, especially if the audience is not specialized in conversation analysis.

In sum, reliability of observations in conversation analytic research (as in any other empirical method) can only be achieved through serious effort. The method itself does not guarantee reliability. In conversation analytic studies, proper attention needs to be paid to the selection and technical quality of recordings as well as to the adequacy of the transcripts.

Validity in conversation analytic research

The validity of research concerns the interpretation of observations: whether or not 'the researcher is calling what is measured by the right name' (Kirk and Miller, 1986: 69; cf. Altheide and Johnson, 1994; Silverman, 1993: 149–66).

In the discussions about validity, especially in the context of quantitative research, there is an underlying background assumption about a separation between the 'raw' observations and the issues that these observations stand for or represent. Responses to questionnaires, for example, can be more or less valid representations of underlying social phenomena, such as the respondents' attitudes or values (cf. Alkula et al., 1994). Conversation analysis is in stark contrast to this kind of approach: the core of its very aim is to investigate talk-in-interaction, not as 'a screen on which are projected other processes', but as a phenomenon in its own right (Schegloff, 1992a: xviii). This commitment to naturalistic description of the interaction order (Goffman, 1983) and the social action taking place within that order (cf. also Sacks, 1984) gives a distinctive shape to the issues of validation in conversation analysis. These include the *transparence of analytic claims, validation through 'next turn', deviant case analysis, questions about the institutional character of interaction*, and finally, *the generalizability of conversation analytic findings.*

The transparence of analytic claims

In *Tractatus Logico-Philosophicus*, Wittgenstein pointed out that philosophy, rightly understood, is not a set of propositions but an activity, the clarification of non-philosophical propositions about the world. The method of this activity is complex because the 'knots' in our thinking are complex, but the results of philosophy are simple (see Kenny, 1973: 18, 101–2). A similar kind of paradox between the complexity of method and the simplicity of results is characteristic of conversation analysis, too.

The results of (good) conversation analytic research exhibit, in a positive manner, what Kirk and Miller (1986: 22) called *apparent validity*: once you have read them, you are convinced that they are transparently true. A conversational activity called 'fishing' may serve as an example. Anita Pomerantz showed in a paper published in 1980 how participants in a conversation can indirectly 'fish' for information from one another by telling what they themselves know. Descriptions of events displaying their producer's 'limited access' to the relevant facts may work as a device for inviting the other party to disclose his/her authorized version of the same issues (assuming, of course, that the other party is in a position of having privileged access to the relevant facts). Such dynamics are at work in cases like the following:

(1) *B:* Hello::.
A: HI:::.
B: Oh:hi:: 'ow are you Agne::s,
→ *A:* Fi:ne. Yer line's been busy.
B: Yeuh my fu (hh)- .hh my father's wife called me
..hh So when she calls me::, .hh I can always talk
fer a long time. Cuz she c'n afford it'n I can't.
hhhh heh .ehhhhhh
(Pomerantz, 1980: 195)

In Extract 1 above, the description based on a limited access to relevant facts given by A (marked with an arrow) works as what Pomerantz called 'a fishing device', successfully eliciting B's insider's report in the next turn. By telling her observations about the line having been busy, A makes it relevant for B to disclose to whom she was talking.

The description of an activity like 'fishing' tends to 'ring a bell' as soon as anyone stops to think about it. 'Fishing' is something in which everybody has participated in different roles. But until Pomerantz's article, this activity has not been described formally. The results of Pomerantz's analysis are very simple. Her argument is transparently true, or, in Kirk and Miller's (1986) terms, it has a genuine 'apparent validity'.

But just as in Wittgenstein's philosophy, 'although the *result* . . . is simple, its method cannot be if it is to arrive at that result' (Wittgenstein, 1975: 52). In conversation analysis, the complexities of the method involve other kinds of issues of validation.

Validation through 'next turn'

As Sacks et al. pointed out, research on talk-in-interaction has an inherent methodological resource that research on written texts lacks: 'Regularly . . . a turn's talk will display its speaker's understanding of a prior turn's talk, and whatever other talk it marks itself as directed to' (1974: 728). In other words, in the unfolding of the interaction, the interactants display to one another their interpretations of what is going on, especially of what was going on in the immediately preceding turn of talk (Heritage and Atkinson, 1984). From this fact arises a fundamental validation procedure that is used in all conversation analytic research:

> But while understandings of other turn's talk are displayed to co-participants, they are available as well to professional analysts, who are thereby afforded a proof criterion . . . for the analysis of what a turn's talk is occupied with. (Sacks et al., 1974: 729)

At the beginning of this chapter, it was pointed out that conversation analysis differs from those forms of discourse analysis and social constructionism which emphasize the open-endedness of the meaning of all linguistic expressions. Now we can see the reason for this: even though the meaning of any expression, if considered in isolation, is extremely open-ended, any utterance that is produced in talk-in-interaction will be locally interpreted by the participants of that interaction. In the first place, their interpretation is displayed in the next actions after the utterance. Hence, any interpretations that conversation analysts may suggest can be subjected to the 'proof procedure' outlined by Sacks et al.: the next turn will show whether the interactants themselves treat the utterance in ways that are in accordance with the analyst's interpretation.

Therefore in Extract 1 shown above, the utterance produced by B in lines 5–8 provides a proof procedure for the interpretation suggested by Pomerantz concerning A's turn in line 4. (What Pomerantz suggested was that 'telling my side' [what A did in line 4] can operate as a 'fishing device', which indirectly elicits an authoritative version of the events from the interlocutor.) And as we see, Pomerantz's interpretation passes the test: in lines 5–8, B gives her first-hand account of what had happened.

In much everyday conversation analytic work, things are not as nice and simple as in Extract 1: the next turns may be ambiguous in relation to the action performed in the preceding turn. However, the 'proof procedure' provided by the next turn remains the primordial criterion of validity that must be used as much as possible in all conversation analytic work.

Deviant case analysis

By examining the relations between successive turns of talk, conversation analysts aim at establishing *regular patterns* of interaction (Heritage, 1995). The patterns concern relations between actions (such as the relations between 'telling my side' and 'giving an authoritative report' in the case of 'fishing' described above). After having established a pattern, the analyst's next task is to search for and examine *deviant cases*: cases where 'things go differently' – most typically, cases where an element of the suggested pattern is not associated with the other expected elements.

The deviant case analysis in CA closely resembles the technique of 'analytic induction' often used in ethnographic studies (see Hammersley and Atkinson, 1983: 201–4; Silverman, 1985: 111–15; 1993: 160–2). For the analyst, those cases that do not fit the inductively constructed pattern are deviant. Rather than putting aside these discrepant cases, the analyst is encouraged to focus particular attention on them.

In her well-known paper on 'fishing', Pomerantz (1980: 186–7) presents a deviant case in which a description of events displaying its producer's 'limited access' does *not* lead the other party to disclose her authorized version of the event:

(2) *A:* . . . dju j'see me pull us?=
1→ *B:* =.hhh No:. I wz trying you all day. en the line
wz busy fer like hours
2→ *A:* ohh:::::, oh:::::, .hhhhhh We::ll, hh I'm g'nna
c'm over in a little while help yer brother ou:t
B: Goo [:d
A: [.hhh Cuz I know he needs some he::lp,
((mournfully))
B: .hh Ye:ah. Yeh he'd mention' that tihday.=
A: =M-hm,=
3→ *B:* .hhh Uh:m, .tlk .hhh Who wih yih ta:lking to.
(Pomerantz, 1980: 186–7)

In Extract 2 above, B reports her experience about A's line having been busy (arrow 1). In terms of the interactional pattern identified by Pomerantz, this kind of telling should make relevant a subsequent disclosure of the details of the event by the other, more knowledgeable party. In the extract above, however, this does not happen. Instead, A shifts the topic in her subsequent turn (arrow 2). Therefore, within the framework of the analysis of 'fishing', we can consider Extract 2 as a deviant case.

In a recent paper, Clayman and Maynard (1994) have outlined three different ways that deviant cases can be dealt with.

(1) Sometimes deviant cases can be shown to exhibit the interactants' orientation to the *same* considerations and normative orientations that produce the 'regular' cases. In those cases, something in the conduct of the participants discloses that they, too, treat the case as one involving a

departure from the expected course of events. If the deviant cases show this kind of property, they provide *additional support* for the analyst's initial claim that the regularities found in the first phase of the data analysis 'are methodically produced and oriented to by the participants as normative organizations of action' (Heritage, 1988: 131).

Extract 2 above is an example of this type of deviant case. After A has failed to respond to B's initial 'fishing' turn by an authorized report of the events, B asks directly to whom A had been talking (arrow 3). Through her question, she openly requests the information which the fishing device (arrow 1), according to Pomerantz's analysis, solicited indirectly. This shift to open information seeking after an unsuccessful 'fishing' attempt indirectly confirms B's initial orientation to the 'fishing' as a device which can be used in indirect solicitation of information.

(2) Clayman and Maynard (1994) point out, however, that there are also deviant cases that cannot be integrated within the analysts' construction of the participants' orientations that normally produce the regular cases. In dealing with these cases, the analyst may need to change his or her construction of the participants' orientations. A classical example is Schegloff's (1968) analysis of a single deviant case in his corpus of 500 telephone call openings. In this single case, unlike the other 499, the caller spoke first. The analysis of that single case led Schegloff to abandon his initial hypothesis (according to which there is a norm obligating the answerer to speak first) and to reconceptualize the very first moves of telephone calls in terms of the adjacency pair 'summons (telephone ringing)–answer'. In the deviant case, the answerer didn't produce the relevant second pair part, and, accordingly, the caller reissued the summons by speaking first.

(3) There are also, however, deviant cases which cannot be integrated either into the existing or into a reconceptualized hypothesis concerning the participants' orientations (Clayman and Maynard, 1994). In these cases, an explanation can be sought from the individual contingencies of the single case. Normative orientations or strategic considerations other than those that usually inform the production of the pattern may be invoked by the participants in single cases, and these other orientations or considerations may explain the deviance. My study on the delivery of diagnosis in primary health care (Peräkylä, 1995b) provides an example. The study focused on the ways in which doctors display the evidence for the diagnostic conclusions that they deliver to the patients. A pattern was found in which the doctors delivered the patients' diagnosis *without* verbal reference to the evidential basis of the diagnosis *only* in sequential positions where the evidence had just been made observably present through the physical examination or the examination of medical records. In two single cases, however, the diagnosis was delivered without that kind of presence of evidence. But observable individual contingencies that made these cases 'different' from the rest of the data were found: in these cases the diagnosis was delivered *for the second time* during the same consultation. The

evidential basis had been present in the first announcements of the diagnosis, and the reconfirmation could be made without such basis.

In sum, deviant case analysis constitutes a central resource for testing of hypotheses in conversation analytic work. Therefore, the researcher should consider the deviant cases not a nuisance, but a treasure. The meticulous analysis of those cases gives impetus, strength and rigour to the development of the analytic arguments.

Validity of claims concerning the institutional character of interaction

In both qualitative and quantitative research, a central dimension of validity involves the correspondence between a theoretical paradigm and the observations made by the researcher. 'Construct validity' is a term that is often used in this context (Carmines and Zeller, 1979: 22–6; Kirk and Miller, 1986: 22). It involves the relations between theoretical concepts and the observations that are supposed to represent those concepts. As it was pointed out above, the primary emphasis that CA places on naturalistic description de-intensifies the relevance of many ordinary concerns of construct validity. However, the recent expansion of conversation analytic research on institutional interaction (see Heritage, Chapter 11 in this volume; and Drew and Heritage, 1992) has reinvoked the need to consider the relation between observations and concepts also in conversation analytic studies.

In conversation analytic research on institutional interaction, a central question of validity is this: what grounds does the researcher have for claiming that the talk he or she is focusing on is in any way 'connected to' some institutional framework? The fact that a piece of interaction takes place in a hospital or in an office, for example, does not *per se* determine the institutional character of that particular interaction (Drew and Heritage, 1992: 18–21). Institutional roles, tasks and arrangements may or may not be present in any particular interactions; they may or may not be present at particular *moments* in particular interactions. If they are, the conversation analytic programme presupposes, their presence is observable to the participants and the analyst alike.

Two basic criteria for the validity of claims concerning the institutional character of talk have been outlined by Schegloff (1987, 1991, 1992b). The first criterion concerns the *relevancy of categorization*. There are indefinitely many aspects of context potentially available for any interaction: we may categorize one another on the basis of gender, age, social class, education, occupation, income, race, and so on, and we may understand the setting of our interaction accordingly. In the momentary unfolding of interaction, Schegloff argues, 'the parties, singly and together, select and display in their conduct which of the indefinitely many aspects of context they are making relevant, or are invoking, for the immediate moment' (1987: 219).

Awareness of this 'problem of relevance' requires the professional analyst to proceed with caution. There is a danger of 'importing' institutional context to data. The professional analyst may be tempted to assume, without going into the details of data, that this or that feature of talk is an indication of a particular context (such as 'medical authority' or 'professional dominance') having affected the interaction. Such stipulation for context may, Schegloff (1991: 24–5) argues, result in the analysis being terminated prematurely, so that the inherent organization within the talk is not thoroughly understood. Phenomena which in the beginning may appear as indications of the workings of an 'institutional context' may in a more thorough examination turn out to be primarily connected to the organization and dynamics of talk which can be even better understood without reference to the 'institutional context'.

Another key issue addressed by Schegloff (1991, 1992b) involves what he calls *procedural consequentiality of context*. He argues that it is not sufficient to say that a particular context is oriented to 'in general' by the participants in interaction, but, instead, it has to be shown how specifiable aspects of the context are consequential for specifiable aspects of the interaction. The goal is to make 'a direct "procedural" connection between the context . . . and what actually happens in the talk' (Schegloff, 1991: 17). What is said, when it is said, and how, and by whom, and to whom, may invoke the context; the goal of the conversation analytic research is to explicate exactly how the things said brought forward the context.

Schegloff's emphasis on the procedural consequentiality of the context has an important corollary. If a piece of research can pin down specific procedural links between a context and talk-in-interaction, it is likely that these observations are not only relevant in terms of analysis of detailed organization of interaction but also that they contribute to the understanding of the context *per se*. Standard social scientific understandings of professional and other contexts are often based on rough generalizations concerning the professionals' tasks, clients' roles and the relations between the two (cf. Hak, 1994: 472). Conversation analytic research goes far beyond such generalizations. Thus, for example, the studies of Heath (1992), Maynard (1991a, 1991b, 1992) and myself (Peräkylä, 1995b) on the delivery of diagnostic news have involved not only a detailed description of the specific practices found in medical consultations, but also a specification of a central aspect of that context, namely the dimensions and character of medical authority.

These two fundamental concerns of conversation analytic research on institutional interaction constitute a validity test for the claims concerning the institutional character of interaction. 'Relevancy of categorization' and 'procedural consequentiality of context' are something to be demonstrated by the researcher. In demonstrating them, the researcher will focus on particular phenomena in interaction, such as lexical choice, turn design, sequence organization and overall structural organization (Drew and Heritage, 1992: 29–45; Heritage, Chapter 11 in this volume). Where the workings of context will be found in a single piece of research cannot be predicted in advance. This unpredictability arises from the inductive character of the conversation analytic enterprise; it causes both the fundamental difficulty and the exceptional fascination of conversation analytic research.

Generalizability of conversation analytic findings

The final dimension of validity of conversation analytic (and any other) research concerns the generalizability of the research findings (Pomerantz, 1990; cf. Alasuutari, 1995: 143–57). Due to their work-intensive character, most conversation analytic studies are necessarily based on relatively small databases. How widely can the results, derived from relatively small samples, be generalized?

This character of the problem is closely dependent on the type of conversation analytic research. In studies of ordinary conversation, the baseline assumption is that the results are or should be generalizable to the whole domain of ordinary conversations, and to a certain extent even across linguistic and cultural boundaries. Even though it may be that the most primordial conversational practices and structures – such as turn-taking or adjacency pairs – are almost universal, there are others, such as openings of telephone calls (see Houtkoop-Steenstra, 1991; Lindström, 1994; Schegloff, 1986), which show considerable variation in different cultures. This variation can only be tackled through gradual accumulation of studies on ordinary conversation in different cultures and social milieus. But let us focus now on the study of institutional interaction, where the problem is posed in different terms.

In some (advanced) studies of institutional interaction, explicit comparisons between different settings are made. Miller and Silverman (1995), for example, applied the comparative approach in describing talk about troubles in two counselling settings: a British haemophilia centre counselling patients who are HIV-positive and a family therapy centre in the US. In particular, they focused on similarities in three types of discursive practices in these settings: those concerned with trouble definitions, trouble remedies and the social contexts of the clients' troubles.

It is likely that as the databases and analyses on institutional interaction gradually accumulate, studies like Miller and Silverman's will become more common. The comparative approach directly tackles the question of generalizability by demonstrating the similarities and differences across a number of settings. For the time being, however, most of the studies on institutional interaction are more like case studies.

Case studies on institutional interaction are based on data collected from one or a few sites only. The number of the subjects involved in such studies can be relatively small. If the professionals involved in the study are theoretically oriented, they may use one theory only, and hence their style may be different from the style that could be found at sites where different theories are applied.[3] For these reasons, it is important to ask whether the results presented in such studies are in any way generalizable. Does everything that is said in case studies on institutional interaction apply exclusively to the particular site that was observed, or do the results have some wider relevance?

In terms of the traditional 'distributional' understanding of generalizability, case studies on institutional interaction cannot offer much. Studying one or a few sites only does not warrant conclusions concerning similarities in the professionals' and their clients' conduct in different settings. In that sense, case studies on institutional interaction have a very restricted generalizability.

However, the question of generalizability can also be approached from a different direction. The concept of *possibility* is a key to this. *Social practices that are possible*, that is, *possibilities of language use*, are the central objects of all conversation analytic case studies on interaction in particular institutional settings. The possibility of various practices can be considered generalizable even if the practices are not actualized in similar ways across different settings. For example, in my study on AIDS counselling in a London teaching hospital (Peräkylä, 1995a), the research objects were specific questioning practices used by the counsellors and their clients. These practices, arising from the Milan School Family Systems Theory, include 'circular questioning' (eliciting one party's description of his or her mind by first asking another party to give his or her account of it), 'live open supervision' (asking questions in such a manner that the delivery of the question is done in two stages, via an intermediary) and 'hypothetical future-oriented questioning' (questions about the patient's life in a hypothetical future situation). These very practices were to a large extent developed in the particular hospital that my data were from, and it is possible that they are not used anywhere else exactly in those specific ways that were analysed in my study (see Peräkylä and Silverman, 1991, for some observations on the wide variety of approaches in AIDS counselling in Britain). Hence my results cannot be directly generalizable to any other site where AIDS counselling is done.

However, the results of my study can be considered descriptions of questioning techniques that are possible across a wide variety of settings. More specifically, the study involves an effort to describe in detail how these questioning techniques were made possible: what kind of management of turn-taking, participation frameworks, turn design, sequence organization, and so on, was needed in order for the participants to set up scenes where 'circular questioning', 'live open supervision' and 'hypothetical future-oriented questioning' were done. The study showed *how* these practices are made possible through the very details of the participants' action.

As possibilities, the practices that I analysed are very likely to be generalizable. There is no reason to think that they could not be made possible by any competent member of (at least any Western) society. In this sense, this study produced generalizable results. The results were not generalizable as descriptions of what other counsellors or other professionals do with their clients; but they were generalizable as descriptions of what any counsellor or other professional, with his or her clients, *can* do, given that he or she has the same array of interactional competencies as the participants of the AIDS counselling sessions have.

Conclusion

At the beginning of this chapter, I pointed out that the specific techniques of securing reliability and validity in different types of qualitative research are not the same. The aim of this chapter has been to give an overview of the imperatives faced and solutions found in conversation analytic research, especially when such research focuses on institutional interaction. At a more general level, however, the considerations of validity and reliability in conversation analysis are similar to those in any other kind of qualitative research: all serious qualitative research involves assuring the accuracy of recordings and testing the truthfulness of analytic claims.

In terms of the division of qualitative methods into three main 'branches' suggested by Silverman (1993), it seems that the specific constraints facing CA are closer to those of observational research than those of text analysis. The questions about the quality and inclusiveness of recordings, for example, arise in both, and deviant case analysis is also used in both.

Kirk and Miller (1986: 21, 42) point out that in conducting and assessing qualitative research (particularly ethnography), the primary emphasis has usually been laid on validity rather than on reliability, whereas in quantitative research the emphasis has been on the opposite. Put in simple terms, this may imply that qualitative research is well developed in terms of validity and underdeveloped in terms of reliability. I hope to have shown in this chapter that this is not the case with conversation analysis: CA can be considered a serious attempt to develop a method for the analysis of social action that is able to combine concerns of validity with those of reliability.

A serious concern about the reliability of observations was at the very core of the initial motivation of Harvey Sacks in beginning the line of research that we now call conversation analysis. The reliability of tape recordings remains an inherent strength of CA – but as I pointed out earlier in this chapter, tape recording *per se* does not suffice as a guarantee of the reliability of the observations. The researcher needs to pay attention both to the technical quality and inclusiveness of tape recordings and to the interplay of spoken language with other modalities of communication and social action.

The main procedures of validation of the researcher's analytic claims in all conversation analytic research include the analysis of the next speaker's interpretation of the preceding action, and deviant case analysis. In conversation analytic studies which focus on institutional interaction, new dimensions of validation have also arisen. These include the validation of the claims concerning the relevance of an institutional context of interaction, and the issue of generalizability of the results of case studies.

Notes

I wish to thank David Silverman, John Heritage and Johanna Ruusuvuori for their comments on the earlier versions of this chapter.

1. For general discussions on the method of conversation analysis, see Heritage (1988, 1995); Pomerantz and Fehr (1997); Wootton (1989).
2. For temporality in organizations, see also Boden (1994).
3. On analyses of theoretically informed work, see Gale (1991), who describes 'solution oriented brief family therapy'; Buttny (1993: 66–84), who analyses couple therapy based on systems theory; and Coupland et al. (1994), who describe medical consultations at a geriatric outpatients clinic operating within the framework of 'holistic' medicine.

References

Alasuutari, P. (1995) *Researching Culture: Qualitative Method and Cultural Studies*. London: Sage.

Alkula, T., Pöntinen, S. and Ylöstalo, P. (1994) *Sosiaalitutkimuksen Kvantitatiiviset Mentelmät*. Porvoo: WSOY.

Altheide, D.L. and Johnson, J.M. (1994) 'Criteria for assessing interpretive validity in qualitative research', in N.K. Denzin and Y.S. Lincoln (eds), *Handbook of Qualitative Research*. Thousand Oaks, CA: Sage. pp. 485–99.

Atkinson, J.M. and Heritage, J. (eds) (1984) *Structures of Social Action: Studies in Conversation Analysis*. Cambridge: Cambridge University Press.

Boden, D. (1994) *The Business of Talk: Organizations in Action*. Cambridge: Polity.

Buttny, R. (1993) *Social Accountability in Communication*. Newbury Park, CA: Sage.

Carmines, E.G. and Zeller, R.A. (1979) *Reliability and Validity Assessment*. Beverly Hills, CA: Sage.

Clayman, S.E. and Maynard, D.W. (1994) 'Ethnomethodology and conversation analysis', in P. ten Have and G. Psathas (eds), *Situated Order: Studies in the Social Organization of Talk and Embodied Activities*. Washington, DC: University Press of America. pp. 1–30.

Coupland, J., Robinson, J.D. and Coupland, N. (1994) 'Frame negotiation in doctor–elderly patient consultations', *Discourse & Society*, 5 (1): 89–124.

Dingwall, R., Eekelaar, J. and Murray, T. (1983) *The Protection of Children*. Oxford: Basil Blackwell.

Drew, P. and Heritage, J. (1992) 'Introduction: Analyzing talk at work', in P. Drew and J. Heritage (eds), *Talk at Work: Interaction in Institutional Settings*. Cambridge: Cambridge University Press. pp. 3–65.

Drew, P. and Sorjonen, M.-L. (1997) 'Institutional dialogue', in T.A. van Dijk (ed.), *Discourse: A Multidisciplinary Introduction*. London: Sage. pp. 92–118.

Fairclough, N. (1992) *Discourse and Social Change*. Cambridge: Polity.

Firth, A. (1995) '"Accounts" in negotiation discourse: A single case analysis', *Journal of Pragmatics*, 23: 199–226.

Gale, J.E. (1991) *Conversation Analysis of Therapeutic Discourse: The Pursuit of a Therapeutic Agenda* (Vol. XLI in the series 'Advances in Discourse Processes'). Norwood, NJ: Ablex.

Gergen, G. (1994) *Realities and Relationships: Soundings in Social Construction*. Cambridge, MA: Harvard University Press.

Glaser, B.G. and Strauss, A.L. (1968) *Time for Dying*. Chicago: Aldine.

Goffman, E. (1983) 'The interaction order', *American Sociological Review*, 48 (1): 1–17.

Goodwin, C. (1992a) 'Recording human interaction in natural settings', *Pragmatics*, 2: 181–209.

Goodwin, C. (1992b) 'Transparent vision'. Unpublished manuscript, Department of Anthropology, University of South Carolina.

Goodwin, C. (1994) 'Professional vision', *American Anthropologist*, 96 (3): 606–33.

Goodwin, C. (1995) 'Seeing in depth', *Social Studies of Science* 25: 237–74.

Goodwin, C. and Goodwin, M.H. (1997) 'Formulating planes: Seeing as a situated activity', in D. Middleton and Y. Engestrom (eds), *Cognition and Communication at Work: Distributed Cognition in the Workplace*. Cambridge: Cambridge University Press.

Hak, T. (1994) 'The interactional form of professional dominance', *Sociology of Health and Illness*, 16 (4): 469–88.

Hammersley, M. (1992) *What's Wrong with Ethnography: Methodological Explorations*. London: Routledge.

Hammersley, M. and Atkinson, P. (1983) *Ethnography: Principles in Practice*. London: Tavistock.

Heath, C. (1992) 'The delivery and reception of diagnosis in the general practice consultation', in P. Drew and J. Heritage (eds), *Talk at Work: Interaction in Institutional Settings*. Cambridge: Cambridge University Press. pp. 235–67.

Heath, C.C. and Luff, P.K. (1997) 'Convergent activities: Collaborative work and multimedia technology in London Underground Line Control Rooms', in D. Middleton and Y. Engestrom (eds), *Cognition and Communication at Work: Distributed Cognition in the Workplace*. Cambridge: Cambridge University Press.

Heritage, J. (1988) 'Explanations as accounts: A conversation analytic perspective', in C. Antaki (ed.), *Analysing Everyday Explanation: A Case Book of Methods*. London: Sage. pp. 127–44.

Heritage, J. (1995) 'Conversation analysis: Methodological aspects', in U.M. Quatshoff (ed.), *Aspects of Oral Communication*. Berlin: Walter de Gruyter. pp. 391–418.

Heritage, J. and Atkinson, J.M. (1984) 'Introduction', in J.M. Atkinson and J. Heritage (eds), *Structures of Social Action: Studies in Conversation Analysis*. Cambridge: Cambridge University Press. pp. 1–13.

Heritage, J. and Lindström, A. (1996) 'Motherhood, medicine and morality: Scenes from a series of medical encounters', in J. Bergmann and P. Linell (eds), *Morality in Discourse*. Hemel Hempstead: Harvester Wheatsheaf.

Houtkoop-Steenstra, H. (1991) 'Opening sequences in Dutch telephone conversations', in D. Boden and D.H. Zimmerman (eds), *Talk and Social Structure: Studies in Ethnomethodology and Conversation Analysis*. Cambridge: Polity. pp. 232–50.

Jokinen, A., Juhila, K. and Suoninen, E. (1993) *Diskurssianalyysin aakkoset*. Tampere: Vastapaino.

Kenny, A. (1973) *Wittgenstein*. London: Allen Lane.

Kirk, J. and Miller, M.L. (1986) *Reliability and Validity in Qualitative Research*. London: Sage.

Lindström, A. (1994) 'Identification and recognition in Swedish telephone conversation openings', *Language in Society*, 23 (2): 231–52.

Maynard, D.W. (1991a) 'Interaction and asymmetry in clinical discourse', *American Journal of Sociology*, 97 (2): 448–95.

Maynard, D.W. (1991b) 'The perspective-display series and the delivery and receipt of diagnostic news', in D. Boden and D.H. Zimmerman (eds), *Talk and Social Structure: Studies in Ethnomethodology and Conversation Analysis*. Cambridge: Polity. pp. 164–92.

Maynard, D.W. (1992) 'On clinicians co-implicating recipients' perspective in the delivery of diagnostic news', in P. Drew and J. Heritage (eds), *Talk at Work: Interaction in Institutional Settings*. Cambridge: Cambridge University Press. pp. 331–58.

Maynard, D. (1996) 'From paradigm to prototype and back again: Interactive aspects of "cognitive processing" in standardized survey interviews', in N. Schwarz and S. Sudman (eds), *Answering Questions: Methodology for Determining Cognitive and Communicating Processes in Survey Research.* San Francisco: Jossey Bass.

Miller, G. and Silverman, D. (1995) 'Troubles talk and counselling discourse: A comparative study', *Sociological Quarterly*, 36 (4): 725–47.

Parker, I. (1992) *Discourse Dynamics: Critical Analysis for Social and Individual Psychology.* London: Routledge.

Peräkylä, A. (1995a) *AIDS Counselling: Institutional Interaction and Clinical Practice.* Cambridge: Cambridge University Press.

Peräkylä, A. (1995b) 'Authority and intersubjectivity: The delivery of diagnosis in primary health care'. Unpublished manuscript, Department of Sociology, University of Helsinki.

Peräkylä, A. and Silverman, D. (1991) 'Rethinking speech-exchange systems: Communication formats in AIDS counselling', *Sociology*, 25 (4): 627–51.

Pomerantz, A. (1980) 'Telling my side: "Limited access" as a "fishing device"', *Sociological Inquiry*, 50: 186–98.

Pomerantz, A. (1990) 'On the validity and generalizability of conversation analytic methods: Conversation analytic claims', *Communication Monographs*, 57 (3): 231–5.

Pomerantz, A. and Fehr, B.J. (1997) 'Conversation analysis: An approach to the study of social action as sense making practices', in T.A. van Dijk (ed.), *Discourse as Social Interaction.* London: Sage. pp. 64–91.

Sacks, H. (1984) 'Notes on methodology', in J.M. Atkinson and J. Heritage (eds), *Structures of Social Action: Studies in Conversation Analysis.* Cambridge: Cambridge University Press. pp. 21–7.

Sacks, H., Schegloff, E.A. and Jefferson, G. (1974) 'A simplest systematics for the organization of turn-taking for conversation', *Language*, 50: 696–735.

Schegloff, E.A. (1968) 'Sequencing in conversational openings', *American Anthropologist*, 70: 1075–95.

Schegloff, E.A. (1986) 'The routine as achievement', *Human Studies*, 9: 111–51.

Schegloff, E.A. (1987) 'Between macro and micro: Contexts and other connections', in J. Alexander, B. Giesen, R. Munch and N. Smelser (eds), *The Micro–Macro Link.* Berkeley and Los Angeles: University of California Press. pp. 207–34.

Schegloff, E.A. (1991) 'Reflections on talk and social structure', in D. Boden and D.H. Zimmerman (eds), *Talk and Social Structure: Studies in Ethnomethodology and Conversation Analysis.* Cambridge: Polity. pp. 44–70.

Schegloff, E.A. (1992a) 'Introduction', in H. Sacks, *Lectures on Conversation*, Vol. 1, ed. G. Jefferson. Oxford: Blackwell. pp. ix–lxii.

Schegloff, E.A. (1992b) 'On talk and its institutional occasion', in P. Drew and J. Heritage (eds), *Talk at Work: Interaction in Institutional Settings.* Cambridge: Cambridge University Press. pp. 101–34.

Silverman, D. (1985) *Qualitative Methodology and Sociology.* Aldershot: Gower.

Silverman, D. (1993) *Interpreting Qualitative Data: Methods for Analysing Talk, Text and Interaction.* London: Sage.

Silverman, D. (1994) 'Ethnography and conversation analysis in the study of professional–client interaction: A question of "how" and "why"'. Paper presented at the RC 25 (sociolinguistics) session at the World Congress of Sociology, Bielefeld, Germany, 18–23 July.

Smith, D.E. (1974) 'The social construction of documentary reality', *Sociological Inquiry*, 44 (4): 257–68.

Smith, D.E. (1990) *The Conceptual Practices of Power.* Toronto: University of Toronto Press.

Strauss, A.L., Fagerhaugh, S., Suczeck, B. and Wiener, C. (1985) *The Social Organization of Medical Work.* Chicago: University of Chicago Press.

Sudnow, D. (1967) *Passing On: The Social Organization of Dying.* Englewood Cliffs, NJ: Prentice Hall.

Whalen, J. (1995) 'A technology of order production: Computer–aided dispatch in public safety communications', in P. ten Have and G. Psathas (eds), *Situated Order: Studies in the*

Social Organization of Talk and Embodied Activities. Washington, DC: University Press of America. pp. 187–230.

Wittgenstein, L. (1975) *Philosophical Remarks*. Edited from his posthumous writings by R. Rhees and translated by R. Hargreaves and R. White. Oxford: Blackwell.

Wootton, A.J. (1989) 'Remarks on the methodology of conversation analysis', in D. Roger and P. Bull (eds), *Conversation: An Interdisciplinary Perspective*. Clevedon: Multilingual Matters. pp. 238–58.

PART VII SOCIAL PROBLEMS

14 Addressing Social Problems through Qualitative Research

Michael Bloor

This chapter explores two case studies which provide illustrative details of two different but related approaches for researchers who wish to address social problems and who are also sceptical of the possibilities of extensive influence on the policy-making community. Both of the approaches aim to influence practitioners rather than policy-makers and both link particularly well with qualitative research methods. In the first case study, an ethnographic research project is viewed as an analogue or partial paradigm of successful practitioner work, in this case outreach work among male prostitutes: in effect, the ethnography may be viewed as a demonstration or pilot outreach project. In the second case study, ethnographic work provides the material and the stimulation for practitioners to evaluate and revise particular facets of their own service provision.

It was rather a shock for me to read in Carey's (1975) social history of the 'Chicago School' of sociology that in the 1920s the foremost practitioners of the foremost school of sociology were divided about how sociological knowledge should be applied: Should it be used to influence policy-makers? Or (and here lay the surprise) should sociologists intervene in social problems directly as consulting professionals, like clinicians or architects? I was vaguely aware that some hundred years earlier Auguste Comte had proposed a similar priestly cadre of sociologists to direct society along enlightened (and Enlightenment) paths. But the realization was somehow monstrous that, as late as the 1920s and contemporaneously with, say Eliot's 'The Waste Land' and a hundred dystopian diatribes, my intellectual forebears could hanker after the power to re-engineer social life and institutions to their nostrums. It was the absence of that power, rather than humility, which thwarted them: in Carey's analysis (1975: 71–94), it was the lack of the kind of institutionalized authority which medicine exercises over a lay clientele, rather than any acknowledged deficiency in knowledge or in technical competence, which determined the path along which sociology would develop. Sociologists eventually opted to set out their stalls as scientists rather than professionals, and the West was largely spared the directive intervention of social experts (the peoples of the Soviet Union were less fortunate).

Since the 1960s, the more limited aspiration of sociologists to influence policy-makers has also been under attack. It was pointed out by various critics that the policy community rarely sought *policies* from researchers: instead, research would be commissioned to confirm a preferred policy option, or perhaps to delay a necessary but inconvenient intervention. Bulmer (1982), in *The Uses of Social Research*, was one of those who sought to redefine an influential role for social science in the face of these criticisms. Taking up Janowitz's (1972) distinction between the 'engineering' and 'enlightenment' models of policy research, Bulmer argued that research cannot engineer changes of policy, but it can have an important indirect impact on the policy climate through processes of intellectual association and influence, providing descriptive accounts and theoretical interpretations. Silverman (1985, 1993) has termed this the 'state counsellor' role and has gently ridiculed how Bulmer's book on 'the uses of social research' turns out to be solely about the uses of social research for policy-makers.

Both the 'enlightenment' and 'engineering' models have long been under attack from advocates of the 'critical social research' model. Becker (1967), for example, posed the rhetorical question 'whose side are we on?' and argued the case for action-oriented research rather than policy-oriented research, for progressive social change achieved through emancipation rather than policy initiatives. He called for a partisan sociology that spoke up for the underdogs against the élites, élites which would include policy-makers in their number. Today Becker's question is widely believed to defy a simple answer, with researchers experiencing cross-cutting responsibilities to their research subjects, to funding agencies, to gate-keepers and to their colleagues in the scientific community. And Becker's rhetoric of sides is thought to be intellectually disabling, embracing what Silverman (1993: 172) has called 'its prior commitment to a revealed truth' (the plight of the underdog, and so on).

Hammersley (1995) has characterized all three models (engineering, enlightenment and critical) as different varieties of Enlightenment models with a capital E, since they all endorse certain Enlightenment ideas originating with the French 'Encyclopaedists' of the eighteenth century, namely that social life can be improved by planned intervention derived from accumulated scientific knowledge, itself the product of social research. In late modern society all three tenets of the Enlightenment paradigm have come under 'postmodernist' criticism: it is no longer universally accepted that planned intervention is capable of bringing about desirable social change, or that scientific knowledge can facilitate this, or that social research can produce such knowledge. Hammersley's review of these postmodernist criticisms leads him to the assessment that they serve to qualify severely rather than demolish the possibility of a social impact for social research: the scope for and feasibility of successful policy intervention has been overestimated in The Enlightenment Project and the role of research in bringing change about has been exaggerated and misunderstood, but this does not mean that social improvement is impossible or that knowledge lacks all authority.

The policy community is not the sole audience for social research. Sociologists who have conducted research on sociological aspects of health and medicine, for example, have long been aware that there is a role for sociologists as participants in debates on public policy, but that there are also other audiences for social research, notably audiences of patients and practitioners (clinicians, nurses and other professionals). Practitioner-oriented social research has also been the subject of revisionist criticism. One strand of such criticism is that the researcher becomes the ally of the practitioner in exploitative relationships with patients or clients, servicing the practitioner in practitioner–client relationships which reinforce patriarchy, say, or white supremacy. This is a topic I shall return to in my conclusion. The other strand of criticism of practitioner-oriented social research is that articulated by commentators such as Schon (1983), who have followed Schutz (1962) in arguing that professional work does not entail the deployment of scientific knowledge, but rather involves the deployment of a different kind of knowledge altogether, knowledge-in-action, which is rigorous but not comprehensive, task-oriented but not systematic, and experiential rather than research-based. In this reading, social research has little of value to contribute to practitioners' work. However, such criticisms hardly apply to that social research which takes practitioners' everyday work as its topical focus: social research which seeks to describe and compare practitioners' everyday work practices self-evidently invites practitioners to juxtapose and weigh their own practices with those reported by the researcher. Qualitative research techniques, with their capacity for rich description, are favoured techniques for research focused on everyday work practices.

The first case study reported in the chapter is a street ethnography of HIV-related risk behaviour among Glasgow male prostitutes. Safer and unsafe commercial sexual encounters were compared: unsafe encounters were found to be associated with control of the sexual encounter by the clients of prostitutes; safer sex was associated with particular techniques of power exercised by prostitutes. These findings indicate possible lines of successful intervention for those engaged in sexual health promotion, while the fieldwork methods and experience offered lessons for the design of successful outreach work in this area. The second case study is a comparative ethnography of variations in therapeutic community practice. The comparative design highlighted a number of features of good therapeutic practice found in particular communities that could profitably be adopted elsewhere, while the researcher's close fieldwork relationships with local therapeutic community practitioners encouraged the practitioners to experiment with particular new methods of working.

Case A: Male prostitutes' HIV-related risk behaviour

The need for services

Prior to the HIV epidemic, targeted services for male prostitutes hardly existed in the UK. There were a few notable exceptions, in particular one should note the London-based charity 'Streetwise' and its pioneering drop-in centre for male prostitutes. But certainly there were no targeted services in Glasgow. Indeed, when I and colleagues first began to inquire about male prostitution in Glasgow, we encountered scepticism in some quarters about whether male prostitution actually existed on any scale in Glasgow (it was thought to be much more the sort of thing that might be found in effete, middle-class Edinburgh). Male prostitution, in fact, is a highly diversified activity: the 'call man' in his own tastefully decorated flat, packing for a trip to Brazil with a businessman client, is far removed from the group of swearing, cat-calling, jostling teenagers warming themselves with their bottles of 'Buckie' wine outside the late-night urinal. Not all male prostitutes have much need of services, but others have multiple and complex problems (legal problems, health problems, housing problems, financial problems) which are sometimes unpresented to, or inadequately addressed by, service-providers. The illegality of male prostitution has made specialist service development difficult: most Glasgow male prostitutes contacted in our study were below the then age of consent for homosexual acts and many of these acts did not occur in private; although the police adopted a stance of qualified toleration to female street prostitution, whereby female street prostitution was 'policed' rather than suppressed, that toleration was never extended to male street prostitution. And male service-providers with an interest in providing services for male prostitutes were vulnerable to misconstructions of their motives.

The harm reduction approach

The HIV epidemic, along with its toll on lives and health, represented an opportunity to change the policy climate in respect of male prostitution. The situation was analogous to that in the drugs services, where a range of services (most notably syringe exchanges) was put in place for existing drug injectors who were not motivated to abstain from drugs or to change their route of administration from injection to smoking or ingestion. This new drugs policy, which became known as that of 'harm reduction' or 'harm minimization', argued that 'the spread of HIV is a greater danger to individual and public health than drug misuse . . . [and that] services that aim to minimize HIV risk behaviour by all available means, should take precedence in development plans' (Advisory Council on the Misuse of Drugs, 1988). In similar fashion, it became possible to argue the case for services targeted at male prostitutes which had as their priority not the elimination of prostitution, but the minimization of individual and public health risks.

Study methods and service provision

These changes in the policy climate are clearer in retrospect than they were in the late 1980s when the fieldwork on male prostitutes' HIV-related risk behaviour was begun. The study was part of a wider programme of research on social aspects of HIV/AIDS supported by the Medical Research Council. The findings and the methodology of the study have been fully described elsewhere (Bloor et al., 1991, 1992, 1993). After pilot work, six different sites – two parks, two pubs and two public lavatories – were selected for time-sampling; non-streetworking prostitutes (escorts, masseurs and call men) were contacted through their advertisements and the study's own advertisement in the gay press. The ethnographic fieldwork was conducted in pairs for security purposes. Prostitutes were contacted by a combination of cold-contacting and snowballing: some of those contacted had never previously spoken to anyone about their prostitution activities. Both gay and self-identified 'straight' prostitutes were contacted, as were both drug injectors and non-injectors, and both novices and experienced prostitutes.

While the fieldworkers' primary objective was research, it was recognized from the outset that the fieldwork also offered opportunities for health promotion: relations between fieldworkers and research subjects can never be scientifically neutral (Hammersley and Atkinson, 1995) and an attempt to preserve a fictional neutrality should never be used as an excuse for failing to attempt to save lives. The Greater Glasgow Health Board provided condoms suitable for oral and for anal sex for the researchers to distribute (when the fieldwork started condoms suitable for anal sex were not freely commercially available); an advice leaflet was also handed out which gave advice on HIV prevention and also gave contact numbers for HIV/AIDS counselling and for other relevant services such as welfare rights and homelessness.

Study findings

If the handing-out of condoms and advice leaflets could be thought to generate a 'reporting bias', discouraging the reporting of unsafe commercial sex, then such discouragement can only have been marginal because at least a third of those prostitutes contacted reported unsafe sex with at least some of their current commercial partners (unsafe sex was defined, following the Terrence Higgins Trust, as anal sex with or without a condom, because of the greater risk of condom failure in anal sex). Unsafe commercial sex was associated with client control. In contrast to female street prostitution, where safer commercial sex is almost always practised and the women assume directive control of the encounter (McKeganey and Barnard, 1992), in many male prostitute–client encounters it is the client who assumes control and decides on matters such as the type of sex and its location. Safer commercial sex among male prostitutes was associated with particular strategies of power to wrest the initiative away from clients.

Seeking payment up front (universally practised by female prostitutes) was one such successful strategy. Getting payment up front was not popular with the clients, who feared (with some justification) that the prostitute might 'do a runner', but that the minority of male prostitutes in the sample who *did* insist on prior payment were all currently practising safer commercial sex.

However, getting the money up front was not the only successful countervailing strategy of power used by male prostitutes to insist on safer sex. Male prostitution is often a highly covert and ambiguous activity, few words are exchanged and it is not even always clear to both parties that the encounter is a commercial one. Safer sex is likely to be associated with any techniques that serve to dispel the ambiguity that surrounds the encounter and make type of sex (and prices) a matter for overt discussion, as in the following fieldnote:

> His procedure was to stand at the urinal. The client would come and stand beside him. When the coast was clear, the client would put out a hand and he would immediately say 'I'm sorry but I charge.' Some would leave at that point. With the remainder he'd negotiate a rate. He would accept 10 pounds but sometimes got 20 pounds. . . . He always did hand jobs or oral sex. . . . If clients asked him for anal sex he told them to eff off.

Encouragement of overt negotiations between prostitute and client is only one strategy (albeit possibly the most effective strategy) for the promotion of safer commercial sex. Another strategy practised by some respondents was to attempt to screen out those clients looking for anal sex by building up a 'book' of regular clients (with whom safer sex was practised) and refusing all casual commercial contacts. But it is difficult for streetworking prostitutes to confine themselves exclusively to 'regulars' (only one streetworking respondent had succeeded in working thus, although another two respondents had some 'regulars' and supplemented their income with additional casual contacts) and one UK study found that anal penetration was actually more common in encounters with regular clients than with casual clients (Davies and Feldman, 1991), possibly because sexual encounters with streetworkers' regular clients are more likely to take place at the clients' houses with more attendant privacy than semi-public locations such as car parks and back lanes, where disrobing may be difficult, uncomfortable and dangerous.

The substitution of overt negotiations between prostitutes and clients for the furtive and largely non-verbal exchanges characteristic of many encounters would have advantages beyond the prevention of HIV infection and of other sexually transmitted diseases. One considerable advantage might lie in an attendant reduction in the levels of violence surrounding male prostitution. Rapes, muggings and assaults (of clients by prostitutes, of prostitutes by clients and of both prostitutes and clients by 'queer bashing' third parties) are commonplace; during the sixteen-month fieldwork period three of our thirty-two research subjects were charged with assault and a fourth was imprisoned. Many (but not all) of these violent altercations are disputes about money. There were no 'going rates' for the various sexual services on offer: prostitutes took what money they could and, without prior agreement on charges (sometimes without even prior agreement that a charge was to be levied), the scope for violent disputes was considerable, as is illustrated in the following fieldnote:

> ['Sammy' said he'd] never been cheated out of his money: he'd make sure he always got his money (this was said with a sudden hard emphasis . . .). He and 'Kenny' laughingly recalled an altercation with one of 'Colin's' punters [i.e. clients]. Colin was demanding twenty-five pounds and the punter swore he was only due fifteen pounds, refusing to hand over the extra ten pounds. Kenny, in his cynical way, was disinclined to believe Colin, but Sammy said he'd rather believe a mate than some dirty old punter. Sammy had intervened, whipped a knife out and held it in front of his face (this was mimed out for our benefit). The punter instantly pulled out the extra cash, shot off and had never been seen at the toilets since.

Implications for service provision

This research project had two possible policy pay-offs. First, it indicated how both unsafe commercial sex and violence could be reduced, namely through encouraging male prostitutes to engage in overt negotiations with clients. And, secondly, it indicated a possible medium for that encouragement, namely outreach work associated with condom distribution at regular prostitution sites.

Outreach work, taking services to clients rather than waiting for clients to attend at agencies, has a long history but has been little evaluated (Rhodes et al., 1991). It is clear that outreach work is the only means of delivering services to clients who are unable or unwilling to attend agencies and the HIV/AIDS epidemic has greatly stimulated the development of outreach services to stigmatized and victimized populations (drug injectors, gay men, female and male prostitutes) who are judged to be at possible risk of HIV infection and transmission. At the time this study was conducted, Glasgow had no outreach project targeted at male prostitutes: there was a drop-in centre for female prostitutes, but no outreach workers were attached to it and no men were admitted to the drop-in premises. Ethnographic fieldwork, in its protracted and regular contacts with research subjects, has much in common with services outreach work and it was therefore possible for the ethnographic study to take on the character of a local feasibility study for a male prostitute outreach service, demonstrating to the sceptical that appreciable numbers of male prostitutes were working in Glasgow, that levels of HIV-related risk behaviour were high and that outreach contact could be established. Moreover, the nature of the fieldwork contact that was established augured well for a future outreach service: large quantities of condoms were distributed (to clients as well as prostitutes); even highly socially isolated individuals with no contact with other prostitutes proved contactable; working relationships were established with important local individuals such as bar-owners and managers, toilet attendants and (at an appropriate distance) the police; and the project proceeded with no threat to the safety of the ethnographers.

Throughout the fieldwork period I had briefed public health personnel, social work staff and AIDS charity workers about project developments and provisional findings. At the conclusion of the fieldwork period, I had arranged (with the permission of my research subjects) to introduce them to a local social worker who was to be employed as an outreach worker, covering the same prostitution sites that I had covered during ethnographic fieldwork. The introductions were accomplished but the planned outreach post was 'frozen' (along with other local authority posts) owing to a local authority budgetary crisis associated with non-payment of the poll tax. Nevertheless, the commitment to a male prostitution outreach service had been made and the establishment of such a service was merely postponed, taking place at a later date.

No claim is being made here that this ethnographic research made a contribution of any importance to national policy debates about HIV/AIDS services. I did participate in a national colloquium organized to discuss outreach services for men who have sex with men, but by this time a number of outreach services for men who have sex with men were already underway in England, funded under the Health Education Authority's MESMAC initiative (evaluated by Prout and Deverell, 1994). The research project did not fulfil a 'state counsellor' role but, thanks to the sustained contact with research subjects afforded by qualitative methods, the project was able to fulfil a dual research-and-health-promotion function and to act as a demonstration project for the feasibility and content of a local outreach service.

Case B: Principles of good therapeutic community practice

Study methods

Therapeutic communities are found in a variety of shapes and sizes (residential and non-residential, long-term and short-term), catering for a range of client groups (psychiatric patients, ex-psychiatric patients, children with learning difficulties, adults with learning difficulties, drug users and alcoholics, prisoners, and so on), with a range of different staffing arrangements, but having in common an approach to therapeutic work as an essentially cognitive activity which can transform any mundane event in the community (be it lavatory cleaning, or complaining about the noise) by redefining that event in the light of some therapeutic paradigm (Bloor et al., 1988). The nature of the paradigm may vary from community to community, but the redefinition of the event (as showing responsibility, say, or seeking out a new and less pathogenic way of relating to others) as an occasion or a topic for therapy sets it apart and transforms it, much as the profane is transformed into the sacred by religious belief and ceremony.

I and two colleagues (Neil McKeganey and Dick Fonkert) conducted a comparative ethnography of eight different therapeutic communities studied by one or another of us over a period of some ten years. Because all the individual studies involved the collection of similar (participant observation) data on the same general topic (the treatment process), it was possible to reuse those data for a single comparative study which avoided the usual constraint of qualitative methods, namely that breadth of coverage must be sacrificed for depth. As a result, we were able to compare practice across a wide range of contrasting therapeutic community settings – two contrasting residential psychiatric units (studied by McKeganey), a Camphill Rudolf Steiner school for children with learning difficulties (McKeganey), a 'concept house' for drug users (Fonkert), a 'foster family' care facility (Bloor), two contrasting halfway houses for disturbed adolescents (Bloor), and a psychiatric day hospital (Bloor). Accounts of the research methods have been supplied elsewhere (Bloor et al., 1988).

Comparison as a stimulus to practice change

Any ethnography is essentially comparative in approach. When the ethnographer is fieldnoting, then he or she is selecting from a cornucopia of continuing sense data those moments that seem to him or her to be of special significance. When analysing the fieldnotes, the ethnographer is juxtaposing and comparing numerous similar and contrasting fieldnote accounts. And when writing the ethnography the writer is weighing various different accounts in order to illustrate and develop the argument in the text. Of course, these comparative judgements are not confined to ethnography: similar evaluative judgements are made on a continuing and routine basis by all research subjects. It therefore follows that one possible *use* of ethnography is to assist in these everyday comparative judgements: rich description of particular kinds of therapeutic practice, for example, can assist practitioners in making evaluative judgements about their own practices, preserving what seems to them good practice and experimenting with the adoption of new practices where this seems appropriate. In effect, reading an ethnography of therapeutic communities can be like visiting other communities and being drawn to reconsider one's everyday routines in the light of contrasted experience: McKeganey has described how a group visit to a second community led staff and residents at the 'Faswells' psychiatric unit to try to make mealtimes much more of a community and therapeutic occasion, such as they had observed to be the case at the visited community (Bloor et al., 1988: 180).

Provided that the practitioner audience retains some autonomy of function and judgement in their everyday work (arguably a minimum definition of professional practice [Freidson, 1970]), then any ethnography can thus serve as a stimulus to practice change and a number of sociological ethnographies have found their way onto professional training courses for this reason (indeed our comparative ethnography is used on at least one therapeutic community training course). However, my fellow researchers and I wished to go beyond merely passively providing opportunities for such comparative practitioner judgements; we wished actively to draw the attention of readers to particular features of practice in one or two communities which, it seemed to us, might be adopted with profit by other communities. The utility of ethnographic texts for practitioner audiences can be enhanced by making explicit for readers those silent and implicit researcher judgements that have led to particular practices being recorded and analysed in the first place. No authoritative scientific judgement is intended here, I simply list below some practices that seemed to my colleagues and myself to be worthy of wider dissemination. The final test of their utility would lie in whether practitioners themselves shared our judgement and found themselves able to adopt them successfully; successful adoption in the unique circumstances of individual communities may not always be possible, perhaps because of a clash with other valued practices, or inadequate resources, or time-tabling problems. The practices we commended were as follows (in no particular order of importance):

1 making fellow residents responsible for keeping residents in treatment;
2 ways of increasing residents' awareness of the changeability of the community structure;
3 the 'after-group' as a way of promoting resident reflectivity;
4 the attendance of residents at staff change-over meetings;
5 the 'tight house' as a way of countering institutionalism;
6 resident selection of participating staff;
7 the offering of alternative sources of satisfaction to junior staff.

There is no space here to enlarge on all these possible means of improving therapeutic community practice (see Bloor et al., 1988: 172–85, for a fuller account); instead I shall simply expand upon the first listed practice, that of making residents responsible for keeping residents in treatment.

Keeping residents in treatment

All non-custodial treatment institutions face problems associated with the premature departure or self-discharge of residents. It is a commonplace that persons who discharge themselves prior to the completion of their treatment may derive less benefit from that treatment than those who stay to complete the course, indeed self-discharge may be part of a process of relapse to those pathogenic patterns of behaviour that led to the resident's referral to the therapeutic community in the first place. In studies of 'concept houses' for the treatment of drug users, for example, high reported success rates in remaining drug-free among those ex-residents who *complete* their courses have to be set against the fact that up to three-quarters of enrollees may discharge themselves prematurely, against staff advice (see, e.g., Volkman and Cressey's, 1963, evaluation of the first concept house, Synanon).

No therapeutic community is more vulnerable to premature self-discharge that a psychiatric day hospital, like Aberdeen's Ross Clinic day hospital, where patients who wish to drop out have the simple expedient of failing to turn up for treatment on the following day. Treatment at the day hospital was conducted on a group basis and followed the principle of 'reality confrontation' (Morrice, 1979), the reflection back to patients, informally and in formal group therapy sessions, that their conduct is unacceptable and the depiction of the therapeutic community as a locale where new and less pathogenic social behaviours can be experimented with and adopted. Although confrontation could be manifest in many forms other than angry denunciation, including gentle irony and hesitant concern, staff were aware that the treatment method put pressures on patients which could lead to self-discharge or even to suicidal impulses. To avoid premature discharge and self-harm, there was a convention in the day hospital (understood by staff and all but novice patients alike) that fellow-patients should provide the necessary comfort and support for patients to remain in treatment. In the first fieldnote extract below, 'Lenny' fled after his first ever public disclosure of his sexual orientation; in the second 'Dawn' fled, threatening suicide:

> [H]e'd remarked that he couldn't face telling his mother he'd had a sexual relationship with another man . . . he'd walked out on Friday lunchtime and a group of patients had run after him and brought him back and got him talking a bit.

> This afternoon considerable pressure was put on 'Dawn': she had spoken of her feelings of hopelessness and depression, her failure to 'work' in the group, and her feeling that she ought to leave the day hospital. Several staff members had already left for prior appointments. 'Edith' (staff) said she had seen Dawn glance at the clock several times: now was her chance to end it (the group). Her voice breaking, Dawn picked up her bag, said she'd end it all right, and rushed out of the room. Edith did nothing to stop her. At 'Harry's' (patient) bidding, 'Olive' (patient) went after her, caught her up in the toilets and made her promise to come again tomorrow. Once before she'd dashed off and her fellow-patients set off after her. Indeed, this dashing after bolting patients is a fairly common occurrence – Edith could predict that Dawn would be looked after.

Moreover, patients who did silently discharge themselves by failing to return to the day hospital could expect a delegation of fellow-patients visiting them at their homes, urging them to return. Determined would-be defaulters had either to announce and defend their decisions in the formal groups or resort to subterfuge – failing to answer the door and even, in one case, leaving the country.

This practice of making patients responsible for keeping their fellow-patients in treatment, albeit effective in the day hospital, is not without potential drawbacks. For example, many patients who stayed away from the hospital were aware that they would be visited and solicited to return: thus, the provision of comfort and support to distressed and defaulting patients could be seen as encouraging attention-seeking behaviour. However, such drawbacks are not overwhelming, since staff who are aware of them can raise them in the formal therapeutic groups.

The patient or resident culture plays an important, even crucial, part in the treatment process in all therapeutic communities: the work of 'reality confrontation', for example, is often seen by practitioners as being more effective when conducted by fellow-patients than by staff, and fellow-residents/patients play an important part in inculcating in new arrivals an understanding of organizational structures and practices. Thus, requiring that patients/residents undertake the responsibility for keeping their fellows in treatment would be simply an extension of the active patient/resident therapeutic role already found in therapeutic communities. Nevertheless, such an extension of patients/residents' responsibilities, if successful, could have an appreciable influence on patterns of self-discharge in many communities. At 'Ashley' for example, one of the two halfway houses for disturbed adolescents in the study, although the residents were prepared to welcome and support new arrivals, established residents who chose to discharge themselves (a procedure sometimes indistinguishable from absconding) were never confronted or persuaded otherwise by their fellows. In one celebrated instance during my fieldwork at the house, almost the entire resident group knew beforehand of one resident's planned 'escape', which involved hanging around on the street outside to intercept the postman and appropriate his 'giro' (welfare benefits cheque) before catching an inter-city bus. No one chose to dissuade him and one fellow-resident even helped him carry his possessions to the bus station.

Feeding back findings

The above list of therapeutic community practices which might be profitably adopted elsewhere (including making residents responsible for keeping each other in treatment) was reported by myself and my research collaborators in the usual way in the academic and practitioner press and in a paper to an international conference of practitioners. But we also fed back findings to individual communities involved in the research. The feedback took various forms: in one community, Neil McKeganey and I used our knowledge of therapeutic community practice at the house to produce a video of everyday practice in the community, which was subsequently used by the house for PR purposes; in the day hospital, I circulated to staff and to some ex-patients (with whom I was still in contact) a research report on the relationship of the patient culture to the formal treatment programme, and that report became the basis for two 'focus group' discussions (Morgan, 1991) with staff and ex-patients; in the two halfway houses ('Ashley' and 'Beeches'), I circulated a comparative report to staff of both houses which was used as the basis for a focus group discussion with Ashley staff and for individual staff interviews with Beeches staff (who had largely dispersed to other posts in the meantime), but also at the conclusion of the fieldwork I had previously given staff some impressionistic feedback. At Ashley, this impressionistic feedback focused on how one might combat premature self-discharge:

> I had previously said that I would give the staff some feedback on my thoughts about the house before I left – not a 'scientific' statement, but simply an informed observer's reflections. I'd given some thought to this in advance and had decided to concentrate on one problem I thought was perhaps inadequately attended to – premature departure by residents 'frightened' of the changes expected of them – and a possible solution – a stronger resident culture. I spent an evening talking about this with the warden last night . . . and she brought it up in the staff group this afternoon.
>
> It led to a lot of discussion: general agreement that the problem was there.
>
> At the end of the [weekly] community meeting [the warden] said that she'd like (after her return from holiday) a special meeting of the community to discuss the problem of people leaving.

Ashley was not the only study community where the comparative analysis acted as a spur to modifications in practice. Sociological description of everyday therapeutic work can act as a stimulus to practitioners to re-examine their practice and perhaps modify it in response to comparative data. This stimulus to change can be increased by choosing certain forms of dissemination in preference to others, for example by explicit highlighting of examples of good practice, and by personal briefings as well as written reports. It is also possible that the close personal ties that are built up with research subjects over the course of ethnographic fieldwork serve to command an interested and committed audience for the fieldworker's findings. Of course, modes of research dissemination that command an audience among therapeutic community practitioners might not be similarly influential with other practitioner audiences: this should be a matter for empirical experimentation.

Conclusion

Policy influence for sociologists is quite possibly a chimera, a unicorn among the cedars which is glimpsed tantalizingly from time to time but always eludes us. Some might say that policy-makers themselves are a chimera: a distinguished epidemiologist of my acquaintance claims never to have met one. In his younger years he would frequently meet senior functionaries in the health service, but they would always claim to be merely implementing policies passed down from above. As he himself grew in seniority, he came to meet the yet more senior functionaries from above, but they, too, claimed merely to be implementing policies passed down from above. Still his seniority grew, but still he encountered only policy implementors. He searched in vain for the fountainheads of health service policy until in old age the truth struck him that no one knowingly makes policy; for reasons perhaps of protective colouration everyone is convinced that they are mere policy-implementors, simply interpreting and elaborating edicts passed down from some more august authority. Analogous, if less colourful, arguments have been constructed by some empirical researchers of policy processes (Manning, 1989; Rock, 1987), namely that policy is a situated discourse, a set of tacit assumptions and implicit meanings found within particular offices and occupational groupings.

It is this policy discourse, this amalgam of committee asides, gossip and unspoken assumptions, that Bulmer would seek to influence through the gentle diffusion of sociological ideas and research findings. But sociologists, particularly researchers, are rare visitors to these social worlds: their capacity for cultural diffusion is minimal. The argument in this chapter has been that the real opportunities for sociological influence lie closer to the coalface than they do to head office, that the real opportunities for sociological influence lie in relations with practitioners, not with the managers of practice.

This role for sociologists as practitioner helpmeets will not be found by some to be wholly satisfactory. All practitioner–client relationships (be they outreach worker–prostitute relationships, or therapeutic community staff–resident/patient relationships) are power relationships. In a Foucauldian analysis (see, e.g., Foucault, 1980), power cannot be wished or legislated away, it is inherent in all relationships. Therapeutic advance has as its corollary the extension of the controlling therapeutic gaze: the growth of public health medicine since the nineteenth century, for example, has brought great health benefits, but it has also subjected populations to increasing surveillance and regulation (Armstrong, 1983). Surveillance as a technique of power ('the eye that knows and decides, the eye that governs' – Foucault, 1973: 89) is increasingly complemented in the late twentieth century by other techniques, most notably that of 'pastoral care' (Foucault, 1981), whereby clients of agencies find themselves 'shepherded' in disciplinary relationships with practitioners whose avowed goals are merely those of care and advice. Assisting in the extension of outreach work to new populations, or suggesting ways to increase the effectiveness of therapeutic community practice, are each alike analysable as endeavours which tighten the disciplinary grip of experts on citizens. In a new twist on Becker's old 'whose side are we on?' question, it may be argued that sociology should be assisting not in the extension of power, but in the extension of resistance – resistance to meddlesome interference in prostitutes' street dealings, and resistance to expert orchestration of patients' private lives. The opposite of power is not its absence, but the resistance it provokes; sociologists, so the argument goes, should be laying the groundwork for citizen resistance rather than fostering the extension and effectiveness of expert power.

However, this critical view of sociological influence on practitioners is a new version of an old song, the song of the Leninist vanguard party which always knows best, having learned the Lessons of History. It matters not, in this critical view, that male prostitutes may welcome the provision of a service where there was none before, or that patients/residents in therapeutic communities may welcome the chance to play a fuller part in the treatment process by providing comfort and support to their fellows. What matters is resistance to experts' disciplinary power. Paradoxically, the critical analyst has become the all-seeing expert: the analyst claims to know better than the practitioners (the outreach workers and the therapeutic community staff), but the analyst also claims to know better than those whose resistance should be stiffened (the prostitutes and the patients/ residents). Yet if the critical analysts are themselves experts, what kind of disciplinary relationship do they have with their audience? Should not they too be resisted? It follows that we can skirt these sophistries: where citizens themselves commend the work of practitioners, then it is not the place of sociologists to murmur of false consciousness and demand resistance to pastoral care.

This issue (of whether or not social research should seek to assist the resistance of clients and patients) is part of a broader debate about the epistemological status of social research, about whether value neutrality can and should remain a constitutive principle of social research. The claim that social research can and should be value neutral is under attack from two sides. On one side, battle has been joined by those who argue that research should be explicitly politically participatory, embracing particular political aims, such as combating racism or patriarchy. On the other side, battle has been joined by those who argue that *no* practice or policy prescriptions can be offered by researchers under any circumstances, since all knowledge is socially constructed and there are no grounds for the researcher to claim superior knowledge.

The argument about participatory research is perhaps seen most clearly in the responses which greeted the publication of Foster's (1990) findings on the lack of evidence for racist practices in British schools. Foster found little evidence that black pupils were treated unfairly in lessons or that they were misallocated to ability groups; moreover, he re-examined the evidence of racism found in earlier studies and found it methodologically flawed. The study generated a considerable critical response from those committed to some version of anti-racism. Hammersley's (1995) review of the controversy firmly supports Foster's position against various implicit and explicit charges, notably that as a middle-class white male he was experientially disabled from collecting and understanding evidence of institutional racism, and that the primary objective of research is not the production of knowledge but the changing of society.

The argument of the 'strict constructivists' (the term is Best's, 1989) that researchers should be silent on social problems (having no basis for claiming superior knowledge) was stated succinctly by Woolgar and Pawluch (1985). Best's edited volume (and especially his own concluding chapter) relates some of the responses to Woolgar and Pawluch's paper. He argues the case for a 'contextual constructivist' position in distinction to the 'strict constructivist' position. Best is unclear whether it is practically possible to achieve the strict constructivists' goal of analyses wholly free of assumptions about objective reality; he cites various examples of how such assumptions may creep in at the backdoor of such analyses. Contextual constructivists, in contrast, may collaborate with collectivity members in examining and debating competing policy claims.

It seems, therefore, that sociologists *may* address social problems and that they can address them most effectively by influencing practitioner practice. Qualitative research has a two-fold advantage in these processes of influence: one advantage relates to influencing practitioners who are the researcher's research subjects, and the second advantage relates to influencing practitioners who are the wider audience for the research findings. In respect of practitioners who are research subjects, qualitative researchers can call upon their pre-existing research relationships with their research subjects as a resource for ensuring an attentive and even sympathetic response to their research findings. A close personal and working relationship, based on lengthy social contact and built up over weeks and months, is likely to ensure that not only will practitioner research subjects have a particular interest in the findings (because of the identity of the researcher as much as a particular interest in the research topic), but also they may be willing to devote an unusual amount of time and effort to discussions of the findings. At the day hospital and Ashley halfway house, staff (and a group of ex-day hospital patients) were willing to read a quite lengthy research report and then make their reactions to the report the basis for a special focus group discussion. Where the researcher has become, for research subjects, a person for whom they have a special regard as a result of long familiarity, then it should come as no surprise that those research subjects will have interest in implementing the researcher's suggestions on changes in practice. In effect, the qualitative researcher may become a part of his or her local practitioner collectivity and trades on that position as a collectivity member to disseminate research findings.

In respect of other practitioners (who are not research subjects), the qualitative researcher has the advantage that the research methods allow rich descriptions of everyday practice which enable practitioner audiences imaginatively to juxtapose their own everyday practices with the research description. There is therefore an opportunity for practitioners to make evaluative judgements about their own practices and experiment with the adoption of new approaches described in the research findings. Qualitative studies of everyday practice, particularly ethnographies, offer sufficiently detailed descriptions of practice to act as a spur to judgement and experimentation. Relatedly, where specialist services (such as male prostitute outreach services) do not currently exist, qualitative research can provide detailed descriptions of the circumstances and behaviour of potential service-users such that material assistance is given with the design of targeted services. In the special case of outreach services, ethnographic fieldwork shares so many similarities with outreach work that a successful ethnographic project can act as a feasibility study or demonstration project for an outreach service. Shaw (1996) has recently developed at length the argument that qualitative methods can provide a paradigm or examplar for practitioners seeking to reflect upon and modify their work practices.

Practitioner autonomy is variable in its extensiveness but universal. Practitioners may not always have the local autonomy to develop new services to new target populations of clients, but all practitioners have the autonomy to modify their everyday work practices. In seeking the chimera of policy influence, sociologists rather neglected how research findings can address social problems through the encouragement of modifications and developments in practitioners' everyday practices. The effectiveness of research in addressing social problems has been increasingly questioned and even the legitimacy of social research in addressing those problems has been queried. Of course, these questions and queries have been raised most loudly *outside* the sociological community, by pundits and politicians. However, this chapter is concerned not with punditry or politics, but rather with those questions and queries raised *within* the sociological community. It is suggested that the addressing of social problems is indeed a legitimate objective of social research and that, although the effectiveness of social research as an agency of social change may be somewhat limited, it is not wholly ineffective. Moreover, if the impact of social research on service-providers' practices is considered alongside the impact on formal policy, then social research clearly has the potential to be more effective yet as an agency of change.

Acknowledgements

I wish to thank Ian Shaw and David Silverman for their helpful comments on an earlier draft of this chapter. All the research reported on here was supported by the Medical Research Council. I wish to thank Marina Barnard, Andrew Finlay and Neil McKeganey for their help as my co-fieldworkers in the male prostitution study and I wish to thank Dick Fonkert and Neil McKeganey for their help in the comparative analysis of the therapeutic communities data.

References

Advisory Council on the Misuse of Drugs (1988) *AIDS and Drug Misuse: Part One*. London: Department of Health and Social Security.

Armstrong, D. (1983) *Political Anatomy of the Body: Medical Knowledge in Britain in the Twentieth Century*. Cambridge: Cambridge University Press.

Becker, H. (1967) 'Whose side are we on?', *Social Problems*, 14: 239–48.

Best, J. (ed.) (1989) *Images of Issues: Typifying Contemporary Social Problems*. Hawthorne, NY: Aldine de Gruyter.

Bloor, M., McKeganey, N. and Fonkert, D. (1988) *One Foot in Eden: A Sociological Study of a Range of Therapeutic Community Practice*. London: Routledge.

Bloor, M., Finlay, A., Barnard, M. and McKeganey, N. (1991) 'Male prostitution and risks of HIV infection in Glasgow: Final report', *ANSWER*, A.212: 1–3.

Bloor, M., McKeganey, N., Finlay, A. and Barnard, M. (1992) 'The inappropriateness of psycho-social models of risk behaviour to understanding HIV-related risk behaviour among Glasgow male prostitutes', *AIDS Care*, 4: 131–7.

Bloor, M., Barnard, M., Finlay, A. and McKeganey, N. (1993) 'HIV-related risk practices among Glasgow male prostitutes: Reframing concepts of risk behaviour', *Medical Anthropology Quarterly*, 7: 1–19.

Bulmer, M. (1982) *The Uses of Social Research*. London: Allen and Unwin.

Carey, J. (1975) *Sociology and Public Affairs: the Chicago School*. London: Sage.

Davies, P. and Feldman, R. (1991) 'Male sex workers in South Wales', *Project Sigma Working Paper No. 35*. Colchester: University of Essex.

Foster, P. (1990) *Policy and Practice in Multicultural and Antiracist Education*. London: Routledge.

Foucault, M. (1973) *The Birth of the Clinic*, trans. A. Sheridan. London: Tavistock.

Foucault, M. (1980) 'The eye of power', in *Power/Knowledge: Selected Interviews and Other Writings 1972–1977*, ed. C. Gordon. Brighton: Harvester.

Foucault, M. (1981) '*Omnes et singulatim*: Towards a criticism of political reason', in S. McMurrin (ed.), *The Tanner Lectures on Human Values II*. Salt Lake City: University of Utah Press.

Freidson, E. (1970) *Profession of Medicine*. New York: Dodds Mead.

Hammersley, M. (1995) *The Politics of Social Research*. London: Sage.

Hammersley, M. and Atkinson, P. (1995) *Ethnography: Principles in Practice* (2nd edn). London: Routledge.

Janowitz, M. (1972) *Sociological Models and Social Policy*. Morristown, NJ: General Earning Systems.

McKeganey, N. and Barnard, M. (1992) *AIDS, Drugs and Sexual Risk: Lives in the Balance*. Milton Keynes: Open University Press.

Manning, P. (1989) 'Studying policies in the field', in J. Gubrium and D. Silverman (eds), *The Politics of Field Research: Sociology Beyond Enlightenment*. London: Sage. pp. 213–35.

Morgan, D. (1991) *Focus Groups as Qualitative Research*. Newbury Park, CA: Sage.

Morrice, J.K. (1979) 'Basic concepts, a critical review', in R. Hinshelwood and N. Manning (eds), *Therapeutic Communities: Reflections and Progress*. London: Routledge and Kegan Paul. pp. 94–111.

Prout, A. and Deverell, K. (1994) 'MESMAC: Working with diversity – building communities: An evaluation of a community development approach to HIV prevention for men who have sex with men'. London: Health Education Authority.

Rhodes, T., Hartnoll, R., Johnson, A., Holland, J. and Jones, S. (1991) 'Out of the agency and on to the streets: A review of HIV outreach health education in Europe and the United States', *ISDD Research Monograph No. 2*. London: Institute for the Study of Drug Dependence.

Rock, P. (1987) *A View From the Shadows: Policy Making in the Solicitor General's Office*. Oxford: Oxford University Press.

Schon, D. (1983) *The Reflective Practitioner*. London: Temple Smith.

Schutz, A. (1962) 'Commonsense and scientific interpretation of human action', in *Collected Papers*, Vol. 1, ed. M. Natansson. The Hague: Martinus Nijhoff. pp. 17–38.

Shaw, I. (1996) *Evaluating in Practice*. Aldershot: Ashgate.

Silverman, D. (1985) *Qualitative Methodology and Sociology*. Aldershot: Gower.

Silverman, D. (1993) *Interpreting Qualitative Data: Methods of Analysing Talk, Text and Interaction*. London: Sage.

Volkman, R. and Cressey, D. (1963) 'Differential association and the rehabilitation of drug addicts', *American Journal of Sociology*, 64: 129–42.

Woolgar, S. and Pawluch, D. (1985) 'Ontological gerrymandering: The anatomy of social problems explanations', *Social Problems*, 32: 214–27.

PART VIII POSTSCRIPT

15 Towards an Aesthetics of Research

David Silverman

I must begin with an apology to readers for what may seem to be the somewhat pompous title of this chapter. The fact is that, once we lift our eyes away from the day to day tasks of gathering and analysing our data, it is difficult to resist the conclusion that an odd type of impulse ultimately shapes the way that many of us work. Of course, many volumes have been written about how theoretical or political positions (either implicit or explicit) shape the research task. However, at root, I feel that such positions have relatively little to do with many researchers' sense of what constitutes a 'worthwhile' research problem, 'interesting' data or a 'compelling' analysis. In relation to these kind of issues, I believe that the most important impulse has more to do with our tacit sense of the sort of appearance or shape of a worthwhile piece of research. In that sense, research is informed by an aesthetic.

Undoubtedly, that aesthetic is encountered in the narratives we tell of our research. Indeed, the style of sociological writing is an issue that has been around for quite a long time. Many years ago, Mills (1959) filleted Parsons's social theories, reducing many pages to a few lines. More recently, Paul Acourt (1987) has raised important questions about the rhetorical methods of the texts of sociological 'grand theory'.

Indeed, such deconstruction of the social science text has moved beyond grand theory to the more humble empirical monograph. Mills' (1959) account of what he called 'abstracted empiricism' – all rigour and minimal content – was hardly less damning than his treatment of Parsons. More good naturedly, Paul Atkinson (1990) has reminded us of the genres through which ethnographers tell their tales of the field, while a whole army of postmodern anthropologists (e.g. Clifford and Marcus, 1986) focus on narrative in order to deconstruct the subjects and objects of the field-worker's gaze.

However, it is not accidental that these issues barely surface in the earlier chapters of this book. For instance, Prior's, Watson's and Atkinson and Coffey's chapters on texts firmly (and delightfully) focus on *using* social science to analyse everyday texts. This is not meant to indicate that I want to downgrade the issues that arise from the narrative organization of social science texts. Rather it expresses my sense that perhaps the reflexive card is now being played too regularly in the social sciences.

In part, my worries relate to the image that we present to the world. A focus on the narrative construction of our texts may be an emancipating activity. However, when carried on too much or too far, it is difficult to resist outside critics who accuse sociology of navel-gazing and, thereby, producing the conditions for a dialogue of the deaf between itself and the community (see Silverman, 1993: Chap. 8).

In part, my resistance to the reflexive turn is also, inevitably, aesthetic. Many years ago, I remember a research student who used to make visiting speakers flounder by asking them: 'how would you apply your own analysis to the text that you have just presented?' As they wriggled, I wriggled too – not from intellectual difficulty but rather from distaste for this sort of wordplay which appeared to make a not very articulate student into a profound thinker.

Moreover, this student and the many texts of the 1980s that invited us to peer behind the curtain of social science narratives or even set out to construct new literary forms (Mulkay, 1985; Woolgar, 1988) may not have been so original after all. In the eighteenth century Denis Diderot was already inventing a novel (*Jacques le fataliste*) precisely directed at deconstructing the tropes of author, character and plot. And, of course, the dialogic form of Socrates anticipated contemporary social science by more than two millennia.[1]

This is not to deny that sometimes it is useful to draw from historical precedents. However, a less than thoughtful repetition of past ploys is hardly to be viewed as the latest breakthrough in social science. Moreover, when it comes to certain rhetorical moves – for instance, the construction of social science texts not just as dialogues but as, say, poetry (e.g. Richardson, 1994) – am I alone in experiencing distaste and even despair?[2]

I am reminded of the illusion that some of us nourish that, just because we are able to turn out some usable social science text, we must have the makings of the great novel lurking within our breasts. Risking the scorn of modern-day deconstructionists, let me suggest that the craft of writing fiction or verse is quite different from the craft of social science. In any event, if I want to read a good poem, why on earth should I turn to a social science journal?

Organization of this chapter

Continuing the theme of how we write, the next section examines the aesthetics of scientific explanations. Drawing upon Polyani and Popper, as well as Wittgenstein, I argue for a passionate commitment to a minimalist aesthetic for social science which celebrates clarity and rigour.

But aesthetics and science can never be apart from the world. I thus set out the political implications of such an aesthetics, referring to Strong and Dingwall's call for social science to offer its skills to the assessment of the efficiency and effectiveness of social arrangements. Such a practical, Stoic position stands in stark contrast to the Romantic oppositional politics with which British sociology has been long associated.

Finally, in the concluding two sections of this chapter, I return to the themes of an earlier paper (Silverman, 1989) to show how Romanticism trades off a dubious 'humanistic' position. Instead, I call for a non-humanist appreciation of the aesthetics of the micro-order.

The aesthetics of explanations

In the 1970s and early 1980s, the weary critique of 'positivism' in science (Adorno, 1976; Filmer et al., 1972) conjured up a version of social science as a hopeless search for universal laws pursued by narrow and naïve technicians. Outside the pages of undergraduate examination answer books, this critique more or less lacked any coherence. First, the term 'positivism' failed to denote any coherent group or set of opinions, functioning rather as a term of abuse for any opinion that one disliked. Secondly, researchers who refused to discard a commitment to a social science were not universally naïve or uncritical. For instance, contemporary demographers are entirely aware of the problematic nature of the realities portrayed by official statistics. In that sense, it is critics of demography who are naïve rather than demographers themselves.

Finally, the anti-positivists failed to paint a convincing portrait of the procedures of the natural sciences which positivists allegedly aped.[3] For instance, Thomas Kuhn's (1970) depiction of 'normal science' need not be treated simply as a critique of laboratory science. Certainly, science needs the theoretical schemes and material structures that Kuhn called 'paradigms'. As Kuhn pointed out, these paradigms are not easily abandoned. On the other hand, the very 'routine' nature of 'normal science' carries with it at least the claim to an adherence to a set of standards which allow some court of appeal in the demarcation of 'fact' from 'opinion'.

Moreover, laboratory science's cautious fact-grubbing by no means describes all natural science or scientists. Theoretical physics is often appealed to as an example of a post-empiricist science. Lacking what might count as data, researchers compete in speculations about the nature of the universe. But theoretical physics is not quite a Tower of Babel. First, researchers share a common language based on a body of agreed, if changing, concepts. Secondly, they use standards to sort fact from fancy. Whether or not relevant data are to hand, the community still has ways of identifying compelling descriptions and explanations. It asks itself:

- Is the account 'economical'? Does it explain multiple phenomena using the minimum of conceptual tools?
- Is the account 'beautiful'? Does it resolve disputes by rearranging the existing pieces in a pleasing way or by introducing a new piece which discloses a previously invisible order?

In this sense, theoretical physics unashamedly appeals to a version of aesthetic standards. However, this should come as no surprise. After all, physics has an intimate link with mathematics, which has long known the link between 'truth' and 'beauty'. As Michael Polyani argues:

> [W]e dwell on mathematics and affirm its statements for the sake of its intellectual beauty, which betokens the reality of its conceptions and the truth of its assertions. For if this passion were extinct, we would cease to understand mathematics; its conceptions would dissolve and its proofs carry no conviction. Mathematics would become pointless and would lose itself in a welter of insignificant tautologies. (1964: 192)

However, aesthetics is not the beginning and end of scientific practice. The 'passion' which Polyani identifies above also demands that descriptions and explanations must be subjected to the hardest tests we can devise. In this sense, Polyani goes on:

> The natural scientist and the engineer are not so free to satisfy themselves; no scientific theory is beautiful if it is false and no invention is truly ingenious if it is impracticable. Yet this merely modifies the conditions of a process of self-satisfaction. The standards of scientific value and of inventive ingenuity must still be satisfied, and these standards are set by the scientist's and the engineer's own intellectual passions. (1964: 195)

Polyani's attempt to develop an aesthetic of passion and constraint echoes an earlier voice. Around fifty years before Polyani wrote *Personal Knowledge*, Ludwig Wittgenstein was engaged in a passionate search for clarity. His *Tractatus Logico-Philosophicus* was a delicate attempt to establish the bounds of sense by distinguishing what could be said sensibly from what could not. As he wrote in his preface to the *Tractatus*:

> The whole sense of the book might be summed up in the following words: what can be said at all can be said clearly, and what we cannot talk about we must pass over in silence. (Wittgenstein, 1961: 3)

This 'minimalist' aesthetic is reflected in the building he designed for his sister, which, like the *Tractatus*, was, on the surface, unadorned and purely functional (see Monk, 1990).

Although Wittgenstein was later to abandon the pursuit of a crystal-clear propositional language, 'clarity' remained his continuing watchword. In his later writings, he pursued clarity through what he referred to as a rigorous intellectual 'hygiene'. This involved asking a very precise set of questions about a reconceived set of phenomena:

> We feel as if we had to *penetrate* phenomena: our investigation, however, is directed not towards phenomena, but, as one might say, towards the '*possibilities*' of phenomena. We remind ourselves, that is to say, of the *kind of statement* that we make about phenomena. (Wittgenstein, 1968: para. 90)

Wittgenstein's new 'phenomena' were grounded in everyday language rather than 'logic' but the pursuit of clarity remained his aim. In all his work, that clarity was to be found by a form of self-restraint which rejected both flamboyant style and the appeal of unanswerable questions (or questions which could only be answered by how one lived).

Of course, as Janik and Toulmin (1973) and Monk (1990) remind us, Wittgenstein was writing in the context of a particular cultural and political constellation. His dislike for the uneconomical use of concepts paralleled the distaste of many contemporary Viennese intellectuals for the baroque and mystifying linguistic forms of the disintegrating Habsburg Empire of the early 1900s.

After the First World War, Karl Popper pursued the fight for clarity of expression within the German-speaking world. In this context, Popper had little time for the convoluted Hegelianism of the Frankfurt School. As he writes:

> Some of the famous leaders of German sociology who do their intellectual best . . . are nevertheless, I believe, simply talking trivialities in high-sounding language, as they were taught. They teach this to their students, who are dissatisfied, yet do the same. (Popper, 1976b: 296)

Popper demonstrates this critique by providing a passage of Adorno, which, *à la* Mills, he then reduces to a few lines. For Popper, the intellectual's pursuit of what he calls 'critical reason' demands clarity:

> One has to train oneself constantly to write and to speak in a clear and simple language. Every thought should be formulated as clearly and simply as possible. This can only be achieved by hard work. (1976b: 292)

But Wittgenstein's project (for clarity, against kitsch) finds echoes in many thinkers who, unlike Popper, are very detached from turn of the century Vienna. In the middle of the nineteenth century, Gustave Flaubert was also attacking kitsch through his critique of the political pretensions and flowery style of the contemporary novel and his demand for a novel of aesthetic forms.[4]

Today, two writers seem to me to pursue Flaubert's and Wittgenstein's aesthetic. Milan Kundera has attempted to unpick the modern world's version of 'authentic' experience in the stirring parades of Soviet Eastern Europe and the 'revealing' biography of chat-show interview of the contemporary media. For Kundera, East and West offer two versions of kitsch dressed up in different clothes (see Silverman and Atkinson, forthcoming).

Like Wittgenstein and Kundera, Nicholson Baker has refused to accept the prevailing version of the 'big' question. Baker's (1997) essays on apparently tiny topics from the history of punctuation to the aesthetics of nail-clippings may infuriate some readers. However, behind such seeming trivia lies what I take to be a serious intent – to seek clarity in place of our often empty accounts of bigger, more spectacular issues.

A reviewer of Baker's book writes that 'the ordinary, in Baker's world, is easily strange enough' (Winder, 1996). This catches the Wittgensteinian thrust of Baker's project, underlined by his injunction to us to 'pursue truth, not rarity. The atypical can fend for itself' ('Rarity' in Baker, 1997).

Baker's essays refuse to take a great analytic sweep, collecting together many phenomena under a single head. Rather beauty and truth can be found in a project which carefully notes apparently minor differences. As Wittgenstein once remarked to a student:

> No, I don't think I would get on with Hegel. Hegel seems to me to be always wanting to say that things which look different are really the same. Whereas my interest is in showing that things which look the same are really different. I was thinking of using as a motto for my book a quotation from *King Lear*: 'I'll teach you differences.' (Drury, 1984: 157)

Wittgenstein's German-speaking contemporary, Walter Benjamin, seems to have been equally fascinated by differences between apparently minor objects. Hannah Arendt tells us that:

> Benjamin had a passion for small, even minute things. For him the size of an object was in an inverse ratio to its significance. . . . The smaller the object, the more likely it seemed that it could contain in the most concentrated form everything else. (1970: 11–12)

Apparently, Benjamin carried around with his notebooks containing quotations from daily living which he regarded as 'pearls' or 'coral': 'On occasion he read from them aloud, showed them around like items from a choice and precious collection' (Arendt, 1970: 45).[5]

Neither Benjamin nor Wittgenstein, nor Popper, Baker, Kundera or Flaubert exemplifies the dry, narrow persona of the caricatured 'Positivist'. Instead, in my view, they point towards an aesthetic in which one passionately commits oneself to both beauty and truth. As Polyani notes, although all acts of understanding involve the personal participation of the knower,

> this does not make our understanding *subjective*. Comprehension is neither an arbitrary act nor a passive experience, but a responsible act claiming universal validity. (Polyani, 1964: xiii)

Polyani tells us that a passion and responsibility is involved in all scientific endeavours. Science pursues an aesthetics of beauty found in its commitment to clarity. At the same time, clarity advances side by side with the search for truth, constrained by the cautious pursuit of validation.

Such caution implies a minimalist aesthetic for social science. As against the flamboyant but unoriginal 'experiments' of new literary forms, I suggest we treat the propositional language of science not as a straitjacket but as the basis of a dialogue with each other and the wider community. Clarity in our writing and economy in our use of concepts does not indicate, *contra* Barthes (1968), a tacit commitment to a specific bourgeois order. Rather, following Polyani, it expresses a timeless, passionate commitment to beauty and truth.

Politics and social science

The preceding argument about a 'timeless commitment to truth' may seem to imply the clearly invalid claim that science can stand entirely apart from society. Karl Popper, while sharing Polyani's commitment to 'truth', will not accept that this implies an entirely free-floating science composed of apolitical scientists. Indeed, his call for 'clarity' owed much to his sense that mysticism and linguistic obscurity, particularly in the work of the Frankfurt School, was dangerously conducive to the charismatic power of totalitarianism.[6]

Recognizing his own partisan position, Popper argues that the elimination of the extra-scientific is neither possible nor desirable:

> [W]e cannot rob the scientist of his partisanship without also robbing him of his humanity, and we cannot suppress or destroy his value judgements without destroying him as a human being *and as a scientist*. Our motives and even our purely scientific ideals, including the ideal of a disinterested search for truth, are deeply anchored in extra-scientific . . . evaluations. Thus the 'objective' or 'value-free' scientist is hardly the ideal scientist. Without passion we can achieve nothing – certainly not in pure science. The phrase 'the passion for truth' is no mere metaphor. (Popper, 1976a: 97)

Popper's treatment of 'objectivity' as a value places him firmly in the tradition of nineteenth-century German thought, which reached its apex in the methodological writings of Max Weber. This tradition welcomes the political and value commitments of scientists. But it also demands the strict separation of scientific generalizations from value statements. As Popper writes:

> What is possible and what is important and what lends science its special character is *not* the elimination of extra-scientific interests but rather the differentiation between the interests which do not belong to the search for truth and the purely scientific interest in truth. (Popper, 1976a: 96; emphasis added)

Such a differentiation means that Popper strongly resists Habermas's argument that theory and practice cannot be separated and therefore 'only one who is a practical critic of existing society can produce serious theoretical arguments about society' (Popper, 1976b: 298).[7] By contrast, Popper argues that the politics of a scientist is irrelevant to evaluating the quality of his/her work or its contribution to society.

Of course, Popper's position, which I share, is inevitably not itself scientific but political. For Popper, the critical debate of science is our best alternative to violence (Popper, 1976b: 292). Equally, one might argue that the examples of Soviet or Aryan 'science' provide a terrible warning of the dangers of introducing what Popper calls 'a sociology of knowledge' approach into our interrogation of science. Ultimately, what should matter is whether a statement is true not who its author is or what interest s(he) 'represents'.

Yet British sociology, much informed by Romantic assumptions, resists most of this argument. To a far greater extent than in other Western societies, my impression is that British journal articles are much more likely to parade the political pretensions of their authors, if only to remind us of their adherence to the expected and acceptable left of centre position.

Note that I am not criticizing candour or left of centre politics – a political position I happen to share. What troubles me is British sociology's apparent need to wear its heart on its sleeve. Such a Romantic politics very easily slips into the kind of self-righteousness which prefers making gestures and taking stands to practical involvement in community issues.

As Strong and Dingwall (1989) have pointed out, this is seen in the way in which British sociology, while quite rightly pressing for the values of equality and humanity, has been relatively silent, or even opposed to, issues concerning the efficiency of social arrangements. They note that this is most apparent in the sociological literature on the National Health Service, where 'managerialism' is used as a term of abuse and where a worthy concern for the sick and under-privileged runs side by side with a reluctance to accept that resources are always finite. As they write:

> [S]ociology has always been suspicious of a wordly concern for efficiency and effectiveness, the stock in trade of the manager or policy maker. In this, it shares the British academic disdain for the *homme d'affaires*. (Strong and Dingwall, 1989: 65)

The very Britishness of this position may make it very surprising to my American or Nordic readers, reared on a more pragmatic position. To them, I may be knocking on an open door when, following Strong and Dingwall, I call for the kind of social science which seeks to make practical interventions which might make legitimate social institutions more efficient or effective.

In the same way, Bloor (Chapter 14, this volume) shows how ethnographic research can be useful to practitioners. The sociology recommended by Bloor, Strong and Dingwall would avoid gesture politics precisely because such a politics faces the academy towards itself rather than towards the wider community.

Of course, my preference is aesthetic as well as political. We see such an aesthetics in the Stoic philosophy recommended to us by Strong and Dingwall. Rather than deny a political dimension to science, Strong and Dingwall's version of Stoicism insists on it. As they write:

> The Stoic programme . . . raises the question of what science is *for*. How does it contribute to the collective wisdom of the community? How can it promote virtuous living, in the sense of a mode of existence which is an expression rather than a perversion of human nature and society? (Strong and Dingwall, 1989: 64)

Precisely because of its modest aims, such a programme rejects sloganizing in favour of practical interventions.

Stoicism's modest, practical programme is not the only relevant source of inspiration for social science. Kafka's (1961) wonderful short story 'Investigations of a Dog' creates a marvellous image of 'Airdogs' (*Lufthunde*), who, like many European intellectuals, get above themselves. However, in this case, this is a literal transcendence – the Airdogs float on cushions above the ground, surveying the world from on high, yet cut off from any contact with it (so cut off that Kafka's doggy investigator wonders how they manage to reproduce themselves!).

In the same way, the Land Surveyor called K in Kafka's (1957) novel *The Castle*, who tries to get direct access to the mysterious castle, only succeeds in over-reaching himself. As Erich Heller (1974) has pointed out, hubris is the fate of those who get above themselves.[8]

By contrast, a more modest form of social science seeks to convince the reader on the basis of its evidence rather than on its politics. Such writing need not deny the political position of its author but, where appropriate, in the Weberian stance, invokes its author's politics precisely so that the reader should *not* be seduced by it.

But explicit political positions are not the most serious seductive forces. Far more seductive are the siren voices of 'humanism' and 'authenticity' that so dominate many qualitative methodologies.

A non-humanist social science?

In the earlier section on the aesthetics of explanations, we saw that Polyani's claim for universal validity derives from a passionate commitment to communally sanctioned methods of sorting fact from fancy:

> [B]oth *verification* and *validation* are everywhere an acknowledgement of a commitment: they claim the presence of something real and external to the speaker. As distinct from both of these, *subjective* experiences can only be said to be *authentic*, and authenticity does not involve a commitment in the sense in which both verification and validation do. (Polyani, 1964: 202)

In Polyani's sense, attempts to ground social science on the basis of 'authenticity' are doomed to failure. Following Wittgenstein, we might suggest that appeals to 'authenticity' confuse two different language-games ('subjective experience' and 'science').[9]

Yet qualitative research is full of appeals to authenticity/experience, and so on. For instance, the rightly celebrated *Handbook of Qualitative Research* contains the following editorial observation:

> This center [of qualitative research] lies in the *humanistic* commitment of the qualitative researcher to study the world always from *the perspective of the individual.* (Lincoln and Denzin, 1994: 575; emphasis added)

Although Denzin has elsewhere drawn attention to how our representations of 'the perspective of the individual' are always 'shaped by genre, narrative, stylistic, personal, cultural and paradigmatic conventions' (1994: 507), the humanistic message present in the Lincoln and Denzin extract captures well the romantic auspices of much qualitative social science.

In *Interpreting Qualitative Data*, I recommended that we reflect on the temptations of the cultural world which might stand behind such appeals to 'humanism', often wedded to a commitment to the 'in-depth' interview:

> Think, for instance, of how much interviews are a central (and popular) feature of mass media products, from 'talk shows' to 'celebrity interviews'. Perhaps, we all live in what might be called an 'Interview Society' in which interviews seem central to making sense of our lives. (Silverman, 1993: xx)

What does the interview society require? First, the emergence of the self as a proper object of narration. Secondly, the technology of the confessional – the friend not only of the policeman but of the priest, the teacher and the 'psy' professional. Thirdly, mass media technologies give a new twist to the, no doubt, perennial polarities of the private and the public; the routine and the sensational.

Newspapers, radio and television thrive on the interview. In both 'serious' newspapers and television 'chat-shows', we expect to be enlightened about the private lives of public figures. For the qualitatively minded researcher, the *open-ended* interview offers the opportunity for just such an authentic gaze into the soul of another with, perhaps, the added frisson of a politically correct dialogue where researcher and researched offer mutual understanding and support.

Here we see the Romantic impulse in contemporary sociology: the elevation of the experiential as the authentic.[10] But a subtle confidence trick is being played in Romantic sociology's appeal to 'authenticity' and 'openness':

> [T]he dialogues of the interview society are precisely the antithesis of the dialogic play of voices and selves that Bakhtin (1981) and his circle celebrated. The interview remains essentially monologic. Interviewer and interviewee collaborate in the reconstruction of a common and unitary construction of the self. When Anthony Clare invites celebrities to occupy 'the psychiatrist's chair' on his BBC radio programme, he has his guests recapitulate a recognizably uniform litany of conversational topics: parents, work, sources of self-esteem or of failure are all explored. These more-or-less standardized discursive domains are used in order to construct the interiority of the subject. The interviewer's gaze thus helps to fix the self of the other. The technology of the interview in such contexts thus generates a type of encounter in which the agenda of questioning and the formulaic patterns of exchange reveal the predictable, in the guise of private confession. (Silverman and Atkinson, forthcoming)

Of course, no method of social research is intrinsically right or wrong. As all methodology texts properly insist, 'it all depends upon what you are trying to do'. So, in their critique of Romanticism, Strong and Dingwall (1989) do argue that the Romantic heritage provided much of sociology's commitment to the creation of a better world. On the other hand,

> the virtues of Romanticism need to be countered by a frank recognition of its vices: the substitution of evangelical zeal for scholarship, the lust for experience over reflection, the elevation of the personal above the communal. (Strong and Dingwall, 1989: 50)

Following Strong and Dingwall's critique of the elevation of the 'personal' above the 'communal', I contend that qualitative researchers who want to use the interview to depict the 'personal' have, in the cockney phrase, 'bought a pup', that is, been deluded. For their worthy aims are precisely the aims of the mass media with their endless 'chat-shows' and 'call-ins'. As Martin Scorcese implies in his brilliant but neglected movie *King of Comedy*, the appearance on a TV chat-show has become the ultimate validation of our existence. Like Scorcese's Rupert Pupkin, who thinks of nothing else, we can all become 'somebody' as we answer the interviewer's questions.

Yet no method of research can stand outside the cultural and material world. As I pointed out in my earlier book (Silverman, 1993), texts depended upon the invention of the printing press or, in the case of television or audio recordings, upon modern communication technologies. And observation is no more unique to social researchers than is the interview. For instance, as Foucault (1977) has noted, just as the method of questioning used in the interview reproduces many of the features of the Catholic confessional or the psycho-analytic consultation, the observation of the prisoner has been at the heart of modern prison reform.

At the very least, however, this involvement of methodologies in the world suggests that we should be a little cautious about the claims we make about our preferred research technique. The appeals of 'authenticity' and of the direct contact with human 'experience' are, I believe, part of the messages of the world we live in. As such, they are to be explained rather than to be relied upon.[11]

Less cautiously, may I admit that my heart sinks whenever I read yet another 'open-ended' interview study claiming to tell it 'like it is'. If this is one's 'bag', why obtain research grants and write scholarly papers? Better by far simply to turn on the TV and wallow in the undoubtedly 'human' and 'authentic' pap.

The aesthetics of the micro-order

All social research faces similar temptations. 'So what did you find out?', we are asked. And, if we are not careful, we recount the moving or shocking story told to us by an interviewee or observed in the 'field'. The danger is that such an answer mistakes what is immediately newsworthy for what is important. Indeed, its very sense of newsworthiness reflects the priorities not of science but of the mass media or of interpersonal gossip. So we succumb to the appeal of the trite and neglect the profound. Journalists, gossips or poets all have their functions. But can't we do better, or at least differently, as social scientists?

Part of what seems to be required is the kind of self-restraint we find in the later Wittgenstein. Time and again, Wittgenstein consciously seeks to reject 'big' questions and global answers in favour of a meticulous examination of apparently unremarkable examples. Rather than shock us with tabloid revelations, he shocks us by reminding us of the complexities of what we know already. As he wrote in his *Philosophical Investigations*:

> What we are supplying are really remarks on the natural history of human beings; we are not contributing curiosities however but observations which no one has doubted, but which have escaped remark only because they are always before our eyes. (Wittgenstein, 1968: para. 415)

What is 'before our eyes' becomes, in Garfinkel's (1967) terms, how indexical expressions are routinely made objective. So ethnomethodology shocks us by pointing to the logical impossibility and yet the routine achievement of a stable, ordered world. Somehow, through methods that await explication, the world-known-in-common is viewed anew as an amazing practical accomplishment.

Of course, Garfinkel's strategy is not the only one available to the qualitative sociologist. Conversation analysis pursues Garfinkel's path through cumulative observations rather than ironic 'demonstrations' (see Heritage, Chapter 11, Heath, Chapter 12, and Peräkylä, Chapter 13, in this volume). And a whole host of other approaches represented in this book exemplify cautious but revealing analyses.

Such approaches have in common their ability to surprise us by making a lot out of a little. So, in the hands of the authors in this volume, we come to see new things in, for instance, a financial statement, a coroner's report, a police file or in a television interview. In this way, theoretical approaches are deployed to reveal new facts and, slowly and cautiously, to build systematic bodies of knowledge.

But there is an aesthetic at work here. My feeling is that the kind of temperament required to take pleasure and find reward in such a social science must separate itself off from many of the messages that are all around us in the world narrated to us by the mass media. That world demands immediate gratification in the form of simple narratives containing exciting 'incidents'. It has no time to gaze around, no desire to take pleasure in the unremarkable, no ability to view without background sounds or to listen without distracting images.

Yet I also believe that a counter-aesthetic occasionally surfaces. I love the kind of cinema with the absence of narrative thrust and the attention to detail that we find, for instance, in Rohmer's *Claire's Knee*. Or the positively ethnographic pursuit of the 'boring' features of the world in Tavernier's *L327*, a police story almost without arrests or car chases but with a strong focus on the routines of police work as we see Parisian drug cops spending most of the time sitting in their offices, 'cooking' their official reports.[12]

Such movies require a certain discipline from their audience just as scientific work is, in a dual sense, disciplinary. So the social scientist, like the moviegoer at a Tavernier or Rohmer film, must forgo the temptation to seek the instant gratifications trumpeted all around. But this does not mean that such a scientist is reduced to a mere technician.

Rosen (1976) tells us that classical composers at the end of the eighteenth century were able to develop their own identities and surprise their audiences by both respecting and playing with musical form. Similarly, we owe it to our audiences to surprise them by inviting them, with great clarity, to look anew at the world they already know. And we owe it to ourselves to respect the discipline (in both senses) as well as the power of social science.

Notes

1. This is not to claim that all writers who explore new literary forms are unaware of this history. Rather I would argue that they fail to make the case that they can achieve any more than previous scholars.

2. As Paul Acourt has commented about such 'poetry': 'the *motive* may be honourable (to dispel difference and give voice to the Other) but the *result* is typically the establishment of yet another layer of difference in the realm of discourse' (personal correspondence).

3. As Popper points out: 'positivistic epistemology is inadequate even in its analysis of the natural sciences which, in fact, are not "careful generalizations from data", as it is usually believed, but are essentially speculative and daring' (1976b: 299).

4. See Flaubert's *Dictionary of Received Ideas*, discussed in Silverman (1989).

5. Arendt reports Benjamin's admiration for two grains of wheat in a museum on which a kindred soul had inscribed the complete Shema Israel: Benjamin's 'delight that two grains of wheat should contain . . . the very essence of Judaism, tiniest essence appearing on tiniest entity, from which in both cases everything else originates' (Arendt, 1970: 11–12).

6. I am grateful for this observation to Paul Acourt.

7. In a simplified form, the argument between Popper and the Frankfurt School turns upon the latter's conception of a contradictory 'social totality', compared to Popper's more restrained focus on specific problems within society. From this follows the value placed upon Theory by Habermas, Horkheimer and Adorno, in contrast to Popper's preference for theoretically generated testable propositions (Paul Acourt, personal correspondence).

8. 'The German for it [Land Surveyor] is *Landvermesser*, and its verbal associations are manifold . . . [it] alludes to *Vermessenheit* (hubris); to the adjective *vermessen*, audacious; to the verb *sich vermessen*, commit an act of spiritual pride, and also apply the wrong measure, make a mistake in measurement' (Heller, 1974: 123).

9. Polyani himself was critical of the later Wittgenstein, arguing that his pursuit of the 'grammar' of everyday language artificially separated form and content (Polyani, 1964: 114).

10. My worries about a discourse of authenticity seem to chime with George Steiner's critique of the 'total utterance', i.e. speech which claims to be a mirror to experience. Steiner writes: 'Could it be that vital resources of inwardness, of disciplined remembrance, of meditative clarity, fundamental to a classical culture, are being eroded by new ideals of extrovert and total utterance?' (1980: x).

11. There are parallels here with postmodern theorists' (PM) rejection of humanism. When coupled with PM's opposition to 'grand narratives' and with their appeals to aesthetics (e.g. Deleuze and Guattari's [1981] appeal for a strategy based on rhizomes) it might look like PM's project is quite close to the project advocated here. None the less, there are also clear differences. First, PM's account of dislocated selves fails to attend to the way in which subjects don't dissolve but, in Gubrium and Holstein's (1994) phrase, are 'reinscribed in local cultures'. Secondly, on Wittgensteinian grounds, I reject PM's tendency to construct complex meta-languages with an unknown relation to ordinary language (see Rorty, 1992; Silverman and Torode, 1980).

12. Arendt reports that, to Walter Benjamin, 'reality manifested itself most directly in the proverbs and idioms of everyday language' (1970: 15).

References

Acourt, P. (1987) 'The unfortunate domination of social theories by "social theory"', *Theory, Culture & Society*, 4 (4): 659–89.

Adorno, T.W. (1976) 'Sociology and empirical research', in T.W. Adorno et al., *The Positivist Dispute in German Sociology*, trans. G. Adey and D. Frisby. London: Heinemann Educational Books. pp. 68–86.

Arendt, H. (1970) 'Walter Benjamin: 1892–1940', in W. Benjamin, *Illuminations*, tr. H. Zohn. London: Jonathan Cape. pp. 1–58.

Atkinson, P. (1990) *The Ethnographic Imagination: Textual Constructions of Reality*. London: Routledge.

Baker, N. (1997) *The Size of Thoughts*. London: Chatto; Berkeley: University of California Press.

Bakhtin, M. (1981) *The Dialogic Imagination: Four Essays by M.M. Bakhtin*, ed. M. Holquist, trans. C. Emerson and M. Holquist. Austin: University of Texas Press.

Barthes, R. (1968) *Writing Degree Zero*, trans. S. Sontag. New York: Hill & Wang.

Clifford, J. and Marcus, G.E. (eds) (1986) *Writing Culture: The Poetics and Politics of Ethnography*. Berkeley: University of California Press.

Deleuze, G. and Guattari, F. (1981) 'Rhizomes', *Ideology & Consciousness*, 8: 49–72.

Denzin, N. (1994) 'The art and politics of interpretation', in N. Denzin and Y. Lincoln (eds), *Handbook of Qualitative Research*. London: Sage. pp. 500–15.

Drury, M. O'C. (1984) 'Conversations with Wittgenstein', in R. Rhees (ed.), *Recollections of Wittgenstein*. Oxford: Oxford University Press. pp. 97–171.

Filmer, P., Phillipson, M., Silverman, D. and Walsh, D. (1972) *New Directions in Sociological Theory*. London: Collier-Macmillan.

Foucault, M. (1977) *Discipline and Punish*, trans. A. Sheridan. Harmondsworth: Penguin.

Garfinkel, H. (1967) *Studies in Ethnomethodology*. Englewood Cliffs, NJ: Prentice Hall.

Gubrium, J.F. and Holstein, J.A. (1994) 'Grounding the postmodern self', *Sociological Quarterly*, 35 (4): 685–703.

Heller, E. (1974) *Kafka*. London: Fontana.

Janik, A. and Toulmin, S. (1973) *Wittgenstein's Vienna*. New York: Simon & Schuster.

Kafka, F. (1957) *The Castle*, trans. M. Brod. Harmondsworth: Penguin.

Kafka, F. (1961) 'Investigations of a Dog', in *Metamorphosis and Other Stories*, trans. M. Brod. Harmondsworth: Penguin.

Kuhn, T.S. (1970) *The Structure of Scientific Revolutions* (2nd edn). Chicago: University of Chicago Press.

Lincoln, Y. and Denzin, N. (1994) 'The fifth moment', in N. Denzin and Y. Lincoln (eds), *Handbook of Qualitative Research*. London: Sage. pp. 575–86.

Mills, C.W. (1959) *The Sociological Imagination*. New York: Oxford University Press.

Monk, R. (1990) *Ludwig Wittgenstein: The Duty of Genius*. London: Vintage.

Mulkay, M. (1985) *The Word and the World: Explorations in the Form of Sociological Analysis*. London: Allen & Unwin.

Polyani, M. (1964) *Personal Knowledge: Towards a Post-Critical Philosophy*. New York: Harper & Row (Harper Torchbooks).

Popper, K. (1976a) 'The logic of the sciences', in T.W. Adorno et al., *The Positivist Dispute in German Sociology*, trans. G. Adey and D. Frisby. London: Heinemann Educational Books. pp. 87–104.

Popper, K. (1976b) 'Reason or revolution', in T.W. Adorno et al., *The Positivist Dispute in German Sociology*, trans. G. Adey and D. Frisby. London: Heinemann Educational Books. pp. 288–300.

Richardson, L. (1994) 'Nine poems: Marriage and the family', *Journal of Contemporary Ethnography*, 23 (1): 3–13.

Rorty, R. (1992) 'Cosmopolitanism without emancipation: A response to Lyotard', in S. Lash and J. Friedman (eds), *Modernity and Identity*. Oxford: Blackwell. pp. 57–71.

Rosen, C. (1976) *The Romantic Style: Haydn, Beethoven, Mozart*. London: Faber & Faber.

Silverman, D. (1989) 'The impossible dreams of reformism and Romanticism', in J.F. Gubrium and D. Silverman (eds), *The Politics of Field Research: Sociology Beyond Enlightenment*. London: Sage. pp. 30–48.

Silverman, D. (1993) *Interpreting Qualitative Data: Methods for Analysing Talk, Text and Interaction*. London: Sage.

Silverman, D. and Atkinson, P. (forthcoming) 'Kundera's *Immortality*: The interview society and the invention of self'.

Silverman, D. and Torode, B. (1980) *The Material Word: Some Theories of Language and its Limits*. London: Routledge.

Steiner, G. (1980) *On Difficulty and Other Essays*. Oxford: Oxford University Press.

Strong, P. and Dingwall, R. (1989) 'Romantics and Stoics', in J.F. Gubrium and D. Silverman (eds), *The Politics of Field Research: Sociology Beyond Enlightenment*. London: Sage. pp. 46–69.

Winder, R. (1996) 'Swizzles, gruntlings and lumber pie', *San Francisco Chronicle*, 14 April.

Wittgenstein, L. (1961) *Tractatus Logico-Philosophicus*. London: Routledge.

Wittgenstein, L. (1968) *Philosophical Investigations*, trans. G.E.M. Ansrumbe. Oxford: Blackwell.

Woolgar, S. (ed.) (1988) *Knowledge and Reflexivity*. London: Sage.

Appendix
Transcription conventions

The examples printed embody an effort to have the spelling of the words roughly indicate how the words were produced. Often this involves a departure from standard orthography. Otherwise:

→	Arrows in the margin point to the lines of transcript relevant to the point being made in the text.
( )	Empty parentheses indicate talk too obscure to transcribe. Words or letters inside such parentheses indicate the transcriber's best estimate of what is being said.
hhh	The letter 'h' is used to indicate hearable aspiration, its length roughly proportional to the number of 'h"s. If preceded by a dot, the aspiration is an in-breath. Aspiration internal to a word is enclosed in parentheses. Otherwise 'h"s may indicate anything from ordinary breathing to sighing to laughing, etc.
[	Left-side brackets indicate where overlapping talk begins.
]	Right-side brackets indicate where overlapping talk ends, or marks alignments within a continuing stream of overlapping talk.
°	Talk appearing within degree signs is lower in volume relative to surrounding talk.
><	'Greater than' and 'less than' symbols enclose talk that is noticeably faster than the surrounding talk.
((looks))	Words in double parentheses indicate transcriber's comments, not transcriptions.
(0.8)	Numbers in parentheses indicate periods of silence, in tenths of a second – a dot inside parentheses indicates a pause of less than 0.2 seconds.
:::	Colons indicate a lengthening of the sound just preceding them, proportional to the number of colons.
becau-	A hyphen indicates an abrupt cut-off or self-interruption of the sound in progress indicated by the preceding letter(s) (the example here represents a self-interrupted 'because').
<u>He</u> says	Underlining indicates stress or emphasis.
dr^ink	A 'hat' or circumflex accent symbol indicates a marked pitch rise.
=	Equal signs (ordinarily at the end of one line and the start of an ensuing one) indicate a 'latched' relationship – no silence at all between them.

Fuller glossaries may be found in Sacks, H., Schegloff, E.A. and Jefferson, G. (1974) 'A simplest systematics for the organization of turn-taking for conversation', *Language*, 50: 696–735; and Atkinson, J.M. and Heritage, J. (eds) (1984) *Structures of Social Action: Studies in Conversation Analysis*. Cambridge: Cambridge University Press.

Name Index

Subject Index